WITHIN
HER

The New World in the Atlantic World
Amy Turner Bushnell and Jack P. Greene
Series Editors

WITHIN HER POWER

PROPERTIED WOMEN IN COLONIAL VIRGINIA

LINDA L. STURTZ

ROUTLEDGE
NEW YORK   LONDON

Published in 2002 by
Routledge
29 West 35th Street
New York, NY 10001

Published in Great Britain by
Routledge
11 New Fetter Lane
London EC4P 4EE

Routledge is an imprint of the Taylor & Francis Group.
Copyright © 2002 by Routledge

Printed in the United States of America on acid-free paper.

10 9 8 7 6 5 4 3 2 1

Library of Congress Cataloging-in-Publication Data

Sturtz, Linda L.
    Within her power : propertied women in colonial America / Linda L. Sturtz.
       p. cm — (The New World in the Atlantic world)
    Includes bibliographical references and index.
    ISBN 0-415-92855-9 (alk. paper) — ISBN 0-415-92882-6 (pbk. : alk. paper)
    1. Women—Virginia—History—17th century. 2. Women—Virginia—History—18th
century. 3. Women landowners—Virgina—History. 4. Women—Legal status, laws,
etc.—Virginia—History. 5. Virginia—History—Colonial period, ca. 1600-1775. I. Title.
II. Series.

HQ1438.V8 S78 2002
305.4'09755—dc21   2001048677

TO JCK

CONTENTS

FIGURES

TABLES

ACKNOWLEDGMENTS

In the preface to the 1931 *Festschrift* honoring Charles McLean Andrews, J. Franklin Jameson described the ideal historian of the presumably British North American colonies. Jameson believed that "he... had better be an American, and born and brought up in the Atlantic states. The outsider perceives some things which the native does not perceive, sees some matters in a juster perspective, but on the whole these advantages are overbalanced by the superior familiarity imbibed from the atmosphere, from old scenes, from continuing folkways, by him who is to the manner born, and which is hardly to be acquired otherwise."[1] Jameson narrowed his definition of that ideal historian of the colonies further, pointing out the advantages if "he" were from New England and descended from English forebears of the "standing order," for only thus would he be likely to obtain sympathetic insights into the ways and thoughts of colonial society, and "it is sounder practice to set out from the point of view of the majority than from that of any minority."[2] Jameson's account suggests that identity politics have had a long and relatively distinguished career. Despite that fact, I must admit I may hope at best to perceive some things the natives do not and "see some matters in a juster perspective," for despite four years' residence in the humid Williamsburg atmosphere I was born in the Midwest and spent my formative years in the Far West and Midwest. I may, at least, claim to be part of the modern gender majority, and I write this book about women, who were a minority in colonial Virginia, from that vantage point. I leave it to readers, whether or not to the manner born, to determine the persistence and significance of continuing folkways in the region.

Anyone who has pursued a project of this nature knows this is no job for rugged individualists. My obligations are numerous. Primary thanks go to David T. Konig for his suggestions on legal history and comments on drafts from early days of researching in Williamsburg to a review of the final manuscript.

The Jamestowne Society funded early research. The Virginia Historical Society generously provided two Mellon Grants and an intellectual home away from home. The American Association of University Women awarded me a writing fellowship in the critical final year of work on the dissertation. William Keefer Faculty Research Fellowships from Beloit College and a grant from the Wisconsin International Outreach Center supported later work. I benefited from having an intellectual home base at the Centre for Gender and Development Studies at the University of West Indies, Mona, under the direction of Patricia Mohammed while I was preparing the draft for publication and at the Huntington Library while I made final revisions.

In libraries I received assistance from Frances Pollard, Janet Schwarz, Nelson Lankford, and E. Lee Shepard at the Virginia Historical Society; Margaret Cook in Special Collections at Swem Library at the College of William and Mary; Gail Greve at the Rockefeller Library of Colonial Williamsburg; Linda Rowe, Caroline Julia Richter, Cary Carson, and Cathy Hellier in the Research Department at Colonial Williamsburg; Sandy Gioia Treadway, Brent Tarter, John Kneebone, Alexandra Gressett, and Minor Weisiger at the Library of Virginia; the staffs of the Library of Congress, University of Virginia's Alderman Library Special Collections, the Huntington Library, the British Museum, and the Corporation of London Records Office. Mrs. Isabella B. Hite generously offered permission to quote from the Mordecai Booth Account Book on deposit at the Virginia Historical Society. Marge Weimer at Beloit College's Interlibrary Loan Department has been a magician in finding materials. Eula Buchanan, Mary Hegel, and David Heesen at Beloit College helped with manuscript preparation.

Family and friends offered tremendous hospitality during my research visits. Mary Beth Taliaferro Huenke opened her home to me and also listened with patience and enthusiasm when I returned from the archives to tell her stories about my "dead people" who came to life in her Richmond apartment. Heather Macdonald and Karen and Rick Berquist also provided homes away from home during the research stages. Jean Mihalyka introduced me to the Northampton County records. Janet and Donald Robertson not only provided a warm welcome when I was still daughter-in-law elect but also fit hospitality around library hours. My parents, John and Bonnie Sturtz, encouraged my efforts from the beginning.

I am grateful to the many readers who have helped shape this book. Jack P. Greene, having heard various conference papers I presented on my research, encouraged me to send the manuscript to Routledge for inclusion in his Atlantic World series. I am also grateful for his willingness to read revisions of the text as the project proceeded to publication. William M. Offutt Jr. read the entire manuscript and made insightful comments for revisions. A portion of chapter 3 was presented to the Southern Historical Association meeting in 1990; I am grateful for comments and suggestions from Gail S. Terry, Jim Horn, and Jean B. Lee on that draft. A portion of chapter 3 was also presented to Bernard Bailyn's 1997 Atlantic World Seminar and I am grateful to the members of the seminar and to Stanley Katz for reading and commenting on that earlier version. At the Many Legalities conference, Allan Kulikoff and Linda Kerber provided stimulating thoughts on chapter 4. Sandy Treadway and Kenneth Lockridge read the entire dissertation and made suggestions on how to revise it into a book. Amber Ault, Heather Schroeder, Virginia Powell, Cheryl Kader, Diane Lichtenstein, Tamara Hamlish, and Ann Smart Martin generously read drafts of several chapters. At an early stage, I benefited from discussions with Jeanne Attie, Mark Kornbluh, and Iver Bernstein. Jean Ensminger and Stewart Banner read an early version of the text. Laura Westhoff and Lisa Gubser Blakeley commented on chapters in their roughest form. Sandy Treadway and Jean B. Lee made suggestions on initial outlines. Gail S. Terry provided constant encouragement and a reminder that good history can still tell a story while offering useful analysis. John M. Hemphill II offered numerous suggestions on how to use imperial and legal sources. Brendan O'Malley started the project rolling at Routledge, made suggestions on the manuscript, and encouraged me in making revisions. Vikram Mukhija at Routledge saw the project through to completion and Brian Bendlin did copyediting; still, any errors remain my own. James Robertson has been involved in this project from the time I began writing the outline until I assembled the bibliography. James remained a constantly cheerful presence even when I was not. He claims he finds reading my work a holiday from his own, but probably wished for a real vacation once in awhile, too.

"AS IF I HAD BEEN

IN A NEW WORLD"

In his 1722 novel *Moll Flanders*, Daniel Defoe created an archetypical colonial woman's success story. Contrasting her life in Virginia with her experience in England, the character Moll declared, it was "as if I had been in a new world."[1] The original novel and popularized versions tantalized readers with the opportunities for upward social mobility in colonial Virginia. In England, Moll turned to a life of crime and suffered transportation to Virginia as punishment. In Virginia, however, life improved. Upon settling in the "wilderness" of her "new world," Moll repented of her life of sin and crime. Ultimately, she became the mistress of a plantation and owner of a white servant and a black slave.

Like actual settlers, Moll Flanders became a powerful woman who acknowledged the class and gender restrictions imposed on her yet still sought to improve her condition. Although *Moll Flanders* does not describe the actual experience of a woman in colonial Virginia, the story does demonstrate a popular English view of what emigrant women could achieve in the colony. Readers and illiterate listeners could hear of the adventures of this New World woman and look at illustrations in abridged, "chapbook" versions of the story (see fig. I.1).

Defoe's popular fictional account portrayed women in Virginia as directing their own lives. Moving from fiction to lived experience, this book evaluates the nature of propertied women's power and analyzes the situations in which colonists allowed, or even expected, women to administer their affairs. Many colonial white women exercised control over their own resources and the lives of others despite expectations of female submissiveness in Anglo-American law and culture. Women who owned property, even if only a small amount, could and often did learn to negotiate economic, cultural, and legal structures to benefit themselves and their families. While some aspects of women's power in Virginia clearly emerged from the seventeenth-century colony's particular environmental and demographic situation, others paralleled wider developments elsewhere in Britain's expanding empire.

FIGURE I.1 *A Chapbook Illustration of Moll Flanders in Virginia.* Note the hills across the bay, quite out of keeping with the flat, swampy terrain of the tidewater region. Anonymous, much abridged chapbook version of *The Fortunes and Misfortunes of Moll Flanders…At Last Grew Rich, Lived Honest, and Died Penitent.* London, [c. 1750], 23. British Library #1079.i.13(21). Reproduced by permission of the British Library Picture Library.

The Chesapeake Bay region's geography and climate differed from any that the colonists had experienced previously. The summers were hotter and the winters colder than anything the emigrants had known in England, and the high humidity of this swampy terrain made the summers almost unbearable and the winter's chill more biting. On oppressively hot, damp summer evenings, the high buzz of cicadas, the chirp of crickets, and the attacks of biting insects reminded settlers they weren't in Kent anymore. Cockroaches, having arrived with the settlers, flourished in the humid climate, and often skittered across the open barrels of cornmeal, the colonists' staple and sometimes only food. Hungry hornworms, also known as tobacco worms, chomped on the cash crop in the field; one of the nastiest tasks of tobacco growing was picking worms off and crushing them between one's fingernails.[2] In the seventeenth century, the region epitomized an "unsettled" first stage of the model of colonial development formulated by Jack Greene. Undoubtedly colonists believed that they, like Moll Flanders, lived in a "new world," though not necessarily in the best sense of the term.[3]

The coastal plain of Virginia, still popularly known as the "tidewater," extends from the fall line west of the Chesapeake Bay to the Atlantic Ocean. The term *tidewater* comes from the large tidal rivers that cross the plain, flowing southeastward into the Chesapeake Bay, which itself opens into the Atlantic. Moving from east to west, the plain rises in stairsteps slowly in elevation until reaching the fall line, exposed rocky areas that mark the westernmost point on the rivers open to navigation. West of the fall line ships found navigation up river more difficult because exposed rocky river beds created treacherous rapids.[4] This upland region, called the Piedmont, ends at the foot of the Appalachian Mountains. Cities eventually developed along the fall line because boats unloaded wares from England and took on cargoes of crops and commodities from the west for export. The banks of rivers at the fall line provided ideal locations for transshipment points and merchants' stores. Towns and cities later developed from these settlements; for example, present-day Richmond has its roots in Henrico, a trading post at the fall line on the James River. The distance from there to the capital at Jamestown was about sixty miles. Both broad leaf trees and stands of fragrant pines grew in this well-watered soil. This Coastal Plain became prime tobacco-growing land early in the seventeenth century, supporting the planters' export-driven economy through the 1740s, when, as a result of soil exhaustion, tobacco planting moved further west (see fig. I.2).

South of the Potomac and roughly parallel to it, three major, navigable rivers—the Rappahannock, the York, and the James—divided the tidewater region into three peninsulas (the Northern Neck, the Middle Peninsula and, simply, the Peninsula, along with a fourth "southside" area below the James). Numerous smaller rivers and creeks, some pooling in stagnant swamps, divided the landscape even further. Rivers simultaneously became water

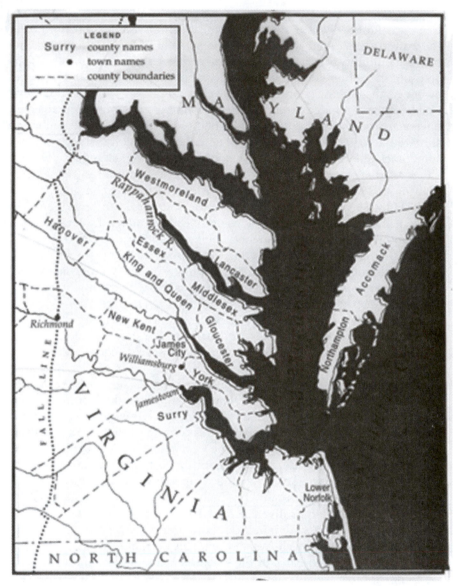

FIGURE I.2 *A Map of Tidewater Virginia.* Counties of Tidewater Virginia in 1774. Drawn by Richard Stinley.

highways for goods and people and barriers to travelers on land. In the seventeenth century, moving along the banks of a peninsula by boat was fairly simple, and settlements tended to move up rivers and creeks, leaving lands away from waterways sparsely settled for several generations.[5]

The landscape of the tidewater is remarkably flat, causing the salinity of the water supply to rise and fall with the ocean tides. Not understanding the nature of local geography, colonists inadvertently located their settlements in unhealthy spots adjacent to the malarial swamps along the rivers that bisected the region. Early colonists succumbed in great numbers to salt poisoning, malaria, and dysentery. In addition to the unhealthy environment, colonists' failure to plant enough food crops, and Indian attacks, further reduced the population of English settlers.[6] As a result of these various causes, life expectancy was low: in one county a woman who reached the age of twenty could expect to die by her thirty-ninth birthday while men who reached the age of twenty-four lived to a median age of forty-eight. Because 73.2 percent of children lost one or both parents before reaching adulthood, step-families predominated in the region. Family formation was further complicated by the nature of migration. Chesapeake settlers arrived as individuals, in contrast to New England's family-based emigration. An exploitative labor system in Virginia, based initially on indentured servitude, kept most English settlers in submission to masters for several years during which they could not marry. Eighty percent of emigrant women from England who came to Virginia arrived as indentured servants, and they faced the possibility of physical and sexual abuse. Only after completing their terms of servitude could surviving colonists start farms and begin families of their own.[7]

Virginia's earliest gender composition made family life difficult if not impossible for many male colonists. A disproportionate number of men were recruited to the colony as servant laborers. In contrast to their Spanish and French frontier counterparts, English men eschewed marriage to indigenous women and, consequently, faced a shortage of available marriage partners.[8] To remedy this situation, the Virginia Company recruited English girls and women to the colony, hoping that family life would make Virginia men more settled. Still, English women remained "rare," and those who have found marriage difficult at home encountered no shortage of potential mates in Virginia.[9] Over the course of the seventeenth century, three to four English men immigrated for every woman. The meager birthrate evened the sex balance gradually, but in 1698 men still outnumbered women in York County 487 to 309.[10] Women operated from a strong negotiating position when seeking upward mobility through marriage. Rather than requiring a dowry, desperate planters could "buy a deserving wife" by paying for her passage in return for marriage.[11] Respectable women could expect to marry soon after disembarking, and sometimes even a felon like Moll Flanders, sentenced as an indentured servant, might marry her way out of servitude.[12] Widows continued to be attractive as potential wives and found themselves with multiple offers of marriage, leading the General Assembly to pass a law in 1624 prohibiting individuals (effectively women) from contracting betrothals to more than one person at the same time. The legislation followed a January 1624 case in which Mrs. Cicely Jordan, a pregnant widow, contracted a secret betrothal with Rev. Greville Pooley days after her husband died, only to betroth herself a second time to another man.[13] Even pregnant, newly widowed women faced multiple opportunities for remarriage.

After marriage, women gained autonomy because high mortality rates left many widowed and in control of family assets at a relatively young age. Young and middle-aged fathers, facing their own mortality and concerned for the well-being of their underage children, wrote wills allocating much of the control over family property to mothers of their underage children, apparently believing them the most trustworthy individuals to watch over the children's assets. As a result, women gained at least temporary control of family property. Virginia women experienced more autonomy and power over family property than did those in England and New England, where women became widows later in life, after their children had reached maturity. Edmund Morgan goes so far as to refer to seventeenth-century Virginia as a "widowarchy." This is an overstatement, but at the same time it is a reminder of the great negotiating power of widows in the earlier period of settlement.[14] Virginia women generally obtained control over land and slaves through widowhood and not, in Moll Flanders-like fashion, through their own efforts.

While historical scholarship in the last twenty-five years emphasizes the role of the Chesapeake region's peculiar demography in providing women with opportunities to exercise greater control over their families' economic resources, these were not the only sources of such opportunities. Within Anglo-American culture wives routinely took responsibility for their families' economic interactions in the wider world during their husbands' temporary absences. This wider cultural phenomenon, while exacerbated in Virginia by the Chesapeake's demography, also occurred elsewhere.[15] Of course, no matter how capable women became, they were still expected to be submissive wives and dutiful daughters to the permanently acknowledged heads of their families—husbands and fathers.

As mortality rates became more stable in the early eighteenth century, the demographic rationale for women's agency declined. Accompanying this transformation, women experienced less opportunity for legal agency, partly because they did not become widowed mothers of young children as frequently. Nevertheless, the need for families with imperial trading interests to manage their businesses in the absence of men allowed women to continue to play an active role in these circumstances. One could hardly justify calling the earlier period of women's greater agency "golden," but the mid-eighteenth-century decline makes sense only if we understand the relative heights from which women's position of economic authority fell.

Refining the economic, legal, and social history of the long colonial period reveals the full extent of women's agency in Virginia. The women who are the focus of this book ran businesses, owned property (including slaves) and participated in the Atlantic colonial economy. They had an impact on both local and imperial structures through their ability to control aspects of their own lives, to influence the lives of others, and to manage wealth.

The theory that provides the foundation for this analysis comes from cultural anthropology, with its focus on ways to conceptualize negotiation among groups in hierarchies. Its focus on individual agency within hierarchal structures proves useful in the analysis of propertied women's power in colonial Virginia. Anthropologist James C. Scott points out that there can be "hidden transcripts" of resistance even within a framework of domination, and that powerful persons "have a vital interest in keeping up the appearances appropriate to their form of domination"; however, "subordinates, for their part, ordinarily have good reasons to help sustain those appearances, or at least, not openly to contradict them." The "mask of compliance and deference," however, conceals subordinate groups's covert actions.[16]

Women's resistances often reveal paradoxes that result from the imbalance in power between women and men. Even a woman who could be a strong, resourceful, competent individual might at other times behave in a weak, deferential, petty, or incompetent manner if acting in such a fashion served her best interests. Drawing on her analysis of oral histories, Bettina Aptheker concluded that even in the most repressive contexts, "while women were deeply oppressed, they were not passive, compliant, victims. Women acted." Women's resistance often occurred within the "dailiness" of their lives, through "accumulated effects of daily, arduous, creative, sometimes ingenious labors, performed over time...." Their efforts remain unacknowledged because women if they have been seen at all, generally have been considered as objects of oppression: either as the victims of circumstances...or as...backward and misguided pawns...." Aptheker quotes a social theorist in reminding her audience that "The fact that their resistance is not generally recognized is itself a feature of the oppression."[17] Declaring women passive and victimized in the histories perpetuates the oppression of women whose activities are made invisible by the historians.

In early North America, women and other subordinate groups negotiated their positions within hierarchies. Here, the work of Ira Berlin, in his history of slavery, is particularly useful for establishing the multiple ways that power relationships occurred. Berlin argues that the masters' vision of hegemonic power was only one of the "many dances of domination and subordination, resistance and accommodation" that shaped the lives of slaves. Relationships between masters and enslaved people included circumstances where white and black people "met as equals," occasions when "slaves enjoyed the upper hand," and times when slaves created their own world beyond the masters' eyes as well as the common and familiar situations where masters dominated. Although "binary opposites fit nicely the formulation of history as written" they "do little to capture the messy, inchoate reality of history as lived."[18]

Recognizing the role of women's commercial undertakings and identifying women's legal options as existing on a spectrum ranging from severe constraint to relative autonomy allows us to reconsider the nuances of coverture in one setting within the Anglo-American world. This should allow us to begin to explain the complexity of gender roles in Virginia in ways similar to those pioneered by historians of slavery who have stressed the problematic nature of seeing "slavery" and "freedom" as absolute opposites.[19] Increasingly, historians are beginning to understand both that Virginia women inhabited a culturally restricted position, and that some women resisted constraints, carving out spaces in which they exercised agency. Identifying complexity in gender relationships and the negotiations embedded in them, likewise, reveals the "messiness" of history as women lived it.

This history of how Virginia's propertied women carved out space for themselves within an oppressive social and legal system cuts across and modifies our understanding of several strands of historical scholarship. Most notable are the classic economic histories of colonial women, geographically situated transatlantic and Chesapeake studies, works on women in early modern England, women's studies scholarship, and legal and social approaches to colonial history. Women's experience was more complex than any single thread in historical scholarship could encompass.

Historians have long argued over the extent of colonial women's trading activities and the significance of their pursuits. In 1924 Elisabeth Anthony Dexter, in her classic work *Colonial Women of Affairs*, pointed out the many ways that women, primarily widows, actively participated in businesses. She immediately faced criticism, but was most "disturbed" by some readers of the volume who "welcomed it as in some sense an attack on the modern women's rights movement." Dexter admitted she was unsure of why her work had been labeled this way. According to Dexter, women's economic activities in the seventeenth and eighteenth centuries provided them with "considerable independence" without any injury to "their family life"; she felt that modern women could learn from the quiet balancing act of earlier generations.[20] Dexter emphasized the New England and Middle Colonies in her work, leaving Julia Cherry Spruill to provide a thoroughgoing analysis of southern women in her 1938 book, *Women's Life and Work in the Southern Colonies.*[21] Spruill covered a wider range of women's experiences reaching beyond their public lives to present both restrictions and opportunities Southern colonial women encountered.[22]

Later historians criticized these early-twentieth-century scholars for suggesting that a "golden age" for women existed in the colonial past. Contrasting her own findings with Dexter's, Mary Beth Norton concluded that women remained sheltered from and ignorant of the commercial world of exchange and credit. Analyzing the rhetoric of the economic claims presented by loyalist women after the American War of Independence, Norton determined that eighteenth-century women "lacked specific knowledge of their families' finances."[23] A further critique of the golden age theory was advanced by Carole Shammas and Alice Hanson Jones, who emphasized that the collective family economic identity mattered more than the individualistic one for this period. Both men and women relied on family capital and connections to get ahead, but women's agency was diminished by being subsumed under the heading of "the family."[24]

Not surprisingly, many scholars critical of the golden age conceptualization of the colonial period have stressed instead the rise of patriarchy. This view emphasizes the emergence of an increasingly rigid race and class system, founded on white male domination of Africans of both sexes and of all women. According to proponents of this view, white masculinity coalesced around a "new constellation of honor and manhood—rooted in property and patriarchy" that defined gender and race.[25] The process of restricting subordinates begun in earnest in the aftermath of Bacon's Rebellion in 1676, and was more or less complete by 1705, when slavery became codified by Virginia law. Guns provided the key symbolic component for white men's display of their power and position in society. Even when sentimental notions of marriage emerged in the middle of the eighteenth century, men continued to draw on the courts to preserve power over women in their families.[26] In current historical scholarship, the patriarchal model has replaced the "golden age for women" framework for understanding the colonial period.[27]

The history of gender in colonial Virginia, as elsewhere, is a history of power. Joan Scott, in her advancement of gender as a category of historical analysis, points out that power emerges from "dispersed constellations of unequal relationships." To understand gender fully, Scott encouraged study of the nature of human agency within social "fields of force"; She identifies human agency as "the attempt (at least partially rational) to construct an identity, a life, a set of relationships, a society within certain limits and with language—conceptual language that at once sets boundaries and contains the possibility for negation, resistance [and] reinterpretation...."[28]

Awareness of propertied women's power forces a reconsideration of the notion of "patriarchy" in colonial Virginia. Women's studies scholar bell hooks specifically addresses the failure of academics to recognize power relationships in which women dominated; she writes, "Narrowly focused feminist ideology tends to equate male development and perpetuation of oppressive policy with maleness; the two things are not synonymous. By making them synonymous, women do not have to face the drive for power in women."[29] hooks describes power as "the right to dominate and control others." She seeks to overcome the "sentimental" treatments of women's power in which the "image of woman as life-affirming nurturer is extolled." Instead, hooks urges us to see that "women, even the most oppressed among us, do exercise some power" and some women gain "material privilege, control over their destiny, and the destiny of others." The privilege of whiteness factors into these power relations.[30]

Seventeenth-century Virginia culture made space for self-willed women.[31] They managed plantations, ran businesses, and saw to legal affairs. They were, according to historian Suzanne Lebsock, "strong willed or rowdy or powerful, women who made their influence felt not only in families but in local communities and in the colony." To illustrate her point, Lebsock invokes the story of Sarah Harrison's creative wedding vows. In 1687, when the minister who read the service asked if she would obey her husband, Harrison responded, "No Obey."[32] An unbalanced sex ratio in this period accounts for only some of the authority accruing to certain women of the supposed "widowarchy."[33]

Through the middle of the eighteenth century, Virginia women still carried cultural baggage from seventeenth-century England that included expectations that men "had the larger share of reason bestow'd upon them" and women were "better prepar'd for...Compliance."[34] Faced with this set of stereotypes and limited opportunities to express wishes openly, women needed to negotiate creatively in phrasing requests. When expressing desires or seeking favors, seventeenth- and early-eighteenth-century English women consciously modeled their behavior on the image of the weak woman and spoke in a self-deprecating manner. This approach worked particularly well when women expressed political views.[35] Furthermore, encountering a dualistic set of ideal behaviors, women could select "when to display their feminine or masculine parts," deploying either when necessary or useful. To accomplish this balance, women, at least in the upper classes, learned both male and female skills, which they drew upon as needed, but they also learned to grant "the preeminent place to their feminine characteristics" and to conceal their own efforts to achieve their goals behind a mask of helplessness.[36] By the middle of the eighteenth century, English prescriptive literature persisted in portraying the ideal woman as passive even as women seized more agency.[37]

By focusing on women's power in the colony's history, this book moves historical scholarship from structures to practices. Law and prescriptive literature advising colonial women constricted their opportunities, but women who enjoyed the privilege of property ownership also gained competence and agency despite these cultural and legal restrictions. The propertied women who are the subject of this book are not necessarily "typical." However, we cannot understand gender—defined as socially constructed appropriate roles for each sex—unless we understand the extent of women's agency, as well as their clearly documented oppression.[38]

The hierarchy of colonial Virginia accorded propertied white women a degree of power despite cultural ideals that demanded subordination to men of their own race and class. One clear example of white women's power is revealed when we acknowledge that slave-owning women's economic power came at the expense of slaves' own autonomy.[39] Women who owned slaves did dominate and control them. The need to refine patriarchy in terms not only of structures but also practices is apparent when considering more theoretical definitions. For example, in concentrating on legal structures, one historian has suggested, "If one defines patriarchy in its purest form as the reduction of women to the status of property owned and controlled by men, then one can find many of its components in Anglo-American domestic relations law."[40] Pitfalls in applying such a definition of patriarchy to colonial Virginia are obvious: How do we conceptualize the power of white women who owned slaves while simultaneously considering these very same individuals as the "the status of property owned and controlled by men" within patriarchy? The relationship of the owners—often female—to the owned, the enslaved, existed within a layered hierarchy. While the hierarchy of colonial Virginia prevented even the wealthiest women from reaching the apogee of the most public of the power structures, it did grant wealthy women great power under certain conditions.[41] In practice, changes in the slave law during the eighteenth century which affected women's claims to slaves made them a particularly secure form of property for women to own, more protected in many circumstances from the grasp of husbands than was land.[42]

Legal histories make clear that concurrent with the rise of a patriarchal race and class system in Virginia was an overall decline in women's power under the law. Legal constraints on women grew in Virginia and throughout the British mainland colonies during the 1740s and afterward as anglicization brought the colonies culturally and legally closer to English patterns.[43] Despite propertied white women's continuing agency within mid-eighteenth century trading families, their actual roles increasingly conflicted with an idealized status that anglicized law and popular literature prescribed. By mid-century propertied women faced conflicting expectations, yet figured out ways to navigate them.

This book examines the restrictions that women with power endured, but also, the ways they exercised control over people and property. Legal records, letters, and economic papers reveal the range and limits of possibility for propertied women. These records demonstrate that there was much overlap in the activities that were deemed appropriate for women and men.[44]

Although Anglo-Virginia women lived within a hierarchical society, many enjoyed benefits of freedom and even property ownership generally unavailable to women in the nineteenth- and twentieth-century British Empire who found themselves "caught between two forms of domination, imperialism and patriarchy."[45] Before the American War of Independence, white women, especially those with property, could take advantage of the machinery of imperial power, right down to the level of the local county court.[46] Even when Anglo-American women experienced a subordinate position imposed on them because of their gender, they nevertheless benefited from their privileged access to bureaucratic power and state-supported personal authority.

Comparing the gender subordination faced by propertied women in Virginia with that endured by women elsewhere in England's empire reveals the relative privileges enjoyed by the former, who successfully acted using the institutions available to them. Recently historians of plantation societies in the Caribbean and elsewhere within European empires have focused on the privileges of propertied white women. Historians of women in the mainland North American colonies have been slow to follow their lead, however, preferring to emphasize the restrictions these women faced.[47]

The English background of the settlers provided the tradition upon which women acted in the colonies. In seventeenth- and eighteenth-century England and Anglo-America, women faced legal and social restrictions not imposed on men in their own class. Even so, scholars of early modern England have revealed gendered "resistances and subversions" within British culture and law during this period and also found inconsistencies in demands for women's subordination. As Sara Mendelson and Patricia Crawford point out, "Patriarchy's very resilience created contradictions which made resistances and subversions more possible. Contradictions inherent in the 'system' (more a ramshackle assembly of prejudices) were exploited by subordinate groups." Women were among those who exploited these contradictions for their own advantage.[48]

Previous analyses of American women's experience focused more on the structures that constricted women and less on the practical resistance individual women offered. Both elements factored into shaping women's lives, and this book shifts the emphasis back onto the ways women negotiated within local tidewater networks and as part of a transatlantic British world.

Clearly, submission and agency were intertwined for women, as they were for other groups of people in early America, but only occasionally do we catch glimpses of any awareness on their part of the double bind within which they acted. These women had to tread carefully between asserting their wills and stating their submission. They faced a tension between what they believed they should do and what they actually did, between normative and behavioral patterns.

The first half of this book examines how propertied women negotiated their roles within the legal system and economic networks of colonial Virginia, covering the legal constraints they faced along with the ways they used local courts to achieve their goals. Chapter 1 analyzes how women, particularly those contemplating a second marriage, sought control over property and drew on various legal means to retain it. Local courts and families supported these women's efforts because they wanted to make sure property descended according to their own wishes. Because young widows with children remarried, courts and women united in protecting the property of the "ghost family" they founded with their first husbands. The legal maneuvering these women initiated provided them authority over their property even when they married again.

The focus of chapter 2 considers how English common law protection of married women's right to dower, a limited share of family property, carried over to tidewater Virginia, and when English tradition and colonial innovation worked in opposition. With the anglicization of the law at the end of the seventeenth and the beginning of the eighteenth centuries, county courts stopped accepting less formally correct transfers of land that failed to protect women's interests and instead increasingly demanded full protection of women's dower rights in land sales. Thus, although demographic stability reduced widows' control over property at the turn of the century, propertied married women saw protection of their rights better supported in the courts during that same time.

This chapter also considers how eighteenth-century anglicization could work against colonial women's property rights under the law. In two test cases, Virginia authorities broke with English tradition to enact bills that granted women individual property rights. Metropolitan authorities vetoed both of the legislature's actions, illustrating the divergence in expectations on each side of the Atlantic. The Virginians found their efforts to adapt to their own demographic situation under review by an imperial legal structure hostile to such changes.

Although widowhood provided the most common means for women to gain control over family property, women in other circumstances had authority to manage affairs during marriage. The economic conditions and Virginia's distance from England left married women with authority normally seen as related to widowhood alone. Chapter 3 focuses on powers of attorney, one means for women to gain agency while husbands were absent pursuing business out of the colony.

As the first three chapters will demonstrate, women had reason to use the local legal system to achieve their goals, primarily within the context of managing family business. Having established the legal framework within which women could pursue their own goals, the next three chapters discuss the economic responsibility and discretionary authority women enjoyed. Some commercially active women required access to the formal structures of law, others operated outside of it. Local court records, personal papers, and merchants' records all provide insights into these transactions.

The second half of the book builds on the legal history from the first three chapters, examining women's economic enterprises within Virginia's restrictive legal system. Chapter 4 links the entrepreneurial endeavors of women who kept ordinary taverns with their need to use the local law courts in the course of operating their businesses. Here, too, local court records and personal papers demonstrate how these women drew on the power of the "state," through the courts, to support their own interests. Chapter 5 focuses on the married and single women whose business interests placed them as active agents within the colonial economy. These women negotiated within local networks and gained access to the consumer economy.

Chapter 6 discusses the roles of women within larger-scale, more formally organized transatlantic trading networks. Women in these family trade webs did not enjoy the independence of the local traders, but had specialized roles within family business networks. The letters merchants and customers wrote to each other reveal the commercial activities of married women who have eluded historians focusing on women's prescribed legal status at the expense of understanding their activities. The structure of the tobacco merchant houses placed women, in practice, in economic roles even when the structures of law and social expectation supposedly kept them from such tasks. Chapter 6 explains how women were significant not only as purchasers but also providers, and acknowledged as such, of goods within the "consumer revolution" that preceded the Revolutionary War. From this discussion, women's negotiated power becomes apparent. As beneficiaries of the hierarchy, the propertied women of this book sought a position of agency within the system, rather than desiring to overthrow it in its entirety.

The life of Susanna Lister demonstrates the contradictions that one woman faced when seeking to advance her own interests while simultaneously attempting to adhere to social norms of the colonial south and a wider English Atlantic world. Her story, like that of many women, remains hidden in manuscripts and in the microfilm made of her handwritten papers.[49]

On October 21, 1743, William Lister met an untimely death by drowning. He left a widow, Susanna, who initially met her financial and family responsibilities with expressions of her own helplessness in the midst of grief. In a family letter she signed herself, "y[ou]r Malincholy and Distres't Sister." Her English in-laws, the Lister family of Halifax, Yorkshire, engaged in international trade exporting wool, selling slaves to the New World, and importing goods from Virginia, Jamaica, and North Carolina;[50] William's drowning plunged Susanna into this Anglo-American commercial world.

William's ship went down with goods valued at nearly £200 and Susanna discovered her husband had left his affairs hopelessly entangled. At first, she claimed she was uncertain about how to protect her "fatherles Babes" and pay off the debt of £650 William had owed his brother Samuel.[51] Susanna requested advice from Samuel about how to manage her business and asked him to send copies of accounts between the two brothers, but she already knew enough to ask Samuel for a receipt when she paid him. Even in these first transactions, she demonstrated her willingness to dive into the management of the estate and to do so with surprising acumen.

Susanna became "Supris[ed] and Terifi[ed]" when a man posing as a creditor to the estate claimed a large demand on the estate. She feared "all might have gon To Destruction" until she discovered the purported creditor had merely been authorized by Samuel Lister to collect payment on a debt she already knew about.[52] The debt in question arose from an agreement her husband had made shortly before his death to purchase town lots and some plantation land "To Be paid at Sundry payments." Payments remained due, but Susanna pointed out that these lands had already increased in value five- and sixfold since the purchase contract had been made and that Samuel Lister would be ill-served by forcing her to break the agreements merely to gain short-term liquidity because this would reduce substantially the value of his brother's estate.

Her success depended on her ability to convince her English in-laws, who were her creditors, of her ability to repay the obligations and that she could manage better than James Murray, the family's agent. She outlined her plan to export local commodities including tar and other naval stores to London, Bristol, and Liverpool, to repay the estate's debts.[53] She also rallied her own family to assist her, persuading her father, John Lewis, to write her in-laws. Lewis did so, bluntly describing the annoying agent as "a proud Deciptfull Scotch man."[54] Immersed in the workings of transatlantic trade, she understood the use of bills of exchange for her long-distance financial transactions.[55]

What is striking in Lister's correspondence is a contradiction between her claims of helplessness and her assertive business ambitions. What explains the apparent shift from her expressions of helpless grief to attempts to competently administer the estate? Because of the debts, Susanna Lister was, in fact, financially obligated to her brother-in-law, and it was she who reminded him of this, in a perhaps manipulative way, claiming, "my Whole Dependence is on Y[ou]r Marcy and Goodness."[56] In early widowhood, at least, she shifted back and forth between claiming helplessness and asserting some knowledge and authority. Although she may have been truly torn, more likely she manipulated the stereotypes and language of the helpless widow to attain her goals. She understood her economic world enough to use the social expectation that widows were ignorant or helpless, but turned it to her own best advantage.[57]

Even while married, Lister and wives of merchants had occasion to learn about business. When William Lister was alive, he would have been absent at times, pursuing his shipping work, and Susanna might well have learned to manage day-to-day affairs of the family then. Still, she recited the tropes of helpless femininity when it was convenient to her, even while acting boldly, but as time went on, her letters suggest that she found it less and less necessary to do so.

When she asked for help Samuel Lister encouraged her to begin with a small undertaking, avoid giving out excessive credit, and deal only with dependable customers along with more platitudinous advice such as "Honesty is the best Policy."[58] None of this rather vague advice would have provided much assistance to a woman who truly had remained ignorant of all aspects of transatlantic trade. He also offered concrete recommendations, such as which merchants to correspond with in England, indicating he trusted her competence enough to propose she work with the family's commercial contacts. With the financial proficiency she presumably gained during marriage, her brother-in-law's advice, and her own savvy instincts, she successfully paid off the land seller.

The experiences of Susanna's sister, Anne, married to another of the Lister brothers, offers a contrast to those of Susanna.[59] Anne's husband also died young, but her letters back to the English family demonstrate a passivity absent in those of her sister. For example, in planning her son's future she wrote, "I Resign him Entierly to your Protection as a second Parent for it is not in my Power to do any thing for him which I beleve you know."[60] Anne had vague hopes that her son would return to Virginia and become a merchant, but she refused to offer her own opinion about how her son should proceed in his career.[61] In contrast to Susanna, who dealt with the problems of managing an estate, speculating in land, and warding off the troublesome Mr. Murray, Anne seems to have had little confidence in her own ideas or opinions.

Juxtaposing the structures that limited women's options with the niches they carved out for their actions allows us to make sense of a growing tendency at the end of the eighteenth century for propertied women to be economically active while simultaneously self-effacing and apologetic about their pursuits. As Susanna Lister's letters reveal, claiming powerlessness on occasion provided a means for women to achieve control over their own lives and those of others. One must not take these claims too literally, or Susanna Lister appears only as a helpless widow.

The goal of this book is to investigate contradictions between the realities and perceptions that propertied women like Lister faced. Their attempts to find autonomy and agency placed these women in a "new world" not only in geographic, but also cultural terms. They encountered inconsistencies in social expectations for their behavior. The prescriptive literature, including law as prescriptive literature, changed over time, as colonists first developed a "creole society" that adapted to the Virginia setting and later adopted English models.[62] Tidewater women, like their fictional counterpart Moll Flanders, learned to operate within the changing framework of their society, pursued their own goals and advanced the well-being of their families.

THE GHOST FAMILY:
INHERITANCE, PROPERTY,
AND STEPFAMILIES

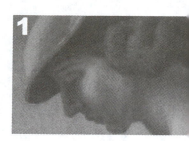

When Chesapeake Virginia women and men retreated into their households at night, they frequently surrounded themselves with their children, their slaves and servants, and often an array of stepchildren as well. In one tidewater county the high death rate meant that men in first marriages tended to die in their late forties while women in first marriages could expect to die in their late thirties. Until the middle of the eighteenth century, two thirds of the children in Virginia's Middlesex County who reached age thirteen had already lost a parent. A similar proportion of children in a York County parish could expect a parent to die before they reached adulthood.[1] Throughout the seventeenth century and into the early eighteenth, young Virginia widows often remarried, forming complicated families composed of step-relations.[2] Members of these families danced a ghoulish minuet of separating at death, then joining to form new, blended families of stepchildren and half-siblings.[3]

Individuals within these complicated families retained a sense of which property properly belonged to whom. Even within the new, blended families that remarriage created, Virginians acknowledged former nuclear families' residual existence in the bundle of property they held. That property fell to the members of the old family, often unequally, but still within the bounds of that family. I refer to this persistent entity as the "ghost family." The ghost family operated within the new blended families, but preserved its own resources. Parents wanted to make sure that the children of the ghost family inherited what was properly theirs, even if stepchildren were added to the new family. This chapter discusses the efforts of women to preserve their former nuclear family's property as distinct from their new family's, thus creating the ghost family.

Women preparing to marry had particular reason to be cautious because English law limited the power of married women over their property. English common law, itself in flux in the early modern period, provided one model for Virginians' notions of marriage.[4] As long as a woman remained single or widowed, the law deemed her a *feme sole*, a woman capable of keeping her own earnings, owning property, making contracts, incurring debts, suing or being sued, and writing a will. Once married, her legal situation changed. English common law held that the husband and wife became one person and that "the very being or legal existence of the woman is suspended during the marriage." A married woman was under both the "protection" and "influence" of her husband. In contrast to the feme sole, a married woman, known as a *feme covert*, had limited opportunity for legal impact on the world around her and could no longer make contracts, run up debts "for any thing besides necessaries," sue, be sued, or make a will. Indeed, she did not exist as a legal actor independent of her husband. According to *The Lawes Resolutions of Womens Rights*, a treatise published in England in 1632, "It is true that man and wife are one person; but understand in what manner. When a small brooke or little river incorporateth with Rhodanus, Humber, or the Thames, the poor rivulet looseth her name; . . . it beareth no sway; it possesseth nothing during coverture. A woman as soon as she is married, is called *covert*. . . clouded and overshadowed; she hath lost her stream."[5] In colonial Virginia, women's relationship to property proved far more complex than the river metaphor suggests. Remarrying widows with minor children created families where individual members had various, and often competing, claims to property held by the family collectively. Historians have accepted the view that powerful Chesapeake Bay women, once they became widows, took on responsibility for the estates of their deceased husbands. As compensation for property they lost at marriage, and as a means for a widow to support herself, common law provided a woman, at the death of her husband, with a dower portion, usually a third, of her husband's real property during her lifetime.[6] She could not sell or give away this property or grant it to anyone else in a will because it would eventually descend to his heirs. If a Virginia husband wrote a will leaving his wife less than her share, Virginia statutes granted the widow the right to protest the terms of the will. A dissatisfied widow could renounce her husband's will in her local county court and claim her legally assigned share.[7]

Rigid as coverture seems as a legal concept, the distinction ordained between the feme sole, who had legal capacity, and the married feme covert, who had none, was not absolute in the colonial setting.[8] From the days of Mary Beard, historians have recognized that common law alone failed to delineate women's actions and that "equity" jurisdiction (with its cases heard in Courts of Chancery) offered a significant means of defining women's property rights. Equity had emerged to mitigate the harshness of common law and to insure justice in cases where a plaintiff feared a powerful opponent could corrupt proceedings at law. In England, the lord chancellor heard equity cases and judged them on their merits. In Virginia, county courts heard both common law and chancery cases. From 1645 a defendant in Virginia could request a hearing in equity at any time before proceedings began on an issue. Once in chancery, a case would be kept from common law until the defendant had answered and the commissioners of the court decided whether the case would be heard in chancery or under common law.[9]

Equity provided various means for families to evade common-law rules regarding women's subjection to coverture. Perhaps most importantly, it enabled married woman to establish a separate estate to be held independent from her husband's control prior to or during marriage. The couple could agree to a "jointure"—a settlement made before to the wedding in which the bride gave up her right to claim dower in her husband's estate when he died in return for accepting instead the property designated in the document. This still did not give her active control over the property during the marriage. When Ralph Wormley of York County agreed in 1645 to a jointure establishing a trust for widow Agatha Stubbings, for whom he proclaimed "unfayned love and affection," he retained a life right to control the six slaves, various cattle, and extensive linens and pewter included in the agreement for his own "use benefitt and behoofe."[10] Agatha could have control of her wealth, but only after her prospective husband, who considered himself a "gentleman," had died.

Equity allowed for the creation of separate estates and provided the means for a couple, or their parents, to negotiate an agreement outlining what property the wife would keep. The property could then be placed in trust, with the wife designated either an active trustee or passive beneficiary. These, and separate uses more generally, were a growing phenomenon in early modern England. Creating a separate estate became simpler with the English publication of law manuals that included sample forms for lawyers and do-it-yourself readers to copy. By the eighteenth century English traditionalists grumbled that separate estates encouraged wives' disobedience toward their husbands.[11]

Widows raising young children and contemplating marrying again found contractual arrangements such as separate estates possible, even necessary, for two intertwined reasons—English legal tradition and distinctive Chesapeake demography. Although a widow as a feme sole possessed some control over property, she lost this power once she entered a new marriage, leaving her a window of opportunity before remarriage to assert control over her property. While this legal framework applied to widows in England, widows in colonial Virginia encountered the possibility of remarriage more frequently than women elsewhere in the Anglo-American world because the high death rate of seventeenth-century Virginia and imbalanced sex ratio, noted in the introduction, left more young widows contemplating the prospect of remarriage than did widows in England or New England during this period.

In New England, by contrast, existing scholarship suggests that women lived to about the age of sixty-three and men to about seventy. The children of New England marriages tended to be in their forties when they lost their parents.[12] Compared to these New England families, seventeenth-century Chesapeake settlers faced greater complications in their family affairs because youthful widows entered new marriages at a time when their young children (technically orphans after the death of their fathers) remained under their care. In both England and Virginia, fathers of young children tended to give their wives greater control over property than did fathers whose children had already reached adulthood and managed their own affairs.[13]

Although the wicked stepmother is a stock character in European fairy tales, colonists exhibited more concern that the evil or spendthrift stepfather would endanger the prosperity of a remarrying widow and her children.[14] Colonial men, aware that their chances were small of seeing their children reach adulthood, enacted legislation to protect their children's interests. The House of Burgesses required that county courts hold an annual session called the "orphans court" to receive an accounting of each child's economic assets. Guardians, including stepfathers and mothers, had to answer to these courts and demonstrate they had not embezzled the estates. At least one widowed mother of small children protested a county court's oversight of her management of her dead husband's estate and its requirement that she offer accounts to her local court. In 1647, Sarah Thorowgood Gookin, later Yeardley, complained to the Lower Norfolk County Court that she "of all others should be marked out to bee troubled in this kynd." Claiming knowledge of the common law, Gookin argued there was no precedent in England for an "executrix in my condition" to give an account before the children reached majority.[15] Even with the orphans' courts "great opportunity existed to despoil the parentless."[16]

Individual Virginia men demonstrated particular concern in their wills about second husbands encroaching on their estates. To protect their patrimonies, individual will writers granted property and executorship to their widows, but then made specific provisions stipulating that their widows would lose their rights to this property if they remarried. The terms of numerous wills reveal that husbands who trusted their wives' abilities during widowhood had less faith in their widows' capacity to protect estates and guard children's interests after remarriage.[17] In addition to relying on the official protection of the courts to oversee children's property, remarrying widows could seek individual measures such as prenuptial agreements to protect their estates from the threat of a stepfather's greed, ineptitude, or bad luck. Court records reveal why such measures were necessary.

In the fall of 1628, Dame Temperance Yeardley West lay on her deathbed. A prosperous woman, she had lived an eventful life, trading in tobacco and marrying George Yeardley, who served as governor of Virginia from 1616 to 1627. Within four months of his death in November 1627, the widow Yeardley made haste to marry Francis West, but only after this cautious bride negotiated a "covenant" with her intended husband.[18] Eight months after her marriage to West, Temperance herself died and her new husband fought her children over the estate.[19] The testimonies generated in this court battle provide an exceptionally full account of Yeardley's business activities during her lifetime, and delineate her plans for the estate after her death.

During her widowhood and subsequent marriage to West, Temperance Yeardley maintained an active interest in her holdings, retaining close control over current accounts. In order to retain her economic power, Temperance kept a separate set of financial records of her estate and her tobacco exports. She appointed William Claiborne to handle her shipments, which were substantial: according to testimony regarding her business, she appears to have exported 322 hogsheads (large barrels) of tobacco in the last year of her life.[20]

As a wealthy widow who brought three young children to her marriage with West, Temperance had reason to be cautious in her negotiations prior to her wedding. Even though West had proven himself as a military leader prior to their wedding, he began his rise to political power in the colony only after allying with her in 1628, the year of their marriage. She insisted upon a prenuptial covenant limiting his access to her property both during her marriage and after her death.[21] According to their agreement, West could count on receiving the substantial, but finite, sum of £1000 from his wife's estate once she died.[22] Even during her lifetime, however, she had no intention of turning her property over to West, and she continued to maintain her business affairs herself after the marriage. West later testified that he approved of this arrangement and during her lifetime "refer[ed] unto her the ordering of all the said Sir George's estate."[23] With the prenuptial contract Temperance sought to assure that her wealth would be distributed according to her own wishes, not those of her new husband.

Despite the covenant, West claimed a share of the estate based upon a reported deathbed whisper. Yeardley's children, represented by her brother-in-law Ralph Yeardley, sued Francis West over her estate, claiming that West secretly conveyed away "great quantities" of tobacco, money, and other goods properly belonging to the orphans. A family servant, Susanna Hall, also believed the accounts fell into West's hands after his wife's death.[24] West claimed that Temperance had changed her mind, increasing the amount of property she left to him. At the trial, witnesses were asked whether Temperance altered the terms of her agreement with West in her final hours: "Did ye said Dame Temperance the night before her death or at any other time . . . say that in case she died before ye def[endan]t he ye said def[endan]t should onely have out of her estate the one thowsand pound menconed in the [covenants] made between them before their marriagdge & noe more and did she expr[ress] also & publi[sh]e the same as her will."[25] Susanna Hall answered that if Temperance changed had her mind, it was "not in the tyme of her last sickness" and believed West was only entitled to the smaller sum provided by the prenuptial agreement. Although William Claiborne claimed he heard Temperance murmur that she wanted him to record revisions to her prenuptial covenant with West, she died that night, before she could make any changes by means of an oral "nuncupative" will dictated to Claiborne.[26] Women who made prenuptial agreements could retain the right to dispose of property through a will, but the Yeardley family asserted that Temperance never made such a will and that her intentions in the covenant drawn up prior to her marriage to West remained in effect at the time of her death, leaving the Yeardley children the bulk of the estate.[27]

Other seventeenth-century Virginia widows taking second husbands took similar precautions before marrying again. In 1679 Elizabeth English agreed to marry Robert Henley, but reserved to herself "liberty" to make a will "when or to which I shall think fit" to dispose of the land she inherited from her first husband. She specifically mentioned that she made the agreement even before the banns were published for her wedding to Henley.[28] Likewise, prior to marrying George Green, widow Sarah Pickett made an agreement with her intended husband that she would retain the right to distribute a specified sum of cash in a last will and testament "as if she was a feme sole" even if her husband survived her.[29] The powers these women exercised were limited, and certainly historians no longer claim, as one did in 1975, that awareness of their "scarcity value induced an imperiousness or even downright tyranny in Virginia's women" during the seventeenth century. Nevertheless, some certainly sought a degree of autonomy, often to guard their children's futures.[30]

Colonists of both sexes could have an interest in circumventing the distinctions made between the feme sole and the feme covert. Some of the considerations were practical and peculiar to the Chesapeake environment: without extended local networks of kin, prudent seventeenth-century parents who worried about dying before their children reached adulthood could designate what would happen to the family property once the surviving spouse remarried. This separate economic identity did not, therefore, always imply individualism or autonomy for the wife: while she retained separate property interests from her new husband, these holdings were not hers alone but shared with her children from a previous marriage.[31]

The degree of autonomy provided to women in prenuptial agreements varied enormously.[32] A few York County women entered contracts to maintain direct control of their property from previous marriages. Documents like Temperance Yeardley West's agreement explicitly outlined the authority these women planned to retain. Mary Stark, for example, used prenuptial agreements before each of her marriages so that she could manage her property for her own benefit and that of her minor children. Stark must have been well versed in these agreements after her five marriages.[33] When her first husband, Henry Power, died in 1692 she was granted executorship of his estate and inherited all of his real and personal estate so long as she did not remarry. If she remarried, the personal estate was to be divided equally between her and her children.[34] After that episode, she found ways to increase control over property during and after her subsequent marriages by establishing separate estates.[35]

In 1656, Richard Parker, of Charles City County, consented to his fiancée, Mary Perkins, "make[ing] over unto her selfe" all of the property left to her by her deceased husband, which included holdings in Virginia and England. In addition, Parker obligated himself to bring up her children and provide for their education.[36] When Elizabeth Lyman, a widow, married William Madox in 1669, the property she was to control after marriage was that which she had received from the estate of her first husband. In the words of their agreement, she was to have "during her life all the estate, property, servants, and lands that her husband John Lyman deceased left to her in his will."[37] Nor did this apparently legalistic precaution seem to dampen Madox's affection for his wife-to-be, since the agreement stated that he made it "in consideration of the love he has for Elizabeth Lyman." In the legalese of the day a transaction made "for love" contrasted with one made "for valuable consideration," that is, in exchange for a monetary sum or property. Lyman's agreement with William Madox "for love" falls into that category of prenuptial contracts created to allow the new wife to retain control over her resources for her own economic pursuits during the marriage rather than merely preserving the property in a trust outside her direct authority. Elizabeth Lyman Madox's 1651 agreement encompassed the entirety of the property she brought to the marriage.

Another York County court case demonstrates the extent of the authority a married woman could retain over her property. In 1672 Mary Croshaw, a repeat bride, prepared a prenuptial agreement that explicitly allowed her to retain, even after her marriage to Clement Marsh, "the same full p[o]wer & authority after marriage to dispose of & settle accord.[ing] to her owne will & desire her s[ai]d estate whether real or personall." She retained the right to grant the property to her children or "otherwise" dispose of it according to the "best advice agreeing with her judgmt."[38] Other women retained specifically designated assets: Rachael Constable Chew held the proceeds from the sale of four servants and some horses as well as retaining the right to the house and plantation where she had lived in 1651.[39] In Norfolk County, a prospective bridegroom gave his bride her own goods, and, in addition, offered to buy his wife a slave as her exclusive property "out of his meere good will and favor to his afore s[ai]d. spouse."[40]

In contrast to the prenuptial agreements that accorded women direct control of property during marriage, some trusts provided a way to maintain property in a woman's possession without necessarily giving her active management of it. A bride or her husband established a trust by making a contract with a third party, usually one of the bride's male relatives and arranged for that third party to hold the designated property for the bride herself. In a 1680 arrangement, Rebecca Travers granted eight slaves and their descendants, substantial numbers of livestock, silver and other household goods to two men to watch over. These two men were to be passive holders of the slaves and property, possessing it only for the use of Travers or whomever she gave it to in her own will or in writing under her hand and seal. Her intended husband, the merchant John Rice, must have considered her a good catch, because he agreed to this and accepted a provision that the slaves and stock would be maintained without charge.[41]

Prenuptial agreements to establish trusts provided one formal means to set aside property as belonging to a woman's children from a previous marriage (the old ghost family), either before or after the woman entered into a new marriage. In 1652, Henry Browne settled a trust on his wife Ann and their three children for their maintenance. The trust included his cattle, chattels, servants, credits, current crops, and future produce of the servants' labors. Unfortunately, there is little information on the Brownes' motivations for creating a trust; it most likely set aside property for the children's and Ann's maintenance in the face of economic adversity. Despite the fact that three men served as trustees and were legally responsible for overseeing this property, they seemed to serve as "silent" trustees because the wording of this particular agreement allowed Ann Browne to retain most of the discretionary authority over the property. She had the power to "dispose of the Cropps, and produce of the Serv[ant]s: Labourer[s] Children, and the Education of them, as shall be by her thought Fit" and expedient, and she should be able to exercise these powers "w[i]thout any contradiction" of the trustees.[42]

The management of trust assets provided women with the courts' protection of their assets during marriage and could necessitate visits to the court house, with the justices overseeing transactions. In January 1669, Robert Jones wanted to sell a horse that was part of the property held in trust on behalf of his wife, Mary.[43] Without a trust, Mary Jones's husband legally could have sold the horse without even consulting her. However, before her marriage, Mary Jones created a trust to set aside some property, including the horse, for her benefit. When it came time for the court to convey the horse to the purchaser, the justices asked Mary "in open court" if the sale was "her voluntary act." Without her permission for the transaction, the sale would have been void.[44]

When a bride worried primarily about her children's estate rather than her own economic autonomy, she could undertake the fairly simple procedure of making gifts to each of her children before the wedding and having them carefully recorded. This is evident in the wording of many of the grants, which start out with the phrase, "there is a marriage suddenly to be solemnized," and then listing the gifts to be given to each child. To secure the grants, the court could also require the stepfather to provide security for the performance of the agreement.[45]

Across the tidewater region, widows on the verge of contracting new marriages carefully worded deeds of gift to preserve their children's property. In 1681, Essex County widow Eve Williams made significant gifts of land and cattle to her two children prior to marrying William Smith, designating each child as residual legatee to the other. As a safety measure, Williams required her intended husband to sign the deed, effectively preventing him from claiming ignorance of the document later. Smith signed it and they had the document recorded at the same time as the marriage.[46] Because the children would inherit the property only after the deaths of Eve Williams and her intended husband, the gift effectively functioned as a will rather than as an outright gift, but as a married woman, Eve Williams would not have had the right to make a will. Two years later, the widowed Mary Day explicitly described the gifts she made to her child on her wedding day. She granted livestock and personal goods of which her son could take possession when he turned twenty-one. She recorded that the gift was made by the consent of her husband to be.[47] This pattern continued into the early eighteenth century. For example, when Sarah Anderson married Peter Vines in 1702, she made a deed of gift providing property for the use of her four children from at least one previous marriage. The property included horses and cattle to be divided among all the children when they reached age eighteen and, in addition, she specifically granted "Indifferent Pewter dishes" and other pots to her daughter. The intended husband also bound himself to honor the gifts.[48]

Widowers as well as widows made gifts to their children on the eve of their remarriages, presumably to prevent conflict over the distribution of property between children of a previous marriage and the new wife. Stepmothers could be a threat to stepchildren, too. When Edward Moorin of (Old) Rappahannock County (now part of Essex County) married a widow, Elizabeth Elder, in 1687, he granted cattle to his son.[49] Also in 1687, John Tiplady, a York County widower about to enter a marriage with Rebecca Wythe, drew up a prenuptial contract to protect his children's property from his wife if he should predecease her.[50] The Wythe-Tiplady marriage agreement proved useful to John Tiplady's daughters when, two years after the marriage, John died and Thomas Beale took up the cause of John Tiplady's daughter, Elizabeth, against the widow, Rebecca Wythe Tiplady. In the case Beale claimed Rebecca Tiplady sought "wholy to dispossess" Elizabeth of a slave that had been given to her. The court decided in favor of Beale and Elizabeth, demonstrating how Virginia prenuptial agreements protected children's property rights as much as wives'.[51] Prenuptial contracts could benefit both spouses and their children, though the agreements had greater significance for women about to marry because it was they who were subject to coverture.

The remarrying widows' prenuptial agreements and wedding-day gifts indicate the desire of women to settle property ultimately on the children of the marriage in which the property was acquired, even if the children would wait years until they received the goods, either upon reaching majority or at the death of the gift-giver herself. These transactions, while an implicit critique of coverture, allowed a woman little independence after she signed the documents.[52] In a few instances, women's autonomy extended even farther, as when, in 1682, a Tidewater County Court allowed Catherine Smith to make a postnuptial gift to her daughter from a previous marriage.[53] Such agreements reveal that though common law stipulated that the husband and wife became one (that *one* being the husband), in certain circumstances a wife could maintain a separate legal identity through careful arrangements.

Another way for parents to leave property to a daughter without a prenuptial agreement was to give a gift or legacy to a daughter, but to place restrictions on it to ensure that it stayed in their daughter's possession and descended to the original donors' grandchildren. From the daughter's perspective, this functioned in effectively the same way that prenuptial agreements did. Parents thereby mitigated the son-in-law's power by skipping his generation when distributing wealth. The daughter still had mere possession of the property, unable to sell or give it away, but she could be sure her children would receive it without its being reduced by her husband. The wording of some of these gifts and legacies, bluntly stating that no current or future husband of the daughter could control that property, make clear the parents' desires. For example, in 1659, William Thomas granted a cow and its increase to his daughter-in-law, Jane Hillier, to be for "Jane and her heirs only" but specifically excluded her husband John Hillier from ownership.[54] The reason for preventing the husband's control over Hillier's cattle is unclear, but the legacy may have fulfilled Thomas's own obligation to stepchildren from his wife's previous marriage, indicating how complicated the overlapping property obligations were in the blended families of the seventeenth-century colony, and demonstrating colonists' corresponding desire to maintain clear lines of descent for property.[55] In this context, a woman became the means to transfer property to the next generation more than she was an individual with autonomous control over property.

Once a second Anglo-Virginia generation was born in the colonies, parents of prospective brides demonstrated an interest in guarding family property and participated in the prenuptial negotiations. For example, in a late-seventeenth-century prenuptial agreement, Alice and Captain Jay bound themselves in a contract with their future son-in-law, James Porter. Their 1683 marriage contract stipulated that at his marriage with their daughter, Mary, James Porter "endued her w[i]th all the worldly goods belonging to her att P[re]sent and also other goods," and lands acquired in her lifetime, and, after her death, the property descended to their children.[56] In addition, the parents insisted that Porter purchase a "convenient" plantation for his wife and their heirs and buy a black servant or slave "out of his meere good will and favor" to Mary, whether she have children or not.[57] This case is interesting in that Mary's mother was listed as an active party in the agreement.

In the first half of the eighteenth century, married and widowed women lost much of their autonomous control over property as the colony's white population became more established. The Virginia-born white population began to live longer, parents reached their midfifties, and most saw their own children grow to adulthood. This had a detrimental effect on widows' power over property because the pattern in both England and Virginia was for fathers to leave more property to widows with minor children than to widows whose children had reached maturity. This alone does not account for the major shift, however, and Lois Carr found that by the 1730s, Chesapeake Bay widows tended to receive reduced portions of the estates whether or not they had minor children still at home.[58] Widows also lost control over property because eighteenth-century men stipulated in their wills that if their widows decided to remarry, they would lose property, thus providing an economic disincentive to remarriage. Eighteenth-century husbands began leaving less generous legacies to their wives, sometimes providing even less than the legally outlined one-third "dower" share, though Chesapeake widows who received less than their thirds could still protest in court and receive their rightful share of the estates. Eighteenth-century widows also lost control over family resources because their husbands were less apt to name their wives as sole executors to oversee the terms of their wills than had their seventeenth-century counterparts since they tended to have more male kin living nearby. Although Anglo-Virginia women began to enjoy longer lives and more stable families, the combination of demographic and cultural trends meant that eighteenth-century widows had less control over property and remarrying widows experienced even greater restrictions on their authority. In sum, as Lois Carr concluded, in Virginia and Maryland "widows on the whole lost ground."[59]

The break was not absolute, of course. Into the early eighteenth century, some propertied women in colonial Virginia continued to function as legal and economic actors. Women attending county court meetings found female company with the other widows overseeing family business. Female litigants were among the throngs on court days during the colonial period. At the York County Court, for example, very few court sessions were held in which no women's business was heard. Many of the widows appearing in the courts continued to be there to probate their husbands' estates, a potentially time-consuming process that included providing an accounting of the estate's assets, arranging for payment on debts the estate owed, and collecting debts owed to the estate.[60] Even after they remarried, widows overseeing estates continued to manage the legal business they had begun in widowhood, and courts recognized these women's actions as legitimate. In a 1721 case, a woman and her husband requested the administration of an estate, and when the court recorded the bond for their proper administration of the estate, it listed both husband and wife as administrators; nevertheless, only the woman ever actually signed the document, thus making her the public figure representing the couple in court.[61] The following year the court recognized the independent action of a married woman in managing estates when Mary (Moody) Atkinson successfully petitioned for the administration of the estate of one relative who died without making a will and for the executorship of the will of her father. The record is clear that Mary Atkinson was married, but it is equally clear that it was she who "came into court" and gave oath to gain administration of the estate. Although her husband was technically responsible, Atkinson took on the practical duties in acting for the couple in court.[62]

Lawsuits arising in blended families demonstrate the continuing importance of prenuptial agreements for preserving family property into the eighteenth century. In two particularly well-documented cases that reached the highest court in the colony, remarrying widows relied on the powers they outlined before marriage when allocating money or land. One such case, *Scarbury v. Barber*, initiated by Anna Maria Timson Barber Scarbury, reached the colony's general court in 1739. Before marrying Mr. Barber in 1731, Anna Maria had driven a hard bargain to protect her property. Like earlier Virginia widows, she undertook her own negotiations as a feme sole before the wedding. Unlike such widows, however, she was marrying a man who had borrowed substantial sums of money from her.[63] When he subsequently wanted to marry her—a good economic decision on his part as a means to cancel his obligation—she very likely suspected his intentions, since she refused her suitor's offer of marriage for several years. When she finally relented and married him, she first negotiated a "Treaty of Marr.[iage]" by which he agreed that she could continue to "enjoy all her separate Estate Notwithstanding the Marr.[iage]," and that he would pay back what he owed. To secure the "treaty," he gave a performance bond for

£1000 which would become due if the court determined he had failed to honor the agreement at any time during the marriage. The "treaty" designated no third party as trustee to hold Anna Maria's estate during the marriage; instead, she directly managed her estate and was to "possess & dispose of as she shall think fit all & every Part of the Estate that she in now possessed of both real & personal without the Molestatation" from her new husband or his heirs. Mr. Barber died first, at which point his widow claimed dower in his land and possessed her separate estate. She then remarried and she and her new husband demanded repayment of Barber's premarital debt to her from his children. The children protested their stepmother's demand, claiming that marriage extinguished all debts due before the marriage. Despite her efforts in the prenuptial "treaty" she had made with Barber to protect her property, Anna Maria faced legal difficulties after he died.

In her suit against her stepchildren Anna Maria brought evidence, consisting of a love letter, various financial documents, including some accounts, a few bills of lading, and some bonds, to support her claim. These miscellaneous records provide an exceptionally full account of the progress of the courtship and the negotiations a remarrying widow undertook to protect her interests prior to subjecting herself to coverture again. Anna Maria had proceeded with extreme caution: Barber courted her persistently and offered her "very good terms" for marriage, but she refused his suit for years. He had written one of his amorous messages in 1722, nine years before they married. In another, undated, love letter apparently written in 1727, he also enclosed a bond.[64] Barber's children claimed that a letter written four years before the marriage could not serve as evidence for the terms under which the marriage actually took place. They questioned whether the husband "remained in the same mind" four years later when the marriage occurred. At this point in the argument, the assumptions of the colonists concerning marriage and the nature of relationships between men and women emerge. The defense claimed that a male suitor's making an advantageous offer once did not suggest that he would be willing to make that same offer later—especially four years later: "On the contrary we know Mens Tempers & Inclinations are very subject to change & especially in Matters of this Sort when a Mistress is obstinate."[65] These negotiations reveal the windows of opportunity during which women had the most control in bargaining. Anna Maria had the upper hand during the courtship, when she could accept or refuse the financial arrangements that went along with contracting a marriage. Once she agreed to marry, she lost all power to renegotiate the terms, and the defense suggested that there was a limit to how much bargaining a man was willing to do with an "obstinate" woman before his temper altered. The agreement still failed to delineate the terms adequately, allowing the suit to develop.

The court sided with the more conservative defense, and it dismissed Anna Maria's suit demanding repayment of the prenuptial debt. Her appeal was also refused on a technicality, because her conniving stepchildren offered her £50, bringing the debt under the £300 threshold necessary for the court to accept an appeal.[66] An unmarried woman had some negotiating power before marriage and could parlay that into autonomous authority over property afterward, but only if she was extremely cautious in her proceedings, and in this case, patient enough to endure a courtship of close to a decade from a man in debt to her. Indeed, it appears in this instance that his wooing lasted longer than the marriage. The courtship lasted from at least 1722 to 1731, and the general court heard the case in 1739, after the husband had died. The period during which a woman could exercise her power over property, and solidify it in legal arrangements, was relatively limited unless she dragged out the courtship period.

A case from the Lancaster County Court reveals the difficulty of protecting assets belonging to individuals in a blended family, especially when they resorted to an oral prenuptial agreement. In May of 1760, the court heard a case in which Frances Blackerby Carpenter sued Thomas Stott, the administrator of her second husband's estate. She believed Stott had failed to provide her with the goods due her according to the terms of a prenuptial agreement she had made with Nathaniel Carpenter prior to their wedding fifteen years earlier. Nathaniel Carpenter, who had at least one son at the time, married Frances, widow of James Blackerby and mother of at least three children.[67] Frances extracted an agreement from Nathaniel, who had been her overseer before the marriage. Her fiancé had orally promised before several witnesses to leave her "as well [off] at the time of his Death as she was when she Intermarried with him" and offered "a Writing" confirming his agreement. The estate Frances received from her first husband had included many valuable goods, but her first husband had also owed many debts, which she was obligated to repay out of the assets. According to his will, she forfeited her legacy from him if she remarried, which she did. A lawsuit arose in 1762, after Nathaniel died, when the family disagreed over what he meant by leaving Frances "as well" off as she had been at the time of Nathaniel's marriage to her. She insisted Nathaniel's estate must provide her with the total value of all the goods she brought to the marriage, with no deductions for outstanding debts, while her stepson claimed the estate only owed her the balance after subtracting for those debts, thereby reducing the sum Frances should receive.

Frances lost her case in 1764, after years of litigation. John, Nathaniel's son from his first marriage claimed Nathaniel spent most of his income paying off his wife's debts. John bitterly spelled out how his father, who had always supported him in a "Decent" manner prior to the marriage, afterward could not keep him "so well maintained" because of his struggle to pay off Frances's debts. The Blackerbys, on the other hand, claimed that Nathaniel would not even house Frances's children from her first marriage without a provision for their support, which Nathaniel took in the form of hogs, money, and tobacco.[68] The Carpenter-Blackerby case also reveals how the courts upheld even informal agreements between bride and bridegroom. Nathaniel Carpenter made his agreement orally before other county residents, who offered depositions at the time of Nathaniel's death, fifteen years after the wedding. Nathaniel also made a written notation of the "articles" of agreement in his pocketbook—the small record book and wallet that colonial women and men used for their financial transactions in an economy with little circulating currency. Nathaniel instructed his son, John Carpenter, to keep this record and use it as evidence to protect his interests because this "Writing . . . would prevent his Wife from giting any part of his Estate."[69]

Nor were prenuptial agreements understood to be subversive to society. Instead, protecting the interests of the ghost family was seen as a moral duty as well as a legal obligation. In one transatlantic family, a stepgrandmother, Jane Metcalfe, insisted that her son fastidiously protect his stepchildren's property to avoid giving even the appearance of dipping into their assets for the benefit of his own children. Metcalfe, writing from London to her son in Virginia, admonished him in religiously toned letters that he had a moral obligation to see that his stepchildren inherited properly from their forebears. Jane, calling her son's stepchildren his "former children," understood the "temptation" for him to seize the property that their maternal grandfather had left them and distribute it to his own children, but Metcalfe warned him "it would not be only a sin but it may [be] a greife to thy wife."[70] The extended family, in extralegal terms, reinforced ideas about the proper devolution of property to the children of a particular marriage.

Judges also believed that a widow had an obligation to watch out for the interests of her children from a previous marriage and thought that remarrying widows who drew up prenuptial agreements merely behaved in a responsible fashion. To their minds, maintaining some separation between the property of the first, ghost family and a new family should be encouraged. The favorable social attitude toward prenuptial agreements is evident in the opinion set out in *Berryman & ux'r v. Cooper & ux'r*, a 1731 chancery case heard before the general court. The Berrymans complained that Mrs. Berryman's mother, Mrs. Cooper, refused to turn over property that she had earlier specified was due her daughters. The Berrymans based their claim on the fact that before Mrs. Cooper entered her second marriage, she required her fiancé to enter bonds promising payment of £100 to each of her two daughters from a previous marriage.[71] The second husband died before his wife and left part of his estate to his widow by will, but also left her the bonds obliging her to pay the £100 to each daughter.[72] Mrs. Cooper then entered a third marriage and refused to pay the sums to the daughters, one of whom, Mrs. Berryman, with her husband, sought payment.

The Berrymans' lawyer argued that Mrs. Cooper's taking out the bond to protect her children's property from the subsequent husband was not only a "very prudent and Laudable Action," but was also "her Duty . . . Because

Children have a sort of natural Right to a share of the possession of their Parents."[73] Rather than being a threat to patriarchal authority, in this case, it was socially admirable for a woman to direct the distribution of family property. Cooper took advantage of the momentary discretionary power she possessed between her marriages to try to protect her interests, but the case also demonstrates the limitation on her power. She was unable to change these bonds later, even after the daughters themselves had married and basic support from the mother's resources was less significant than it would have been if she had died while they still lived as minor orphans in the household of their stepfather. The court sided with the daughters, revealing the value it ascribed to the prenuptial arrangement.

Official expectations that widows ought to take active roles in managing the property of a ghost family persisted in the eighteenth century. In a 1761 York County court case, the justices allowed a widow to manage her family's legal business, even when she tried to shirk this duty. In this example, the local county court granted a certificate to two men for the administration of an estate and omitted the widow from this original certificate, but the court added a provision in its order that the executrix named in the dead man's will should have the "liberty" to join in the probate of the will "when she shall think fit." In this instance the court, while not delaying the administration, provided the opportunity for her to take on this traditional widow's task later even though it designated other executors to take over in the meantime.[74]

By the eighteenth century, prenuptial agreements defined property holding for first-time brides as well as for remarrying widows. These arrangements could be made by parents watching out for their daughters' interests. Agreements initiated by parents on behalf of first-time brides reveal their suspicions about losing property to sons-in-law. Although these contracts provided the wives with little independent control over property, the prenuptial agreements drawn up for first marriages reveal a far greater hostility to the implications of coverture. Creating provisions for separate estates at women's first marriages suggests a powerful critique of the legal custom which collapsed the woman's identity into that of the husband. Some of the difference in the tone of seventeenth- and eighteenth-century agreements may merely reflect the more detailed records of disputes that survive from the later period, but the nature of the agreements themselves seems to differ as well.

The bride's parents often initiated prenuptial contracts written on behalf of their daughter, suggesting that fathers, perhaps more than the women themselves, considered coverture detrimental to their interests, at least where sons-in-law were concerned. When negotiating with his daughter's prospective husband in January of 1776, Landon Carter wanted to settle on Lucy the six slaves he intended to give the couple, in part because the property the groom brought to the marriage was entailed and thereby descended in his family exclusively. In Chesapeake Bay families, sons tended to inherit land while daughters received slaves and moveable property, so this couple followed the common pattern of accumulating property to begin a new plantation. As a cautious father, Carter wanted to be "satisfied" that his daughter would be provided for if her husband died. He believed that to rely on the law to protect his daughter's property would be no different from "a Parent throwing his child into a river that some kind hand might save her from drowning." Carter's son-in-law claimed Lucy considered a settlement unnecessary, to which Carter replied, "Your wife out of weakness might, seeing your uneasiness, tell you so; but no Prudent parent ought not to do so." Carter worried that after the "full shine of the honeymoon . . . the moons of others" might shine on Lucy. According to Carter's account, Lucy remained innocently ignorant of her need to protect her property rights; only her crumudgeonly father prevented her from potential distress.[75]

A fairly simple means of preventing family property from falling into the active control of a son-in-law was for a will writer to grant property to a daughter's children, sometimes providing the daughter with the use of the property during her lifetime.[76] Families could also use a more elaborate mechanism to keep property under several generations of female descendants' control, even during the anticipated coverture of those unmarried girls. In 1768, Susannah (Rogers) Reynolds, who earlier herself had inherited a Yorktown lot from her father, left her own property encumbered on behalf of her daughters.[77] Reynolds was the widow of a Yorktown merchant, and by her own will she established a trust for the "separate use" of her land to benefit her daughter Anne (Reynolds) Savage. She also established a trust for the separate use of her daughter, Susanna, even though she specified that Susanna was not "yet" married. As an heiress herself, the elder Susannah apparently recognized the usefulness of a woman holding onto her own property, and valued this independence enough to establish a trust on behalf of her daughters and granddaughters even to the point of covering all options, including the younger Susanna's eventual marriage.[78]

A more ethically suspect use of trusts emerged during this period, too. After a marriage, a family could settle a trust on the wife to the benefit of the family as a whole. Husbands as well as wives had reason to take advantage of this maneuver because it prevented creditors from seizing family assets listed in a woman's name. In 1771, during a period of economic instability, Anna Catherine Moore and her husband, Bernard, established a trust for Anna and her children. Anna reported that Mr. Moore's "unhappy circumstances" put his creditors at their door, and since at the time Anna's aunt planned to leave a legacy or make a gift to the family, both Anna and Bernard wanted the gift to be protected from Bernard's creditors. They hoped to do this by means of a trust held by their factors (business agents) for the use of Anna and the children. This trust was not created for female independence, though the measure had this ultimate effect, but rather to protect the family's assets.[79] This sort of arrangement retained a suspect quality into the nineteenth century, when it became more common, because it was thought to be a means by which men fearing bankruptcy could hide from creditors behind their wives' financial skirts. Using trusts in this manner usually signaled a family's downward mobility.[80]

Cajoling mothers and fathers, and even more distant family members of prospective spouses, participated in negotiating the marriage agreements. Love, money, and family influence could stir up a heady brew. In calm prenuptial arrangements, a relative merely needed to grant approval for a marriage to proceed. A 1753 example of this appears in the account book of one man who, along with his more mundane financial arrangements, recorded the payment he made to Colonel Presly Thornton as a "portion to your wife my Cousin Charlotte." Charlotte Thornton had been promised this £500 if she "marryed to please" her cousin.[81] Parental strong-arm tactics led to the late seventeenth-century marriage of one Mrs. Slate of York County. In 1691, Mrs. Slate reported to a neighbor that although she believed her husband loved her, "truely she had never any reall love for her husband." She claimed that her parents, who lived nearby, forced her into the match. The dangers of a marriage without the woman's love and consent were apparent, however, when Mrs. Slate proclaimed her independence within her new family, boldly bragging "lett me goe & come when I will my husband will not controle me."[82]

Parents who did negotiate on behalf of sons and daughters might proceed in underhanded as well as transparent ways in order to speed along their marriages. In a not-quite-conspiratorial tone, the mothers of Mary Pricket and Robert Green worked on their children's agreement. Before Mary and Robert married, Robert's father announced that he had given his son a deed of gift. Mary's mother took on an air of caution, wisely inquiring if the deed had been acknowledged officially in court. Robert's father responded that it had not. Mary's father, when he heard that his potential son-in-law had no official record of receiving the land, refused to allow his daughter to marry. Robert's mother, anxious to see the young couple married, encouraged her husband to give his son the land. Initially he refused her request because he was then "in Drink," but by the next morning she had succeeded in bringing "the Old Man (her husband) into a good humour…and the deed was read, signed, sealed." Robert's mother kept the document for safekeeping.[83]

Robert's father later claimed he had not intended to give his son the land and that the gift had been made "in a great Passion." Unless Robert's father had a short memory, this suggests that Robert's mother struggled to bring her husband "into a good humour" either while he was sober or still "in Drink." This story reveals the various ways in which women could exert power. The bride had little voice in the transaction, though she had little need to speak as long as her father and mother stood firm on their demand, presented on her behalf, that the young couple possess land before their daughter could marry. The groom's mother could only use indirect influence to bring her own husband around to making the gift,[84] but eventually she convinced him to follow her wishes. The power of the women in the senior generation was indirect, but their efforts brought about the desired result of providing the newlyweds with the means to begin their own plantation.

The significance of a mother in negotiating to protect her engaged daughter's property is apparent in the case of Mary Latané (1685–1765). Mary Latané and her future son-in-law, Dr. John Clements, disagreed from the time they began discussing the property that Mary's daughter, Mary Anne, would possess after the wedding.[85] Prior to the wedding Dr. Clements came to Mary Latané and asked what she planned to give the couple as a gift. She responded that she intended to provide her daughter with four slaves. Not satisfied with her answer, Clements pressed the issue by asking if the slaves were an outright gift or if he would have to wait until Latané's death to obtain the slaves. She replied that she planned to give three slaves "when they went to house-keeping" and the fourth at her own death. The less-than-tactful Clements started the wedding day by bringing Latané a document to sign that he had composed himself stating that she would give him, rather than Mary Anne, the slaves. Latané declined this emotional blackmail, refusing to accept his wording because she planned to "secure" the slaves to her daughter and then to any grandchildren that would be born to the marriage. She explained her reasons for doing this, but noted that Clements seemed "disturbed" about the terms. After a pause he said he would proceed with the marriage and "take her att all Hasards" but "would not hear of an Intail," which would have limited his control over the property and prevented him from selling it. His blustering failed. Latané then wrote her will, in which she gave her daughter a portion of land, and "lent" the slaves to her daughter and Clements during their lives, after which the land and slaves would be divided among her daughter's children.

This plan initially pleased Clements, but he later "flew from all this" and demanded that she write another will. He "then dam'd the Land and said he would hardly thank any for it and if it was Escheatable [in danger of being lost to the Crown for unpaid taxes or public obligations] he would not be at the Expence to save it." Instead, he brought Latané a deed of gift and asked her to sign it. She refused and proposed an alternative solution whereby the slaves would go to her other heirs if her daughter had no children. Clements at first acquiesced, but after she drew up the document, "his mind was quite changed." Latané said she would not alter the document, but agreed and had it recorded after the persistent Clements again "Dam'd the land" and asked for a deed of gift. In an undated letter to Clements, she attempted to reverse the deed, describing the events leading to its writing and asking for reconsideration. She complained, "how you would like to be us'd after this manner as I have been and for what I have don[e] the worst word and the contemptible behaveour that ever a mother-in-law met with."[86]

The slaves and land provided the means by which Mary Latané retained her power in the family and also provided the vehicle for ensuring that the property remained in her daughter's line of descent. Clements and Latané were of the same race and class. In gender terms alone, Clements should have dominated, but the relationship was complicated by further details. Latané possessed property Clements considered his due by his marriage, and with that property she retained a powerful position in the relationship until she deeded it away. Latané's authority over her son-in-law derived from several factors. Her position as mother-in-law, possibly her age, and certainly her property, all granted her a position of power over a man of her own race and class.[87] Clements resented this situation.

Latané's ownership of property and her ability to decide how property would descend in the family were the other sources of her power. Furthermore, Mary Latané's strategy for settling her land and slaves over the next two generations, despite her son-in-law's protests, reveals her awareness of the property's importance in maintaining her power, and perhaps even her independence and authority. Clements should have lost nothing but direct authority when his mother-in-law encumbered the gift of the land and slaves to his wife. Presumably, the couple and their children would share in the benefits of income they derived from the productivity of the land and the work of the slaves. The problem remained, however, that he would be required to share control of the wealth and income with his wife during their lifetimes. Clements would never have absolute control over the land and slaves in his lifetime and had no right to have such control or to make a will disposing of the slaves at his death. It was not the benefits of wealth per se that he stood to lose, but independent authority over it, potential to borrow against it, and, perhaps, the social standing and family position that wealth accorded the individual in control. These would, however, be particularly sensitive issues to someone like Dr. Clements, whose social status was initially based upon his education and who, through this marriage, placed himself in a position on the edge of acceptance into the colony's landed elite. But this would have been an incomplete integration into the elite if his wife's wealth remained encumbered so that he obtained no direct management of the property. Matrilineal devolution of property threatened to impose matriarchal authority, a possibility that bothered Clements, but was quite acceptable to Latané. Power over property, then, complicated the equation of male dominance over female family members.

The actions of the women in another family, the Holladays, demonstrate the limitations and range of options women had in taking legal action. In this eighteenth-century family, Elizabeth Holladay protected the family against a prospective son-in-law who attempted wedding-day blackmail. Holladay used prenuptial agreements to preserve her own and her daughter's property. She had good reason to be cautious in making negotiations for her own second marriage and for her daughter's first: when John Littlepage, her first husband, died he willed most of his property, including land, the home plantation, a mill, and his slaves, to his sons from a previous marriage. Refusing to accept the terms of the will, Elizabeth demanded instead her full rightful share—that is, her customary dower rights.[88]

Refusing the limited allocation to her in her first husband's will was only the beginning of Elizabeth Littlepage's legal activities. During her widowhood she bought additional slaves from her deceased husband's estate. She purchased 480 acres of land that had been her brother Ben's patrimony. According to contemporaries, "her exertions were constantly used" in providing for the two Littlepage children.[89] Having striven to improve her economic position, she sought to protect her interests by establishing a trust before she married Lewis Holladay, installing another brother, John Lewis, to act as her trustee.[90]

She was equally cautious when she began negotiations prior to her daughter's marriage. Robert Spilsby Coleman courted Elizabeth Holladay's daughter, Mary, and by December 1782 had raised the topic of marriage. Coleman took advantage of Mary's stepfather's wartime absence to visit the house and then courted Mary without her mother's permission. Mary's mother worried that he wanted to marry her daughter "for Lucrative and disingenuous motives" rather than "from those of esteem and affection." Mrs. Holladay's suspicions were further aroused when she discovered that Coleman had been at the center of a scandal in which he had betrayed and dishonored a young woman of a reputable family and "afterward was ungenerous enough to forsake her."[91]

Coleman failed to endear himself to his future stepfather as well, treating him rudely and announcing that Lewis Holladay had been a "common overseer" and possessed of only a single horse when he had married Elizabeth Littlepage Holladay. Not willing to let this accusation stand, Mrs. Holladay countered that her husband descended from a reputable family and enjoyed the respect and esteem of the neighborhood. Ultimately, Mrs. Holladay permitted Coleman's marriage to her daughter only when she discovered her daughter's "affections to be fixed" and that the marriage was "prudent for reasons unnecessary to mention"—presumably pregnancy.[92]

One day the tension grew when Mrs. Holladay walked into a room where Coleman sat with Mary and found Mary crying. She asked what was wrong and then told Mr. Coleman "you know what is the occasion of Pollys [Mary's nickname] oneasyness, she expects you are going to leave her." Mr. Coleman said he intended to marry her but that he could not without a gift from her parents. At that point Mrs. Holladay told her daughter "see Polly what you have brought yourself to by this sorry fellow you may plainly see that it is property he wants."[93]

Coleman refused the terms of the first agreement the Holladays offered and claimed that his own father refused to grant the couple anything if Mary's parents would not provide for them something for setting up housekeeping. Coleman still wished to marry Mary, but would not unless her parents would "Speake freely and Candidly what you Design to lefe on your Daugter."[94] Eventually Coleman married Mary anyway, claiming that Elizabeth Holladay verbally granted her daughter two slaves as a gift at their marriage. A lawsuit erupted when the timing of the Holladays' gift came into dispute and then continued by appeals into the nineteenth century.[95]

In order to win her case Elizabeth Holladay had to claim that she had no independent right to give the slaves to her daughter—that she needed her husband's approval before she could legally make any gift. Coleman could claim the slaves only if his mother-in-law had separate power over those slaves through the trust she established before her own second marriage. Otherwise, Coleman had to wait for Holladay's death for Mary to inherit the disputed slaves. Elizabeth Holladay's side attempted to claim the trust was fraudulent because Coleman had taken "*improper advantage*" of Lewis Holladay in forcing him to execute the deed of trust the day before the marriage and nearly two weeks after the license was out, implying that "there was a surprise on his part," placing an "undue influence" on Holladay.[96] This strategy was sufficient to void the trust and prevent Coleman from receiving the slaves he claimed as his due. Ironically, a separate estate for Elizabeth Holladay protected her property from misuse by her second husband, but, in this case, exposed her property to a claim by her son-in-law.

By July 1783 the Colemans had a son, and Richard Coleman used the occasion of his wife's lying-in to attempt to manipulate his mother-in-law again. He reported that during Mary's labor she thought she was dying and called out for her mother, who did not attend the birth. Coleman scolded her: "If you as a mother have lost of all bowels of Compassion Over y[ou]r. daughter as a Child, I think that she to you as a mother seems to bair a deeper sence of the humane mind."[97] Coleman was willing to cite gender conventions to get what he wanted from his mother-in-law.

The testimony by both parties and by deponents on their behalf reveals the power struggles within the families, especially between Elizabeth Holladay and her son-in-law, but also how Elizabeth Holladay manipulated social expectations concerning gender to achieve her own goal of thwarting Coleman in his attempt to control her property and that of her daughter. The depositions spell out some of the contradictory gender ideals of the period. According to the Holladays, Mary had always been a difficult daughter with an "obstinate temper," which the Holladays tried to amend by impressing upon her "the purest principals of morality and virtue." They thought they had succeeded and believed Mary had "no reason to swerve either from the influence that the authority of a Husband might have over" her or "from any other motive."[98] The Holladays' testimony provides a telling account of the limits of how far a husband was expected to influence a virtuous wife when she still was expected to be "dutiful" to her parents' competing desires.

In contrast to the Holladays' hopes that Mary would rely on her own sense of independent moral duty, Elizabeth herself hid behind the terms of subservient wifehood in arguing her side of the case. In another incident, Elizabeth Holladay invoked the trope of helpless femininity as her own defense against her daughter. When Mary Coleman went to her mother to inquire if she might have two specific slaves her mother responded, "I am but a woman I shall give nothing or do nothing" to explain why she would not give them to her.[99] Elizabeth, too, could manipulate assumptions about women for her own benefit.

The contested Holladay, Yeardley, and Latané disputes all turned on the inability of a married woman to reassign her assets once she had executed a document that bound herself as well as her husband to her prenuptial economic wishes. Women had power over property, but like Mrs. Cooper (of *Berryman & ux'r v. Cooper & ux'r*), found they had a limited window of opportunity to exercise that power and only within legally defined circumstances. Once Cooper made the bonds, she found she had limited her own options as well as restricting her husband's freedoms.

The ways property was transferred from individual to individual and from the collective family to a particular individual demonstrates the ways colonists understood women's positions within families.[100] While the law had always limited married women's power over property, in the seventeenth century some women, especially remarried widows, managed to create ways to keep even a modicum of authority over wealth for as long as possible. The opportunities for women to take advantage of even this limited autonomy decreased, however, in the eighteenth century, when the divide narrowed between the prescriptive literature of common law (with its emphasis on the subordination of the feme covert) and the practices of Virginia wives, who found fewer chances to control their property. Fewer Virginia brides had opportunities to exercise such power once families became more stable. The remarrying widow with her obligation—and opportunity—to oversee the assets of the ghost family became less common.

"HARDSHIPS UPON WOMEN": ANGLICIZATION AND PROPERTY LAW

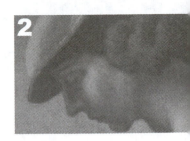

2

*O*ver the course of the colonial period the property rights of women, particularly those of married women and widows, changed as a result of county courts' practices, deliberate legislation at the colony level, general court decisions, and imperial directives from the king and Privy Council. While court records reveal that changes began in the seventeenth century, innovations became more obvious when the Virginia Assembly overhauled the colony's statutes in 1705 and then enacted further large-scale changes and clarifications in 1727, 1748, and 1752. Any colonial legislation required dialogue between colony and mother country because the crown retained the option to "disallow" (veto) colonial legislation. As a result, legal innovations in the colony played out against the backdrop of English expectations, making the transatlantic framework significant for understanding the history of women's property rights. While some changes brought women's property rights in Virginia more in line with English expectations, others did not and risked rejection by imperial authority. This chapter considers the extent of "anglicization"—the process of bringing colonial law into conformity with British practices—in three different areas defining Virginia women's property ownership: married women's power over family land, married women's claims to their families' slaves, and finally, legislation that established married women's access to their own earnings and property.[1] What these three aspects reveal is that women's property rights followed no easily discerned trajectory toward "improvement" or "decline," or even "innovation" or "anglicization."[2] Instead, two different trajectories developed. On the one hand, colonists anglicized their legal procedures; on the other, the second and third generations of colonists diverged from English assumptions about property, which included land and the slaves who made land ownership valuable. These trends affected the ownership of property by married women. The contrast between English and colonial attitudes became apparent when Virginians attempted to float two mid-eighteenth-century test cases about married women's right to dispose of property, and these cases ultimately reached the English solicitor general's office. In these two final cases, colonists diverged from their English counterparts, only to have imperial authorities undermine their efforts.[3]

Protection of women's dower rights in real estate at the county courts demonstrates one way that Virginia women's property rights became "anglicized." These changes in form affected married women's rights over property and increased the veto power married women wielded over family property in the courts. The surviving records of the county courts of tidewater Virginia reveal that these courts consistently documented their protection of married women's dower rights at the end of the seventeenth century.

To provide for a woman's support during widowhood, English common law guaranteed a widow a portion of her dead husband's estate as her "dower." It usually constituted a life estate in one-third of the real property the couple owned during their marriage.[4] Dower claims traditionally acknowledged the financial contribution that a bride's family made to the couple when they married. As historian Carole Shammas points out, "The existence of dower claims widows could make on estates and the practice of daughters inheriting from fathers were, at least initially, due to the status accorded a woman's kin group, not the woman herself."[5] *Dower*, a widow's share of the family property at the end of the marriage, contrasts with *dowry*, the property a bride brought with her into a new marriage. As we saw in chapter 1, a married woman (a feme covert) legally was considered to have no will independent of her husband and lost control over her property when she married unless she made a prenuptial agreement. By allotting the widow some rights to land that the couple owned during the marriage, the law ensured that a widow could support herself either directly from the crops harvested on the land or indirectly through some other type of agreement.[6] She might, for example, permit a child to have use of the farm in return for an annuity or a place to live. The growing proportion of widows among the recipients of poor relief at the beginning of the eighteenth century suggests that these efforts did not always succeed, and only widows from landed families would benefit, but setting aside some land for the widow's use was a gesture toward providing for her.[7] A widow's attractiveness to a new husband also could be increased by this lifetime possession of land, an important consideration for a society that encouraged its members to be settled in families. If her husband wrote a will leaving her less than the dower share as outlined in Virginia statute, she could sue to recover her prescribed allotment.[8]

This system became more complicated if a couple sold land during their marriage. In a practice dating back to the Middle Ages, one way that English

courts frequently recorded land sales was through "fine and recovery" conveyances. This involved a fictitious lawsuit in which the purchaser, as the
purported victor in the suit, acquired secure ownership of the land after a
period of time (usually a year and a day) had elapsed. Sellers found this
process expensive and time-consuming, so they began to adopt a simpler
form of conveyance, through the "bargain and sale," which in England was
becoming more common, especially in urban areas, during the eighteenth
century. Virginians found sales by fine ill-suited to their rudimentary court
system and, some time before 1674, had adopted the system of "bargain and
sale" procedure for land transactions. Both bargain-and-sale and fine-and-
recovery transactions required the private examination of the wife to ascer-
tain if she agreed to the sale. If a husband sold land without his wife's agreement, she could, at his death, return to claim a third of the family's real
estate and possess it during her lifetime.[9] Purchasers would be wary of
acquiring land if they realized the seller's widow might return to haunt them
for the "thirds" to which she was entitled during her lifetime.[10] To solve this
problem, a buyer could require the seller's wife to renounce her dower rights
at the time the land was sold. In order for the sale to be valid, the wife had to
renounce her claims and agree that she did so without coercion from her
husband. The courts developed a procedure to examine the wife privately
(with her husband absent) to verify that she granted her consent to the sale
without his compulsion. If she freely consented to conveyance, including
the sale of her dower rights, the court recorded that fact.[11]

A 1685 sale of Virginia land recorded in the London Lord Mayor's
Hustings Court offers a contemporary example of how English courts
recorded transactions of this sort. Elizabeth Osborne, the wife of an
Englishman who had inherited a Virginia estate from a relative, used the
London Mayor's Court to acknowledge her approval of a sale in a private
examination where she specified she had made the decision without
"threats constrain[t] Compulsion or other meanes" by her husband.[12] This
very precise acknowledgment regarding Virginia land was made at a same
time when Virginians themselves remained more careless in procedures
protecting women's rights.

Although a wife's assent to the surrender of her dower rights in a land
sale represented the ideal under English and Virginia law, the reality sometimes strayed considerably from this practice in the colony.[13] Before 1700,
the records reveal that wives did not always acknowledge by private examination the alienation of lands in which they had rights or, at least, the court
did not record examination. For example, some York couples sold land in a
variety of ways without always bothering with the wife's traditional acknowledgment. They were permitted to accomplish the same goal by having the
wife and husband be recorded as cosellers or cograntors of the property.[14]
The format of this type of grant varied, but generally the husband and wife

were both listed on the deed as cograntors.[15] The husband's name was always given, but in some transactions the wife was simply listed as "my wife." Deeds in this form were usually signed by both husband and wife. In other sales, only the husband was named in the deed, but the wife signed or made her mark at its close. Sometimes an attorney-in-fact made the acknowledgment for the couple jointly without private examination of the woman.

In the middle of the seventeenth century, problems remained in the examination process and it appears that individual colonists misunderstood the process of acknowledging deeds even when they attempted to follow the correct form. At the end of the seventeenth century and beginning of the eighteenth, tidewater courts sometimes recorded women's alienation of "dowry" instead of "dower," suggesting some confusion about the meaning of the terms.[16] In 1657 William Crumpe sold a substantial amount of land in which his wife, Anne Crumpe, had dower rights, to Charles Woodington. Anne appointed an attorney to acknowledge the assignment in the common Virginia manner, but the person she designated as her attorney-in-fact was none other than her own husband.[17] Clearly, appointing her husband as her attorney in this transaction circumvented the purpose of protecting her from his potential coercion. Another example of a deed that deviated from the norm was one careless or perhaps even fraudulent sale. In 1670, Bryant Smith sold the land that his wife, Dorothy, had inherited from her father. Instead of including his wife's approval, Smith promised that "his wife [would] acknowledge the assignment" at a later date. Yet the buyer apparently accepted this procedure.[18] Legally, Dorothy retained her rights, since there is no record of her acknowledgment. Although the York court recorded transactions that approximated English customary form, it did so without demonstrating understanding or concern for its intended purpose of protecting the wife's property rights from the husband's coercion and merely followed the form of common law procedure without regard for its substance.

Sales were recorded in several different ways. In one, a woman, along with her husband, signed the bond to keep the deed, though she did not make a separate acknowledgment for the sale.[19] Rather than using private examinations of wives' consent, courts accepted public acknowledgements if they took them at all. This, too, circumvented the wife's opportunity to protest the sale in her husband's absence. Generally, when the court displayed any attempt to meet common-law requirements, the acknowledgement was merely an in-court assent to the transaction. Although the court increasingly mentioned the wife's "free and voluntary consent," "voluntary act and deed," or the fact it was made "without compulsion" in the 1670s, the record does not record the wife's private examination or her approval.[20] While these transactions did not meet the strict standards of common-law land sales, none seemed to be contested later by widows claiming they had not received their rightful lands.

By 1701, the York County clerks often indicated that a woman was "att lawfull age & Did freely acknowledge all hir right of Dower to the Within: mentioned land and primises."[21] This form fails to record details about private examination for the alienation of the land, but does report that the woman had a right to her dower share and that she was of age to alienate it. Despite a few attempts at improving the process of alienating women's ownership of land, the court continued to demonstrate a flawed understanding, or lackadaisical concern, for protecting women's property rights in these transactions.

By the late seventeenth century, even Virginians noticed the general failure of their county courts to adhere to English examples. Henry Hartwell, James Blair, and Edward Chilton, three colonists who had returned to England, criticized the disorderly way that law courts worked in the colony in their 1697 report to the board of trade: "These County Courts having always been held by Country gentlemen, who had no Education in the Law, it was no Wonder if both the Sense of the law was mistaken, and the Form and Method of Proceedings was often very irregular." Furthermore, rather than improving as the colony became more established, the report indicated that "of late the Insufficiency of these Courts has been much more perceiv'd and felt."[22] Other colonies experienced a similar fate. Cornelia Dayton has found that in Connecticut, litigants who came to court before the 1690s escaped rigid courtroom rules about orderly pleading but, between 1690 and 1720, began to encounter a "jarring" set of new rules.[23]

Greater concern for regular procedures and proper documentation of transactions appears in York County between 1700 and 1725, and the courts recorded women's acknowledgments more consistently. The gradually increasing formality of land transactions was an uneven trend, as records with no indication of a woman's assent are interspersed with those with complete acknowledgments. Judging from the varieties of handwriting in the records, different deputy clerks may have recorded these acknowledgments as they understood or misunderstood the procedure. Despite the technical imperfections, however, the York County court clerk, William Sedgwick, signed all of them, assenting to them in some way. The catalyst for change seemed to emerge locally rather than being directed from colony-level instructions because the counties shifted their practices for examination of women at different times. York County seemed to be slower than other tidewater counties in making the shift.[24]

By the early eighteenth century, several more carefully crafted documents were filed alongside the slipshod sales records and suggest a trend that would emerge full-blown by the middle of the century. In 1702, when John and Elizabeth Rhodes sold land to Stephen Fouace, only John personally acknowledged the documents. However, a month after the release papers were entered, a clerk copied the same into the record again and added Elizabeth's acknowledgment, which read "Elizabeth the wife of John Rhodes did this Day in Open Court Confess all her Right of Dower to the Land Within Menconed to the Use of Mr. Stephen Fouace according to Law."[25] This suggests that Fouace was skeptical about the validity of the transaction as it stood, and may have requested the later acknowledgment. At about the same time, another purchaser, Major Lewis Burwell, one of the colony's richest planters, seemed to have demanded more certainty in his land acquisition because the seller's wife, Mary Hill, when examined, "confest" that "without compulsion" she specifically "did acknowledge all her reight of of [sic] Dower of the within lands & P.r[e]misisses to Major: Lewis Burwell."[26] In both of these examples, the purchasers, Stephen Fouace and Lewis Burwell, were prominent, well-educated Virginians. Fouace was the rector of York Hampton Church and one of the first trustees at William and Mary College. Major Lewis Burwell served as a member of the Governor's Council for a short time.[27] Since it was the responsibility of the purchaser to guarantee a clear title, more knowledgable purchasers, such as the prominent Burwell and the relatively well-educated Fouace, appear to have demanded increasingly secure titles to their land. These two strict acknowledgments were unusual in the first decade of the eighteenth century, but foreshadowed what was to follow.

After 1710, the York County court increasingly recorded that a wife "being first privately Examined Voluntarily Relinquished her Right & Title of dower in & to the s[ai]d Lands." By 1711, the court imposed some demands on a seller who attempted to circumvent the procedure protecting his wife's rights. A seller's lack of proper acknowledgement was sufficiently rare that by 1711, when Mary Athy, the wife of a seller, could not "come down to the s[ai]d [York] Court to acknowledge her consent to the s[ai]d Sale of ye s[ai]d Lands & to give up her right of Dower in the same although thereunto freely" willing, Edward Athy, her husband, had to include a statement that he and his "heirs Exec[uto]rs, and adm[inistrato]rs:" would "defend ye s[ai]d Tract or Parcell of Land . . . ag[ain]st ye s[ai]d Mary Athy" for "right, title or interest of Dower or any other right."[28]

Clerks and English-trained lawyers provided more formal legal documents in Virginia during the early eighteenth century, as is apparent from the records of Godfrey Pole, who studied law in England, served as a county court clerk on Virginia's eastern shore, and practiced in several tidewater county courts. Pole represented Elizabeth Dawson in a 1717 Gloucester County dispute over her dower rights and in his own notes on the case, he copied passages about dower from English legal authorities and cited references from English cases when making his own.[29] In the 1720s, York County acknowledgments were done according to a standard form, although in one case the clerk squeezed in lines in both the lease and release indentures stating that the woman had relinquished her dower on private examination. The line being added to both documents suggests that a clerk forgot, but the error was now significant enough to be rectified upon proofreading.[30]

The frustrating Virginia custom of citing how law "has always been" without citing specific dates when innovations occurred prevents us from knowing when county courts actually demanded acknowledgments to honor a deed. The process of acknowledging women's approval of land sales that alienated their dower rights became more formalized between 1650 and 1720, but why did the transformation occur? An obvious reason was that Governor William Berkeley attempted to set a good example in one of his own land sales. In September 1674, a bill confirming Governor Berkeley's land transfer described the way such transactions should take place. The bill said Frances, Berkeley's wife, was "first privately examined by the court whether she acknowledged the same freely," that this was "the legal way in England" and was "the usual way in this country for many yeares."[31] More directly, the 1705 revision of the statutes confirmed that wives were to give consent to written deeds. However, the law may have qualified this when it stated that deeds were valid even if sloppy in execution. Whether the lack of a wife's acknowledgment was considered acceptable or not under this 1705 law is uncertain.[32]

Because the county courts finally began to record dower alienation consistently only several decades after the law required the changes, statutes alone seem to have had only a marginal effect on improving women's property rights. Therefore, other factors had to be at work to encourage Virginians to adhere to English procedure. One explanation for the change is that the statutes were haphazardly implemented in the seventeenth century, and only when the courts became aware of, or concerned with, the proper methods of execution could the statutes have any effect. Because legal administration in Virginia became more bureaucratic and court personnel better trained in the early eighteenth century, this is a plausible explanation for the increased enforcement of women's right to acknowledge land sales. By the beginning of the eighteenth century, the colony's government began issuing procedural instructions to the county courts on how to operate. Apprentice clerks were taught by the secretary of the colony and sent out to the counties, ensuring that the untrained "country gentlemen" of the 1697 report would have some informed assistance.[33] In addition, the colony encouraged increasingly formalized procedure by distributing books of sample forms that enabled county courts to issue consistently worded, legally correct documents.[34] In September 1696, the law stated the fees for recording deeds and included a sum for both the order and the recording of the relinquishment of dower, giving clerks a vested interest in recording the procedure. The inclusion of these costs suggests that some Virginians

believed the formal step of alienating dower rights was important in the procedure for selling land, particularly because such procedure had not been
mentioned earlier.[35] The 1696 imposition of the fee schedule indicates that
Virginia county courts increasingly came under centralized guidelines
within the colony and that colony-level statutes outlined greater conformity
with English expectations. In protecting married women's property rights,
Virginia statutes moved closer to the English model at the end of the seventeenth century and regional variations died out.

Courts that continued to omit any documentation of the examination
left the buyer in a vulnerable position. Without record of the examination,
the buyer had no guarantee that the woman consented to the sale freely and
she could return to reclaim the property once she became a widow. Unwary
buyers protested. As late as 1734, courts' decisions to reject conveyances
that failed to document the wife's private examination had been "much
questioned" by Virginians, but the House of Burgesses remained adamant
that only recorded acknowledgments protect a purchaser from a widow
returning to claim her dower rights to the land. The burgesses reiterated
their stance in the 1748 revision of the law, claiming, "it has always been
adjudged, that when any deed has been acknowledged by a feme covert
[that is, a married woman], and no record made of her privy examination,
such deed is not binding upon the feme or her heirs."[36]

The colony-level general court backed up the burgesses in April 1740,
when it heard the case of *Jones, &c v. Porter* over the issue of proper documentation.[37] Earlier, a county court had failed to record Jane Porter's private
acknowledgement that she agreed to the sale of 499 acres of land. Although
Porter stated during her widowhood that she had "intended to convey, and
she always acquiesced under it; never pretended she was not privately
examined; but on the contrary, in her widowhood, declared she had joined
freely and voluntarily in the sale, and was satisfied with it,"[38] her approval
had not been recorded with the deed at the time of the sale. As a result, the
court "by a great majority" determined the purchasers' heir could not seek a
more secure title to the sale. But old habits died hard. In a more peaceful resolution to a similar land purchaser's predicament in 1764, the seller's widow,
Margaret Scott, admitted she had never officially made over her dower
rights, but that she wanted to record her wish to have the rights assigned to
the purchaser.[39]

Increased legal bureaucracy alone was insufficient to address all the
detailed nuances about women's rights entirely, and a modicum of confusion persisted. As late as 1803 a Virginia legal scholar, St. George Tucker,
wrote that there remained a common misunderstanding that a woman was
barred from her dower lands unless she renounced all benefit under the will,
rather than at the time of sale.[40] Still, the records indicate that as county
courts became more bureaucratic at the end of the seventeenth century,

they greatly improved their observation of women's dower rights at the time of the sale. Furthermore, even though Virginians' adoption of dower protection occurred late in the seventeenth century, it occurred earlier than in other colonies. In historian Marylynn Salmon's exhaustive study of statutes concerning women's property rights in the various colonies, she concludes that Virginians adhered more strictly than settlers of other mainland colonies to the procedure of privately examining married women before alienating land. Salmon also points out that "in the earliest days of settlement in all the colonies, women's rights were overlooked, sacrificed to the need for secure land titles even though some of the titles resulted from unfair dealings."[41]

Economic and demographic shifts also affected legal practices concerning women in colonial Virginia. The lack of step-by-step common law acknowledgments of sales of land reveals as much about how wealth was held and how land was valued in seventeenth-century Virginia as it does about the role of women and their power within the family. Concern for a woman's dower rights assumed that land would allow a woman to maintain her status during widowhood. However, land was not necessarily the most stable means of guaranteeing her well-being, since in the seventeenth century the continuing availability of land slightly further upriver could keep the value of land in the settled areas low.[42] Relatively speaking, land in seventeenth-century Virginia was cheap.[43]

By the eighteenth century, the differences between the mother country and the colony had narrowed as the tidewater region became more densely populated.[44] This transformation affected women in a variety of ways. Studies on inheritance indicate that when land was plentiful, daughters inherited land more equally with their brothers; however, as land became scarcer, colonists began excluding daughters from land inheritances.[45] It is not surprising, then, that at this time when land was becoming increasingly valuable, purchasers of land began to require more careful records that ensured the validity of their purchases. At the turn of the century, only a few well-informed buyers, such as Stephen Fouace and Lewis Burwell, demanded these recorded assurances. But by the 1770s, even transactions held away from the courthouse recorded that "We did personally go to the within named...Wife...and Examined her privily and apart from her husband and before us she acknowledged the Indenture within mentioned to be her Act and Deed and declared that she did the same freely and voluntarily without his persuasions or threats."[46] This was a far cry from a husband going to court as attorney for his wife to acknowledge her approval of a land sale. In short, as land values increased, purchasers of real estate wanted greater adherence to legal forms as a means of protecting investments. Perhaps more significantly, as better-trained officials and lawyers became part of Virginia's society, colonists adopted the more formalized procedures that Hartwell, Blair, and Chilton complained did not exist in 1697. Women's dower rights became one element in the Virginia colonists' efforts to bring their legal practices specifically and cultural norms more generally in line with those in Britain.[47] As an indirect result, the courts made greater efforts to record women's alienation of their dower and, by this means, indirectly protected married women's rights to family land.

Ironically, when legal procedure became more regular at the end of the seventeenth century, land alone no longer accounted for the bulk of Anglo-Virginians' property holding. Virginians turned to slave labor in earnest during the last quarter of the seventeenth century, and as a result, families invested in bound labor, and increasingly in slaves, as well as land. Labor systems in England and Virginia grew markedly different during the eighteenth century and although England was a "society with slaves," Virginia became a "slave society."[48] While colonists brought their land law in line with English norms, they innovated in slave law, and there were implications for women to this.

In the eighteenth century, Chesapeake Bay families disproportionately gave their daughters slaves while they tended to leave legacies of land to their sons. As daughters increasingly benefited from ownership of slaves, women's claims to property in slaves grew in importance. Women like Mary Latané, Lucy Carter, and Mary Holladay (described in chapter 1) often received family property as a portion at the time of their marriages. This made the women attractive brides to men who had inherited land but "needed wives with slaves."[49] The Latané, Carter, and Holladay families attempted to retain control over the descent of slaves to their daughters' offspring, but the law defined dower rights to slaves for families with less foresight.

Legally defining slaves as property for the purposes of inheritance changed over the course of the eighteenth century and, not surprisingly, lawsuits arising from women's claims to dower rights in slaves occupied a prominent place in the general court, the highest level of Virginia's legal system. In addition, Virginia families invested in livestock and imported goods which all could be relatively valuable legacies for daughters. Control of labor, as well as land, continued to be a significant factor in creating and maintaining wealth into the eighteenth century, and Virginians in the seventeenth century were acutely aware of the need for servants, and later slaves, to succeed in the colonial economy.[50] Thus, wealth and well-being in seventeenth-century Virginia were defined in different ways than in England due to economic and demographic differences, even if they shared a similar legal heritage. Colonists deviated from the English model when enacting laws about slavery in general and the property rights of women over slaves in particular.

Slaves became a significant portion of family capital, and one colonist went so far as to argue that a slave was "worth as much as the ground he cultivates" and legally had been put on "a footing with lands."[51] To meet the needs of property-owning colonists, the Virginia Assembly enacted laws defining slaves as a type of property. The most sweeping change came in 1705, when Virginians passed a law one historian has seen as "removing blacks from the family of man and reassigning them to the classification of real property."[52] Over the course of the eighteenth century, up to the time of the Revolutionary War, Virginians debated whether slaves should be classified as chattels real, chattels personal, or real estate.[53] Each definition had implications for women's slave ownership.

In 1705 the legislature defined all "Negro, Mulatto, and Indian" slaves as real estate, and, explicitly, "not chattels." As such, they would "descend unto the heirs and widows of persons departing this life, according to the manner and custom of land of inheritance, held in fee simple."[54] By making their slaves real estate, planters could protect their "property" from being easily seized for debt repayment and could pass their slaves along to their heirs. Making slaves real estate benefited some women, particularly femes coverts.[55] As we have seen, at her husband's death a widow would inherit one-third of his real estate for her lifetime. If a husband left a widow less than a third of the real property she could renounce his will and take a legally prescribed larger share of his property. If slaves were declared personal property, she did not enjoy these benefits, and could well receive a smaller share of the personal estate because her husband, if he chose to do so, was permitted legally to leave her only a child's portion of the personal estate, which would be less than a third if the couple had three or more children together. On the other hand, declaring slaves personal estate benefited femes soles who owned slaves because they could sell, grant, or will property as they pleased.[56]

Although the advantages to married women of having outright ownership of property is obvious, there were counterbalancing disadvantages. If a widow remarried, her new husband could not dispose of real estate, though he enjoyed any income it produced. Like the women discussed in chapter 1 who made prenuptial gifts or trusts, remarrying widows with real estate could rest assured that the ghost family's property would not fall into the hands of the second husband. In contrast, personal property became the property of a new husband at marriage. As a result, outright ownership of property, beneficial to the feme sole, could be disadvantageous to the feme covert.[57]

What constituted the most valuable form of property for men was not always the same as for women. For example, a man might prefer to own land outright rather than hold it under an encumbrance like entail. He could sell, will, or give away unencumbered land more freely. For a married woman, encumbered property might be more advantageous to her personally because restrictions kept the property in the woman's lineage while a husband could sell off unencumbered property. Parallels from Maryland, where slaves were personal property, demonstrate how slave owners dealt with the issue. Historian Jean Lee points out that Maryland parents preserved a daughter's right to her slaves by granting her only a life right to the slaves so that neither the women themselves nor their husbands could dispose of the slaves. The desire of parents to protect their daughters' slaves from the control of sons-in-law is even more striking in Maryland, where parents used the language of entail when granting slaves because Maryland law, unlike Virginia's, did not permit the entail of slaves.[58] The Virginia legislature obtained a similar outcome by declaring slaves real estate.

By 1727, the disadvantages to husbands of declaring slaves real estate had become apparent, and the Virginia Assembly sought to resolve this.[59] It claimed that the 1705 law created confusion about a widow's right to the slaves because slaves became real estate for some purposes but not for others. To remedy the situation, the assembly passed a law in 1727 to clarify and delineate what dower rights widows could claim in slaves.[60] After 1727, a slave owner could transfer slaves by sale, gift, or inheritance as chattels. Slaves were treated as personal property insofar as a husband gained control of the slaves a feme covert brought to the marriage or inherited during the marriage.[61] If a widow believed she had been cheated out of her proper inheritance, she could seek a remedy. The new law collapsed the rights of widows with the rights of orphans to preserve their estates, suggesting the emergence of a paternalistic approach to this law.[62]

But the 1727 act was not necessarily a step forward for women's property rights. The least encumbered form of property may seem the most beneficial but for women, more restriction in property rights could be preferable, especially to married women. For comparison, colonists used another form of encumbrance—entail—to maintain property within a lineage. With entailed property, descendants could enjoy the profits and products of the estate but did not enjoy complete control over it. Colonists built on the English notion of entail and enacted legislation permitting slaves to be entailed if they were annexed to land in a serf-like fashion.[63] Encumbered property, including property in entail or reserved for dower reduced the liquidity of assets in a commercial or speculative economy.

Colonists' awareness of the value of encumbered property for women is apparent in the "surprisingly large" proportion of tidewater will writers who chose to entail land when leaving property to daughters. Sometimes the same testator would give unencumbered land to sons while making bequests of encumbered property to daughters, with the succession established on the daughter's male descendants. As Holly Brewer notes, entails "often" originated when fathers entailed their property on daughters. By entailing property on their daughters, parents protected their daughters' property from their sons-in-laws, a phenomenon that functioned as "the equivalent of a prenuptial agreement."[64] Other gender-specific aspects of statutes concerning entail indicate the particular value of entail to women's property holdings. Even when the 1727 law reduced slaves to personal property generally, it created a loophole for shrewd slave owners to protect the property rights of women in their families, permitting them to entail slaves by annexing those slaves to entailed land. This law permitted creditors to take entailed slaves on a man's or a feme sole's estate for payment of debts, but specified that slaves annexed to a married woman's estate could not be taken to pay the debts of her husband.[65] Women benefited most from owning encumbered property at a time when men could value fee-simple lands more.

The best indication that the colonists realized that their 1727 clarification of the law would have a negative impact on women's property rights appears in a letter the governor, William Gooch, sent to the board of trade in support of the bill in June of 1728. Gooch bluntly stated that many colonists believed it "hard to vest all the slaves of the wife in the Husband who may squander away his Estate, sell her slaves, and leave her a beggar." He countered that a married man endured a greater hardship if his wife brought only slaves to the marriage and he "after maintaining her many Years suitable to her Rank and Degree" should lose the slaves if she died without children.[66] Confusions created in the 1705 law continued beyond the 1727 "clarification" and even greater complications arose in 1748 when the Virginians repealed the 1705 law entirely, returning slaves to the status as chattels and making their sales easier, thus turning slaves into a more liquid form of wealth.[67] Widows, however, continued to possess only a life interest in slaves inherited from their husbands under the 1748 revision.[68] The crown disallowed the colonists' repeal, but word of the veto reached the colonists only after they had printed and distributed copies of the law in 1752.[69]

Again, the gender component of the law was secondary to the legislators' consideration, but nonetheless factored into the debate between colonists and colonial officials. When Gooch wrote to his English superiors about the 1748 legislation he encouraged disallowal, pointing out the advantage to the King's revenues, but also stressing that making slaves real estate had "enable[d] the Planter to annex Negroes to Land to make Settlements on Daughters in Marriage; to keep Estates in Familys."[70] Gooch feared the repeal of the laws would also cause many lawsuits, and encouraged the king to disallow the repeal.[71] The colonists' 1752 petition stated the gender implications of the law more explicitly. They believed that "Widows marrying second Husbands and carrying with them a property in so many of their first Husbands Slaves" would bring the children's share to "ruin." In order to prevent remarrying widows (and their new husbands) from destroying "some of the best estates" in Virginia, the colonists claimed it was "necessary to insert a Clause to keep widows to their Old Allowance of only an Estate for Life in a third Part of the Intestates Slaves."[72] No matter which way the colonists changed their laws, they made sure that women's share in slave inheritances would be limited.

Not surprisingly, the revision, repeal, and disallowal created even more confusion, and reports of cases heard in the colony's general court reveal that within the resulting disputes, lawyers understood the gendered implications. Edward Barradall, a Virginia jurist and law reporter, argued in support of a husband's right to claim his wife's slaves during marriage in *Jones v. Langhorne*. In this case, Barradall supported the husband's right to mortgage his wife's slaves, arguing, "It is absurd to talk of the Hardships upon Women unless it be a Hardship that any Thing should vest in the Husband by the Marriage."[73]

Conflict over slaves' classification as property continued into the 1770s and was one of the first issues that Virginians addressed once, with Independence, they were no longer accountable to imperial legal opinion. In November 1776, revolutionary Richard Lee wrote to inform a fellow Virginia planter, Landon Carter, that the new state legislature determined "Negroes are to be made personal Estate, widdows to have their Dower for life."[74] Thus, with the Revolution, slaves were to be personal property for all purposes except that widows still possessed a limited, life right to slaves.[75] Virginia's assembly and court granted widows no right to sell or give away slaves, even during widowhood, but they did protect against a second husband seizing slaves from his wife's first family. The back-and-forth trading of the two possible benefits—alienability or protection—that occurred under the statutes, revisions, and disallowals ended with the Revolution, when women lost both.[76] The legacy for slave-owning men was more mixed: Virginia abolished entail in land in 1776, permitting landowners to sell more easily, but waited until 1796 to prohibit entail in slaves.[77] Individual men found themselves with more autonomous control over land and slaves that came to them by will or marriage after Revolutionary-era changes went into effect. Once independent from imperial control Virginia legislators could define the gendered nature of property in humans freely. They did so by removing legal encumbrances, allowing men to sell land and slaves more easily.

Although slavery persisted in England until it was undermined by Chief Justice Lord Mansfield, in the 1771–72 case of *Somerset vs. Stewart*, slave law in Virginia did not anglicize and colonists knew this. In fact, by the end of the colonial period, one English legal expert warned of the reverse danger—that of the mother country taking Virginia law regarding slavery back to England. In the watershed *Somerset vs. Stewart* case that ended English courts' enforcement of full-fledged slavery within England, William Davy, arguing on behalf of the slave, posed the issue at the heart of the matter: "If the Laws having attached upon him abroad are at all to affect him here, it brings them all, either all the Laws of Virginia are to attach upon him here or none—for where will they draw the line."[78]

Edward Barradall rationalized Virginia's innovations in slave law and emphasized the distinctive nature of slave laws to the colony, stating, "There is no estate in England resembling that of slaves."[79] When Thomas Jefferson took careful notes of general court cases, he concentrated on cases "peculiar to our own Country" and not derived from English law because these were the issues for which Virginia law was the "conclusive authority."[80] The central role of women as slave owners within Jefferson's study of legal innovations in Virginia is apparent from the number of cases he included in his collection. Of the forty-one cases Jefferson described, twenty-two dealt with issues arising from slavery, and twelve of those concerned women's property rights to slaves. Distinctive legislation in the colony had powerful repercussions for women as property owners of slaves, and Jefferson's notes reflect this.[81] Insofar as legislators recognized that they were creating new laws, reports for Virginia emphasized slave law precisely because these cases differed from anything in England. Combined, the major Virginia law reports from the colonial period (those by Barradall, Jefferson, and Sir John Randolph) reveal the degree to which women's stake in one of the colony's primary forms of wealth—bound human labor—were subject to dispute and change in the eighteenth century.[82]

Thus, although the colonists moved to bring women's dower rights in land in accord with British patterns, slave property could not be so easily anglicized because other colonies, not metropolitan expectations, provided the precedents.[83] Lawyers like Jefferson knew they innovated when they defined and redefined slaves as a form of property and spelled out the gender implications of their legislation, allowing colony and metropole to proceed on two separate legal tracks with little interference from England until the colonists tried to backtrack in 1748. Matthew Lamb, who wrote the legal report to the lords commissioners of trade on this act, encouraged disallowal because "inconvenience" was an insufficient reason for making slaves chattels personal rather than real.[84] Imperial authorities did not always receive such colonial innovation in women's property rights in an accepting fashion; in this chapter's final example we shall see how they soundly rejected colonists' innovations regarding women's property rights.

In other respects officials in the colony and those at the metropole differed in their expectations about women's property rights. In the middle of the eighteenth century, three Virginia women deserted by their husbands initiated private bills to free themselves from the restrictions common law imposed upon them. Virginia's representative assembly attempted to use two of the cases as an opportunity to establish new precedents about law affecting women's property. To do so, the burgesses presented the two bills in heartrending terms. Their arguments reveal that, by the eighteenth century, colonists and imperial authorities had developed distinctive attitudes toward women's independent control over property. While other historians of women have stressed the significance of these particular cases as indicators of women's lowly status under common law in the Virginia colony, the arguments used in the cases demonstrate how powerful Virginia government officials desired married women to have a modicum of control over their property. In this, their wishes grew apart from those of the imperial authorities.[85]

The first case in which a married woman sought a bill from the legislature to permit her to dispose of her property occurred in 1704, when the Virginia Council deliberated over a petition from Mary Greenfeild requesting control over some family property.[86] She specifically wanted permission to sell part of her land "for her Subsistence, her husband having left her."[87] The Council forwarded the petition on to the House of Burgesses, who then sent the petition on to their Committee on Propositions of Grievances, whose opinion led them to reject the proposal. Neither the committee nor the burgesses recorded any explanation for refusing the request, but what is significant is that the burgesses deemed the bill unacceptable and refused to forward it to England for approval.[88] Colonists and imperial authorities were still in agreement when the Virginians rejected Greenfeild's 1704 bill.

Official opinion in the colony changed by the time Frances (Taylor) Greenhill and Susanna (Sanders) Cooper submitted their petitions in the 1730s and 1740s. Like Greenfeild, Greenhill and Cooper, both still married, sought permission to dispose of property even while still under coverture. In contrast to the Greenfeild case, however, the House of Burgesses voted to support the Greenhill and Cooper causes. Many aspects of Greenfeild's unsuccessful 1704 attempt foreshadowed key elements of Greenhill's and Cooper's petitions.[89] The cases all had three characteristics in common: the husband had deserted his wife; the petitioner had access to property in the colony that could be liquidated to provide for her maintenance; and the primary motivation for the action, according to the official record, was that the abandoned woman needed to dispose of the real property for her subsistence, not for any more ambitious economic goals or dynastic testamentary plans.

A sympathetic version of the details of Frances Taylor Greenhill's marriage emerges from the records sent from Virginia to London as part of her case. Frances Taylor's troubles began when she married Joseph Greenhill in 1716 and brought to the marriage a personal estate valued at two hundred pounds "and upwards" and over a thousand acres of land situated across three counties.[90] Joseph Greenhill, on the other hand came to the marriage "a person of no fortune, or circumstance" and proceeded to spend his wife's personal estate and contract debts. Less than two years after the marriage, he departed the colony, leaving her to pay the bills, and reducing her to "the utmost misery and distress." To dissuade her from joining him, he wrote to inform her that if she followed him he would not provide for her or "look upon her as a wife." She remained in Virginia. Frances depended on the charity of friends during her husband's absence. Over a decade later, she petitioned for free control over her estate. She claimed she had no idea if Joseph was alive anymore. In his absence she had "by her industry, and the assistance of her friends" purchased slaves and goods, but she would be unable to support herself in her "declining years" because technically the property belonged to her husband. In addition, she claimed she was "exposed to many injuries, by trespasses" on the land. As a result she wished to obtain permission to sell land or grant it away in her will. She had no children to inherit the land. Without obtaining this power, "no purchaser will treat with her, on account of the incertainty."

Frances Greenhill's case began to wind through official channels in June of 1730, when her petition reached the House of Burgesses. In the relatively brief initial record, she simply stated that her husband, Joseph, had been absent about twelve years, that he had left her "without any subsistence"; that she lived on "the Charity of Her Friends"; yet she had an estate consisting of nine-hundred acres of fee-simple land with buildings in Prince George County and she requested permission from the House of Burgesses to sell the land in order to have a "proper maintenance" for herself. In her 1730 petition, she further sought to guard her assets by requesting that the proceeds from the land sale be vested in trustees solely to provide for her own support "without the Intermeddling of Her Husband or His Creditors."[91] Considering Joseph's lengthy absence, his creditors, quite likely irritated, no doubt posed a greater threat to her financial well-being than to her husband. Significantly, the case potentially provided a precedent for the colony as a whole. The issue of a married woman (feme covert) acting on her own account potentially threatened the smooth operation of economic exchange in the English common-law tradition. Women's property rights were a matter of increasingly open debate in legal circles in eighteenth-century England, and conditions in Ireland, the West Indies, and Britain's mainland North American colonies compounded the issues.[92]

After hearing a debate over Frances Greenhill's 1730 petition, the House of Burgesses voted to send the 1730 petition on to a committee. The assembly ordered the committee to prepare a report on the case, but only after it had alerted another Greenhill family member, Paschal Greenhill, of the petition.[93] The case disappeared in committee for over a decade, and no record of the committee's action, information on the matters the burgesses debated, or subsequent action on the part of the burgesses appears to have survived until the case reappeared in 1742.[94]

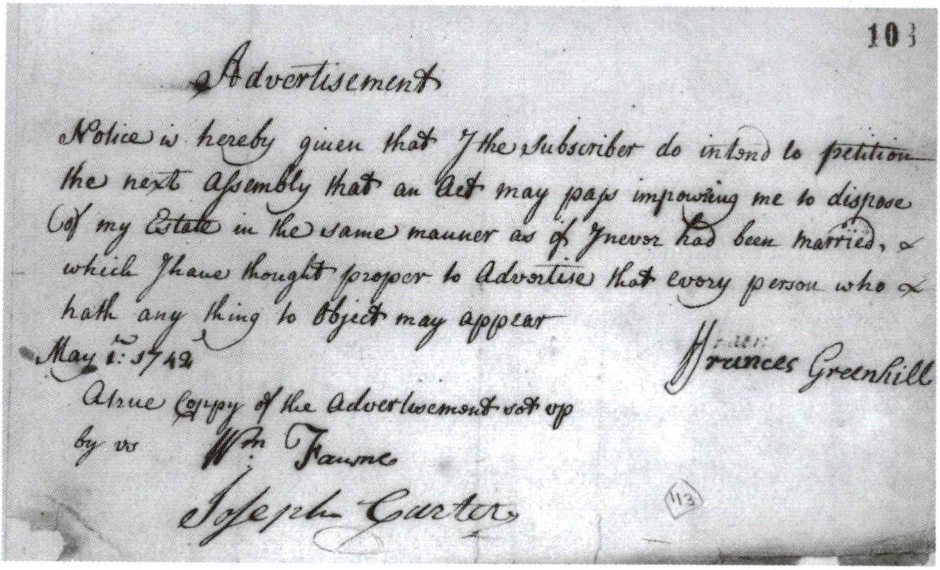

Advertisement

Notice is hereby given that I the Subscriber do intend to petition the next Assembly that an Act may pass impowring me to dispose of my Estate in the same manner as if I never had been married, & which I have thought proper to Advertise that every person who & hath any thing to object may appear

May 1: 1742

Frances Greenhill

A true Copy of the Advertisement sett up by us Wm Fawne

Joseph Carter

FIGURE 2.1 *"Advertisement" for Greenhill's separate property.* Copy of Frances Greenhill's signed "Advertisement" presented to her local parish of Merchants' Brandon in Prince George County stating she intended to petition the next Virginia Assembly to regain control of her property "as if I never had been married." The clerks of the parish, William Fawne and Joseph Carter, then "published" the information to the congregation on three successive Sundays immediately after worship services, allowing any person who had objections to appear. This procedure was consistent with the way that intended marriages by "banns" (in contrast to marriages by licenses) were announced to communities to allow individuals the opportunity to explain if any impediments existed to the wedding. Another type of legal maneuver, breaking entail, also required publishing individual intentions to the larger community. PRO CO 5/1325 f. 103.

Frances Greenhill petitioned the assembly again, but only after she secured community support for her action. With the assistance of two church clerks in the neighborhood, she wrote an "advertisement" giving notice that she planned to petition the Assembly, "empowering [her] to dispose of my Estate in the same manner as if I never had been married" and requesting anyone with objections to the move to "appear" (see fig. 2.1). Officials from two of the parish churches in her home county then "published" the note on three successive Sundays to the members of the congregation immediately after services, in a manner remarkably similar to the publishing of the banns for couples wishing to marry. Using the church to obtain community consent extended to other procedures, too, and Virginians wishing to break an entail through a private act also proclaimed their intentions at three meetings of the local parish church. Greenhill's "advertisement" is also consistent with the pattern of divorces that would be granted in North America after the War of Independence. To demonstrate community support of divorces in the post-Revolutionary period, neighbors submitted collective petitions advocating the legislatures to grant the dissolution.[95] In all these instances, petitions reflected community, as well as individual desires.

Having obtained the tacit approval of the local community, Greenhill proceeded to petition the Assembly. In May of 1742 the House of Burgesses passed the bill and forwarded it on to the council, which agreed to hear the interested parties present their side of the case and, in June, after amending the bill, the council sent the approved bill back to the burgesses.[96]

Finally, Greenhill had succeeded in obtaining a private bill allowing her control of her property, including her land. She gained other legal powers denied femes coverts, including the right "to make contracts and agreements in her own name; and to sue, and be sued, in all courts of judicature within this colony, as a feme sole may, or can by law, notwithstanding the said Joseph Greenhill shall happen to be living." In return, Frances Greenhill was barred from her right to dower and gave up her right to claim any share in Joseph's estate.[97] The latter may have been of little or no value in itself, especially if she did not know of his whereabouts. The only remaining hurdle for Greenhill was getting the bill accepted by the imperial authorities, because the bill also included the usual clause suspending the execution of the law until the king approved the bill.

The governor at the time, William Gooch, encouraged approval in August 1742 on the basis that the facts stated in the bill were correct and because the case deserved "compassion" from the lords commissioners for trade and plantations, the body in England responsible for overseeing colonial administration on behalf of the king.[98] Before making a recommendation, the lords of trade sent the bill on to Francis Fane, one of the king's counsel, to obtain an opinion on it.[99] Fane responded favorably to the case, stating that although he believed this case was the first instance where a legislature in any of the colonies "have taken upon them to a law in so settled and known a point, as giving a power to a Feme Covert" to sell or grant her real and personal estate "in the supposed lifetime of her Husband," he believed, nonetheless, that "perhaps no case ever happened before attended with such Compassionate and equitable circumstances," and that he had no reason to believe the circumstances were returned incorrectly. Fane encouraged the council to advise the king to approve the act, since it was "highly probable" the husband was dead, and especially because Greenhill would sacrifice any claim on the husband's estate in return for the right to dispose of the property then in her hands. "Surely," Fane pled, "No Case evermore deserved the interposition of the Legislature."[100]

The board received Fane's opinion on January 31, 1744, read it on March 1 that same year, but postponed making a decision until "application is made by the party concerned."[101] Contrary to Fane's recommendations, however, they encouraged the king to repeal Greenhill's private bill.[102] The members reported to the king that they had consulted with Fane, but astonishingly enough and for mysterious reasons, they edited information they forwarded to the king and thereby reversed the meaning of Fane's opinion.[103] Although the lords commissioners quoted Fane's argument that Greenhill's was the first attempt in the colonies by a feme covert to "alter the Law in so settled and known a Point as giving a Power to a Feme Covert" to sell or dispose of land, they then omitted Fane's conclusion that the circumstances of the case demanded that Greenhill's bill be allowed to stand. The commissioners' selective reporting completely changed Fane's recommendations, using Fane's own language to urge the king to do the precise opposite of what Fane recommended. Their records do not explain their reasoning, but they believed the king should disallow the bill as "it may not be advisable to countenance any Attempts of this kind."[104] The king in council, on receiving this advice of the lords commissioners for trade and plantations disallowed Greenhill's bill in 1747, leaving her once again at the mercy of the common law.[105] In this case, the colonists, from Greenhill's fellow Merchant's Brandon parishioners on up to the governor of Virginia, believed she should have the right to dispose of her property as a feme sole would. The imperial authorities, with the exception of Fane, believed the colonists, in doing so, would establish a dangerous precedent, and rejected the law.

Not to be dissuaded by a single case, the House of Burgesses persisted in their efforts to allow a married woman who had been deserted to have control over her own property. Two years later, they approved a second private bill that allowed a feme covert, this time Susannah Cooper, to gain control over property. Cooper's tribulations began in 1717 when, as Susannah Sanders, she married Isles Cooper. At the time of the marriage, she, too, was "possessed of a personal estate" while her new husband was "a person of no fortune or circumstance." Less than three years after the marriage, Isles Cooper disappeared "to parts unknown to her." Before he left, Isles spent most of her estate and contracted debts that allowed his creditors to seize the rest of her estate, leaving Susannah and her son "reduced to the utmost misery and distress" and dependant on the charity of friends and relations. Like Mrs. Greenhill, Cooper claimed she had not heard from her husband in twenty years, but she did report that Isles had married again and, after this second wife died, he married a third wife with whom he had children.

After Isles left, Susannah "by her industry" purchased slaves and a small estate "though not sufficient to support her, in the decline of life." Even without the backing of the law, she conducted business outside the purview of the official legal system and engaged in transactions with her neighbors. Although she had de facto autonomy to conduct much of her business she needed de jure power when she wanted to dispose of her real estate. Once again, she submitted her bill to the assembly when she wanted to sell property, including land she had acquired herself, because "no purchaser will treat with her on account of her coverture." To obtain the legal power to sell, she petitioned for permission to take action in her own name, to make contracts, and to sue and be sued "as a feme sole may." She, like Greenhill, agreed that in return, she would sacrifice her claim to dower or right in Isles's property if he should still be alive. Considering the description of Isles given in the act, there was little danger he would have property she could claim, anyway, but gaining a clear title to the land would allow her to sell or give her own land away.[106]

The governor of the colony was still William Gooch, and he strongly supported Cooper's bill, arguing that it reflected social norms more widely and claiming "The allegations exhibited in the Bill were so well known in the Country, that upon application made to them, the [Virginia] Council and House of Burgesses immediately Passed it."[107] Cooper's bill confronted her derelict husband's power more directly than Greenhill's earlier bill had, and Gooch supported the bill in his letter to the Board of Trade because of this element, not in spite of it. Gooch warned the board, "I must likewise beg leave to recommend to your Lordships the Bill...for should her Husband return before this Bill is confirmed by His Majesty, all that she has, with great Industry and Honesty gott, since he left her, will be forced from her."[108] Gooch, in providing the board with this information, suggested that the return of Isles Cooper and any attempt on his part to play the patriarch to his wife and child endangered their well-being unfairly. In this construction, Susannah Cooper would only become the poor, helpless woman because of the unfairness of the law, not because of any defect in her own industry, competence, or honesty.

Governor Gooch's letter to the Board of Trade included Cooper's predicament with a more general indictment of patriarchy, or, at least, of patriarchy run amok. A good patriarch recognized his responsibilities as well as his rights. In the discussion of Cooper's bill, Gooch also sought the board's approval of wealthy planter Mann Page's private bill permitting him to sell land to pay his father's debts. Page's father, who had been a member of the council, had "almost ruined his Family by taking up Land, in order to be respected as the richest man in the Country; which [is] the true reason he was in possession of such large Quantities in several Parts of the Colony."[109] The son, by contrast, was a worthy man possessed of the "reverse of his Father's temper." Gooch begged relief from the imperial authorities for Page, the suffering son, as well as for Cooper, the wronged wife, suggesting a subtle critique of the wayward patriarchs in the Cooper and Page families.

Cooper's bill, and Gooch's argument in favor of it, fit within the larger trends of imperial governance of the colonies in the first third of the eighteenth century. The colonists danced a minuet between invoking local custom and relying on English tradition. Jack Greene has argued that, although by the 1730s colonists were subject only to those English statutes that explicitly mentioned the colonies' residents, they nevertheless gained legal guarantees to English rights in practice. Gooch, perhaps by virtue of his long residence in the colony as lieutenant governor between 1727 and 1749, believed the balance worked and the legal system of the colony became "exactly suited to the Circumstances of the Respective Governments, and as near as possible [as] it can be, conformable to the Law and Customs of England."[110]

In describing Susannah Cooper's predicament to the board, Gooch argued that local opinion supported allowing Cooper to have property rights in a fashion that seemed to tip the balance in favor of colonial innovation over English tradition. Both Cooper and Gooch were disappointed in their efforts. Unfortunately for Cooper, the imperial administration retained the trump card. In June of 1745, as soon as the bill arrived in London, the Board of Trade wrote to the governor to inform him that Cooper's bill was "liable to great Objections" and would be rejected.[111] The implications of the bill's progress are less clear cut. Imperial authorities never accepted Cooper's bill, but her cause seemed to have survived long enough—more than a decade—to suggest it had been accorded a grudging consideration at the metropole, even after Greenhill's bill had been disallowed outright.[112] It is also important to remember that Cooper's case threatened legal principles less than Greenhill's because Cooper sought access only to personal property while Greenhill sought to wrest authority over real estate as well as personal property.

Francis Fane dawdled in providing an opinion on Cooper's bill, perhaps to demonstrate his exasperation with the commissioners' earlier refusal to take his suggestions on the Greenhill case seriously. In July 1745 the lords commissioners for trade and plantations had forwarded the bill to Fane, along with the forty-five other acts of the Virginia legislature for the preceeding year.[113] Almost two years later Fane had responded to all but two of the bills, and Cooper's bill had to be sent on to a second king's counsel for an opinion.[114] In February 1754, Matthew Lamb reported on "a Private Act Passed [in Virginia] in April 1752"—Cooper's bill again. Lamb was more succinct in his one paragraph opinion of Cooper's case than Fane had been earlier with Greenhill's. Although Lamb thought the "circumstances of the case may appear to claim some Favour in regard to the Hardship the Wife laboured under," this bill of an "unusual and extraordinary Nature" should not be confirmed because "the Right which the Law invests in the Husband of the Personal Estate of his Wife cannot be taken away without his consent by Act of the Legislature."[115] The bill was rejected.[116] Twenty-four years after Cooper's husband left, she still had no access to her personal property.

So what are we to make of these two cases? In contrast to Greenfeild, Greenhill and Cooper enjoyed the support of officials within the colony, and the fact that the Virginia government returned Greenhill's and Cooper's cases for approval within a decade of each other suggests the colony was using them as test cases. Furthermore, the conditions and wording of Cooper's act closely resembled that of Greenhill's earlier bill. In both cases, the women were very clearly the wronged party, having brought property to the marriage or acquired it after separation and suffering from desertion.

Cooper's presence in financial records of other colonists demonstrate how far she was integrated into the local exchange economy within Virginia. She operated her own business in New Kent County providing lodging, stableage, and refreshment to travelers while also selling small items on the side.[117] She purchased three dozen almanacs wholesale from the printer in Williamsburg to sell to her local customers and obtained large quantities of sugar, tea, and coffee to supply her customers.[118] She provided the treats, worth over £27, to William Bassett's supporters during his New Kent County elections.[119] Another indication of Cooper's success in the economy was her purchase of a "quire" of forms for making bills of exchange.[120] Whether she expected to use the forms herself or provide them to her customers is unclear from the surviving record, but they do demonstrate that Cooper's business located her in the midst of a geographically far-flung economy.

Even without an allowed bill, Cooper, a feme covert operating on her own behalf, ran her business by forming a close business relationship with Bassett, who provided her with a long line of credit and who, in turn, drew on her occasionally for paying his own bills. Cooper sold hogsheads of tobacco to Bassett, provided board, leased skilled slaves to him, and allowed bills to be drawn on her to pay wages to two of his employees. Bassett and Cooper allowed their respective obligations to run in each others' account books, and they only settled the 1735 to 1740 exchanges in August of 1740 and then allowed their accounts to run again for four more years before reconciling the obligations.[121] The prominent merchant Francis Jerdone also extended credit to Cooper.[122] Cooper's ambiguous marital status failed to deter Jerdone and Bassett from doing business with her.

Individual colonists' willingness to include Susannah Cooper within the credit networks of the Virginia economy even without her regaining status as feme sole suggests that the colonists recognized women's status as economic actors in informal ways that extended beyond the strictest interpretations of coverture outlined by statute and the imperial administration. Nor was Cooper the lone beneficiary of colonists' recognition of such a woman; Mrs. Greenhill, who earlier petitioned for feme sole status after desertion by her husband, was able to purchase large quantities of beer from Mr. Bassett's imported inventory in 1739.[123] She was probably not merely drowning her sorrows but instead sold the beverage as a means of generating income.

In choosing to advance Cooper's case, the colonists may have felt themselves on safer ground. Cooper, who lived in New Kent County, ran her own financial affairs even after her husband abandoned her and their son. Technically she operated within a legal limbo since, as a married woman, she was considered to be a feme covert. Cooper managed, nevertheless, to participate in the economy on her own terms and to maintain an economic identity separate from that of her husband despite the fact that she had no clear-cut legal status. Cooper succeeded moderately in her efforts to establish her own economic identity, and other colonists recognized her as an economic actor. Her covert status failed to provide an absolute deterrent to her business, and she secured and extended credit within the colony, even when the imperial authorities refused to permit her to sell her property. In the short term her resourcefulness, competence, and the acceptance of other colonists of her de facto independent status allowed her to survive. Her main problem, according to her petition, was having the means to support herself in old age.

Virginians resembled Londoners in defining women as independent actors—legally single—in certain situations. The medieval "custom of London" permitted married women who engaged in business on their own account to operate as "feme sole traders." Historian Amy Erickson claims that other English boroughs also accepted women in this "anomalous" role and suggests that Northampton, England, like London, may have been a town whose customs formally or informally treated married women as feme sole traders, producers and providers of credit.[124] In Connecticut, at least, colonists knew of the London practice of married women carrying on trade as single women.[125] The Virginia burgesses granted that Cooper and Greenhill had reasons justifying de facto independent status in a commercial but rural context; in England, however, feme sole trader status tended to be an urban phenomenon.

In England as in America, feme sole trader status remained contested during the late eighteenth and early nineteenth centuries. Case law in mid-

and late-eighteenth-century England suggests that Lord Mansfield struggled to define the circumstances under which a married woman would be recognized as an independent economic actor. Significantly, perhaps, the residence of one spouse outside of England made acceptance of feme sole trader status easier. In other cases the key to establishing distinct legal identities was for the wife to have a "competent separate maintenance that was regularly paid to her."[126] Both elements appear in the case of *Ringsted v. Lady Lanesborough* (1783), in which Lord Mansfield deemed the defendant responsible to her creditors. Mansfield thought she acted as an independent agent, despite her married state, because when she and her husband agreed to separation, she received a regularly paid separate maintenance and because of the geographic separation of the two parties (Lady Lanesborough remained in England while her husband lived in Ireland). Mansfield revealed his concerns in his opinion, noting "If she was permitted afterward [after contracting] to say she should not pay because she was a wife incapable of contracting, it would be contrary to the truth of the transaction, & a fraud & deceit upon her creditors. After having got credit as single, she shall never be permitted to say, I am not liable to pay because I was married."[127] For a woman in late-eighteenth-century England to be recognized legally as a feme sole trader, then, she needed to be living separately, have her own maintenance, and be accepted as trading on her own behalf. Mansfield's 1785 decision in *Barwell v. Brooks* broadened his earlier position and allowed that both spouses could live within England and still have the wife considered responsible for her debts. In his opinion on a subsequent case, *Corbett v. Poelnitz* (1785), Mansfield argued that a woman could contract for goods other than mere necessities and "that where a woman has a separate estate, and acts and receives credit as a 'feme sole' she shall be liable as such."[128] Beginning in 1800, however, English common-law judges began a conservative reaction against Lord Mansfield's acceptance of married women behaving as femes soles. The reactionary response occurred after independence made these decisions irrelevant in the U.S. context.[129]

In the late-eighteenth-century cases, creditors and jurists in England debated the rules concerning married women's separate legal identity and, specifically in these cases, their liability for debts.[130] What is interesting in the transatlantic context is that American colonists, imperial bureaucrats, and legal specialists all dealt with the issue of married women's responsibilities and opportunities within a larger context of trade and residence abroad, whether "abroad" meant Ireland or Virginia. The Virginia House of Burgesses did not require proof that the husbands of Cooper and Greenhill lived "abroad," but it certainly indicated that the two men had vanished. In attempting to define Cooper and Greenhill as de facto femes soles in the 1730s and 1740s, the colonists led the mother country in establishing law that Mansfield's court would adopt for England only in two cases from the

1780s. In the meantime, the imperial authorities had found the Virginia innovations unacceptable.

The transition from early modern to modern gender constructions, at least under the law and in terms of the economy, was positioned within the empire. Britain's growing commercial and colonial enterprises, in which Virginia played a key role, complicated legal notions of property during the eighteenth century. According to Susan Staves, changes in English chattel property rules after 1660 "were designed to promote business, colonial, and imperial enterprise."[131] These changes, not surprisingly, affected women's property rights and were under consideration in England as well as the colonies, but the Virginia Assembly, in the Greenhill and Cooper cases, grew increasingly liberal in attempting to extend property rights to married women. As with slave law, these innovations diverged from the law developing in England and imperial authorities overturned the assembly's bills, granting Virginia married women more control over property than their English sisters possessed. The wrangling over the Greenhill and Cooper bills, because they were relatively well-documented as they proceeded through the channels of mid-eighteenth-century political bureaucracy, does reveal the growing division between colonial and imperial attitudes toward access of married women to family property.[132] These two examples are not surprising as private bills easing property restrictions per se, because colonists succeeded in proposing many similar bills to break entail in order to free encumbered property. Furthermore, the English courts at the highest levels also grappled with a femes covert's contractual capacities in the late eighteenth century.[133] Both English and Virginia courts considered the issues, but, in the end, they disagreed with colonists over how to define the property of feme coverts. As a result, colonists disagreed with the king and the Board of Trade and seemed more interested in "Americanizing" (or at least, "Virginianizing") the law regarding married women's property rather than "anglicizing" it. The Virginia burgesses proceeded cautiously, however, by limiting their innovations to private bills. Neither public statutes nor general court decisions framed new autonomous roles for women in Virginia, suggesting colonial authorities' reluctance to initiate more radical change. Still, the Board of Trade deemed the issue of married women's property significant enough to send these two private bills to the Privy Council, indicating they mattered as test cases establishing precedents about the nature of women's property in the colonies. The role of Greenhill's bill as a "test case" is apparent in the decision of Board of Trade to send it on to the solicitor general for an opinion.[134]

In all three of the Virginia examples—those of Greenfeild, Greenhill, and Cooper—the colonists recorded the issues at stake in the formula that Mansfield still considered later in England: all the women were married and had been deserted by their husbands, and all three phrased their requests in terms of subsistence, even if their larger goals extended beyond "necessaries" to, in Greenhill's case, the right to sell significant tracts of land. What distinguished Greenhill's case from the other Virginia cases and indeed the cases Mansfield considered, was that Greenhill wanted access to her real as well as personal property. Perhaps this was the reason Greenhill's case particularly threatened metropolitan English notions about women's property despite the support of the colonial council, assembly, and governor. By raising Cooper's case two years after Greenhill's, the Virginians selected a safer course; Cooper's situation more closely resembled that of the English feme sole traders in that she had an ongoing series of exchanges, she received credit for wholesale purchases, and she did not overtly request permission to sell real property.

Although leading lawyers at the metropole themselves wrestled with the problem of married women as independent actors, this did not preclude imperial authorities casting the Virginia colony as an innovator in this concern. In writing his legal opinion, Francis Fane, the king's counsel, claimed that he believed the Greenhill case was the first instance where a legislature in any of the colonies "have taken upon them a law in so settled and known a point, as giving a power to a Feme Covert" to sell or grant her real and personal estate "in the supposed lifetime of her Husband."[135]

The cases of Susannah Cooper and Frances Greenhill demonstrate very visibly the contrast between the colonists' own views on women's autonomous power over property and that of imperial authorities. The cases seemed eminently reasonable to the colonists, the Virginia representatives, and even the royal governor. As precedents these bills, had they been allowed to stand, indicated how colonial married women in similar predicaments could have claimed real estate, a right not extended to married women at the metropole. From the vantage point of the imperial personnel in London, the innovations seemed unacceptable because they granted married women too much authority to dispose of property, establishing a dangerous precedent.

The War of Independence allowed for the reopening of debate within the various new states, but with the Virginia government's earlier willingness to pass Cooper's and Greenhill's private bills, American readiness to attack the most severe limitations to female autonomy preceded the Revolution by at least a generation. Despite these potential precedents, improvement of married women's property rights—including a woman's access to her own earnings, her right to make a will, and reconsideration of feme sole status leading to more equal property relations between spouses—occurred only later in the nineteenth century.[136] Indeed, antebellum changes in married women's rights left women in "a legal twilight zone," that only increased confusion and litigation,[137] a phenomenon antithetical to Lord Mansfield's late-eighteenth-century goal of clarifying the trading status of the feme covert to make commerce easier.

This chapter steers a course through developments in gender and imperial history on both sides of the eighteenth-century Atlantic. While much of the scholarship on women in the second (post-1783) British Empire analyzes the relationship between imperial authority and colonial gender constructions, this same relationship seems inadequately delineated for the first empire.[138] Anglo-Virginia women experienced male and imperial domination as a mixed blessing or half curse. Down to the level of the county court, propertied Anglo-American women could take advantage of the machinery of imperial power and use that power to protect their own interests. Still, as Greenhill's and Cooper's cases show, even propertied Anglo-American women experienced the subordinate position accorded their sex in colonial society. When Virginia women married, they became, in a strikingly commercial description Jefferson recycled from John Milton, "joint traders for life," but, under the legal system, they still remained junior members in the partnership.[139]

"AS THOUGH I MY SELF WAS PR[E]SENT": WOMEN WITH POWER OF ATTORNEY

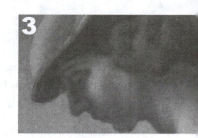

3

n 1716, William West planned to leave his Essex County, Virginia, home. Prominent among the arrangements he made for the management of his affairs during his absence was a grant to his wife Elizabeth of a power of attorney allowing her to do "all my business whatsoever Relating to me as though I my self was pr[e]sent." Thereby, Elizabeth West, even as a married woman whom the law defined as a feme covert, gained the authority to manage property and legal matters as she deemed appropriate. She was not alone. Judging from this and similar grants in the seventeenth and early eighteenth centuries in tidewater Virginia, colonists did not believe sex defined or precluded competence in the legal sector. Historians of the colonial Chesapeake region have understood that women managed property, but they have concentrated on widowhood as the period in women's lives when they took on these responsibilities. Even during coverture, however, some Virginia women, especially in families with far-flung economic concerns, handled legal affairs and administered property. Courts recognized married women's various legal actions by recording powers of attorney.[1]

Individuals operating under powers of attorney, including married women acting on behalf of their husbands, were different from professional lawyers, referred to as "mercenary attorneys" in early Virginia statutes. Lawyers who served professionally were prohibited in Virginia in 1645 and were suspect in the early years of settlement. There were few professional lawyers in the seventeenth-century colonies and, in colonies where lawyers were allowed to practice, the legislatures limited what a lawyer could earn for a case.[2]

Not all, or even most, women in colonial Virginia held power of attorney, since these tended to serve the distinctive interests of commercially active families.[3] Men who granted powers of attorney primarily did so when they planned to be absent pursuing trade or other interests that took them out of the local vicinity. Thus, the women who possessed power of attorney came from relatively prosperous families who had geographically dispersed economic concerns. Some men also assigned power of attorney to widows they planned to marry to allow them to control their former husbands' property even after marriage. A women acting under power of attorney in these circumstances maintained some responsibility over the ghost family's assets even after marrying a new husband. (For an examination of the "ghost family," see chapter 1.) In most cases, however, a woman with power of attorney provided her current husband with a responsible local agent authorized to serve in the family's best interests. In either case, these grants remained exclusively the province of women from propertied families.

Another, anomalous type of power of attorney in Virginia developed in an extraordinary case in which the couple established arrangements for distinct control of property in a de facto separation agreement that, the husband hoped, would allow him to establish a new household with a different woman and their children. Although exceptional, the case illustrates how a power of attorney could delineate property relations to keep a married woman's property separate from that of her husband, essentially establishing a separate maintenance for the wife.

Power of attorney permitted married women to act as separate legal persons under the specific terms established in the documents. A husband like William West could designate that his wife had legal responsibility to act on his behalf by recording his grant to her of power of attorney. The instructions in these documents varied from very specific, limited powers to more general discretionary authority. Usually men granted power of attorney to their wives in anticipation of travel outside of the county or, especially out of the colonies. The men who granted these powers clearly believed their interests were best served when their wives had the legal authority to pursue the families business in the local courts.[4]

Although Virginia widows' economic activities are well known, it is clear that during both marriage and widowhood, many women managed economic and legal affairs and propertied women actively pursued their economic and legal concerns. For example, even after marriage a very limited number of women in the colonies acquired feme sole trader status in order to maintain economic autonomy, and Pennsylvania and South Carolina enacted statutes defining feme sole trader status. While other colonies did not pass similar statutes, legislatures "developed other methods of dealing with women who worked outside the home" and colonists found other ways to grant women economic agency. This chapter investigates one means—the recording of power of attorney—that provided femes coverts with legal agency.[5] That agency could be restricted or extensive, according to the designs of the parties and the activities women undertook in court under power of attorney demonstrate that a spectrum of possibilities was open to women under colonial law. At one end of the spectrum, a power of attorney could grant a married woman legal authority to undertake a discrete task or list of tasks. In such cases women were confined to following directions outlined by men, gaining them the status of what Laurel Ulrich has termed the "deputy husband." This provided women no real initiative or autonomy and merely confirmed the patriarchal nature of family authority.[6]

An example of power being delegated to include only limited action is Elizabeth Dale's case. In April 1667, Elizabeth Dale granted to Edward Mosse "the same power that I have from my husband," to record an agreement made "between us" concerning some land. In this instance the power apparently extended to a single transaction and might have been undertaken for convenience, to streamline the land transfer. In any event, Dale refused to undertake the power but instead assigned it away immediately. In the early eighteenth century, Kezia Henshaw, the "well beloved wife" of Essex County planter Samuel Henshaw, received a power of attorney from him that left her little discretionary authority. Her husband gave her a list of legal chores she should complete, including representing him in two specific lawsuits and making a conveyance for four hundred acres of land to a specified buyer. Women could be preferred family representatives in court, but, like other representatives, women could also be left with very limited discretionary authority.[7] At the other end of the spectrum, a few women won greater freedom to act according to their own wishes, without direction. For example, the apparently illiterate Christopher Pearson made his wife, Margrett, attorney "in all manners" to manage business in York County as she saw fit in 1693.[8] Other women seized large-scale independent authority over a long period of time.

Earlier in the seventeenth century, when the colony was still fairly new, married women acted for their families as part of the everyday mechanics of operating businesses even without power of attorney. As historian James Perry observed, on the eastern shore "women frequently acted on their own or in behalf of their husbands in and out of the county courts," in some instances behaving as if they had de facto feme sole trader status. Such activities were not always recorded, however, so we have no way of knowing how common this practice was. There are examples of this less formal way of proceeding, especially in the early to mid-seventeenth century. For example, in York County, Mary Smith recorded an obligation in court "by order of her husband" once in October 1647 and again in December that year. Apparently she did so in both instances without the benefit of a power of attorney, since none was recorded. The York court again accepted a married woman acting as agent for her husband without officially recording power of attorney in 1660. With the introduction of more formal legal procedures in

Virginia at the end of the seventeenth century, this practice appears to have died out.[9]

Grants of power of attorney had a variety of implications, and local authorities could use the procedure of recording a power of attorney as a means of extending short-term credit. When Winifred Martin purchased goods from an estate sale, the court granted her credit by declaring her to be attorney for her husband, George Martin. On the same day that Winifred Martin obtained goods from the estate sale, other purchasers obtained temporary credit from the county through the process of a "confessed judgment," acknowledging the debt to a county official. For Martin, the court recorded that she also confessed judgment, but, in addition, that in so doing she acted as attorney for her husband. The court itself recorded her as attorney as a means of guaranteeing her obligation. By this means it recognized her action independent of a husband's direct orders. Winifred Martin had no specific instructions from her husband about what she was to accomplish as his attorney. Indeed, she seems to have purchased goods (ribbons, ruffles, women's clothing, and jewelry).[10]

In the York County Court women acted officially as attorneys in numerous cases, and these are much easier to document. Elizabeth Disarme appeared for her husband in November 1679. Alice Page received the confession of J. Mathews in a debt suit in January 1675 while serving as attorney for her husband. Frances Weeks was given power of attorney from her husband in February 1666 and confessed judgment for a debt in January 1668. Anne Clopton served as attorney for her husband in 1681. Charles Bryan made his wife Susanna his attorney to collect his debts, though the records reveal no more details on what she managed.[11]

In other tidewater counties, too, women in the seventeenth and early eighteenth centuries obtained power of attorney from their husbands. For example, in Charles City County, Warham Horsmonden made his wife his attorney with broad powers to make and receive all debts and "to arrest sue and imprison any Debt'r and at her pleasure againe to release and Discharge, and to do all and every such act and acts...as I my selfe could were I personally here present." Were she to die in his absence, the plantation's overseer was to take her place. Anne Wilkins served as "lawfull Attorney" of her husband in a 1644 Northampton County court case. In Lower Norfolk County, Colonel Francis Yeardley appointed his "welbeloved" wife Sarah, and a friend, attorneys in 1653. Sarah was at least a decade older than her young husband and, because her father had been a London merchant and her grandfather lord mayor of London, she had strong family trading connections long before she took Yeardley as her third husband.[12]

Husbands who lacked confidence in their wives' abilities appointed men as assistants to their wives in managing the family legal affairs. In 1669, Samuel Plowright, a surgeon, requested that two men assist his wife "in my business whatsoever that belong to me" and recorded the request in the court documents. Sometimes women with power of attorney, in turn, delegated authority to their own attorneys. Ann Dixon, wife and attorney of William Dixon, appointed James Crabtree her attorney to represent her in an action "between me" and Samuel Dowse in York County. She may have done so because she lacked the confidence to pursue this particular case, because of her illiteracy. Perhaps she engaged an attorney because she realized she would benefit from the expertise of an agent who could handle some of the business while she managed most of the work herself. She limited her attorney's action to one specific case, retaining control of the rest of the business herself. Even after designating an attorney, she continued to consider the suit her own. Distance from courts also factored into women's decisions to appoint attorneys for some of their cases while maintaining control of disputes that could be handled locally.[13]

Single transactions could involve multiple appearances at the courthouse. Jane Mountfort (also Mountford) acted in court as attorney for her husband, Thomas, in numerous instances over a long period of time. In 1689 she sold a servant boy, William Marshall, to John Hatton, but Jane, acting for herself and her husband, subsequently blocked Hatton's attempt to resell the boy by claiming Hatton had not completed the terms of the bargain. Hatton sued the Mountforts unsuccessfully, and the court ordered Hatton to fulfill the terms of the contract. Similarly, Jane Mountfort was a party in a suit and a countersuit as attorney for Thomas Mountfort. Both concluded in nonsuits, though the cases were subsequently reintroduced and continued. A seemingly simple transaction required Jane Mountfort to make numerous court appearances before the affair was over.[14]

Husband-to-wife powers of attorney demonstrate that family property was understood to be the responsibility of several members of a kin network, not just the male head of the household. Especially when men had to undertake extensive travel to maintain a family business, proximity to courts became a primary motive for assigning a family member of either sex power of attorney. Thus, seventeenth-century women with power of attorney often appeared within trading families whose economic concerns extended beyond a single county.

Local knowledge and proximity often made a wife the best representative for the family. A self-described gentleman from James City County, Thomas Broomer, granted his wife broad power of attorney in 1691 before he left for England.[15] Another traveller to England, Thomas Gentle, appointed his "loveing wife" Mary, who lived in Gloucester, to be his attorney and to manage "all my reall & personall estate in Virginia," indicating that she was to act in such a manner as "shall be in my best interests & profit." Gentle, the commander of a ship in the final stages of preparation for departure to London in 1698, appears to have procrastinated when making his arrangements, because he admitted his ship was already "now rideing in Yorke River" when he made his wife his attorney.[16] Another woman whose husband travelled for business, Sarah Harrison, obtained a letter of attorney from her husband, Robert, which explained that he was "late in York Town" and granted her power to act, apparently in his absences. Robert Harrison, a carpenter, spelled out the extensive powers he granted to his wife to oversee their business — she could independently sell the cattle and household goods, collect debts by bills, bonds, accounts, "or otherways," and could sell their house "and Lot or Lotts" in Yorktown. On the very day that the power of attorney was recorded, the court heard cases involving her.[17] In the 1640s Anne Littleton acted as attorney for her husband, Nathaniell Littleton, "Esquire," while he was in England, prosecuting suits against individuals who owed Littleton money on wholesale accounts. At one of her court appearances, after serving on behalf of her husband, she took care of some of her father's legal business, indicating that her legal experience made her valuable to her more extended family. (Since she was at the court already, her father perhaps decided to let her take care of his affairs at the same time).[18]

Using female family members to represent the family's interest in court was hardly limited to Virginia or the Chesapeake region. Records suggest that, shortly after the English capture of the island of Jamaica, women served in courts there under power of attorney from both related and unrelated men, but most commonly on behalf of husbands. Within the specific context of Virginia, the career of Elizabeth Jones further illuminates the various legal activities of women with power of attorney. Jones obtained power of attorney from Richard Jones, her husband and a planter, when he left Virginia. Elizabeth was to "act in all ways" assisted by Richard's friend George Light but Richard stipulated that if Elizabeth died before he returned to the colony, the estate was to be left unaltered, demonstrating that Richard did not trust his "friend" to act without his wife's guidance. In practice, Elizabeth acted alone, and Light's name did not appear in the records for this case. Elizabeth began her legal activities a month after the power of attorney was recorded, winning a suit against a tardy debtor who had refused payment to her husband. By invoking the power of the court, Elizabeth succeeded in obtaining payment for a bill her husband had been unable to collect. Later cases provided her with additional experience in the courts.[19]

Less than two years later, the relationship between Light and Jones took a turn for the worse. By December 1660, Richard Jones was dead, and Elizabeth acted as his executor. At that juncture, Light claimed the estate owed him "severall somes of money" and that Elizabeth should pay him £8 for Light's work as a carpenter in building her a tobacco house. The court appointed a group of "viewers" to examine it when it was completed and, after hearing the report and Light's deposition, ordered Elizabeth Jones to pay the reduced sum of £5 for the structure. A month later the court heard

Jones's own deposition that she had paid most of the debt. After examiners reviewed the accounts the court settled the dispute between Light and Jones, ordering Jones to pay £1.5.6.[20]

Elizabeth Jones's actions under power of attorney exposed her to the family's commercial affairs and allowed her to gain practical knowledge about the legal system. Jones certainly knew how to manage family affairs well before she became a widow: her first accounts, presented in 1660 for goods and services she purchased in 1658, indicate she acquired them "in the time of hir husband Richard Jones being gone for Eng:[land]."[21]

By the end of 1661, Jones, now her husband's executor, initiated a long and, according to the court's own description, highly complicated, suit over a debt owed by one Richard Longman, Sr. As executor she continued to hold many of the same responsibilities she already exercised before her husband died, when she acted under a power of attorney. As a widow, she faced Longman's son and John Achley, who described himself as a factor for "his Master" Longman, over obligations each claimed the other owed. The court declared the case "a business of great concernment and difficulty." Jones subsequently presented interrogatories to pose to Longman and his associates about the twenty-eight hogsheads of tobacco consigned to Richard Longman, the price obtained for the tobacco in London, the costs incurred in selling the tobacco, and the payments credited to the Jones's accounts. In January 1662, the court ordered two examiners to go to the home of James Bray to examine the accounts and receipts in the case. The suit, listed with Longman as plaintiff and Jones as defendant, concluded in March, the court balancing the accounts in Longman's favor. Jones's obligations totaled £374.2.2 and her credits totaled £353.0.9. Jones then turned to pressing a suit against John Whiskin for the proceeds of tobacco her husband had sent through him to Longman, claiming Whiskin had taken an excessive share of the proceeds. She won the suit and also asked that she not be held responsible for the legal costs of the suit. It appears, then, that the discrepancy in the transaction arose not from Longman's underpayment, but from Whiskin's gouging the Jones family, a maneuver that Jones uncovered and successfully redressed by using the court system.[22]

The progress and variety of Elizabeth Jones's activities in the York County Court demonstrate the significance of a woman within a family's transatlantic business and why it was necessary for women to use the courts to try to protect those interests.[23] Although women were most visible in the courts as widows, where they acted in their own names, their participation in the exchange network could begin before widowhood. Indeed, for women who had no experience with the courts, serving as an attorney could provide the transition toward taking more responsibility for family affairs later in life. "Mrs" Anne Calthorpe was summoned to court as attorney for her husband, Colonel Christopher Calthorpe, to answer the suit of James Bray for a debt of forty pounds of tobacco due by bill, evidence of community awareness of Anne Calthorpe's responsibilities. A month later, Christopher was dead, and Anne Calthorpe was named administrator of the estate. In families with property, women with written power of attorney took responsibility for business in the courts, which included presenting receipts and demanding evidence for the prices of tobacco sold overseas. Competent women could learn about business earlier in their lives, before they became widows.[24]

Trading enterprises, especially those requiring ties to other counties, other colonies, or to England, benefited from the combined efforts of members of extended families. The ways that women exercised power of attorney in the local courts show how women served as local representatives in larger, kin-based trade webs. Elizabeth Vaulx, a particularly visible woman within a mid-seventeenth-century family trade network, operated in several Tidewater county courts but was especially active in the York County court. Vaulx, born Elizabeth Burwell, sister of wealthy planter Major Lewis Burwell, married Robert Vaulx, a leading merchant in London and one of four brothers who immigrated to Virginia. They became merchants dealing in trade between the colony and mother country, as well as with Holland. Elizabeth and Robert Vaulx lived on a five-hundred-acre York County plantation complete with its own warehouses. Robert frequently traveled from Virginia to England to manage his business and to defend himself in lawsuits, and it was for this reason that Elizabeth's business achievements became visible in the county courts in Virginia.[25] In his absence, she managed some of the Virginia side of the family enterprise. She oversaw repayment on a sizable number of debts and occasionally appointed her own attorney to represent her in cases.[26]

In addition to the trading business, she managed substantial land holdings both in York County and in Northern Virginia. The extended Vaulx network placed family members and unrelated representatives in various locations in the colonies and mother country to supervise exchanges of English finished goods for colonial products. Family records indicate that Elizabeth Vaulx corresponded with these representatives in other counties and cultivated additional links. She settled relatives on land near her own substantial tract, ensuring that someone she could rely on would keep watch over her holdings. On at least one occasion, she traveled to England herself, leaving her accounts in the hands of an agent. Before long she returned to Virginia and handled more cases, including a dispute that was ultimately sent up to the colony-level general court in Jamestown.[27]

The Vaulx family had extensive commercial concerns in other tidewater counties. Although men with power of attorney oversaw some of the business in other counties, Elizabeth Vaulx managed northern Virginia affairs. When one purchaser was interested in a plantation, she was told that she should "speak to Mrs. Vaulx" to see if the land was available. Mrs. Vaulx, if willing to sell, would send the patent and orders on to a local representative to lay out the land. The extended family placed members in various locations to receive the goods imported from England and to export tobacco, fur, and other colonial products. Elizabeth Vaulx predeceased her husband in 1666. All of her extensive legal actions, then, occurred during her marriage, since she never became a widow.[28]

Into the eighteenth century, protecting a family's collective interests in trade and property demanded the efforts of women, both as femes soles and femes coverts, as well as the management of the men, to advance the family's well-being. Two generations after Vaulx's cases, the geographic location of the frontier had moved from the tidewater region, and tidewater families no longer relied on women to serve as frequently under power of attorney. However, families in what was by then the frontier again required women to participate in legal affairs when husbands left the home region for extended periods to pursue their interests.[29] Elizabeth Cabell provides us with an example of a woman who left extensive records documenting the ways in which she advanced the Cabell fortunes in the 1730s and 1740s. Elizabeth worked closely with her husband William; fragments of letters reveal her capable position in the family business. A receipt indicates she paid their quit rents and legal fees and other scraps of correspondence describe both selling a slave and the proceedings of the local court.[30]

William Cabell, like Robert Vaulx, had business that took him out of the colony. When he left Virginia for Britain in 1735, he left Elizabeth power of attorney "for the better managem[en]t" of his affairs. William consoled her about his extended absence, reassuring her that she should not "think it occasioned by want of Respect" but that the delay was only to improve "both our Interests." He asked her to pay an account from Major William Mayo, suggesting she turn to her Father or "Richard" to pay it off "to prevent a Sute." The business in Britain required his full attention and prevented him from returning but he hoped that in the meantime "your and my other attorneys Prudent care will Cary my bisn[es]s on with the same life as tho I was with you."[31]

The relative power of each of William Cabell's attorneys and Elizabeth's role in managing the land then became part of a protracted legal dispute itself. Elizabeth sought to protect the family's business in a long-running lawsuit with the Carrington and Mayo families over the management of a tract of land. The Cabells claimed Elizabeth was to serve along with William Mayo and George Carrington, and her husband reported that he granted the two men the power of attorney mostly to "aid and assist" Elizabeth, that she was to have the "principal managem[en]t of the family's affairs. "Mayo then claimed that Cabell originally did not plan to leave the "principal managem[en]t of his affairs to his wife" and that Cabell only added her name to the letter of attorney after Mayo's "earnest request."[32]

By August 1739, Elizabeth Cabell reported that Mayo and Carrington had undermined her efforts, seizing control of the Cabell land and family legal affairs. She wrote to Edward Barradall, a prominent Virginia lawyer, to ask for advice in the case. She forwarded Barradall a copy of her husband's grant of power of attorney and related the recent turn of events. She complained that Mayo wanted to collect fees he was owed as a land surveyor, so that even though he had an interest in the case he "artfully" confessed a judgment that indebted Cabell to him at the local court. He did this without Elizabeth's "knowledge, consent, or presence," despite the fact she was a party in the power of attorney. All this happened to Elizabeth's "great surprise." She concluded her request for help from Barradall by saying, "If such an extraordinary proceeding as this is justyfiable, I must submitt to it;" otherwise, she wanted to retain Barradall to act on her behalf.[33]

Barradall apparently agreed to take the case and advised Elizabeth Cabell to enter an injunction, which she agreed was acceptable when she wrote him again two months later. She also asked whether she actually needed to attend the case "at Town," which she preferred to avoid. The case was heard and appealed to the colony's general court in 1744, where the accounts were settled in Cabell's favor. Other matters remained in dispute among the Cabell, Mayo, and Carrington families into the 1760s, when the case was continued against Mary Mayo and her children after William Mayo's death.[34]

Elizabeth Cabell accepted significant power and responsibility when she served as attorney in her husband's absence, and her work had an impact on the family's economic success. The cases that went to court indicate on what grounds that power might be questioned: Was the power of attorney left equally to all three or, instead, to Elizabeth individually, who was provided with the power to veto actions of the other two, who were merely to serve her as advisors? Apparently either option was possible, but William and Elizabeth took the stance that the power ultimately remained in her hands. This is not surprising since, in this particular dispute, the family would benefit more by claiming the coattorneys possessed no power to proceed without her approval. Still, for the Cabells, delegating the power over immense tracts of land to Elizabeth during William's protracted absence seemed an acceptable division of labor in a family with transatlantic trade concerns. "Temporary widowhood," the situation where a capable woman took over the family business in wartime, could exist in peacetime as well if a husband were absent for equally long periods of time because of economic obligations. Perhaps here "economic widowhood" would be more descriptive; some of these "economic widows," like Vaulx, never became widows in fact. Technically, they remained "deputy husbands" who held their authority from their husbands. As husbands remained absent for longer periods of time, women could gain competence in economic affairs and the legal realm.[35]

Powers of attorney granted to women in family trade networks allowed colonists with commercial interests to preserve a family's prosperity by having competent women in place to oversee the operation of business at various points in the network. However, in other instances, the practice of men's granting their wives power of attorney might have an alternative function; instead of commingling legal interests, power of attorney could permit the separation of the two spouses' legal identities.

A common reason for a woman to seek a legal identity independent of her husband was to protect the interests of her children from an earlier marriage, retaining the economic viability and legal authority of this family. As chapter 1 explains, the demographic situation in early Virginia meant that women often maintained multiple family allegiances resulting from a series of marriages. A responsible widow with children could seek, on remarriage, power of attorney from her new husband as a means to keep the claims of a first family and its children distinct from the interests of the woman's second, or subsequent, husband. In these instances, a married woman could appear in court independently from her current husband (or "now" husband, in the Chesapeake phrasing). Women's legal identities were not singular and fixed but existed along a spectrum of legal statuses. Marriage to a new husband did not completely obliterate the woman's link to her previous husband and their children. Even during marriage, the boundaries between the restrictive prescriptions of feme covert status and the legal freedom of the feme sole were less absolute than those fixed categories would suggest, particularly in the seventeenth century, when remarrying widows with children sought to protect their interests.

Women who used powers of attorney in this manner were similar to those who used prenuptial agreements to keep family property distinct. With a power of attorney, a remarried widow could manage business that primarily concerned assets acquired during a previous marriage without the new husband's active meddling. She also could watch over property that she perceived as hers. In December 1666, Elizabeth Woods, the remarried widow of Robert Frith, received power of attorney from her second husband, John Woods, to enable her to collect debts. She had children from her marriage with Frith and took the precaution before marrying for the second time to obtain a prenuptial agreement to protect her children's interests. She did this by demanding a performance bond from her new husband and by requiring him to acknowledge that he was indebted to her or her heirs for the land she owned. Woods promised to deliver the land and cattle to her children when they came of age. Furthermore, if the children died before reaching maturity, Elizabeth was still left with the right to dispose of the property. Elizabeth supervised her family's business during her marriages and continued her activities after Woods's death. A deposition in a 1675 proceeding indicates that she "knew viewed & accepted" an account concerning a debt.[36] The court's approval of remarrying widows maintaining control of the ghost family's estate, with or without official power of attorney, is apparent in the 1660 case of Elizabeth Alvis. Although she had no official power of attorney, the court recorded that Alvis appeared on behalf of her current husband. It added, however, that she was acknowledging a debt that her late husband had incurred, suggesting that her legal obligations simply had less bearing on the new husband and stemmed, instead, from these previous responsibilities.[37]

Other York County women followed paths similar to Woods's during widowhood. The career of Susanna Brookes Vergett Davis, an apparently illiterate woman, demonstrates how powers of attorney worked for remarried women. She was granted the administration of the estate of her first husband, Thomas Brookes. Less than a year later, after she had married Job Vergett, she was sued because she had not returned an inventory of Brookes's estate and because the court had received reports that much of the estate had been "disposed of imbezelled & wasted" at the orphans' expense. Susanna Vergett first confessed judgment "in open court" on behalf of her husband, Job Vergett. Her representation of her current husband in the July 1669 court by power of attorney must have been merely a continuation of her supervision of the first husband's estate. The court's written comment that she pursued legal business "in behalf of her husband" simply protected the creditor from any later claim by Susanna's current husband that his wife had no right to take on the debt for her family. By September 1672, Job was dead, too, and two months later, Susannah Vergett "relict of Mr Job Vergett dece[ase]d & relict of Mr Thomas Brookes dec[ease]d" efficiently presented inventories of both of her dead husbands at the same court before leaving the county.[38]

In these cases, Susanna Vergett's power of attorney allowed her to continue her already-initiated legal affairs without the meddling, or perhaps much interest, of her new husband, Edward Davis. She returned to the court again in February 1679/80, when Davis appointed her his attorney to conduct business in the York court. She and Elizabeth Brookes, probably her daughter from the first marriage, leased the land. The Davis power of attorney might have been recorded to give her the legal capacity to do so. The fact that mother and daughter cosigned the lease suggests that this was property from the Brookes marriage. Davis might well have seen this as primarily his wife's business.[39]

Susanna's powers of attorney from her various husbands allowed her to pursue management of her deceased husbands' estates. Property from one nuclear family could continue to be seen as a unit and identified with those family members even after the widow remarried. By this means, a ghost family and its property continued as an entity even after the father died and the mother remarried, leaving the mother responsible for directing its management. As the thrice-widowed Susanna Brookes Vergett Davis demonstrated, a woman could manage business from a previous marriage. The court recognized that a woman or her family ought to preserve a separate economic identity or to use legal mechanisms to gain a measure of control over property. Property interests, rather than being defined individualistically for either women or men, could be seen as a bundle of assets held by a family, with both women and men involved in their management.[40]

Powers of attorney thus ranged from restrictive, one-time instructions that allowed the appointed attorney little autonomy to grants that gave women, as attorneys, relative independence. A final, extraordinary, and well-documented example, that of Jane Parke, demonstrates that power of attorney could, even more dramatically, function effectively as a separation agreement in a time and place where absolute divorce with right to remarry was impossible to obtain. In the first power of attorney that Daniel Parke II granted to his wife Jane (Ludwell) Parke, he provided her with limited legal identity; a later power granted her a de facto separation agreement that gave her extensive authority over property and legal affairs. Her legal career demonstrates how far a woman could go in exercising power over property, sometimes out of necessity, sometimes reluctantly, and often to the chagrin of the men in the family.[41]

In 1689, Daniel Parke II, "gentleman" of York County and later governor of the Leeward Islands, made his "deare & loveing wife" Jane Parke, along with his brother-in-law, Major Lewis Burwell of Gloucester, his attorneys to collect all debts that were due then or later. Before being designated as attorney, Jane Parke's formal court experience was limited to her making oath to a will in 1688. As attorneys, Jane Parke and Lewis Burwell initiated two suits in late 1689 and early 1690.[42] In September 1690, Daniel Parke added another attorney to manage his affairs in Virginia, but Parke's instructions indicated that the new attorney should, "if need be," receive directions from Jane Parke and Lewis Burwell. During this time Jane Parke responded to several suits, including payment of a fine on behalf of a servant who had given birth to a child born out of wedlock and faced a whipping if she could not pay the fine. Jane appeared more frequently after Daniel once again left her in charge of his affairs when he left for England in April 1697; he recorded a second power of attorney to his wife, and this time he did not designate an assistant. He granted her more limited discretion in this document because he provided her with no authority to sell or dispose of his land or slaves without his specific instructions. Most of the cases she managed were heard after her husband's departure in 1697.[43]

While acting as sole attorney for her husband, Jane Parke both initiated and defended herself in various suits concerning debts and obligations. She worked, not always successfully, to advance the family's position. She rented land to William Gibbs and sued him when he failed to pay.[44] Like other colonial parents concerned with creating an estate to support and advance the position of their children, she invested in livestock. She purchased cattle from a man named Thomas Steare and employed him to care for the stock. She cultivated corn on her land and purchased an additional sixty-two acres. She sold slaves, but on one occasion she was sued for damages by a purchaser who claimed she sold slaves who had already won their freedom. In this particularly long trial, the jury agreed with her accuser and awarded the plaintiff the cost of the slaves and damages against her.[45]

In another suit, she had more luck in resolving business her husband had initiated earlier. In this case Daniel Parke, before his departure, had hired James Ming to survey land, and Ming claimed payment. A Parke attorney, Stephen Thompson, said the action was invalid. Ming countered, responding that on July 20, 1702, Jane Parke, in her role as wife and attorney of Daniel, asked Ming to wait until the next fleet arrived, at which time she would be able to pay him. She still did not pay, and Ming initiated a suit. The court dismissed the case, making Parke's stalling techniques effective.[46]

Jane Parke's career came to an end when, at about the age of forty, she predeceased her husband in 1708. Although at first she appears to be like other women married to prominent men with political or economic interests overseas, the Parke family was more complicated. Daniel Parke clearly had transatlantic business, and like Elizabeth Vaulx, Jane Parke played a part in her family's undertakings. The testimony in the Ming case revealed that Jane Parke used delaying tactics to hold off creditors. Only her disputed business shows up in the court records, but it demonstrates her many roles. Both alone and with the assistance of other attorneys, Jane Parke participated in the legal and economic activities of the county, advancing her business when she chose to do so and protecting assets when necessary, just as Elizabeth Vaulx had done fifty years earlier.[47]

Daniel Parke's absence from the colony was due to his service as governor of the Leeward Islands, and his wife did not accompany him there—for good reason, it appears. In his will, Daniel Parke acknowledged a female companion and child in the Leeward Islands and left that family land and other property.[48] In the context of this shadow life, the power of attorney that Daniel twice granted to Jane Parke takes on a distinctive meaning. In other families, powers of attorney indicate the ways that women played a part in trade networks. Jane Parke's powers of attorney, especially the second, seem to have served as an effective separation agreement. In a colony that allowed no absolute divorce, a separation agreement delineating rights and obligations of each party was the best that this unhappy couple could hope for.[49] The 1697 power of attorney allowed Jane Parke enumerated, but relatively wide, rights. She had the authority to manage all of the plantations, lands, slaves, stock, and all other real and personal estate in Virginia, with the exception of selling or giving away the land. This last clause proved irrelevant, because she added to the acreage rather than disposing of any real estate. In effect, this power of attorney allowed Jane Parke much of the power of a separation agreement but without the complications. Daniel hoped that distance and the sexual double-standard would allow him the freedom to start a new family in a fashion that was no more and no less effective than if he had obtained a separation. He did not entirely succeed, however, and a protracted dispute after his death prevented him from disinheriting his Virginia daughters.[50]

In July 1705, Jane Parke felt overwhelmed by the responsibilities left to her in Virginia, especially after a "dying-sickness" of four months duration left her incapable of "taking the worldly care" of the Virginia business any more. As Daniel prepared to take up the Leeward Islands governorship, she wrote to him, hoping he would stop in Virginia on his way to take up office and begging him to release her from the obligations and instead settle "as small a competence as you please" on her so she could live quietly. Her letter revealed she was particularly concerned about placing her daughters, then young women, in proper circles for them to meet spouses of their own and about negotiating the offers of marriage that had already come their way. As she well knew from experience, "married life is the best or worst of lives" and she hoped her daughters "will be careful in the liberty they take." Daniel, she believed, undermined her efforts on their behalf by complaining the three women lived extravagantly when Jane believed "it is expected we should live equal with the best in the country" and to look "tolerable like other people." Jane reminded her husband of her economies, including having her daughters' dresses remade and their limited consumption of expensive imported sugar and wine. She expressed her frustration with her husband in her reminder that he should "remember[] who it is [that] has for these twenty-odd years made your home so uneasy for you; in which I have been so great a sharer as [to have] brought my life with sorrow to the grave."[51] Further evidence demonstrates that the Parkes' marriage had broken down by 1707, if not before, and that Daniel was alienated from his daughters by then as well. In that year, Jane's family discussed Governor Parke's attempt to disown his daughters on the pretext of being offended at their marriages. This, according to Jane's relatives, was merely an excuse, which "save[d] him the trouble of finding" another reason to quarrel with his children. Jane's family believed Parke would welcome news that his wife was dead. More immediately, Jane's family was concerned that she "[wa]s in want," though she said "nothing of shame" in her treatment by her husband. She had some slaves and "7 or 8 working hands may keep a single body from starveing being well employed," but the soil of the plantation was already worn out. The family's English agent attempted to protect Jane Parke's interests and offered suggestions for providing for the daughters.[52] Still, Governor Parke's vindictive will and complicated family life plagued his Virginia daughters and their families well into the next generation. During her brief life, the Parke power of attorney provided this family with a means of maintaining themselves despite the actions of a problematic patriarch. Daniel Parke II learned little about dealing humanely with subordinates in his encounters with his family. Leeward

Island colonists also found him overbearing while he served as their governor, and an even less forgiving violent Antiguan mob attacked him and dragged him through the gravel streets, leaving him in the sun to die of his wounds.[53] The mob provided, perhaps, a suitably horrific ending to the life of a man who tormented family and subordinates for so long.

Not all women who acted under power of attorney did so as representatives of family members. Although Virginia women acting under power of attorney most commonly did so on behalf of their husbands, others did business for unrelated men pursuing commercial interests in England. In 1683, Anthony Hall, a former resident of Virginia, "now of the Boogge in England Gent," made Rebecca Hethersall, a widow living in York Old Fields, his attorney to collect all his Virginia debts. Because she possessed property both in Virginia and England and had used the court successfully to collect debts in her own suits in the 1680s, Hethersall's reputation as a litigant no doubt appealed to Hall. She lived up to that reputation when she successfully defended Hall in a debt suit in 1684. Similarly, Mary Croshaw appeared as attorney on behalf of Thomas Holder in a suit initiated by Jonathan Newell. Elizabeth Duke served in Prince George County in 1722 for John Woof, a London merchant who had legal business in Virginia.[54]

The most intriguing cases of power of attorney held by women in Virginia remain those granted from husbands to wives. William Blackstone, in his 1765 *Commentaries on the Laws of England* confirmed and delineated the proper procedure of a wife acting as attorney on behalf of her husband, and he claimed her doing so "implies no separation from, but is rather a representation of, her lord [the husband]." Women's acceptance of power of attorney, even while under coverture, allowed them to learn about finances and legal procedure and to oversee portions of family business.[55]

The choice of a wife as an attorney declined in the tidewater counties by the middle of the eighteenth century, though they did not cease entirely. Benjamin Smith of Essex County still granted his wife power of attorney in 1752, though she was to serve with the assistance of Smith's friend. Robert Hockley, also of Essex, appointed his wife his attorney, but indicated he did so because of his illness, now that he was "Rendered incapable of any service," not because he was entrusting her with the whole of the family's transatlantic business. Increasingly, men from the tidewater involved in transatlantic trade appointed other men who were merchants, mariners or others traveling out of the county to serve as their attorneys.[56]

This is consistent with the time of change in other colonies as well. Before 1740, North Carolinians used powers of attorney to delegate legal responsibilities to married women who sometimes had legal "careers" during which they became involved in a series of lawsuits in the process of managing estates and protecting their own business. Similarly, in West Jersey, attorneys were "not trained lawyers at all, but men—and women—of affairs" who lost access to legal processes with the rise of the legal profession. Women there became decreasingly significant figures during the 1720s and 1730s, when serving as a professional attorney became a profitable enterprise. Simultaneously, women were prevented from becoming professional lawyers by being denied access to training in lawyers' offices and to licensing by the colony's superior courts. Historian Peter Hoffer concludes that the rise of the legal profession "went hand in glove with the increasing complexity and frequency of litigation" at precisely the time that women were refused access to that more formal training. In a vicious circle, the untrained representative could no longer successfully represent her family's interests in court, and she could not gain admission to more formal means of education that allowed her to become an attorney-at-law.[57]

By the time of the War of Independence, colonists and residents of the mother country were reconsidering the position of women under the law. Even before the eighteenth century, England's growing commercial and colonial enterprises complicated legal notions of property, and these changes, not surprisingly, affected women's property rights. When Lord Mansfield, chief justice of the English Court of King's Bench from 1756 to 1788, heard the case of *Ringsted v. Lady Lanesborough* (mentioned in the previous chapter) in 1783, he decided that if a married woman behaved as a single woman for commercial purposes, the merchants and others dealing with her should be able to sue and be sued by the acting-as-sole woman. Trading interests were at the heart of Mansfield's innovative approach to women's property rights.

Following independence from England, at least one prominent Virginia jurist, St. George Tucker, also reconsidered the nature of women's public status, reflecting on the difference between the English and Virginia practices. Tucker published an annotated version of *Blackstone's Commentaries* in 1803 to assist lawyers in the new state of Virginia to understand the law, and in his edition, he attacked English common-law construction of women's legal rights. Tucker disagreed with Blackstone's editorial remarks that the disabilities of coverture were "for the most part intended for her [the wife's] protection and benefit. So great a favourite is the female sex of the laws of England." He then proceeded to enumerate how English law made unfair legal distinctions between men and women. After the Revolution, according to Tucker's argument, women should be released from the bondage of British common law to enjoy instead the power to protect the interests that their colonial mothers and grandmothers had guarded only under power of attorney. Tucker was not immediately successful, and circuitous routes for protecting women's autonomy remained the norm in postindependence Virginia.[59]

Colonists sought to redefine the options married women had for controlling property and pursuing their legal interests in various ways in the colonial period, and extending power of attorney should be seen as only one means colonists had to accord married women power over property.[60] Historians of women in Virginia have pointed out that, prior to the middle of the eighteenth century, colonists used a variety of methods to avoid the strictest of common-law restrictions limiting married women in the colony. The grants of power of attorney to married women are consistent with this trend. Only with closer adoption of English patterns in the law in the middle of the eighteenth century did these opportunities disappear.[61] The variety of powers of attorney that husbands granted to wives suggests that earlier in Virginia history, men, as well as women, occasionally saw the advantage of according women agency under the law.

THE "ORDINARY" WOMEN: BUSINESS OWNERS AND THE LOCAL COURTS

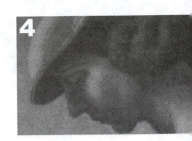

*A*s the eighteenth-century capital of Virginia, Williamsburg attracted numerous travelers who came to attend the House of Burgesses, the colony's general court, or merchants' meetings. Other colonists came to seek out the governor, to study at the College of William and Mary, and to take advantage of the shopping. Today, visitors to Williamsburg are familiar with the reconstructions of Jane Vobe's King's Arms and Mrs. Campbell's taverns, but other women also kept ordinaries (the customary Virginia term for taverns before the middle of the eighteenth century) and rented rooms, as well.[1] These women who maintained their own enterprises learned to use the legal system when necessary. As women with business interests and personal financial obligations, ordinary keepers resorted to legal action when necessary, demonstrating the frequent link between a woman's autonomous legal affairs and her entrepreneurial efforts.

The appearances before the courts of female ordinary keepers reveal how power relationships worked and hierarchies were maintained in the colony. Many of these were fairly prominent women. Had they occupied lower positions on the social scale, the courts could easily have ignored their plights. All the litigants occupied a distinctive place within the society because they had their own businesses and enjoyed more autonomy as a result, but it also made them vulnerable.[2] They had goods worth stealing and also represented challenges to male domination. Just as women with autonomous ownership of property in New England were disproportionately vulnerable to witchcraft accusations, so women in colonial Virginia who had their own means of support could suffer legal and physical attacks from neighbors.[3] When women lived in their own households they relied on the courts rather than men in their households to sustain a race-based order that granted them a relatively privileged position.

This chapter argues that ordinary-keeping women, a particularly well-documented group of businesswomen, employed the local county court to protect themselves from attacks and to seek redress from injustices. Even within an Anglo-American culture that voiced a desire for docility and submission from women, especially "covert" married women, certain groups of women still publicly confronted opponents, using the very legal apparatus that, at other times, served as the means to oppress them. Autonomous women suffered attacks, but they fought back with the legal and bureaucratic resources at their disposal. Propertied women entered into an implicit bargain with their society: in return for their subordination, they received certain kinds of legal protection against those people who, in turn, threatened them.[4]

Determining "typicality" is always difficult. Here I concentrate on the group of women who "typically" had cases to manage before the local court. The typical woman in court was a litigant, not a criminal defendant, and as such, she represents a specific kind of ordinary experience (see table 4.1). Furthermore, these ordinary women's cases demonstrate the link between women's business interests and their activities before the bar. This makes Virginia women's experiences similar to those of colonial South Carolina: Elizabeth Marie Pruden has discovered that the majority of South Carolina women's lawsuits centered on financial issues and provided the motivation for women to participate in "public arenas." In South Carolina and Virginia, women, limited by coverture, used the law less frequently than men did, but they still found ways to assert their rights within the limits imposed upon them. Pruden has found that historians have left these forms of participation "unexplored."[5]

Ordinary owners who used courts to resolve issues often engaged in business exchanges outside the legal system and only resorted to litigation in trade gone bad. Law was not the only way to collect and prosaic references to women's uncontested dealings appear frequently in colonial records. Williamsburg tavern owner Jane Vobe purchased two barrels of flour through a Fredericksburg merchant firm.[6] She presented an account to Henry Marse for numerous meals and drinks provided in 1772 and 1773, prior to coming to an accounting with her customer on August 17, 1773, and offering Mr. Marse a receipt for the settled payment.[7] Similarly, Carter Burwell of Carter's Grove ran long-term accounts with Anne Pattison, who obtained large quantities of pork, wood, cider, "old" china, and glassware from Burwell. Both Burwell and William Lightfoot supplied Mrs. Campbell on credit for her supplies of beef, veal, and numerous bushels of wheat.[8] The nature of women's credit and exchanges in the local economy will be analyzed in chapter 5; here, however, it is important to recognize that women only resorted to legal remedies to resolve their disputed or tardy payments; most business did not require actual intervention on the part of the court.

TABLE 4.1 BREAKDOWN OF FEMALE DEFENDANTS IN CRIMINAL AND CIVIL
CASES IN THE YORK COUNTY COURT

YEAR	FEMALE CRIMINAL DEFENDANTS	FEMALE CIVIL DEFENDANTS
1646	1	11
1661	8	5
1671	3	5
1681	2	17
1691	2	10
1701	9	6
1711	3	5
1721	6	26
1731	6	20
1741	19	11
1751	5	27
1761	9	15

Women who kept ordinaries often had to put some pressure on debtors
when obligations went unpaid. Even when cases did not go to court, the
threat of going to law could be useful to business owners who wished to
pressure customers to resolve unpaid balances. Jane Vobe sought repayment
by resorting to advertisements to warn her debtors in advance that she
would initiate prosecution for unpaid debts. If successful, she could avoid
expensive litigation.[9] Other owners avoided collection problems by accepting only cash payments for food or lodging.

Even if a case never went to trial, the legal system provided a source of
implicit power for women, who could use even the threat of litigation to
their advantage when other solutions fell short. If an ordinary-keeping
woman sought legal remedies to collect overdue payments or to enforce
other types of obligations, the creditor faced her recalcitrant debtor. In these
circumstances, the law provided women who had businesses with agency by
enforcing legal obligations between the women and their customers.

Ordinaries, like those run by Williamsburg businesswomen Susanna
Allen or Jane Vobe, were licensed. The regulation of ordinaries by the county
courts made these establishments a particularly visible type of business
enterprise. County courts set the prices for all establishments in their juris-

diction twice a year, and ordinary keepers needed to use set weights and measures in selling their goods. Because this extensive regulation required that ordinary keepers obtain a license each year (and pay a substantial fee), we can trace the owners of these businesses, including the female-owned establishments.[10] This chapter will concentrate on the taverns in the tidewater counties, particularly in York County, with its concentration of establishments serving travelers, including, in the eighteenth century, those with political interests or business to conduct at the colony's capital in Williamsburg.[11]

Because officials believed taverns served as a location for disorder—drinking to excess, loafing out of sight of a master, or engaging in inappropriate "disorderly" sexual behavior—they enacted laws regulating these establishments. In 1668 the postrestoration colonial administration sought to curtail the "excessive number" of ordinaries seen as encouraging "idleness and debaucheryes, in a sort of loose and carelesse persons who neglecting their callings misspend their times in drunkenness" merely for the private gain of the ordinary keeper.[12] Because legal ordinaries had to have licenses, historians have the means for tracing the owners of legal businesses. When the governor complained in 1721 that his own servants patronized Catherine Craig's ordinary against his desires, the court intervened. Two justices of the county court temporarily "suppressed" Craig, taking away her liquor license. She evaded prosecution after she promised to "keep more regular order in her ordinary" in Williamsburg after a complaint to the court.[13] The York County grand jury presented another ordinary keeper, Elizabeth Moody, on the charges she was "extorting in the price of her Liquors." Through her attorney, Moody managed to convince the trial jury that the court had insufficient proof to convict her.[14]

The licenses controlled women's businesses, but also benefited existing establishments by limiting access to the trade. In the seventeenth century, county courts used the licenses as an informal means of self-help poor relief: In 1696 Robert Leightonhouse successfully petitioned for an ordinary license on account of his "low & mean condition" and his affliction, resulting in the "loss of his limbs."[15] By 1705, the colony attempted to halt this practice and specifically ordered the county courts *not* to give licenses to a "poor body" to keep him off the parish charge because this measure was "very Prejudicial" to legitimate business.[16] Here, though, the statute was likely to remain prescriptive rather than descriptive.

After 1644, Virginia required individuals who kept ordinaries and "victualling houses" to obtain a license from the governor of the colony after obtaining permission from the county court.[17] This allowed the government to regulate the quality of the food, control the prices of meals and beer, and ban the sale of strong liquor.[18] Over the latter part of the seventeenth century, officials regulated selling various beverages and attempted to control the "exorbitant" prices on drinks. In one instance several York County ordi-

TABLE 4.2 GENDER DIVISION OF ORDINARY LICENSE RECIPIENTS: YORK COUNTY ORDINARY LICENSES[25]

YEAR	TOTAL #	# MALE OWNERS	# FEMALE OWNERS	% FEMALE OWNERS
1701	1	0	1	100%
1711	12	8	4	33%
1721	19 (one granted to husband and wife jointly)	15	5	26%
1731	6	5	1	17%
1741	5	5	0	0%
1751	2	1	1	50%
1761	4	4	0	0%
TOTALS	49	38	12	22%

nary keepers banded together to petition the county to influence the list of prices. They accepted that they should sell meals, known as a "dyett," at the single set price of one shilling per person in 1711, no matter whether the ordinary keeper put delicacies or slop on the table. They thought the list of fourteen different beverages from "Virginia Mid[d]ling Bear & Cyder" at three and three quarters pence per quart to French Brandy at four shillings per quart was inadequate. The petitioners wanted to add "Roger's best Virg[ini]a Ale" to the list and to be able to charge six pence per quart for this drink. The court complied.[19]

In York County ordinaries were particularly important to a local economy that included both the busy port of Yorktown and half the city of Williamsburg. Women as well as men obtained licenses to operate ordinaries in the tidewater region during the colonial period (see table 4.2). As the pioneering women's historian Julia Cherry Spruill points out, during the colonial period, southern women commonly kept taverns and boarding houses, especially in cities like Edenton, North Carolina; Charleston, South Carolina; and Baltimore and Annapolis, Maryland. In 1770, Mary Davis even offered women a room of one's own in Williamsburg: "Ladies that may choose to spend a few weeks in private times, whether for pleasure or education, may do it here both reasonably and with convenience."[20] "Microenterprises" that provide food and drink continue to be a significant source of income for women in the developing world.[21] Although the skills necessary for providing hospitality on the market closely resembled domestic undertakings within a private household, a recent critique of gender-biased definitions of the public sphere suggests that taverns served a more complex function, especially when women operated taverns that served as venues for political debates. The two views can be reconciled: hospitality "straddled the boundary" between public and private. Taking this more expansive definition of public life, tavern keeping could function both as domestic and as public.[22] Elsewhere in the eighteenth century women made up 22 percent of tavern keepers in Charleston in 1790 and 71 percent of the boarding house operators. Boston women had 24 percent of the tavern licenses in 1765, though this declined to 21 percent in 1789 and 0 percent in 1798.[23] The latter trend also occurred in Virginia, and in Petersburg, a city located just south of Richmond, Suzanne Lebsock has found that women still operated about 20 percent (11 out of 54) of the licensed ordinaries between 1780 and 1800. These women operated smaller, less prestigious enterprises than men did there. Furthermore, women increasingly lost their foothold in the tavern and innkeeping business after 1820, when more pretensions hotels took over the hospitality industry. Men owned all of the new-fangled hotels.[24]

Unlicensed ordinaries operated, as well, though these are more difficult to document. In 1692, the York County court summoned Christopher and Margrett Pearson, "his wife," jointly for selling liquor without a license.[26] In 1705, Sarah and Thomas Sclater were summoned to answer for their illegal selling of drink by a competitor who operated his own ordinary nearby.[27] Again, in August 1708, ordinary keeper Elizabeth Moody used the York County court to ward off unlicensed rivals when she complained that "sev[era]l persons about the Court house door" sold liquor without licenses. On hot summer days, especially, informal court-day vendors presented cut-price competition to the legal and more established ordinaries, including Moody's own. She won her case and the court "speedily remove[d]" her competitors.[28] Other occasional events provided vending opportunities. An Essex County grand jury presented three men and one woman to the court for selling rum or cider without licenses at the end of the race grounds. These sellers operated out of informal, temporary booths. A fifth offender was presented for allowing liquor to be sold at his house without a license. All five appeared in the November 1727 grand jury presentments, suggesting a "sweep" of illegal alcohol retailing.[29] Petersburg between 1780 and 1800 again offers a useful contrast: there, 30 percent of ordinary keepers accused of operating without licenses were women.[30] This suggests that an underground economy probably existed for the earlier period as well.

According to the York County sample, based on one year's worth of licenses issued for each decade between 1700 and 1762, women were most likely to run ordinaries in the earlier years of the eighteenth century. Women there and in other counties who had capital could use their houses and skills to operate ordinaries. In the 1720s in Essex County, Virginia, the widowed Mary Coleman obtained a license to keep an "ordinary at her house" at the town of Tappahanock.[31] Ady Booth obtained her first ordinary license and proved her husband's will in the same year—1711. The next year she also purchased an urban lot in Yorktown and obtained a license to keep at her "now dwelling house" in Yorktown.[32] Booth established her business and attended to her husband's estate between 1711 and 1713, using the court to collect debts owed to her both as businesswoman and as executor.[33] In October of 1711 she presented a claim to the court for payment on an official, county purchase for "entertaining sev[era]l labourers in the time of their working on the fortifications at Yorktown" and presented a signed certificate from the project overseer to prove the obligation.[34] In January 1712, she sought payment from a debtor to her husband's estate and reported that she possessed an account she found "amongst the papers of her dece[ase]d husband" in January of 1712.[35] Her move into legal affairs and ordinary business coincided as she began to make a new life for herself.

Even when married women operated ordinaries, they may have run the businesses as largely their own, and they may have been publicly recognized for doing this. For example, in March 1721, the York County court recorded that George Luke "Esqr." and Mary "his wife" were awarded a license to keep an ordinary in Williamsburg.[36] However, when the court transcribed the bond for the license into the official records, her husband disappeared, leaving only Mary Luke with a third party, Thomas Jones, as obligor to the bond. The court also left her husband out when it issued the license and listed only Mary when describing her right to keep the ordinary at "her now dwelling house." The supporting performance bond also held only Mary, individually, responsible for providing good, wholesome food and lodging for travelers, and provisions for the animals.[37] Further evidence than she ran the business herself is a receipt she wrote for a customer, attorney Godfrey Pole; on it, she signed her own name on the record of payment Pole retained.[38]

Other evidence suggests that even while married women worked as partners, at the least, in family-operated ordinaries, the court issued the official license to the husband.[39] When the York County court charged both Thomas and Sarah Sclater with selling drink "contrary to law" in 1705 and again in 1708, both were listed as defendants. One historian has suggested that Sarah was the guilty party, or that the couple ran an ordinary together. As long as Sarah was married, however, she was prosecuted with her husband.[40] Married women, like Anne Sullivant, may have kept ordinaries while their husbands pursued other occupations.[41]

Prospective spouses (male and female) of ordinary keepers sometimes had experience running such businesses before entering their new marriages. Ann Marot, was the daughter of two ordinary keepers, Jean Marot and Ann Marot Sullivant, and the stepdaughter of a third, Timothy Sullivant.

(See table 4.3). Ann herself married her second husband James Shields, a tavern keeper. Her third husband was Henry Wetherburn, also in the same business. Wetherburn was the widower of Mary Bowcock Wetherburn, a tavern keeper whose first husband had been Henry Bowcock, a tavern keeper.[42]

Members of the Bowcock-Wetherburn-Marot-Shields network operated some of the best ordinaries in Williamsburg during the eighteenth century. This is the best indication that in Williamsburg, widows and widowers recognized the skills, knowledge, and assets that a future bride or groom could bring to an existing business in the extended family network of intermarried tavern keepers in the eighteenth century.

Women in tavernkeeping households learned the business well enough so that once on their own they could continue to maintain the family enterprises. Ann Marot observed the business firsthand in the ordinaries of her parents, Jean Marot and Ann Marot Sullivant.[43] As the daughter of an ordinary keeper, Christiana (Burdett) Campbell knew about ordinary keeping, so she returned to the business and her hometown of Williamsburg after her husband, a doctor, died.[44] Mary Maupin learned enough about ordinary keeping to continue to run the family ordinary during her widowhood and after she remarried.[45] Mary Smith had a tavern in Yorktown in the 1710s after she separated from her husband, a former Williamsburg tavernkeeper.[46] Elizabeth Leightonhouse, the widow of Robert, took out a license for her own ordinary in Yorktown after her husband, who had the business earlier, died.[47] Two of the most prominent Williamsburg tavern owners, Jane Vobe (owner of the King's Arms) and Anne Pattison, had been married to men who owned taverns before setting themselves up as sole operators during their widowhoods in the middle of the eighteenth century. Campbell and Vobe ran two of the "finer" establishments, and each could claim that George Washington had slept there. A 1765 traveler reported that "all the best people resorted" at Mrs. Vobe's.[48] Securing rights to an ordinary mattered enough to Mary Swann in 1681 that after her husband died she traded away dower rights to various lands, and, in return keeping a house to her self and a share in the family ordinary.[49]

Taverns seemed to be desirable investments. In 1680, when Agnes and Andrew Reader sold their land and house to York County on the understanding that it would serve as the courthouse for the county, they received an ordinary license in return. For the Readers, the ordinary would provide a source of income that made sacrificing their land worthwhile, especially since the ordinary was to be located near the new courthouse where travelers in town to use the courts would need food and possibly lodging.[50]

Securing a profitable location for the business mattered enormously. Anne Pattison established herself just west of the Capitol building in Williamsburg, appealing to slightly less extravagant patrons.[51] Simple ordinaries provided stopping-off places for travelers en route to other destinations, and were situated along the main roads or at the ferry stops on the

TABLE 4.3 THE BOWCOCK-WETHERBURN-MAROT-SHIELDS NETWORK

Jean Marot m. Ann Marot (later Sullivant) m. (2) Timothy Sullivant in 1718

Henry	+ Mary	+ Henry	+ Ann (Marot)	+ James	+ Eliz (1?) Cobbs
Bowcock	(1) Bowcock	Wetherburn	(1) Ingles	Shields	(2?) Shields
	(2) Wetherburn	d. 1760	(2) Shields		(no ordy. lic. of
	d. 1751		(3) Wetherburn		own)
			m. 1751		

banks of the major rivers. York County's Half-Way ordinary no doubt received its name for its location. Because major rivers bisected the landscape, ordinary keepers often situated their establishments on the banks of the river near a well-used ferry.[52] In addition to lodging persons with official business or traveling overnight, ordinaries provided entertainment, including gambling and dancing, as well as a place for pleasant conversation.

In county seats and the capital cities, destination ordinaries tended to offer a range of levels of comfort, from the relatively lavish to the crowded and dirty. In September, 1668, each county was permitted a maximum of two ordinaries, to be located adjacent to the courthouse. Additional ordinaries could be licensed, where necessary, at sites near ports, ferries, or "great roads" with the express purpose of serving travelers, not locals. Restrictions on ordinaries increased in June 1676; the colony suppressed all ordinaries except at the capital (James City), and at the ferry sites on either side of the York River. Even these could serve only beer and cider. The colony's capital, first at Jamestown and after 1699 in Williamsburg, attracted a regular clientele during times when court was in session or the legislators met. At the county courthouse, a "complex" of buildings, including taverns and offices, developed to serve people who traveled to vote, conduct business, or gawk at proceedings. An assortment of people, including itinerant preachers, converged on court days and an architectural historian has described the scene of court day, with men and boys hanging out of the courthouse windows listening to arguments, and vendors milling about selling goods and refreshments.[53] In the eighteenth century, auctions could be scheduled on the steps of a tavern and tavernkeepers could host upscale "clubs," sell tickets to balls and dancing assemblies, and encourage horse racing.[54] Women and men, even children, all stopped at the house ordinaries. After Elizabeth Burt concluded her August 1691 case in court, she, her husband, and her newborn baby headed to the French Ordinary adjacent to the York County Courthouse for a celebratory round—or several. We only have records of this event because she then ran into difficulty after her husband, still imbibing, refused to take her home. She accused the neighbor, who had agreed to carry her and her baby home on his horse, of the seventeenth-century equivalent of acquaintance rape.[55] Normally this type of postcourt tavern party escaped the historians' records.

The most opulent ordinaries were near sites associated with official administration and assured the owners they would have a steady flow of wealthy (and status-conscious) customers. After the Virginia capital moved from Jamestown to Williamsburg, it became a magnet for taverns and board-inghouses. In prosperous York County, Yorktown became a desirable loca-tion for taverns because it served as the location for the York County court as well as the site of the ferry between Gloucester and York Counties. Yorktown became increasingly significant as an economic base after legislation estab-lished the town as the inspection center for exported tobacco, and it pro-vided an ideal location for offering services to travelers concerned with tobacco exports. These more cosmopolitan locations may have been partic-ularly appealing to women who sought to establish taverns. By contrast, Lancaster, a more remote tidewater county situated on the north side of the Rappahannock River, listed only men as keepers of legal ordinaries after 1721, when the series of relevant records began.[56]

Proximity to the courts meant that ordinary keepers could benefit from public contracts. The significance of official contractors for lodging and food is apparent in the 1711 county records, when both Susanna Allen and Ady Booth claimed funds from the colony for "entertaining" several of the labor-ers working on the Yorktown fortifications.[57] Taverns could provide the ser-vices of a livery stable, renting out a chaise for local transportation, and could take on official colony business as well providing for private individuals. Anne Pattison provided horse and chaise hire from her Williamsburg tavern during the 1740s.[58] Elizabeth Moody presented a claim to the York County court to obtain payment from the public budget for providing "horse hire" for two days to convey Morris Cockland, "a Criminal," to the public jail. The county approved the request for fifty pounds of tobacco and forwarded it to the colony for payment.[59] Susanna Allen, likewise, essentially provided a tem-porary jail when she housed several "French prisoners" in 1711.[60] Other indi-viduals in the county provided food and lodging to both travelers and inmates. Public business could provide female tavernkeepers with an addi-tional stream of income to supplement business. Occasionally, women pro-vided more formal food and lodging to prisoners, including runaway slaves.[61]

Situating an ordinary near a county- or colony-level administrative cen-ter meant that in addition to selling provisions and lodging, women could contract to sell domestic services, including cleaning, directly to the govern-ment outside the tavern building proper. Essex County paid Mary Pritchett 460 pounds of tobacco for "tending" the court for seven months in 1727.[62] In

York, Elizabeth Moody received her payment for "sweeping the courthouse" and for "cleaning the courthouse." Moody probably contracted the services rather than doing the scrubbing herself, since she owned land, ran an ordinary, and owned slaves and indentured servants; the court no doubt paid her for sending over a worker to accomplish the tasks.[63] In 1712, she received 100 pounds of tobacco to clean up after the legislators, when, by contrast, burgesses received 130 pounds of tobacco to serve in the House of Burgesses.

The opportunities for ordinary keepers in the Jamestown-Williamsburg-Yorktown vicinity grew with the importance of these settlements to the local and Virginia-wide government and economy. Protecting their interests involved more than shutting out rural ale sellers on court days. Ordinary keepers in general, and women owners in particular, had good reason to turn to the courts for protection, especially when they suffered physical and legal attacks on their characters or businesses.[64] Women who kept ordinaries faced hostility and occasionally even violence from their neighbors, perhaps because of the perceived links between drinking establishments and so-called disorderly houses, or brothels. This could be a reasonable assumption: elsewhere in the colonies and in the Caribbean, inns and taverns served as brothels. There is less overt evidence to support this connection in Virginia, but it must have occurred at some locations. In the popular opinion of the time, at least, neighbors of ordinary keepers occasionally enforced "informal justice" on the proprietors they disliked and whom they believed to be operating disorderly houses.

Elizabeth Woods, who apparently kept an unlicensed ordinary, successfully defended herself in August 1675 against Nicholas Toope, who accused her of retailing liquor without a license.[65] Neighbors, encouraged by Nicholas Toope, harassed her outside the courtroom as well. That same August, Woods prosecuted a trespass case against the men who had attacked her establishment and shattered her glass windows, split open the doors, and inflicted other damages.[66] In this case she collected cash to pay for repairs on her house.[67] She had numerous opportunities to learn the use of the courts during her marriage and widowhood: Woods's career as a focal point for trouble began earlier, when she was accused of distributing libelous notes accusing the church wardens' wives and vestrymen of being mirkin makers,[68] and in a later case she and her daughter were implicated in hog thievery. Later, to protect her own property from her second husband, she contracted with him for land and cattle for herself and her children even after their marriage.[69] Elizabeth Woods's appearances in court with her attempts to sell drinks dovetailed with her experience for other legal business.

These contests and competitions for authority and autonomy demonstrated the difficulties in creating a social hierarchy. When slave women and men challenged their own roles within the local hierarchy they targeted certain types of white women for their challenges—those who had, themselves, stepped beyond the most circumscribed, protected roles in society and independently owned property. Ordinary keepers fit this description. Jane Vobe and Ann Shields, both Williamsburg ordinary keepers, were involved in cases before the oyer and terminer courts, the courts with jurisdiction over slave crime. The particulars of these oyer and terminer cases demonstrate how colonists perceived weak spots in their hierarchy. The local courts had an interest in protecting white women's power and property when they deemed such action necessary to upholding social order.

Elsewhere in the American slave world, white women have been described as "pro-slavery agencies within the world made by the slave holders," an appropriate description of Virginia white women, too.[70] All of the women discussed here lived without men because they were widowed or remained single. While male victims of thefts could resort to more direct, summary justice without turning to the legal system to provide the social control and authority they wished to impose on their plantations, white businesswomen, by contrast, had to turn to the courts.

Slave defendants were denied the same criminal justice procedures that white people accused of crimes enjoyed.[71] In 1655, Virginia counties stopped hearing criminal cases locally and sent white defendants' cases to the colony-level general court, theoretically providing white defendants with greater protection against local elites.[72] By contrast, in 1692 Virginia established local oyer and terminer courts to hear felony cases of accused slaves. Significantly, these courts could impose sentences concerning life and limb on slaves while local courts could not impose comparable punishments on whites.[73] The legal system of Virginia permitted masters "nearly unlimited legal authority to punish their slaves for misdemeanors and lesser offenses," and the courts backed up the "day-to-day" power of slave masters and mistresses.[74]

The cases heard at the March 1751 court are particularly interesting for revealing the court's response to slave crime against property-owning women.[75] The first accused man, Simon, belonged to Ann Shields, who kept a tavern. Simon faced felony charges for breaking into the "Mansion House" of Jane Vobe of Bruton Parish between nine and twelve P.M. on February 7, and stealing five gallons of rum, valued at ten shillings sterling and one box of candles valued at twenty shillings sterling.[76]

At the same meeting the court heard the case of Natt, a slave belonging to William Drummond, of adjacent James City County, who also was accused of the February burglary at the house of Jane Vobe. At this trial, the court heard testimony of the victim, Jane Vobe, and that of Betty, "a Christian Negro Slave" who belonged to Frances Webb.[77] After hearing the testimony of the two women, the court determined that Natt was not guilty of the stated crime, but was guilty of "divers misdemeanors" which were not enumerated in the record. For this, the court ordered Natt to receive the relatively mild punishment of thirty-nine lashes at the public whipping post, after which he could be released to "go home."[78]

Another slave named Matt broke into the dwelling house of Ann Shields (twice widowed and soon to be Mrs. Wetherburn) on December 22 between nine P.M. and midnight. While there, Matt stole five gallons of wine and ten gallons of rum.[79] In court he pleaded he was not guilty, though he had earlier given a confession to John Holt, one of the county justices of the peace. Ann Shields herself came to court, where she gave testimony under oath. The court decided that Matt was guilty. Simon and Matt faced a harsher sentence: they were to be hanged. As a final statement, the court recorded a memorandum that Simon and Matt were worth fifty-five pounds (current) each, a notation that allowed their owners to make claims for their losses.[80]

On the one hand, the proceedings in these cases demonstrate the power these white women could invoke even when fractures opened in social order.[81] Women played significant parts in these cases: the victims of these crimes were female, as were the witnesses who testified on Natt's behalf to keep him from hanging. In this instance the court even listened to and believed an enslaved woman, albeit one specifically designated as being "Christian."[82] Why were women and their enterprises such tempting targets of crime? The easy answer could be as simple as the question of why robbers rob banks and its rejoinder: because that is where the money is; or, in these cases, the ordinaries were where the rum was. In addition, people moved in and out of ordinaries frequently. The influx of guests and their servants provided a constantly changing population under the women's roofs. In addition, supplying guests required that the ordinary keepers have substantial stocks of provisions on hand, including large quantities of rum, wine, and, apparently, candles. Natt and Simon, as slaves of tavernkeepers, may well have understood the workings of the victims' ordinaries, since the victims were competitors of their own mistresses in the business.

Yet one is also left with another question: How well did slaves themselves, especially male slaves, perceive that white women were a weak point in the hierarchy of white over black when the society also placed male over female? How much did they resent the expectation that they would be submissive to white women? Ann Shields was not only a woman, but a widow who had no man to provide protection or legal impediment of coverture. She was, nevertheless, a property-owning woman, which gave her the power that derived from that class. Tensions remained in the hierarchy of the colony. These crimes suggest ways that the powerless attempted to exploit the tensions in this system as well as the ways that, through the oyer and terminer court, white men sought to bolster the power of slaveowners, whether those owners were male or female.

The court took the side of upholding the order of society by protecting victims—when those victims were white. If the courts stepped in when they perceived that women who owned slaves could not keep control over their slaves, then society, through the power of the men on the courts could exert its pressure to maintain the hierarchy of white over black. Like other instances of court power in protecting female victims, this suggests a paternalistic role for the court.

This array of crime, and the ways that courts supported women's interests, illuminates the problems and possibilities that women who ran businesses faced and the ways they used the courts to obtain a satisfactory conclusion. The next portion of this chapter traces the career of Susanna Allen, who lived in the early eighteenth century, and demonstrates the circumstances that would require a woman to have frequent—in Allen's case almost constant—contact with the county court over the period of a decade. Allen ran her own ordinary (tavern) in Williamsburg when it served as Virginia's capital city.

Allen's name first appeared in the court records on November 24, 1710, when she was granted a license to keep an ordinary on the York County side of Williamsburg. Unlike many men and still more women of the period, Susanna Allen was able to sign her name, rather than simply a mark, to her documents.[83] As was customary for ordinary licensees, Susanna Allen offered security to the court that she would provide "good Wholesome & cleanly lodgeing & dyett" for travelers and shelter for animals, as well as pasturage or fodder for the horses as the season required. She was not to allow "unlawful gameing" in her house and was not to allow anyone to "tipple or drink more than is necessary" on the Sabbath although she was not subject to restrictions on serving those who tippled excessively on other days of the week. In 1711, Allen was relatively new to the business and a competing tavern owner complained to the court that she did not follow the letter of the law requiring ordinaries to post publicly the officially established prices for liquors. In 1712 she defended herself successfully in a jury trial against the accusation. In this instance, Allen was a defendant; however, she was no passive by-stander and actively used the local county court in the 1710s and 1720s to collect from her debtors and to protect herself in lawsuits. The 1711 case merely signaled the beginning of her appearances in court to protect her business interests. Allen's cases came before the court frequently: she usually had a case at every court, and at many meetings she had several cases pending.[84] (See table 4.4).

Allen's lawsuits personified the whole range of harassment a female ordinary keeper might face from a local man about the proper operation of the ordinary according to the regulations of the colony. William Smith, proprietor of a competing establishment, sued as informant against Allen. Virginia colonial statutes offered informants a reward, usually half of the fine, for bringing evidence against certain types of wrongdoers. Smith, who brought information against male and female ordinary keepers during the 1711 county court session, accused Allen of failing to obtain and post a "fair

TABLE 4.4 SUSANNA ALLEN'S YORK COUNTY COURT CASES

YEAR	NUMBER OF MONTHLY COURTS W/SUSANNA ALLEN'S BUSINESS IN THIS YEAR	CASES PENDING OR HEARD IN THIS YEAR[86]
1711	4	6 cases of her own 2 claims for payment
1712	9	7 cases (1 as assignee)
1713	9	11 cases (including 1 jury trial) 2 suits: served as evidence bought land
1714	9	23 cases of her own gave oath served as estate administrator
1715	8	28 cases of her own 6 cases as estate administrator 2 cases as witness
1716	7	14 cases of her own 3 cases as estate administrator sold land
1717	9	6 cases of her own 1 jury trial: trover
1718	10	15 cases of her own
1718	6	11 cases

copy" of the rates of liquors and not "continually keeping them up in the common entertaining room" of her ordinary. Allen did not appear at this November hearing, and the court ordered the sheriff to take her into custody until she entered a bond. Allen appeared to plead "not guilty" on December 17, 1711, and the case was referred to a later court for a jury trial. That same day the court renewed her license for another year, suggesting the accusation did not prove a decisive threat to her business.[85] On June 16, 1712, the jury heard the case of Allen not posting the liquor prices within one month of their being set, and for not keeping them posted "continually." After repeating her "not guilty" plea, the jury heard the evidence in an apparently long trial.[87] Unfortunately for the opportunistic Smith, the jury, after receiving its charge and "being agreed," found for Allen and the case was dismissed.[88]

Smith's trial was time-consuming, but Allen made efficient use of her attendance at the June court. While there, she served six days as a witness for John Brookes, who was a defendant in his own suit against William Smith.[89] She also served as evidence for Mary Whitby, who was executor of a will, in a suit against William Taylor. Allen was listed as security in an action on the case between two men and allowed a case against Richard Hall to be dropped.[90] Indeed, many of the disputes in which Susanna Allen acted as plaintiff were settled out of court; this indicates that Allen used the threat of legal action to force delinquents to observe their obligations and allowed the suits to lapse when the result proved satisfactory to her. Nor was she alone in this: at least one other woman who kept an ordinary in Yorktown seems to have used the same strategy.[91] All in all, Susanna Allen knew her way around the courthouse. In the process of protecting her businesses, she learned how to use the courts.

Ordinary keepers drew on the court's authority to force their suppliers to meet their obligations. In 1714, Susanna Allen sued Timothy Metcalf, a meat supplier, for £12 due by bill. The court ordered Metcalf to make his payment in beef at a set price.[92] Creditors prosecuted ordinary keepers, too, and Susanna Allen's suppliers used the court as means to recover payment for goods she acquired from them. Thus, Francis Sharp resorted to legal action against Allen in recovering payment for forty-nine loads of firewood, building materials, wages for a builder, and use of a cart and horse.[93] In this particular case, a jury found for Allen, and the case demonstrates that in operating a business, even a conventionally female-run business such as an ordinary, a woman would be required to appear in court to settle affairs.

Allen was involved in numerous routine suits in the courts in 1712 and 1713, serving as plaintiff, defendant, and witness. The court clerk, accustomed to dealing with male litigants, inadvertently listed her as "him" in recording the forty pounds of tobacco she was to be paid as witness in a suit on May 18, 1713.[94] On that day, and others on which she appeared, she was paid the customary rate paid to all witnesses, regardless of gender, equally—forty pounds of tobacco per day plus travel expenses for those coming from outside the county. She also bought a town lot in Williamsburg from Jacob and Magdalin Flournoy in February of 1713.[95] She conducted an active but prosaic, public life in the courts and her ordinary license was renewed yet again.

But the round of litigation and business dealing ended in June 1713, when the grand jury presented Allen for "keeping a marryed man company." She pleaded not guilty and trial was set for the next court. At the July court she was accused of not only keeping a married man "constant" company, but also for operating a so-called disorderly house.[96] Even a prosperous, property-owning woman like Allen suffered from prosecution when she flouted social mores. She did not appear for this hearing, but the court fined her five hundred pounds of tobacco for her action.[97] Considering the brutal whipping of servant women for fornication and bastardy in the seventeenth century, this punishment was relatively minor.

The court recorded society's displeasure, but Allen never suffered similar accusations again during her public legal life. The man in question was apparently allowed to remain anonymous. It is possible he was David Cunningham, an apparently illiterate barber and peruke (wig) maker who lived in Williamsburg and who had served as security for Allen when she obtained her 1713 ordinary license.[98] The strength of the alliance between Allen and Cunningham emerges from their mention of each other in their wills. When Cunningham died in late January or early February of 1720 his will ordered that his servants, slaves, the Williamsburg lot and houses, and his shop tools be sold at auction and that Susanna Allen was to be in charge of managing the proceeds to use for educating and maintaining his daughter and son.[99] After designating what his children were to receive, Cunningham left the rest of his estate to Allen.[100]

Earlier in her life Susanna Allen had attempted to establish a more conventional relationship with a man, but she planned to retain her autonomy even after her intended marriage. She had a lawyer draft a marriage contract between herself, defined as a "spinster of Williamsburg," and Joseph Seward of Surry County. In the contract she agreed to sell her Williamsburg land if Joseph Seward would sell his land in Surry County. She offered to give her husband-to-be all her personal estate except what was listed on the back of the document. In this, she recorded goods suited for running a tavern—her capital—as her prime concern, including a fairly extensive stock as her personal property. Overnight guests could have taken advantage of comfortable sleeping arrangements on one of her fifteen feather beds, complete with pillows and bolsters. Some could enjoy a bit of privacy and warmth behind one of the six pairs of bed curtains. She had fifteen pairs of sheets and bed quilts, as well. She decorated rooms with one "large" looking glass and two smaller ones at a time when mirrors remained uncommon in all but the wealthiest tidewater homes.[101] For preparing and serving food, she listed a variety of brass and copper kettles and pots, and "an iron jack for a spit." Guests could relax in one of the dozen "large turkey work chairs" or one of the dozen leather chairs. They could imbibe at the large oval table or one of the three smaller ones. She also owned bound labor, including an indentured servant and two slaves, a man named Aggy and a woman named Mary Aggy.[102] Apparently she never married, but Susanna Allen's drafting of a marriage agreement signified her intention to retain control over her property, and especially the property that provided her with the means of earning an independent living, even after marriage.[103]

Allen's insistence on using the law to protect her interests rather than being controlled by legal norms appears in other instances as well. Others in the community recognized Allen's abilities and familiarity with legal proceedings and made her responsible for business brought before the court. When John Timberlake, another ordinary keeper, died without a will, Allen made oath to that fact and became the administrator for his estate.[104] The court ordered the appraisers to meet at Allen's house to value Timberlake's goods, and she presented the records and accounts for the estate over the course of the following year.[105] In the process of administering the Timberlake estate, Allen prosecuted a case against Timberlake's runaway servant, John Spicer, and recovered the cost of capturing him in addition to obtaining an order for Spicer to serve her for double his time of lost service.[106] The court had good reason to appoint Allen as administrator of Timberlake's estate. As an ordinary keeper herself she understood the business Timberlake had left unfinished. The condition of her own business and her status as a creditor to the estate rather than her gender provided the primary reasons for the court to place Allen in charge of the Timberlake affairs. In addition to taking on that estate, she was called in to make oath to the inventory of the "small estate" of an unrelated person, Elizabeth Brodbank, who died leaving an orphaned child and without a will.[107]

Susanna Allen's life and legal activities demonstrate how women became involved in litigation through mutually reinforcing ways: as Allen had more business before the court she became more knowledgable about procedure, and as she became more knowledgable about procedure she could pursue her interests more effectively. Some of Allen's notes and correspondence about her various York County court cases survive in the collection of legal papers kept by attorney-at-law Godfrey Pole. Pole served as attorney for several of Allen's opponents and evidence that remained in Pole's hands indicates that as a plaintiff she maintained an active interest in pursuing the cases.[108] Allen attempted to settle a case against a Mr. Stoner, a man with whom she had done business, before going to court. She wrote that she was sorry her opponent proved himself "so wicked A man" but warned him that she had obtained "good Evidence" against him when she first accepted the debt. When the debt was made, she "made [him] a drink" and called a third party to "witness a pone your a some sett," her phonetic spelling of "assumpsit," a legal term for a type of financial obligation.[109] Her knowledge of procedure may have been gained from the oral tradition of law—hearing about it in the local court or from customers, thus limiting her to a phonetic spelling—but she knew the way to advance her case. By 1716, Susanna Allen had been in business long enough to know how to proceed with recording a debt so that would stand up in court, though she eased this transaction with a drink from her stocks. Later, Allen used the court as a last resort and was willing to use threats against Stoner, warning him that if "thar is a god and you may be Sure i will have my money of you and befor i Rast [arrest] you i give notis." She did conclude politely with a "so god blas you"—presumably meaning "bless" rather than "blast."[110]

Allen died in 1720, shortly after she proved the will of David Cunningham, Sr. In her own will she left the proceeds of her Williamsburg lots and houses as well as several slaves to David Jr. and Jane Cunningham. She also specified that each of the "orphans" were to receive specific objects made of silver and designated Bibles, apparently items with sentimental value that were excluded from the sale of the other property, suggesting the emotional ties that existed between Allen and the Cunningham children.[111] Her life demonstrated how a propertied woman could use the courts to protect herself and her business.

Over her eleven years as an ordinary keeper and active litigant in Williamsburg, Susanna Allen became involved in an exceptionally large number of cases for a resident of either sex in York County. Two of her cases required full jury trials, relatively rare events in the Virginia legal system, where "months passed in many counties between jury trials." (Even York County had only thirteen jury trials between 1681 and 1686; less populous Lancaster County had only two cases sent to juries in the same period.[112]) Yet other women who maintained taverns, although involved in fewer cases than Allen, still needed to resort to the courts to answer to protect their interests. These women provide examples of how running an ordinary required that they work frequently with the local courts and, by this means, gain experience in the operation of the law.

Elizabeth Leightonhouse accumulated experience in the legal system while running an ordinary and, simultaneously managing her three husbands' estates after they died. Her husband, Robert Leightonhouse, had obtained an ordinary license in 1694, referred to himself as "innholder" in a 1699 document, and, like other ordinary keepers, received payment for providing "dyet & tending" to prisoners several times in 1701.[113] He was involved in legal cases as both a debtor and creditor in the 1690s and engaged in large-scale trade. At the time of his death in 1701, he left his widow burdened with numerous debts on protested bills of exchange and accounts.[114] In order to improve her financial situation, she took out an ordinary license in her own right to operate an establishment in Yorktown.[115]

The same day she obtained her ordinary license she had three other cases before the county court. Over the next year, she took over her dead husband's legal cases. During her widowhood, she paid off what she could, but remained in debt at the time of her marriage to Mungo Somerville some time before March 1702.[116] The couple managed the cases, through an attorney, from 1701 until Mungo Somerwell's death in February 1707.[117] In late February 1707, she was in court to take on the administration of Somerwell's estate.[118] In this capacity, she also pursued debts owed to the estate.[119] She married again sometime before August 1710, when she and her new husband, Edward Powers, were defendants in a case stemming from her role as administrator to Somerwell.[120]

After her remarriage, there are no records that Elizabeth Leightonhouse again turned to legal ordinary keeping, though she owned a town lot in Yorktown. This may have been economically motivated: Robert Leightonhouse seemed to be unlucky financially and the family downwardly mobile when he admitted publicly that he faced pecuniary difficulties in his petition for an ordinary license toward the end of his life. By contrast, Elizabeth seemed more comfortably situated economically in her last two marriages: she died a wealthy woman and had eleven slaves in her estate inventory. She also had the furnishings one would expect in a well-stocked ordinary, including eleven beds, twenty-one blankets, thirteen tables, forty-five chairs of varying quality, and large quantities of beer, wine, rum, and brandy. Furthermore, she also owned two sets of weights and a pair of stilliards that would be useful in a place where commercial exchanges occurred.[121] In her later court cases, she was creditor, while earlier she sought to delay payments to her creditors. In her legal "career" Elizabeth Leightonhouse managed her first husband's estate and established her own ordinary simultaneously. Most of her experience came from serving as administrator for her husbands' estates as well as from keeping an ordinary, though both brought her to court at a moment of crisis.

By contrast, Elizabeth Moody's cases concerning her ordinary and the administration of estates indicate that the tavern continued to be a prime concern. Moody first encountered the legal system when she and her first husband, Humphrey Moody, sold their plantation in 1694, and again in 1696 when they sold another tract of land. They, too, may have been downwardly mobile, because in each case they sold the lands where they currently lived. By Christmas of 1700, tension between the couple exploded, and Elizabeth left "her own house and family," so Humphrey Moody publicly announced he would no longer pay his wife's bills amounting to more than a sixpence, though the couple later reconciled. In 1707 she faced a complaint that Anne Duvall initiated against her, claiming she was a bad mistress to her servant. Duvall's daughter was a servant in the Moody household and Duvall complained of the "ill usage" Elizabeth inflicted on the girl. Within a year, Humphrey Moody died, but he had reconciled with his wife by then and chose to leave her all his "worldly goods," real and personal, and to make her his sole executor.[122]

Her ordinary keeping may have begun with her widowhood. In 1708, as a widow, she pursued cases on her own. Once she had her own ordinary, she increased the pace of her legal actions, beginning with a suit and countersuit with Robert Crowley for a settlement of accounts.[123] She proceeded to complain about illegal liquor sellers and to purchase lots of land in Yorktown and the port land. She also "renewed" her ordinary license in January 1709.[124] Within a year she was accused of charging too high a price for her liquors. Through her attorney she pleaded not guilty and the attorney general sent the case to trial. Witnesses appeared on both sides, but the court determined that there was insufficient evidence to convict.[125] After that, her cases were more tame, and she introduced additional cases.[126] She also renewed her ordinary license each year until 1716.[127] Between 1715 and 1719 she took a hiatus, but in 1719 she again had ordinary licenses every year until 1729.[128] There is a parallel gap in the county's payments to Moody for the courthouse cleaning: she received payments for 1711 and 1712, then none until 1719, when she received payments for four years.[129] The four-year period in which she had no ordinary corresponds to the time of her second marriage, to Edward Powers—suggesting that he, she, or both thought she had other obligations as a wife that interfered with operating a business.[130] Still, the experience served her well when she went back to supporting herself until her death in 1733. Once she regained her legal footing, she also took on the administration of an estate and several other cases, including a financial dispute that went to a jury trial.[131]

Moody may have been considered an easy target for crime and she, like other propertied women on their own, suffered a theft from her household in 1722. Zephaniah Martin and Ann Sawser were arrested and sent to the general court in Williamsburg for stealing money, and probably other goods, from Elizabeth, requiring her to go to Williamsburg to give evidence in the case.[132] Moody herself was arrested for evading her poll tax and the county court ordered a jury trial; the verdict was one penny damage, and her attorney postponed the final judgment. At that court she "exhibited her reasons" for not paying to the court, facing John Clayton, the king's attorney, who decided not to prosecute her further.[133]

Elizabeth Moody possessed a strong will, temporarily leaving her first husband, much to his chagrin, and tormenting a servant girl placed in her care. This aspect of her personality predated the experience of running a business by herself. Undaunted by these two conflicts, she escalated her participation in the court. In business as well as in her household, her own sense of entitlement, in bringing a case against her competitors, for example, demonstrates that once she had practice with running a business and using the legal system, she aggressively pursed her interests there. Experience with the law and business went hand in glove for this ordinary woman.

Several of the York County ordinary-keeping women, including Catherine Craig, Mary Hunter, Elizabeth Moody, Elizabeth Leightonhouse, and Susanna Allen, became embroiled in lawsuits related to their businesses and other concerns—particularly estate management—for which they were responsible. The experiences varied widely, from Elizabeth Leightonhouse's gradual withdrawal from business to Elizabeth Moody's four-year retirement during marriage, to Susanna Allen's long and aggressive legal wrangling; all, however, demonstrate that these ordinary women developed expertise, and sometimes confidence, to manage their businesses, resorting to the institution of the law courts to do so. Like chicken-and-egg causality, it is difficult to say which came first, the ordinary or the court experience, because circumstances varied for each of the women. More probably, law experience in one pursuit carried over to the other, and the two reinforced each other, regardless of which came first. This increasing experience, in range as well as number of cases, no doubt occurred in other businesses, as well. For example, Mary Seale had acted as attorney for her husband and that same day was asked to provide evidence in a case in which a widow gave birth to a child out of wedlock.[134] Still, keeping a business, especially an ordinary, provided women with some property with the obligation and opportunity to use the courts for their own advantage.

County courtrooms were spaces controlled by male officials, including the sheriffs, justices of the peace, clerks, and prominent men. Yet the courts were not entirely a male domain, and not just because women organized the cleaning or sold ale at the door, but still more because propertied women used the courts to record their own transactions and enforce obligations owed to them alongside male litigants. "Middling" and upper class women with businesses could become familiar with a range of legal procedures in order to accomplish their goals. These ordinary-keeping women resorted to the courts frequently, and with this contact they gained knowledge about and power within a legal system that restrained many, but not all, of their female compatriots.

"A LITTLE PURSE TO HERSELF": CASH, CREDIT, AND SHOPPING

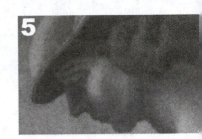

5

In early modern England, pamphleteers and theologians debated the desirable allocation of power between husbands and wives. Economic control, in particular, symbolized the competition between spouses, and English popular literature lampooned the war between the sexes and women's desire for individual economic power.[1] In one inexpensive chapbook offering advice to newlyweds, the fictional young couple discussed control over finances:

> The husband-to-be, J[ohn], envisioned their future life together: "we will keep poultry too; you shall have cocks, hens, ducks, geese and turkeys, and the increase of them shall serve thee to go to market with."
>
> His fiancé, K[ate], had a practical question about this enterprise and asked "Who must have the money made of those odd things?"
>
> J[ohn], replied "My pretty rogue, I find thou understandeth the way of a farmer's wife already, for they had rather have a little purse to themselves, than the knowledge of five hundred pounds of their husbands"[2]

After this exchange, John, whom the reader is told is "Honest," assured "Loving" Kate that her market income would remain under her own control. To what extent did colonial women during the same period successfully gain discretionary power over even a portion of their families' economic resources?

To delineate the outer limits of possibility, the exceptional instances, not the typical, prove the most revealing; it is therefore important to move beyond an attempt to find the "typical" behavior of statistically average women.[3] In summarizing the historiography on this subject, Laurel Ulrich points out that the earlier strand of colonial women's history, advanced by Elisabeth Dexter, looked at "what was permissible" in colonial society while more recent scholars, notably Mary Beth Norton, have looked at "what was probable." Ulrich herself rephrased the problem for Northern New England and has found that work revealed more about female responsibility, "which was often very broad," and less about economic opportunity, which was "limited" for these colonial women. In Virginia, women's activities ranged from shipping tobacco to mending shirts—making searching for means and medians more difficult. How far could women behave autonomously, or even in opposition to the desires of men and other family members, in their economic pursuits? How constricted were women in a society whose stated legal restrictions on them were severe? In short, how could women partici- pate in local economic networks in colonial Virginia?

Sources such as account books, daybooks, and receipts all indicate that women participated in economic exchanges, even if those same documents fail to reveal what women thought about their undertakings and the extent to which they had to negotiate with men to retain their incomes. In addition to these personal or household accounts, merchants or their assistants recorded transactions made in the stores. Account books recorded each cus- tomer's account over a period of time. Daybooks recorded transactions as they occurred, sometimes indicating who came to their shops to take the merchandise, what they bought, who was ultimately responsible for pay- ments, and what the merchandise cost. Those same merchants then trans- ferred some of the information from those daily records into their ledgers and account books, a more permanent type of record that showed a cus- tomer's accumulated debts and payments over a longer period, sometimes years or generations. The daybooks, by contrast, reveal more information about the *processes* of buying, selling, and paying for goods and include indi- viduals, like women, who do not often appear in the pages of account books listing purchases made on credit. Ledger entries reveal only a few traces of the day-to-day conducting of business. Although merchants varied in the amount of detail recorded in each line, weaving together threads of informa- tion unraveled from accounts allows us to detect general patterns in their customers' economic behavior. This chapter draws on the long runs of records from several shopkeepers in tidewater Virginia, including the Jerdones in Yorktown; Thomas Partridge, Mordecai Booth, and Edward Dixon in Caroline County; Ritchie and Company in Essex County; the Granbery Family of Nansemond and Norfolk; and unidentified shopkeepers in Hanover and King and Queen Counties. The *Virginia Gazette* Daybook, listing printing and stationery expenditures, the Pattison tavern account books, and a weaver's account book cover more focused trades, but reveal the purchasing habits of some women. Finally, financial records of wealthy persons, including those kept by two planters, William Lightfoot (for 1747–1764) and Carter Burwell (for 1738–1756), and those of Edward Taylor (for 1775–1789), a farmer and entrepreneur in Accomack County, demonstrate the local trading networks that included women who were producers and purchasers.[4] These and other sources indicate that women had considerable discretion to acquire goods in Virginia's growing consumer economy and demonstrate the extent to which they could gain independent economic identities, if only in the short run.

In some settings, women and men had separate and distinctive economic responsibilities while in other situations exchange networks created interconnected webs that incorporated both male and female participants. In this, aspects of women's participation in the local economy in tidewater Virginia during the colonial period resemble those of rural northern New England that Laurel Ulrich describes for 1785–1812, even though the specifics of commodity production in the regions differed. While the New England women often remained invisible in the surviving account books, Ulrich's close reading of midwife Martha Ballard's records reveals that women and men worked in a family economy "based not only upon cooperation" between them, but also a "division of responsibility." As a result, "what is most striking is the independence of men's and women's labors, not only in production but in management and utilization of resources."[5]

In the nineteenth century, aspects of the gendered nature of economies differed in New England, and indeed in rural New York, from practices in Virginia; for example, northern men often accounted for exchanges—even those where no cash changed hands—in monetary terms, while women more often traded "in kind" with less interest in the financial accounting that might be used to record the transactions.[6] In Virginia, women's accounts appear with cash values assigned. Even the 1694 account of the Granbery Family of Nansemond lists "John Peoel [probably Powell] Detter to Sarah Granbery" for his multiple purchases of butter by the pound, meal by the peck, and cider by the gallon. The next year he bought cheese, wheat, butter, cider, and a hoe. In the earliest exchange, the debt to Sarah Granbery listed both currency values (in tobacco prices) and sterling costs, but after that she only listed the sterling prices.[7] In this respect, Virginia women's accounting resembles that of northern men more than northern women.

This chapter borrows from Ulrich's pathbreaking methodology in teasing meaning out of snippets of economic information. Despite the differences in women's lives in the north and south, Virginia women, like those in northern New England, had selective economic autonomy even as they lived within a culture that expected submission of wives to husbands and treated the family as an economic unit. In addition, a Virginia wife could act as "deputy husband" when she took on her husband's responsibilities because poor health, travels, or other impediments prevented him from accomplishing his tasks. In this conceptualization, active women confirmed rather than threatened the household gender hierarchy because they only accepted properly delegated authority.[8]

Before turning full attention to the topic at hand, a caveat is necessary. Although women contributed to the colony as reproducers and producers, they did not automatically gain discretionary authority as a result of those roles. Assuming that productivity accorded elevated status would be fallacious if one considers that the economy was based first upon indentured labor and later upon slavery, and producers derived little benefit from their output. Instead, authority rested on individuals' ability to make decisions about how resources, including labor, would be allocated. Economic power was based more on the ability of plantation mistresses and masters to compel other people to work rather than their engaging in productive labor themselves. Furthermore, the extent to which women gained access to resources depended on their race and class position as well as on their proximity to towns and markets.

That said, women sometimes gained authority over resources from their income-generating pursuits even though they often did not. This chapter considers women's productivity insofar as it provided the means for them to then gain control over resources. Women's economic autonomy rested on the limited opportunities they wrested to control the link between consumption and production more than their productivity. Like Loving Kate, some Virginia women, both femes soles and femes coverts, enjoyed the "little purse" containing the proceeds deriving from the sale of the cocks and hens, cider and eggs, or even tobacco and cloth that they, their families, and their subordinates produced. Financial accounts from the period show how.

The nature of trade and credit in the colonial economy made the interdependence of individuals within their families a significant element in the success of their transatlantic enterprises, as will be discussed in chapter 6. In those large-scale businesses one should not expect individualism from either men or women; reliance on extended family provided a better basis for success. Locally focused undertakings, on the other hand, offered women opportunities to control cash and, in some cases, to develop independent economic identities. Women living on plantations with access to urban areas sold goods produced for local markets and often controlled some of the income from those sales. In addition, women who resided in the towns began small-scale businesses or brought their produce to market for sale.[9]

Several exceptionally visible examples suggest the range of women's economic exchanges. Male accounting systems occasionally considered female exchange networks, indicating that male and female economic worlds were computed separately but also overlapped. Sometimes, women paid bills for men unable to attend to a transaction for example, Sarah Lush went to collect cash from merchant Neil Jamieson on account of one of the Lushs's debtors when her husband, Andrew, attended to business in Portsmouth in 1765. This Virginia "deputy husband" could travel to the port city of Norfolk to claim the obligation.[10]

Another way that overlap occurred was when men stepped in to remedy problems in agreements between two women, perhaps because men had greater access to the legal system than did married women. One such case began when the wife of Liveing Denwood made a "bargain and agreement" with the wife of George Willis. Mrs. Denwood offered to give Mrs. Willis a hat in return for doing the washing for a year. Mrs. Denwood gave Mrs. Willis the hat, but Mrs. Willis failed to do the washing. The dispute became a legal case on July 6, 1640, when the court ordered George Willis to pay the court costs, and in return, Liveing Denwood was to "acquite and discharge [the] said Willis of all differences between them."[11] Willis bore some accountability, reflected in his responsibility for the court charges, but it appears that the Denwoods never received the washing services.

As this case demonstrates, when two women made an agreement, the bargain was sometimes difficult to enforce. This arrangement is exceptional, however, only in that one participant took it to court. More important is the way that this recorded exchange illuminates informal transactions between women that occurred in less contentious circumstances—transactions leaving no trace in the written record. Women's economic pursuits often remained invisible in the official records. The exchange shares characteristic features with women's work in the informal sector of developing economies. Mrs. Willis's washing undertaking was of small size, required intensive labor (her own), little capital. Her business lacked organization or formal contracts, and relied on in-kind payments.

The records of Elizabeth Bassett and her husband, William, prominent tidewater planters, demonstrate not only the independence of each spouse, but also the intersections in their family's day-to-day economic undertakings. Mr. Bassett kept his own records of financial transactions as did Mrs. Bassett. The fact that her surviving accounts seemed to start after his death might lead to the conclusion that she did not engage in independent trade until she was widowed, but his records show otherwise. In 1736 William noted Elizabeth's trade with another woman, indicating that he was transferring to his account the balance "in my Wifes Book." This reference not only reveals that William and Elizabeth Bassett kept separate records during his lifetime, but also suggests the outlines of a female economic network. In the end, the exchanges among the women were not totally independent of William's reckonings. He accounted for the transaction in his own records when computing the third woman's balance with him.[12]

A more complete set of a woman's account books survives for a plantation mistress, Rebecca Coles, who kept records of household production and expenditures at Enniscorthy plantation, further west of the tidewater in Virginia's piedmont. Her portion of the accounts begin in 1774, when she was twenty-five years old; run through the Revolutionary War years, during which her husband was frequently absent on military service; and conclude late in her life in the 1820s.[13] In the colonial era accounts, she listed long-term series of exchanges in the account book. For example, she traded in hogs with Mrs. Muler for years. She paid various individuals, apparently slave women and men, for chickens.[14] She weighed out cotton to be spun and noted the cotton weighed out to the spinners. She bought cotton "of different Negroes" in about 1773–1774. Most of what she acquired she put to use on the planation, listing the clothes made for the slaves, for her children, and for Mr. Coles by season.[15]

Shadow references, like those of the Denwood/Willis transaction and Elizabeth Bassett's exchanges, and more overt records, like the Coles' account, suggest both the separation and the overlap of spouses' duties and transactions. In the Coles accounts, Rebecca kept most of the records, but John noted the pork butchering completed one year. Elsewhere, men could be brought in at a later stage of account resolution, but in more placid transactions, both members of a couple participated in distinct trade networks.[16] In this manner women could control the returns on their labor by bartering goods and labor with other women and retain a modicum of economic autonomy even though, or perhaps because, they resorted to a cashless trade.[17]

A further example of a husband's and wife's set of parallel but distinct records appear in the account book of a merchant from King and Queen County. Although his name is not recorded, the merchant sold fabrics, powder and shot, shoes, rum, tools, sewing goods, spices, and sugar. He accepted payments in tobacco, cash, eggs, and chickens. The poultry trade loomed large enough in this merchant's accounts that he kept a separate "chicken book" to record those transactions. Unfortunately, the chicken book does not survive, but customers' running accounts in the chicken book were eventually transferred into the general account book and this volume provides some information from the lost book. (See fig. 5.1)[18] Many Virginia women, like the fictitious "Loving Kate," received credit from this King and Queen County merchant for their eggs, chickens, and other farm produce, allowing them to purchase goods from his store. Exchanges were recorded in monetary terms rather than being pure barter.[19] The merchant maintained separate accounts for women in the chicken book, even if the women's families had combined accounts in the general account book. For example, John Harwood had an account in the general Account Book, but his account included a debit for "your wives Account in the Chicken Book."[20] The King and Queen County merchant registered a distinct account for Mrs. Harwood in the chicken book under her own name, and she purchased goods on that account. Eventually, the merchant transferred her chicken-book balance to her husband's account in the general account so that ultimately the transactions became Mr. Harwood's responsibility. In the meantime, however, his wife maintained her own running totals. Married women also kept accounts in their own names, as when Jane Lumpkin "wife of Rob[er]t" purchased one of the two leghorn hats sold that year.

Comparable references suggesting a woman's separate account for her poultry production appears in the account book of planter Carter Burwell. Several times he recorded that he paid cash for geese, turkeys, chickens, and "fowls" to several women, including Ann Reynolds, Mrs. Mason, and Mrs. Buck. Like the King and Queen merchant, Burwell combined an account, the Jones's, under the husband's name. The credit for this family came from "Mrs. Jones's account for chickens."[21] The family spent the proceeds from the sale on fabric and men's shoes, though it is not clear if Mrs. Jones bought the shoes for her husband in the same spirit that Moll Flanders made her purchases for her husband.

Chicken and egg money and other production for local consumption provided women with some small incomes to be spent at their own discretion. Anne Gregory went to the store on August 7, carrying three chickens to sell for an iron pot—most likely not an impulse buy. When she arrived, the shopkeeper must have told her that, at current prices, she was three shillings, two pence short; either denied credit or refused to allow the balance to accumulate, she paid the sum in cash.[22] Another supplier, Hannah Kelly, exchanged her labor in making rough "negro Cloth" for the merchant's own household consumption in order to acquire more yards of fashionable Irish linen and "check" fabric along with a thimble and the notions to allow her to make up her garment.[23] A more regular trader, Elizabeth Hall, purchased linen, pins, handkerchiefs, knitting needles, indigo and oznaburg fabric in five shopping trips over the course of a year. Every time she came to the store to buy, she also brought something to sell, including chickens (anywhere from two to ten squawking birds per visit), eggs by the dozens, and sometimes both, allowing her to count her chickens both before and after they hatched. She never bought without selling, but twice that year went home from a selling trip without purchasing something new. All of her sales and purchases were recorded in cash equivalency terms and allowed to run to credit or debt in the merchant's books, so this particular set of exchanges were not even-exchange barters. Furthermore, she received different prices for her poultry over the course of the year, suggesting market forces affected even this level of trade.[24]

Many other transactions in this account book did occur as even exchanges, though most of these still included a cash reckoning, and the merchant listed these as "Household Expenses"; indeed, many of the goods were foods. These transfers included cheese for chickens, rum for sugar, "chex" for chickens, a wash basin for two chickens, ribbon lace for chickens, thread and ribbon for chickens, and a variety of other goods for chickens. They did not generally list the name of the customers.[25]

In eighteenth-century Virginia, colonial equivalents of "Loving Kate" undertook market activities, and these women gained economic autonomy even in a hierarchy that placed them, as a group, in a subordinate position.

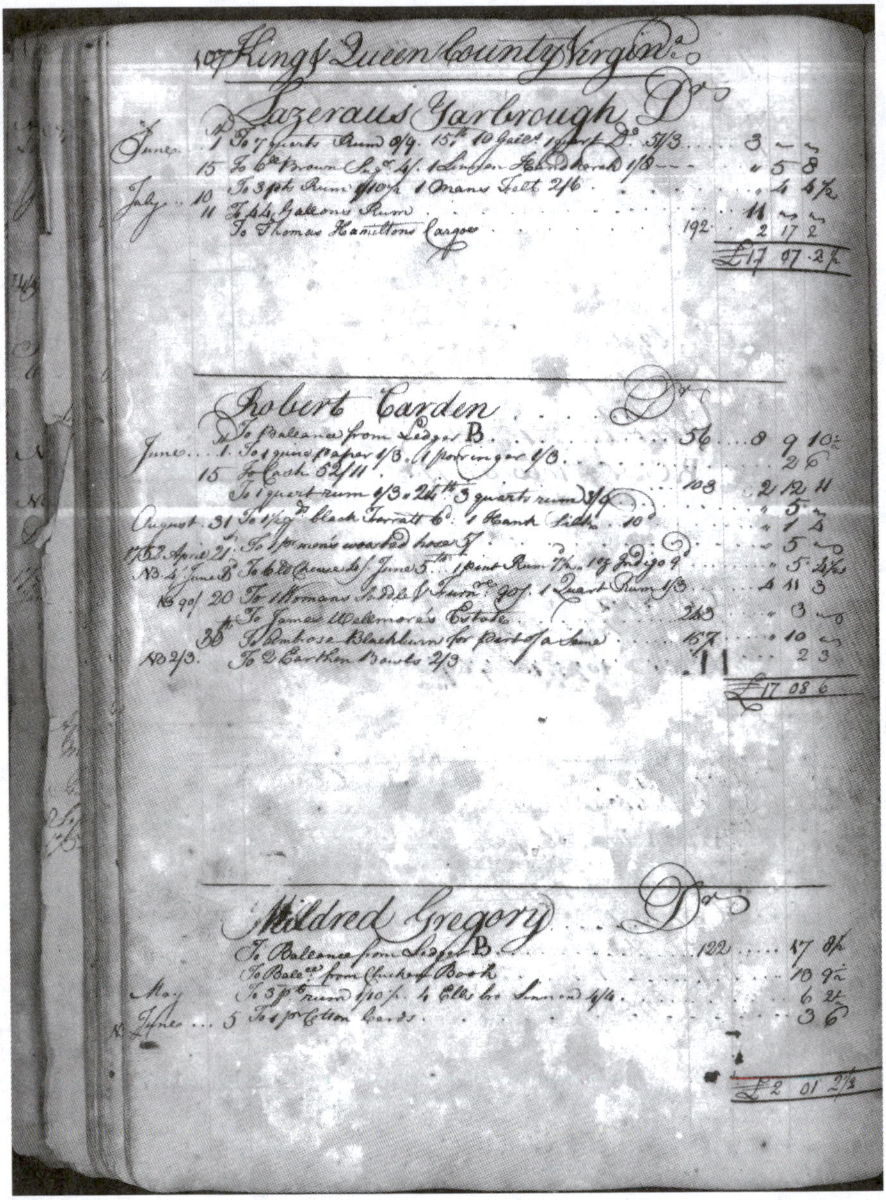

FIGURE 5.1 *Ledger Entries.* Mildred Gregory's credit and debit entries in a 1750–1751 ledger belonging to an unknown merchant from King and Queen County. On the left page, the merchant recorded the charges against her account, including old balances from a previous ledger and from the "Chicken Book" and new purchases of rum, linen, and tools for carding cotton. On the facing page, the merchant indicated she sold him chickens and pears in May and eggs in June and October. She also made a cash payment against her account in June. After totalling the two pages, the merchant recorded a balance on her account of thirteen shillings and nine pence,

which could be carried over to the next book or paid off. Notice that these accounts ran for years and balances could be transferred from book to book. Also, few transfers of cash occurred, but this merchant, like many others, still recorded the transactions in values calculated in cash.

Mildred Gregory account in Merchant (unknown), King and Queen County, Business Ledger, 1751–1752, Business Papers Collection, Accession 28893, Library of Virginia, Archives Research Services.

Married as well as single women who had income of their own had agency to allocate the proceeds as they saw fit. It was this discretion that gave them power within the colonial economy.[26] There were other ways that some married women could obtain a modicum of discretion over other, often more local, economic exchanges. Women's de facto control over disposal of goods on the market shows up in several sources outside the account books, including official records. In 1737, Elizabeth Beverley determined what meat on the plantation could be sold for official use. Her husband William refused to send corn, it "being scarce with me." The power to dispose of the meat he ascribed to Elizabeth, who, he claimed, was unable to spare any of the "beeves."[27] In this prominent planter family, Elizabeth ultimately made decisions about the allocation of precious meat supplies on the plantations, a fact that, in this instance, adversely affected the provisions available for public use.[28]

In other instances women themselves discussed their control over family resources and production. When Robert Carter wished to purchase wheat from a neighboring farmer, he inquired if the wife of Rev. Thomas Smith had grain to sell rather than asking the parson himself.[29] Within Carter's own household, Robert's wife Frances was responsible for managing the produce. When a newly hired tutor arrived at their home, Mrs. Carter gave him a tour of the plantation, pointing out "her" stock of "Fowls & Mutton" for the winter and, like "Kind Kate," stressing the fact that they were under her management.[30] Raising small fowl with an eye to the market could be useful both as a means of gaining income in the short term and as a longer-range investment in the case of widowhood or during uncertain times.

In other families, women had discretionary authority over local marketplace exchanges. Although women who received income for goods or services constituted a minority of the female colonists, the presence of their names in merchants' account books suggest the possibilities—and limitations—of women's economic undertakings. Not all Virginia women visited stores and made purchases, but many did, demonstrating that women participated in the colony's commercial exchanges and the emerging consumer culture. It also confirms the weakness of conceptualizing the commercial world of colonial America as inherently "male."

Women's work in the colonial period reflects some of the same trends as women's work in the informal sector in the twentieth-century developing world. In her classic study of women's work in developing nations, Ester Boserup found women trading, sometimes traveling long distances to buy and sell. Traditional women's trade coexisted with established stores because women sold more cheaply than their larger competitors. To this day, in many developing countries "the modern [formal] trade sector remains small compared to the traditional [informal] trade sector, at least outside the big cities."[31] Women's work is not always visible, especially in the "informal sector." In eighteenth-century New England, oral transactions coexisted with official merchants' records, and "a broad middle space" between the two developed.[32] In the more recent past, the United Nations characterizes enterprises in the informal economy by their "small size (usually not more than four persons), intensive utilization of labour with minimal capital, use of simple technologies, ease of access to such units by workers, . . . predominance of the family-owned property system, use of unskilled labour, lack of organization and of formal contracts, and frequent use of payments in kind." In addition, a "hazy area" of unpaid jobs carried out "by own-account workers or family members who collaborate in small family enterprises" parallels the informal economy.[33]

These seem to be the characteristics of many women's undertakings in colonial Virginia as well. Women's economic activities remained less visible than men's because of the physical location of women's work (in or near the dwelling space) and the resemblance of women's economic activities to their domestic chores: washing, ironing, food preparation, and the production and sale of goods. Most colonists did not keep the proverbial laundry receipts, but Henry Morse was an exception and his records indicate the ways that women could earn cash in the Virginia economy in 1772 from this endeavor. His most formal receipt came from tavernkeeper Jane Vobe, of Williamsburg, who provided him with meals. In addition, Mary Major made him ten shirts, Anne Jones did his washing, and a Miss Blair mended his shirts. Blair reminded him of the £1.10.0 he owed her and appealed to him to pay more quickly because she was "in want of a little money." With the exception of Vobe's accounts, the bills for services women provided were written on small pieces of paper folded into rectangles. More formal accounts, including Vobe's, were recorded in lined ledger sheets.[34] The Morse account reveals the ways that women's work could be integrated into a cash economy and that, even when these enterprises were small in scale and local, women could undertake "own-account" business. For the purposes of this chapter it is not the work per se that mattered; after all, women did washing, mending, cooking, and sewing more frequently without compensation. What is significant in this context are the ways that women could gain access to a cash or cash-equivalent economy. In the Morse examples the women traded on their own accounts. The rest of this chapter examines the ways that colonial women participated in the more local networks both as managers of resources and consumers of goods.

Merchants' accounts indicate that women frequently browsed through merchandise at some stores, and these accounts shed light on women's day-to-day roles as consumers in the stores of colonial Virginia, a particular kind of public space at the onset of the consumer revolution.[35] These entries locate women as customers in the spaces that served as public meeting places in the neighborhood and qualify modern views that present male domination of spaces beyond the household as a key element in the male hierarchy of eighteenth-century Virginia. According to this depiction of the colony between 1740 and 1790, women in all but the poorest families centered their lives around the home. They rarely traveled and then only to attend church, a wedding, a christening, or a housewarming, and they certainly did not visit stores. In Rhys Isaac's account, for example, "Women—even widows who controlled property—did not, it seems, go into stores to make their own purchases. Those were places where men gathered, drank, swore, and even boxed or wrestled among themselves." This is an evocative image. A study of stores and taverns (the two were often combined) in adjacent back-country North Carolina suggests that women had only a "narrow" role in "the public economy of the southern frontier." In contrast, Darrett and Anita Rutman do place women in the stores that developed in Urbanna (Middlesex County), Virginia, between 1650 and 1750, claiming the stores "offered variety to the men and women of Middlesex and a more stable source of goods than had the planter-merchants. A Middlesex man (or his wife) in need of a particular item could count more readily on its immediate availability and judge its quality on the spot" rather than waiting for a future import.[36] The Rutmans' assessment for Middlesex County rings true for other stores in tidewater Virginia. In these shops, women selected merchandise, and, on occasion, they made purchases on their own accounts.[37] Furthermore, women continued to do so in the middle and late eighteenth century.

The apparent dearth of female customers in payment books may result from their use of cash as a form of payment. Some North Carolina store accounts did not identify customers who paid cash at the time of purchase.[38] In Virginia, store accounts recorded that women often paid cash for their purchases, and, in addition to the accounts in the aforementioned chicken books, some married women seemed to have had pocket money allotted to them for household and personal purchases.[39] A summary of women's visits to the Yorktown store operated by the Jerdones between October 1750 and April 1751 reveals the degree to which women shopped there, purchasing goods for themselves and their households.[40] The Jerdone daybook, kept by the person actually minding the store at any given time, suggests how frequently women made purchases in cash. Five times within less than a year, the shop minder posted a transaction to a woman's individual account, only to cross it out and record it as a cash purchase instead.[41] This complicated procedure indicates that the women often chose to pay in cash for purchases that the shopkeeper had already listed to a credit account. The anonymous category of "cash" records in ledgers conceals the previously invisible women's transactions.

At other stores in Virginia, women's methods of payment varied somewhat. For example, at the Partridge Store, women purchased using cash,[42] on their own credit,[43] or on someone else's account.[44] Customers at a Hanover

County store followed a similar pattern, though the female customers also made payments by offering various kinds of goods and services in exchange for merchandise. There, in one year, Jane Carr bought sugar and "sundry goods" on three occasions and paid for her purchases by her labor: "by Making 2 P[ai]r sheets" as well as by making a cash payment. Sarah Slaughter paid "by 9 months washing." "Widow Bogg" paid by 2 casks of butter. The most significant accounts were paid in tobacco-denominated sums, then the currency of Virginia.[45] Still others allowed their accounts to run on the credit of the merchant.[46] Only three of the Hanover merchant's female customers paid by credit from men.[47] In the Booth store accounts, 32 percent of the women paid in cash (24 accounts), though not necessarily at the time of purchase. Men paid accounts directly in cash 35.5 percent of the time. Women used tobacco as payment for 7 percent of the accounts. Elizabeth Garner, who worked for Mordecai Booth, applied her wages to pay her account.[48]

The Jerdone records indicate that women of various classes came to the store. These particular shopkeepers kept remarkably complete notations of each customer's transactions, indicating the date of purchase, whose account was charged, the items purchased, the value of each item, and the total for that person's transaction. More intriguingly, the Jerdone shopkeepers, like other Virginia store owners, also wrote down who actually set foot into the store to pick up the items, entering a notation "P[er]. herself" when an individual selected her own goods and took them home with her. Goods delivered through a third party appeared as "dd. by," indicating by whom the merchandise was delivered. From these records, then, we know who came to the store in person and who sent a servant, slave, or other agent to pick up goods.

Throughout the Jerdone store's Account Book (October 1750–May 1752), individual women's shopping patterns become apparent. For example, Jean Ansell came to the store herself to purchase goods on her own account or by paying cash. Ansell was one of the most frequent shoppers in the Jerdone store, appearing in the Account Book sixteen times in a twenty-month period. On her excursions, she acquired a padlock, cheese, silk, fine muslin, coffee, bed cords, silk cloaks, Glasgow checks, worsted hose, gilt buttons, and, most frequently, sugar and Bohea tea.[49] These goods allowed Jean Ansell to live in the height of fashionable consumption for her time, not only in her clothing, but also in the supplies for tea drinking.

Free white women appeared in the stores to obtain goods, sometimes taking goods charged to a husband's or father's account. In contrast to the servants and slaves obtaining goods at a master's behest, free women could buy items at their own discretion, and the goods purchased under their own names indicate that the store owners recognized women as economic actors in their own rights. The goods they acquired consisted primarily of various types of fabric and apparel, tea, coffee, sugar, molasses, cheese, writing paper, and household goods.[50] Mrs. Moss bought ginger, molasses, small china bowls, fabric, and silk lace at the Jerdone store in 1752, charging her purchases to her husband.[51] More specialized goods were in order when, in mid-June of 1751, public mourning for the Prince of Wales brought several women into the store. Mrs. Digges charged "Queens Crape" and a pair of black knee garters to Colonel Dudley Digges's account on one trip and some ribbon on a second trip.[52]

A similar pattern emerges in the records of the Dixon store in Caroline County. There the accounts specifically noted when women obtained goods in the store on men's credit. The storekeeper noted when "yr. Wife" or "yr daughter" purchased goods on the family account. Sometimes the merchant only noted a first name, suggesting a servant or slave woman had obtained the merchandise.[53]

Not all women went to the stores themselves and some sent a man to make purchases on the women's own accounts.[54] Women could be the errand runners as well as the senders: servant and slave women came to the store frequently to pick up items for their masters and mistresses. The Jerdones seemed to consider white customers the norm, and accounts only record racial identifiers for African-American customers or whites when they were in service to a household. Slave women and girls commonly visited stores. Slaves, referred to as the "negro wenches" of an account holder, or by their own names prefaced with "Negro" (as in "Negro Lucy"), bought green tea, fabrics, rugs, jacket buttons, snuff, thread, corks, sugar, and molasses at various times, charging these to their masters' or mistresses' accounts. Other female household workers acquired goods at the store, and nurses and housekeepers bought fabric and kidskin gloves on the accounts of their masters.[55] In these daybook accounts the storekeepers frequently left the customers nameless, only identifying them by their relationship to the household, either by their position as "nurse," "housekeeper," or "servant," or less specifically as "negro," implying slave. Nevertheless, this list indicates the degree to which women did visit the stores. Servant and slave women purchased goods frequently, and African-American women and girls seemed to visit the stores more often than African-American men and boys.[56]

Women from all classes came to the stores, and when they did, they purchased merchandise using various forms of payment. Accounts of several Virginia stores indicate that women did come into the establishments to shop, sometimes for a practical item, like an iron pot, sometimes for luxury goods, such as silk lace. It remains unstated in these accounts whether or not the female customers had to step over the cursing, wrestling, inebriated men described above.

The form of payment women offered was linked to their position in the local economy. Women who worked as midwives, tavernkeepers, and cloth producers accepted in-kind credit, and most of their payments were recorded in terms of cash—cash they most likely earned in practicing their trades. Here, too, the Jerdone daybook accounts are unusually full, indicating the items purchased, the person who actually obtained the merchandise from the store, and the person responsible for paying the account. In these accounts women frequently participated in the economy at the most local level of the neighborhood store, and shopkeepers would need to consider their customers' choices and keep up with fashions if they wished to sell to this market.[57] While women bought many of the goods from stores for their own consumption or households in which they worked, much of the other purchases were supplies for businesses such as tavernkeeping or clothing production. In these transactions, individual women exercised their discretion in selecting which goods to buy.

The nature of the accounts suggests a range of women's integration into the local, neighborhood economy. Women with their own businesses or a large degree of autonomy to make purchases existed at one end of the spectrum. At the other, women who purchased on husbands' and fathers' accounts suggest greater dependence on male authority. For the latter, a shopkeeper's decision to record purchases by a man's full name and to note a woman simply by her relationship to the man would, at first glance, seem to subsume women's identities in men's. The shopkeeper, however, clearly had a practical reason for this type of record keeping. Since under Virginia law, the shopkeeper needed to know the name of the husband to recover the debt from a wife, the man's identity appeared at the top of each account. Married women continued to participate in economic exchanges even when their husbands ultimately had responsibility. This is apparent in those instances where married men renounced their responsibility for their wives' debts. When a man wished to announce his unwillingness to pay for his wife's purchases, he could record his refusal in a public place, such as the court records or in newspapers. For example, in May of 1703, Thomas Pate warned that no one should give credit "upon any Manner of Accounts" to his wife, Elizabeth. Anyone who did give her credit "by Trucking or tradeing or any other Maner of Dealing" did so at their own "Loss and Detriment." Thomas denied Elizabeth credit because she had left their house near Yorktown.[58] This announcement and many others like it demonstrate the degree to which married women could and did participate in the economy under more peaceful circumstances.

While women's subordination in such a system is obvious, it needs to be considered in the context of a collective family identity for both men and women. Men as well as women found themselves defined by family relationships. A 1716 reference in the Granbery journal records distribution of corn to the wider family network, including quantities sent to "my mother" and "yalls son," possibly an early transcription of a southern speech pattern.[59] Merchants' record books noted who should be held responsible for repayment of questionable men's debts well as women's. Ann Powell had her own account at the King & Queen County store and also served as security for Elizabeth Powell when she purchased fabric on credit. At that same store, Elizabeth Jones offered to serve as security for James Gregory's account and was stuck with a balance when he failed to complete his repayments.[60] Ritchie & Company's accounts from Essex County listed the means by which the company expected to collect from debtors. In some entries, the shopkeeper reported that the debts were hopeless, indicating which account holders were poor risks. Examples of these assessments include, "This small balance if not bad is certainly very doubtful;" "he has nothing left;" another lived near the prison bounds for two years "and will continue there;" another was "supported by the charge of the parish."[61] The shopkeeper also reported when family members might well be tapped for payment. For example, when the shopkeeper for Ritchie and Company kept a column in the Account Book of information he needed to collect payments, he noted that Ann Ramsey was the sister of Francis. In the same column, he wrote "enquire Elias Harrison" for Eliza Harrison and "enquire of Joshua Donahoe" for Elizabeth McCormack.[62] He used this same sort of notation in describing men's accounts, listing family relations who might pay the debt. Sometimes legal ties reinforced those family ties, though they too could be worthless, as when the shopkeeper wrote that he was afraid one debt was hopeless because the father would "not agree he is security & is not good pay if he did."[63] Other shopkeepers adopted similar practices. Dixon's Caroline County store also identified some men by their family relationships in the accounts in the middle of the eighteenth century. William Smith appeared as "Thos. Smiths Son," Hugh Bankhead was "the Doctors Brother," and William Marshall was identified as "Son of Edward."[64] In these entries, the company emphasized the significance of family connections over individual identity in economic networks for men as well as women.

This system of accounting worked well in incorporating women into trade, especially in face-to-face local exchanges. Account book debts assumed a degree of trust shared between the two parties and did not require a promise to repay, though they assumed settlement at a future date. Debts on account, or "book debts," allowed for more flexibility in local trading than did more formal written contracts. For example, there was no limit on the number of exchanges that could be tacked onto the list and balances could run for years. No interest was calculated.[65]

Account book exchanges and informal debt incorporated a variety of colonists, even married women and enslaved men. The gender inclusiveness of "book debt" occurred elsewhere in the colonies. Cornelia Dayton concludes that for Connecticut, "the locus of the account book and the informality of local debt relations made men's dealings familiar to women." During the 1720s, colonists in Connecticut continued to rely on this form of exchange, though by the middle of the century book debt as a means of recording and litigating exchanges had declined, reducing the presence of women both in stores and in court rooms, where their disputes were aired.[66]

In tidewater Virginia, the inclusion of women in the exchanges continued through the eighteenth century, and merchants assumed that women shared responsibility for purchases with men in their families even when these sellers did not explicitly record this expectation with the original obligation. This assumption is apparent in a lawsuit a young customer, Richard Ball, initiated against his merchant, James Gordon, once Ball reached the age of majority. Ball claimed the merchant consistently overcharged for goods during his youth and wanted redress. Gordon offered in his defense that the goods he sent to Ball were suitable to his "station and Estate." Even more, Gordon claimed Ball's mother knew of her son's dealing at Gordon's store "and never intimated to [Gordon] her disapprobation thereof." Gordon assured the court that if he believed Richard Ball dealt with him "contrary to his Mothers orders he would not have trusted him" because other customers paid their debts more promptly.[67] The case included other elements as well, but the merchant defended himself by claiming the mother of his young customer resided in the neighborhood; that she tacitly accepted the exchanges suggests their legitimacy.

Acknowledging the degree to which colonial Virginians described men as well as women by those kin relationships provides the appropriate context for discussing the female dependence on family by placing a comparable stress on a more limited, but very real, male reliance on family connections to give them credit and power. Searching for female independence from family connections seems anachronistic within a context of universal dependence on family ties.

These store accounts offer other insights into the gendered assumptions about debt in colonial Virginia. In some cases, descriptions of misfortunes following men's and women's bad debts appear in merchants' accounts. In the 1750s, one King and Queen County merchant simply recorded that Elizabeth Barclay was "Dead Insolvent," that Elizabeth Dunnahoe ran a small balance "Not worth Transferring," and that Mary Robins's account could not be collected, noting in the margin "Runaway."[68]

Elsewhere, shopkeepers recorded bad debts in gendered terms, and annotations on men's refusal or inability to pay more often included descriptions of fraud or ineptitude on the part of the debtor. Women's accounts stressed helplessness and bad luck. Ritchie and Company recorded one woman as "very poor" and assisted by the parish, and simply listed another as "a poor woman." In memoranda after men's bad accounts the shopkeeper sometimes used similar terms. The Ritchie and Company agent wrote that George Brabner was supported by the charge of the parish, as was Thomas Sullivan, and Thomas Gibbons was "wr[e]tchedly poor &

lives upon charitable neighbors."[69] One male debtor was described as "a worthless gamester now commonly in North Carolina." Samuel Sale, with a rather large unpaid balance of over forty pounds, is listed as "a young spend-thrift" and his debt was "at least very doubtful." The shopkeeper described George Turner as "a lazy worthless fellow" and wrote that Richard Conquest "deceived me last year about his crop" making the shopkeeper "not a little uneasy" about recovering the debt. The shopkeeper also noted that Jessiephron Clark had a family and was "worthless, indolent & wretchedly poor."[70]

While it is possible that women escaped falling into irresponsible bad debt because only the most dependable women ever secured credit in their own names in the first place, or that women truly were more honest customers, the situation was probably otherwise. The distinctions the store-keepers made in their descriptions of bad debts suggest that colonial Virginians had different expectations for men's and women's economic success. Commentary on men's debts that a creditor feared might not be repaid—so-called doubtful debts—often carried moral overtones that descriptions of women's unpaid sums lacked, even in the same account book. Both men and women could be counted among the understandably poor and even supported by neighbors or the parish, but only men's economic failure could be considered moral failure resulting from laziness, deceit, excess, or simply in being considered "worthless." Certain groups of women had more access to the consumer economy than others. Although women who received income for goods or services constituted a minority of the female colonists, their frequent presence in the account books does suggest some of the limitations and opportunities open to women. Which groups of women successfully integrated themselves into this network? Again, the account books suggest the answer.

Women gained a modicum of autonomy when they also controlled the revenue and resources gained by selling or exchanging their goods or labor, or by taking advantage of family resources. Considered separately, productivity did not grant women more autonomy; however, the results of productivity *could* when women retained control over the goods and services they produced and exchanged. Men and women were not yet divided into separate spheres in colonial stores, and if drunken men brawled in the stores, female customers went about their business despite the disorderly fellow shoppers.

Midwives, tavern- and ordinary keepers, cloth producers, and women employees paid wages for work were the women most likely to appear in the accounts alongside wealthier widows operating plantations.[71] For example, Martha Baviol ran a ferry and took in a substantial cash income from this work between 1750 and 1759. She took further advantage of her prime location at the ferry landing, which served as a bottleneck for travelers traversing the terrain of tidewater Virginia, and sold ducks, geese, and chickens by the dozens to passengers waiting to make their river crossings. As a result, she had cash with which to buy indigo, wool, sugar, shoes, fabrics, and the cost of "smiths work." She also purchased two gallons of rum, though it is not clear if this was to resell for refreshments or for her own consumption.[72]

Another woman who relied on multiple sources of cash income was Catherine Blaikley, a prominent Williamsburg midwife who had accounts with several local merchants, integrating herself into the cash and credit networks of colonial Williamsburg. She purchased "sundries" in April and May of 1747 at a Yorktown store, paying cash on one occasion, and took goods on credit during another shopping trip. When she decided a hat she purchased did not suit her, she returned it for credit. On a later shopping trip, she purchased fifty oranges when the winter fruit arrived in town.[73]

The degree to which she possessed an independent economic identity is apparent from material culture, as well. In 1769 she lost a red Morocco pocket book. Pocket books served as personal organizers, and many contained paper calendars or memo books stitched into one half and dividers sewn into the other to hold slips of paper or currency (see fig, 5.2). In the memo book portion, a debtor could sign (or make a mark) to a note promising to repay an obligation. A seller of goods could ask for a receipt and know where to find it if a dispute arose. Blaikley's misfortune is the historian's fortune because when she sought assistance in retrieving the book, she placed an advertisement in the newspaper, describing in detail its contents. At the time it disappeared the pocket book held seven or eight pounds in paper money, some bills, some silver, "sundry receipts; and other papers and memorandums," including one about some drugs. In her pocket book, Blaikley recorded a transaction involving "three hogs and a half" of pork.[74] The variety of transactions she reported indicates the wide circumference of her sphere, and the memorandum on drugs highlights her role as a midwife to the mothers of Williamsburg. She probably began her career as midwife by at least 1739, a little over three years after she became a widow.[75] At the time of her death, the *Virginia Gazette* praised her as "an eminent Midwife" who brought "upward of three Thousand Children into the world."[76] In addition, she ventured further still into the exchange economy by offering lodging and board to men attending to legal and political affairs in town.[77] Catherine Blaikley's demonstrates how a woman's life could, simultaneously, incorporate pursuing a distinctively female way of making a living through midwifery, engaging in a business that appealed to both men and women in providing bed and board to paying customers, and enjoying the benefits of labor by purchasing goods from Williamsburg's luxury market.

Certainly productivity alone was not the critical element in women's efforts to securing economic autonomy. The payments for "Negro Sarah's"

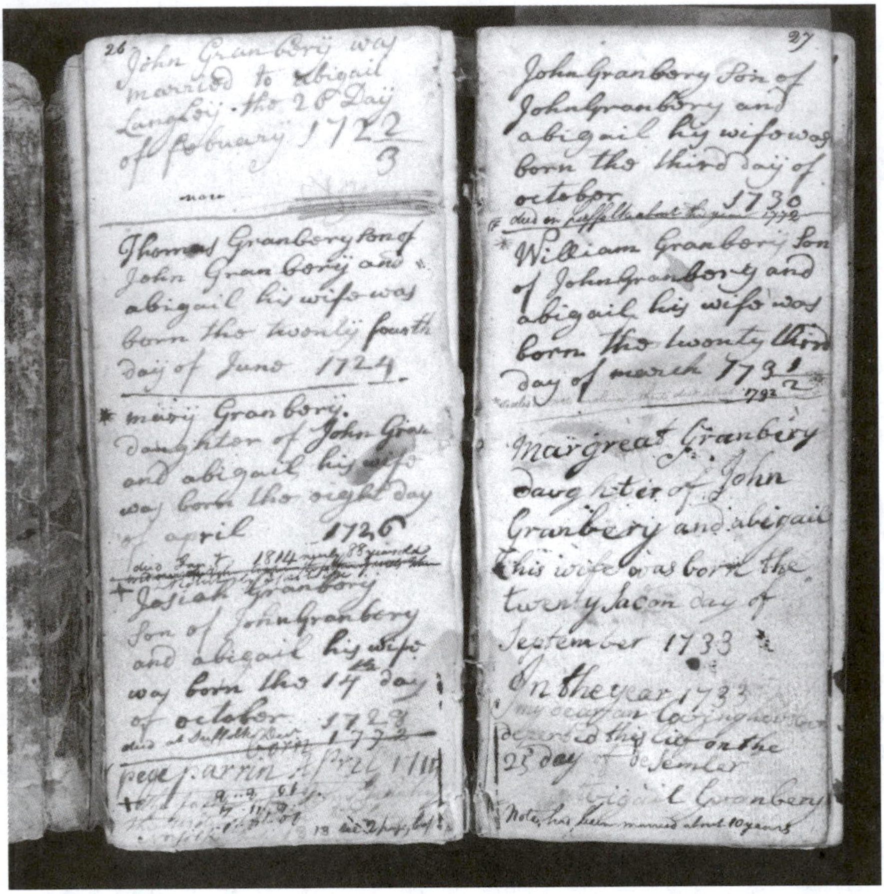
26 John Granbery was married to Abigail Langley the 28 Day of february 1722/3

Thomas Granbery son of John Granbery and abigail his wife was born the twenty fourth day of June 1724

mary Granbery daughter of John Gran and abigail his wife was born the eight day of april 1726

Josiah Granbery son of John Granbery and abigail his wife was born the 14th day of october 1728

27 John Granbery son of John Granbery and abigail his wife was born the third day of october 1730

William Granbery son of John Granbery and abigail his wife was born the twenty third day of march 1731/2

Margreat Granbery daughter of John Granbery and abigail his wife was born the twenty second day of September 1733

In the year 1733 … departed this life on the 25 day of desember

Abigail Granbery

FIGURE 5.2 *Abigail Granbery Pocket Book.* Pocket books, owned by both women and men, included a pocket under one cover for holding cash, loose notes, or receipts, and a book of blank paper stitched into the spine. Colonists commonly recorded financial or personal information in the pages. This particular pocket book is open to pages used for recording information. When the book is closed, the flap to the left folds over and fastens with a clasp to the outside of the opposite cover.

Several members of the Granbery family of Nansemond used this pocket book over the course of four decades. Sarah Granbery documented a business exchange in 1694. Abigail Granbery recorded personal information in the 1720s and 1730s, by which time the pocket book may have achieved heirloom status, removing it from the realm of day-to-day transactions. Sarah Granbery could have been either the wife or mother of John Granbery, Jr., who was listed as owning the book by 1708.

Abigail (Langley) Granbery Hargroves journal and pocket book. Accession Mss5:5H2244:1. Reproduced by permission of the Virginia Historical Society.

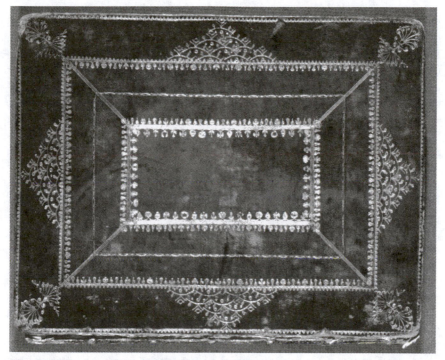

FIGURE 5.3 *Prayer Book belonging to Catherine Blaikley.* Catherine Blaikley's Book of Common Prayer, cover image. This volume is covered in red calf skin and is decorated with gold tooled patterns. Accession 1990–59. Reproduced by permission of the Colonial Williamsburg Foundation.

work in delivering babies went to her master, Edward Taylor of Accomack. Sarah served as midwife for both African- and European-American women in the 1770s and 1780s. Intriguingly, Sarah delivered the child of Dr. Jon Boicourt's wife. In exchange, the doctor provided bleeding for Taylor and one of his slave women when they fell ill.[78]

Still, women with regular incomes could be integrated into the exchange economy and certain occupations allowed for this. Both ordinary keepers' and midwives' names frequently appeared in merchants' account books as purchasers of goods because they had access to the cash-denominated economy even if they did not carry coins or currency. Even when women's occupations were not listed in the account books, their economic pursuits may be discerned. For example, female account holders at the Jerdone store in New Kent County fell into several categories. Some primarily purchased large quantities of liquor, sugar, and spices, and paid cash for the items at regular intervals, suggesting they kept taverns or small ordinaries. Other female customers with long accounts were credited for their services in delivering babies.

Midwives carried accounts at the Dixon store in Caroline County. There, Martha Hellier incurred debts for purchasing household goods, fabric, powder, and shot. She and other store customers also used the store as a means of making payments to third parties, including Dr. Allison. Hellier's selections reflected rather modest tastes, and she bought shoes "out of the cask," in contrast to her neighbor's purchase of grander "fine Shoes [out] of [the] Pidgeon Holes."[79] In return, the Dixons credited Hellier's account for payments from other men and women for her services as a midwife, most frequently to slave mothers. She received £3 from one man "by bringing six negro women to bed" and payment from someone else "for bringing 5 wenches to bed" and in other instances for attending individual births.[80] Another midwife, Anne Graves, patronized the Jerdone store from 1760 to 1771, purchasing fabric, cotton cards, sugar, rum, and paper. Anne Graves apparently enjoyed more colorful attire than Hellier, judging from her selection of "womens purple calamancoe shoes" from the store.[81] The payments her clients made to Mrs. Graves's credit in the store accounts indicate the sort of network that surrounded her. She apparently was married at the time she had accounts, since the Jerdones listed her as "Mrs. Anne Graves wife of Thomas Graves," yet her six pages of income and expenses continued to list the accounts under her name, not her husband's.[82] She, like Hellier, received fees for attending various African-American women listed as "Negro"; these were probably women in the Jerdone households, and Graves likely received the standard midwifery fee of ten shillings per delivery. Graves also received cash credits of ten shillings, almost certainly for midwifery, posted to her account from various other women and men.

These indicate the ways that stores served as clearinghouses for payments and exchanges among local residents, and the accounts for Hellier and Graves demonstrate how integrated midwives were into the exchange networks of the colony. With coins and currency in short supply, colonists exchanged goods and services through local stores, but these were still translated into cash equivalencies. Rather than collecting her midwifery fees directly from each client, Graves received cash-denominated credit at the store through her clients' payments to the third party of the storekeeper. She then purchased goods for herself, withdrew cash from the surplus on her account, and in one instance, paid the store owner for services, such as "weaving" woolen and cotton cloth rather than for the fabric as a finished product.

Although colonists did not always purchase goods with money, merchants affixed relatively "set" prices to commonly available consumer goods. This practice is apparent in a customer's complaint about price gouging in a lawsuit deposition. In this case, the parties claimed that "Goods were charged at a moderate price particularly a small parcel of ozna[burg fabric] which is charged at 8 1/8 p[er] yard it being an article the price of which is well known."[83] A cashless exchange system was not necessarily an informal web for women consumers and producers.

Other, even more shadowy, networks can be glimpsed through the Account Book from Anne Pattison's tavern, which records that on April 14, 1748, "Mrs. Lewis the oyster woman" bought a bottle of beer and charged the cost to her own account. Several weeks later, she charged six bottles of ale to her total. More significantly, her husband bought punch the same day and charged the cost to his wife's account.[84] Mrs. Lewis should have had an account in her husband's name since, as a married woman, she could not be sued and few individuals would choose to enter a contract and allow her to incur debts in her own name. Nonetheless, for some reason the tavernkeeper decided to record the debts under Mrs. Lewis's name. There are several possible explanations for why this happened. As a seller of oysters, Mrs. Lewis probably peddled her goods for small amounts of cash, permitting her to pay off her debts in cash in an economy that depended largely on recorded barter transactions and credit.[85] She likely supplied the Pattison tavern with oysters. This sort of vending remains in use in developing countries today. If Mr. Lewis had no similar access to credit, the tavernkeeper may have decided that Mrs. Lewis was a better credit risk. Another possible explanation is that despite official, legal restrictions on married women's autonomy, married women could, in practice, be recognized as independent economic persons who would dependably pay their obligations without recourse to the law. Women who were lower on the social scale could also still maintain credit and accounts in their own names, especially if they were involved in the exchange economy. Mr. Lewis, like "Honest John," may have decided there were certain advantages to his wife's economic situation, especially if it gave him convenient access to punch at the local tavern. The tavernkeeper could also have seen Mrs. Lewis as the more reliable member in the couple to repay the debt.

Production also provided women with a means of entering the exchange economy, but the tasks associated with cloth production took on particular political significance as colonists turned to nonimportation as a political measure during the Stamp Act crisis in 1765 and continuing through the Revolutionary War years. Even "local" production adjusted in response to transatlantic political circumstances. In the context of nonimportation, women began to discuss politics more openly, even to the point of attacking the taxation without representation that women suffered.[86] For the most part, southern settlement patterns inhibited public recognition of women's domestic labor, including spinning and weaving so that, according to historian Cynthia Kierner, cloth-producing slave and free southern women "toiled in obscurity" in the 1760s and 1770s.[87]

Women who exchanged their products in local stores are slightly less obscure because they appear in merchants' records. On the eastern shore, Sarah Mackallin received credit in 1778 for spinning "toe" in her account with her merchant, Edward Taylor. Thomas Randolph recommended a weaver woman he had hired previously and spoke of her ability to weave fine quality cloth herself as well as her skill in teaching weaving and in managing spinners and weavers. His letter suggests that the war years opened new opportunities for women because he said that he hired this versatile woman even though Mrs. Randolph desired a male worker for the task. It also suggests that women, in this case Mrs. Randolph, could be the sustainers of the glass ceiling preventing other women's advancement.[88] Even before the Revolution, women as well as men were weaving. In 1747, Abigail Granbery of Nansemond noted that "Sary hancok begin to wef the 29 day of october her first Web of lase 1747."[89] At the most local level, plantation mistresses sometimes hired workers or ordered their slaves to make cloth.[90] Elizabeth (Lewis) Littlepage Holladay, a wealthy widow, hired Sarah Jones to live with and work for her for the sum of five pounds a year in 1767. Most of the payments to Jones were in yardage of Virginia cloth and cash.[91] Holladay kept strict records of various payments and of the money her own father, Zachary Lewis, owed her for making shirts and jackets for him. She even recorded trade with her family in cash terms.[92]

Other accounts recorded exchanges among women who produced cloth for the market in some locations. A type of "putting out" system developed, with families and individuals completing steps in the process of cloth production. Weaving, for example, could be sent out. The Jerdone Account

Book lists a woman named Millie Webb at the head of an account that included the men of the household. It was, in fact, a family account with a woman identified as the holder of the account. The Jerdones credited Webb's account for weaving over two hundred yards of fabric in 1760 and Webb received credit for her weaving expenses in 1763, and again in 1765.[93] In return, Millie Webb herself drew on her account for pins, sheeting, and cash. Her father and brother took cash from her account on two different days, and the shopkeeper noted that they did so with her permission and carefully noted that she offered them her receipt authorizing the transactions.[94] Here, by drawing on her skill at weaving cloth for the larger market, a woman had access to the cash economy and she provided cash to both her brother and father.

Other women wove cloth for market exchange, working through the Jerdone store. Initially Judy Belsches oversaw the cloth production and the Jerdones took over the operation after she died. At the time she managed the textile weaving, Judy Belsches was the widow of Patrick Belsches, a merchant of Louisa County. She was relatively wealthy, having inherited all of her husband's land in Louisa, five slaves, and the remaining term of service of an indentured servant.[95]

Only rarely does full documentation of this sort of exchange survive, but a book that appears to contain Belsches's records has been preserved among the Jerdone papers (see fig. 5.4). The cover of the book says "Ledger" and has an identifying triangle over a letter "B," though the rest of the writing on the cover has been worn away. The Account Book, really a small booklet, contains two different sets of accounts; one, written in a very labored, childish handwriting, consists of records dated before 1768, and the other is recorded in a tidy merchant's hand similar to Francis Jerdone's.[96] Another Jerdone Account Book recorded that one of the weavers, Mary Macon, had a balance "on the sales book of the deceased Mrs. Judy Belsches."[97] There is good reason to believe the Account Book in Francis Jerdone's possession was originally Judy Belsches's and was transferred to him after she died. This volume seems to be the book that Jerdone called Belsches's "sales book" and describes her business dealings as well as her agreement with her overseer, providing further evidence of the book's provenance.[98]

A separate portion is entitled "Account of What Cash I Make use of in 1764" and another, for 1766, described expenses. Belsches paid for quantities of food, small consumer goods, and expenses such as ferriage and repairs to her "chair"—a type of small, wheeled single-horse drawn vehicle. Belsches also paid other women for work. She listed expenses "To weaving 53 y[ar]ds of clouth," payments to Margery Ellyson, to Mrs. Overton for knitting, and Mrs. Garland for weaving.[99] Another section of the Belsches book, headed "Account of What Clouth I have wove began 1762" and running to 1767, includes a variety of different types of cloth—"Negroes Clouth," a

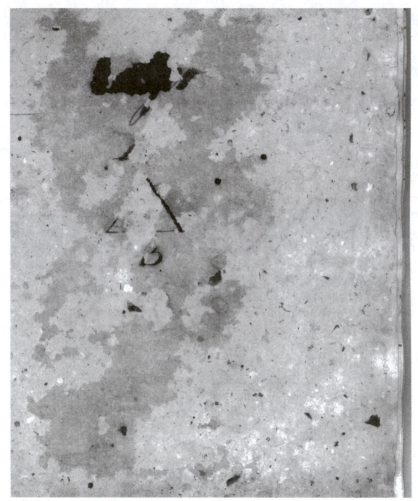

FIGURE 5.4 *Belsches Account Book Cover.* The cover of the book has a worn title "Ledger" and an identifying triangle over a letter "B." The rest of the writing on the cover has been worn away.

Jerdone Family Papers, 1762–1866, Personal Papers Collection, Item 208, Folder 6, Library of Virginia, Archives Research Services. Reproduced by permission of the Library of Virginia, Archives Research Services.

rough fabric sold for slave clothing, "counterpins" (counterpanes), sheets, curtains, woolen cloth, and bed ticking.[100]

It remains unclear exactly how much of the cloth Belsches made herself, though she listed it all as cloth "I have wove." The inventory for her estate lists two flax wheels, spinning wheels, cotton cards, a variety of fabrics, forty pounds of "Spanish Brown," a quilting frame and a shoemaker's tools and leather, but no looms. According to her account of cash payments, she paid Mrs. Garland for weaving in June and July of 1766, yet included entries for "53 yds at 4d Mrs. Garland for sheats" and "53 [yards] at 4d Mrs. Garland for Negroes."[101] Two other entries in the "Clouth I have wove" list the bed ticking as "Cosbeys weaver" and thirty-three yards as "Mr. Jerdones Weaver."[102]

The accounts seem to indicate that instead of weaving all the cloth herself, she directed the work through a putting-out system, as the middlewoman. It is also possible that she merely recorded production of cloth intended for household consumption, but this is unlikely considering the quantities she listed. In this set of records, Belsches appears at the center of a production network that incorporated both men and women. Supervising cloth production provided Belsches with an admittance to the exchange economy in the way that midwifery and tavernkeeping did for other income-earning women. For example, she paid two other women who wove for her. One of these weavers also supplied her with seventeen pairs of shoes and some other goods. In return, the supplier received a coat, some lining fabric, pins, salt, a padlock, hosiery, and four pounds of wool.[103] The Account Book indicates that one man was in her debt for shoes, making a suit of clothes, and making shirts for which Belsches received "credit upon the store books."[104] One woman bought a type of fabric called "roles," and paid for her purchases in cash and "By weaving 21 y[ar]ds Cloth."[105] Anther woman named Mrs. Pondexter bought shoes, a paper of pins, ribbon, a half a yard of calico, a "pare of spectakels," and lining fabric "to Line a gown," and was also in debt to Belsches for her "making a gown." This same customer paid her debt over the course of two years by exchanging her labor. During 1764, she wove thirty yards in March, nineteen yards in November and another fifteen yards at other times. In 1765, the account listed her as weaving cloth "at different times," and perhaps it was this extensive weaving that initially created the need for the newly purchased "pare of spectakles."[106] Pondexter's account also listed that "Ben went to Mr. Jerdones December th[e] 30 1766" as well as the days he was at home over the course of the year, so Pondexter may have leased a slave to the Jerdones, and the deductions for the time the slave was home were debited to her account. Slave as well as free labor could be quantified and accounted for in monetary terms.

The account book, which debited customers for shoemaking, sewing, and purchases of small finished goods also documented the extension of credit for weaving, thereby describing a small, local economic network with Judy Belsches at its nexus, directing the exchanges. For all the entries, the account keeper assigned a cash value to weaving done by women. In return, customers received cash, store credit, or other services. The shopkeeping Jerdones entered this network, at first as proprietors of a local store importing English goods and, later, as executors to the Belsches estates. Eventually, the Jerdones contracted women and girls to weave for them directly. The store provided the location for colonists to exchange the goods they produced for items for consumption.

The pattern of "putting out" cloth production occurred elsewhere in Virginia and slave as well as free women completed steps. Thomas Jefferson continued to put out finishing steps in the production of cloth rather than completing all of the steps of production on the plantation. Cloth production and spinning, in particular, seemed to be tasks assigned to enslaved women and girls.[107] At Monticello, spinning was assigned to girls between the ages of ten and sixteen, before they "went into the ground" to work the fields.[108] On Green Spring plantation, William Lee instructed the plantation manager to have the slaves produce their own clothing from flax, cotton, and wool produced on the plantation. Lee wanted the girls and "infirm old women" to be taught to spin flax and be "kept constantly at it."[109] On smaller plantations, spinning may have occupied slaves only part of the year. In 1762 a planter's contract with an overseer instructed him to employ the plantation's slave woman in spinning until March, and then transfer her to laundry duty for the slaves, and then to field work.[110] The woman may have been pregnant and expected to return to heavy work after delivery, but spinning could have been an indoor task assigned when little other work was available, since the enslaved men's work was also divided by season, with brick-making occupying the fall months.

Cloth production could be a seasonal complement to the agrarian calendar in rural parts of Virginia. Mary Belsches's weaving accounts suggest little seasonal variation in weaving. While total production in the recorded years indicates that the highest monthly totals occurred in December and the smallest in July and September, the work was otherwise spaced fairly evenly throughout the year.[111] The Jerdones seemed to act as agents for weavers in this putting-out system, and for a time, several orphan girls who did weaving lived in the Jerdone household. Cloth production provided one means for Virginia women, or their masters, to enter the cash economy.

This chapter has demonstrated that Virginia women became individual economic actors in a variety of ways, including making purchases in their local stores and selling items to local consumers. Recognizing women's presence in the stores and in the shopkeepers' account books also allows us to see the degree to which some women gained economic autonomy as producers and consumers, even in a hierarchy that placed women in a subordinate position. By the time of the War of Independence, colonists more explicitly described consumption in gendered terms. From "Poor Richard's" jibes at his wife for her extravagance to the organization of societies encouraging boycotts of British goods, colonists understood consumption, especially excessive and frivolous consumption, as "feminine."[112] Conversely, according to T. H. Breen, "The acquisition of goods by women in this economy was an assertive act, a declaration of agency, and male writers found these aggressive expressions of personal independence intimidating."[113] The surviving economic records for the pre-Revolutionary period do not reveal how colonial Virginia women perceived their own economic activity; however, we do know that women participated in economic exchange networks that included both men and other women not only as producers but also as consumers who made informed choices about what they would acquire. Merchants and neighbors trusted women to honor their obligations and extended credit to married women as well as widows. This allowed women a degree of economic autonomy, though clearly women enjoyed enhanced economic choices when they controlled the proceeds arising from their own labor or the labor of others in their households in income-generating enterprises ranging from weaving to midwifery to tavernkeeping to oyster selling. The tidewater local economy, in practice, allowed women to deal with each other as well as with men, and the gender boundary in exchanges for tidewater Virginia seem less dramatic than they were in northern New England, where Martha Ballard traded. Lowering the boundary potentially benefitted male as well as female colonists: a merchant could allow a local boy to acquire goods in a shop by counting on his mother's tacit approval of the exchange to support claims for repayment.

Having access to accounts of their own or relying on family accounts accorded women a degree of agency as consumers. Their travel to stores suggests some geographic freedom as well. Women moved in and out of social spaces, including stores. Rather than being immured in the restricted bounds of the home, women were part of the economic world around them. The accounts indicate women came to stores in part to select from the wide variety of fabrics available in tidewater Virginia. Some account books from the region list silks, Irish linen, muslin, printed linen, plain lawn, calico, and cheaper cloths such as oznaburgs among the choices. With access to accounts in shops, women could acquire these goods and, no doubt, socialize with fellow shoppers or the shopkeepers. These eighteenth-century Virginia women participated in the consumer revolution, both as customers with an economic identity and as suppliers of goods and services to other colonists. The latter will be discussed in greater detail in the next chapter. It is clear, though, that in getting and spending at the local level, women participated in the larger economic world beyond the household while simultaneously remaining enmeshed in an accounting system that recognized all individuals as part of family networks.

The economic agency that allowed some women to be consumers within local trade did not emerge from productivity alone. Productivity could, however, be a source of women's agency if women maintained the proceeds from their enterprises, especially if they received cash or credit accounted in cash terms. In the practical experience of day-to-day life in Virginia, some married women could wrest discretionary authority within the economy, even if they only gained the small pleasure of donning purple calamanco shoes after a long day's work in the way Anne Graves could.[114] Marital status did not necessarily bar women's local economic pursuits and married women continued to trade on their on accounts, either in "chicken books" or in merchants' shop books. At the local level, a woman in colonial Virginia could enjoy having "a little purse," or at least, "a little account," to herself.

"MADAM & CO.": GENDER, FAMILY, AND TRADE ENTERPRISES

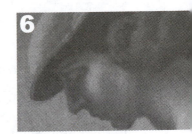

n one of the early chapbook versions of *Moll Flanders*, the transplanted plantation mistress orders servants and goods to be shipped to her from England. She also purchases two long wigs, two silver-hilted swords, three or four fowling pieces, a fine saddle with holsters and pistols and a scarlet cloak. As Moll explains "I had taken care to buy those things for my husband, which I knew he delighted to have...everything I could think of to oblige him, and to make him appear, as he really was, a fine gentleman."[1] In this mid-eighteenth-century adaptation of the fictional Flanders for a popular audience, the heroine believed that through conspicuous consumption, her husband, also a transported criminal, would appear to be the fine, swashbuckling gentleman that "he really was." Within the eighteenth-century consumer revolution, it was Moll Flanders, not her husband, who decided which goods best signaled her husband's high status in a setting where clothes, wigs, and silver-hilted swords worked together to signify gentility.

Chesapeake residents enjoyed two periods of relative material comfort during the colonial period, one brief moment of luxury in the 1620s, and a steady improvement beginning in the eighteenth century. The first, a short period of heady consumption, occurred during the 1620s boom when tobacco prices hit "dizzying heights," but ended with a return to simplicity after the price bubble burst before the end of the decade.[2] During the 1620 tobacco boom, even the tenants on the Virginia governors' farmland accumulated costly, nonessential goods, including mirrors, books, and the latest fashion in early seventeenth-century luxury imported goods—Chinese porcelain. These tenants had a pet cat (nonindigenous to Virginia), whose remains were discovered in an archaeological site dating from this period. Archaeologists suggest that the feline helped the settlers to recreate familiar English surroundings in their new homes. Merchants supplied the settlers with luxury fabrics, streams of drink, and tempting porcelain wine cups, the latter most likely acquired more for conspicuous consumption than regular use.[3]

Consumption declined after this boom period, however, and Virginians suffered an extremely low standard of living, even when compared to English households of the same period. While poor households in England during the early seventeenth century had "bare necessities" such as basic furniture, pots and pans, Virginia colonists did not. Even further up the social scale, they had a living standard that was "remarkably, almost unimaginably primitive." In the lower middle class, half of all households had no seating furniture, and 70 to 80 percent had no bedsteads but relied on mattresses on the floor. Sheets, pillows, and blankets were a luxury. Meals were often one-pot dishes, boiled. Family members shared a common cup.

Only in middle- and upper-middle-class households did each diner enjoy a plate and dish of her own. The family might own lighting equipment such as candlesticks or lanterns, allowing them to continue activities into the evening. The majority of individuals owned sheets and bedding while cooking equipment allowed for frying and roasting as well as boiling foods. Wealthy individuals in both England and the Chesapeake area consumed many of the same types of goods that middling and lower class people did, so possessions did not distinguish markedly different ways of living. James Horn points out, "Differences in standards of living between the rich and middling classes were…a matter of degree rather than kind." In the eighteenth century, however, the distinctions became progressively clearer, especially at the upper ranks of the social order. Colonists' lives gradually became more segregated by class, gender, and race as space in households became more specialized with separate spaces for cooking, relaxing, preparing meals, and washing.[4]

These trends in consumption continued during the eighteenth century in the Chesapeake area and Britain. Lois Carr and Lorena Walsh have concluded that by 1770, demand in the Chesapeake area for new kinds of goods expanded down the social scale so that "the social definition of what was a luxury had changed. Even poor will writers possessed coarse ceramics, linens, and books."[5] Archaeologists, material culture scholars, and architectural historians are expanding our understanding of what and how goods were consumed.

Historians have noted that with the arrival of a "consumer revolution" in late-seventeenth and early-eighteenth-century England and British North America, growing desire to acquire goods conforming to rapidly changing styles provided the means for producers and sellers to create demand among consumers.[6] Certain kinds of goods were considered "fashionable" while others remained more utilitarian. Wealthy consumers acquired both kinds of goods, but fashionable goods appeared in drawing and dining rooms, while other commodities made their way into barns and kitchens.[7] In addition, a new category of objects associated with "comfort"—the moral balance between luxury and bare necessity—in the consumer revolution became associated with respectable, middle-class life and displayed women's success at domesticity within their households.[8] In a process that began as early as the opening of the eighteenth century and continued through the Revolutionary War period, colonists were buying larger quantities of consumer goods and persons of "middling" status were purchasing items previously considered extravagant.

Several historians have commented on women's importance as purchasers of the new goods, but their significance to marketing has received less attention.[9] Left unsaid is the degree to which women in the mercantile houses provided the means to stimulate consumption among colonial customers. This chapter analyzes the role of women in acquiring goods, both fashionable and quotidian, at the beginning of the consumer revolution, and considers how far women understood and participated in trade supplying this market. Women's roles included, on the one hand, serving as marriage partners in alliances between families with common concerns on both sides of the Atlantic and, on the other hand, putting their skills to work in this new setting.

Merchants in the transatlantic tobacco market understood that their success depended on "intensely personal" relationships with their customers. Regarding the transatlantic tobacco trade, Jacob Price refers to three "systems" of trade: the market, administrative logic, and "the much looser quasi system or 'human comedy' of interpersonal connections or relationships (including kinship, marriage, dependency, reciprocal obligation, and partnership)."[10] Marriage alliances certainly strengthened trading ties, but this chapter examines the role of these women once they became members of these webs. Women had more active roles in those family businesses selecting goods for their firms' customers. The chapter illuminates how gender functioned in the period before industrialization, when other historians argue the concept of separate spheres ascribed "private" roles as the ideal for women. In the early modern period, commercially competent women acted within colonial trade webs and English and Anglo-American men worked together with women in transatlantic family enterprises. Family firms depended on women's expertise in supplying their long-term customers in the colonies and solidified the firms' personal and business connections with the Virginians.[11] These businesses required the contributions of various family members and developed from the capital of extended family networks.[12]

Economic historians have long understood that marriages provided the means by which merchants solidified their trading networks across the Atlantic. For example, among Glasgow merchants trading in Chesapeake tobacco, junior partners in firms "commonly" married the daughters of the senior members. This chapter will demonstrate that the significance of women in the economy can be taken further still: merchant families called on female family members when cultivating personal connections to suppliers and customers. Women were more than symbols of links among families and conduits for wealth within business partnerships, though they served those functions, too.[13] Like Moll Flanders, trading women served as arbiters of taste in purchasing goods.[14]

Structural restraints certainly hindered women's autonomous access to transatlantic commerce. Law restricted married women's undertakings; additionally, women's desire to participate in the commercial world could be dampened through socialization in a culture that allowed women to claim ignorance or infirmity based upon sex, claims that then confirmed the legal conceptions of women's roles.[15] Despite those limitations, the hierarchy of colonial Virginia distributed power to individuals according to class as well as sex, and merchant and planter women found themselves with responsibilities within their extended families' economic undertakings.

There is English evidence to suggest that during the late seventeenth and much of the eighteenth centuries, contemporaries recognized the importance of women gaining knowledge about economic activities. Daniel Defoe's *The Complete English Tradesman* (1726) acknowledged the value of women's understanding of their families' businesses in a backhanded way. He commented on the significance of a wife's contributions by pointing out the potential for the failure of the whole family's business if the woman were allowed to remain ignorant of affairs.[16] Similarly, the English merchant Sir Josiah Child discussed the dangers of estates left in the hands of ignorant wives. In 1693 Child wrote, "if a merchant in England arrives at any considerable estate, he commonly withdraws his estate from trade before he comes to the confines of old age." Child explained the merchant's rationale for this retreat: land was a safer investment because English wives were ill-equipped to manage a mercantile empire, in contrast to the well-prepared wives of Holland. As a result, "if God should call him [a merchant] out of the world while the mass of his estate is engaged abroad in trade, he must lose one third of it through the inexperience and unaptness of his wife to such affairs, and so it usually turns out." According to Lawrence Stone, "English mercantile wives seem to have been withdrawing at this time [the late seventeenth century] from the counting house to become genteel ladies, as Defoe, complained, so there may be some grain of truth in Child's argument."[17]

A transatlantic family with members in London, Jamaica, and Virginia expressed similar concerns in their late seventeenth-century correspondence. Jane Metcalfe, widow of merchant Gilbert Metcalfe, wrote from London to her son, a planter in Virginia, warning him that his wife should

TABLE 6.1   THE METCALFE NETWORK: THE CHILDREN OF JANE AND GILBERT
METCALFE, LONDON MERCHANT

GILBERT JR.	ANNE	JANE	MARY	RICHARD	m.	ANNE (STONE)
Jamaica		m. Ambrose Talbott	m. Samuel	Virginia		Metcalfe
merchant		London merchant	Remington	merchant		Barrow
				Gilbert Metcalfe III		

understand how to run their family business. In language that makes her
statement sound like a biblical Eleventh Commandment, Jane Metcalfe
warned her son in a 1697 letter, "thou would not keep thy wife ignorant of
thy affairs." Richard should teach his wife, and "informe hur Judgement, and
advise with hur in all matters of moment indevouering to [involve?] hur in
busines." Jane understood the limitations her daughter-in-law faced in
learning the business, but assumed these were related not to Anne's inferior-
ity or necessary submission to her husband, but the practical context that
Anne only participated "as hur family occasions and the strength of hur as is
so often breading and bareing of Children will Permit." As a warning, Jane
Metcalfe prefaced her statement by giving Richard's sister as an example of a
poor widow who had been held in ignorance during her marriage: "Sister
[Jane] Talbott" reaped the "sad Effects" of her London merchant husband's
not letting her know the circumstances of his business. "She knows to hur
sorrow" the importance of a wife understanding family undertakings. Jane
Metcalfe encouraged her son to be sure his wife and children were provided
with a source of income after his death, "sumthing that may be
Improvement be a suppley to them."[18] The other risk, Jane understood, was
that her daughter-in-law, Anne Metcalfe, faced the possibility she would
have to manage family affairs even during her husband's lifetime if he
needed to return to England to take care of the extended family lawsuit then
underway. In the end, the family did not require him after all because the
English Metcalfes handled the lawsuit without his presence, but Metcalfe's
mother recognized that this was a distinct possibility in transatlantic families.[19] Anne Metcalfe escaped "economic widowhood" because the lawsuit
did not demand her husband to travel, but within a year her fortunes
reversed when he died, leaving her a widow in fact. He did not leave a will,
and Anne Metcalfe took on the administration of the estate and handled
lawsuits related to that administration.[20]

Despite Defoe's and Child's grumblings, Virginia and English merchants'
widows may not have been uniformly disastrous. British historian Linda

Colley argues that shrill defenses of separate spheres emerged at the same time English women moved into wider interests—in the third quarter of the eighteenth century.[21] In America, the demands for educating women to be good at business tasks continued after the War of Independence. American physician and educational theorist Benjamin Rush thought women should be educated in order to teach their citizen sons, but also encouraged women to study practical subjects including English composition and bookkeeping.[22] Rush's rationale for teaching women the practical subjects was that a family with women poorly equipped to undertake family business placed its economic well-being at risk, and conversely, that women's ability to manage trade on both sides of the Atlantic had allowed English and Anglo-American traders to succeed during the seventeenth and eighteenth centuries.

At the end of the eighteenth century, at least one Virginia planter father agreed, and taught his daughter to understand, hands-on the financial operations of marketing tobacco. Colonel Randolph devised an exercise by which his daughter learned the system, giving her two hogsheads of tobacco "as a venture, to purchase dresses and ornaments."[23] Rather than simply purchasing consumer goods for his daughter or providing her a cash allowance with which to acquire the merchandise for herself, Colonel Randolph thought that his daughter should grasp for herself the operation of the transatlantic tobacco trade that provided income to her family and the colony, as well as "dresses and ornaments," to herself. Within an export-based exchange economy, she as plantation mistress (and possibly as planter's widow) would need to understand how to manage her tobacco exports to obtain goods necessary for her household.

The individualistic nature of the *tobacco marks* in identifying goods by a particular person indicates that single women and widows, like male planters, relished the reputation accompanying a good crop. Single and widowed women who exported tobacco in eighteenth-century Virginia and who actively studied their financial affairs managed to retain some rudimentary identification of themselves as producers within this larger scale exchange. One indication of their pride in their own crops was their use of personal marks, early precursors to trademarks, in identifying their casks of export tobacco. Historians have described the significance of the male colonists' social ranking as being founded upon public acknowledgment of their skill as producers: "The planter's self-esteem depended—in part, at least—upon the quality of his tobacco."[24] Quality also affected price, certainly a matter of great importance in its own right to the ever-indebted tidewater planter, and "personal" tobacco marks signified the connection between personal reputation and crop quality. Various records on tobacco shipments indicate that women also used their own marks for identifying their crops; after all, some women were themselves planters, not planters' wives. The Virginia auditor of public accounts listed tobacco exports by the name of the crop's owner, then recorded his or her tobacco mark. Once again, most of the accounts list individual men and occasional collective accounts, but here, too, when the auditor recorded women's exports, their tobacco marks incorporated the women's own initials (see fig. 6.1).[25] These women were not simply continuing to trade under their husbands' names. When the colony tried to determine the proper relief payments to make up for damages that individual planters suffered when their tobacco burned in a public warehouse, the 1756 allocation bill providing a remedy identified both men's and women's tobacco by the owners' initials.[26] The widowed Gertrude Harmanson, a self-taught student of the law, shipped tobacco to her agents in hogsheads marked GH.[27] Hannah Major's tobacco appeared in her local county merchant's accounts under her mark, HM, which she had stamped on the hogsheads.[28] The identification of women with the goods they offered for sale is especially apparent when the colonial authorities linked trade goods to the women who bought and sold them. In a similar manner, in William Beverley's accounts for the rents he collected from his tenants, he recorded that Eliza Vaughan and Edward Lovell paid their rent with a tobacco note from a local warehouse for a crop marked EV, suggesting the pair recorded their tobacco with her mark.[29] Beverley also credited the accounts of three other women with tobacco marked with their respective initials.[30] Containers of goods purchased for consumption in Virginia were also marked this way and a parcel of "biskit" that one woman imported from England was stamped with her own mark.[31]

These marks were taken seriously in the larger public economy: one woman's use of her own tobacco mark when shipping crops from her deceased husband's estate became part of the evidence in a suit between her and her stepchildren.[32] Often, tobacco marks identified a widow's crop as distinct from that of her husband's estate. An exception was Martha Custis's continued use of Daniel Parke Custis's mark even after his death because his estate was left undivided. This was a world where individual women in planter and merchant circles constructed economic personae for themselves, as well as serving as competent traders within their families. Merchant and planter families in the transatlantic trade relied on women to advance the family firms precisely because they developed interests in the economic workings that surrounded them.

Husbands and wives cemented many of these relationships. Within England, women and men who were engaged in colonial trade used marriage as a means to advance their interests. Information about one such early-eighteenth-century alliance emerges from a lawsuit between an English merchant trading to Virginia and his wife.[33] According to the depositions, Thomas Colemore carried on a good trade to Maryland and Virginia for about three years before his marriage and he enjoyed "great reputation or

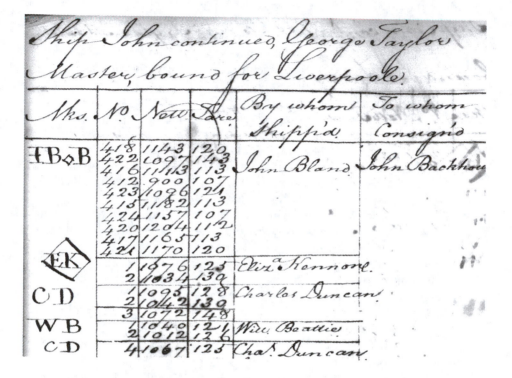

FIGURE 6.1 *Eliza Kennore's Tobacco Mark.* On July 8, 1774, Eliza Kennore consigned her tobacco to John Backhouse on a ship bound for Liverpool, England. Like other planters, she had her two hogsheads (large barrels) containing the tobacco stamped with a distinguishing personal "mark." Kennore's mark consisted of a pattern enclosing her initials, "EK," inside a diamond. In this same 1774 record, two other women, Eliza Fitzhugh and Lydia Jones, were listed as consigning tobacco for export under distinctive marks incorporating their initials. State Records, Auditor of Public Accounts (RG 48), James River Naval Office Records, 1773–1789, APA 301 (Miscellaneous Reel 257), Archives Research Services. Reproduced by permission of the Library of Virginia, Archives Research Services.

credit" in his business.[34] His friends testified that when he married he could expect a wife with a "very considerable fortune." The woman he selected, Ann Milner, was the widow of Isaac Milner, who also had been a merchant trading to Virginia. The Milners were believed to have "considerable effects" in Virginia and Maryland. Neither Ann Milner Colemore's widowhood nor her subsequent remarriage put an end to the Milner enterprise, and a witness described to the court how Ann continued her business in the time between her marriages. John Moore, Thomas's clerk or bookkeeper, testified that he did "verily believe" that during her widowhood Ann carried on the "Trade of a Merchant or trader as such to Virginia and Maryland."[35]

After Thomas Colemore's marriage to Ann, he took on her trade as well as his own. When a dispute developed over the boundaries of the two enterprises, the bookkeeper was called upon to report on Ann's record books from her earlier, independent trade. The bookkeeper believed that Thomas Colemore carried on the trade at Ann's request to recover her dead husband's estate. The Colemore marriage demonstrated how trade alliances and family connections overlapped. This case became visible in the court records only because their marriage of economic convenience failed to meet the standards of behavior deemed acceptable for husbands and wives, even in these circumstances. The couple began fighting when Ann maintained her own circle of friends and continued her less-than-frugal spending and drinking habits, to the chagrin of her new husband. Even when married for business reasons, a couple was expected to live in a "quiet loving or affectionate way." Witnesses testified that this merchant woman carried herself in a "fretfull peevish & uneasy manner" and continued to spend money as she pleased.

Evidence produced in the Colemore lawsuit illuminates how family trading alliances worked. Merging capital and connections allowed two individuals with investments in trade contacts and shared expertise in the field to pool their resources to create a more substantial trading empire. Although the Colemore marriage seemed less successful in fulfilling social demands for an affectionate and profitable union it nevertheless demonstrates how economic interests revolved around family ties while women's roles allowed family businesses to succeed, even in transatlantic enterprises. The family link, not the individualistic enterprise, permitted women and men to succeed in large-scale trade. Men and women both benefited from their family relationships when trading to colonial Virginia.

In Virginia, women in the seventeenth and eighteenth centuries also participated in their families' businesses, though the nature of that participation changed over time. Economic pursuits in colonial Virginia were often family enterprises, requiring contributions from various relatives to make the businesses succeed.[36] In trade, fathers and adult sons of bourgeois or "middling" families formed networks that extended from Britain across to the American colonies and Caribbean islands and on to continental Europe and ultimately into India. Family connections extended farther through the intermarriage of sons and daughters of the mercantile houses, expanding the networks of personal contacts necessary for successful trading endeavors.[37]

When distance separated couples who were establishing their family enterprises, married women took care of the business on both sides of the Atlantic. Englishman John Godfrey preceded his wife, Sara, in emigrating to Virginia and establishing a plantation in the mid-seventeenth century. Before she joined him, Sara went to a London shop and purchased several parcels of goods worth at least £48, including linen, hardware, haberdashery, and grocery items. She took the goods on credit and endorsed the receipt in her own name, noting the "Price of makeing due returnes thereof." Later, when Sara herself eventually emigrated, the shopkeeper gave her a parcel of clothes to take to his brother in the colony. John Godfrey died soon after-ward and Sara married again.[38] Because distance separated the Godfrey fam-ily, Sara Godfrey, a married woman, went to the English store, selected a large quantity of goods, signed her own name to the note recorded in the shopkeeper's account book, and took the goods with her to Virginia, clear evidence that some women knew how to proceed with outfitting themselves materially for the journey. Women left behind on one side of the Atlantic undertook business because the circumstances of early colonization pre-vented men who had already emigrated from convenient access to London stores and credit. Women had more access to the economy in these situa-tions. Their relative power and freedom also benefited the family enterprise as a whole, including the men within those businesses.

Women in England who lived in households connected to Virginia trade also possessed knowledge about transatlantic business matters. Even female shop servants spoke knowledgably of the export business to Virginia. Early in the English colonization of Virginia, Lucretia Laneare, identified as a twenty-four-year old spinster who worked in her master's store, testified to the financial affairs of her master, a citizen and armorer of London, who "sometime us[ed] the trade of bondseller." She reported that her master was creditor to Lawrence Evans, a citizen of London and a carpenter who had worked as a merchant and died in Virginia. Laneare reported on the exact sums that Evans owed her master for goods he purchased in 1637 and 1638. When asked about the extent of her familiarity with the transactions, Laneare responded that she "well knoweth" about the goods and their prices because she had "the use & right of the shopp booke." She examined the books for the court and pointed out the remaining unpaid sums Evans owed her master.[39]

The reverse situation, wherein men traveled to England and left wives in Virginia, also forced women to take on additional responsibilities. In the sev-enteenth century, married women took on family businesses when their husbands were away. When a man planned to leave his home, and perhaps even the colony for an extended period, he designated a substitute to take his place in the business that came to hand in his absence. He recorded his transfer of legal authority by writing a power of attorney indicating who was to act as his representative. Married women who operated business under power of attorney appear in the seventeenth-century records.[40] Sometimes men designated male friends or relatives to take on the business, but often they indicated that their wives were to step into their shoes.[41]

It was hardly surprising, then, that women in merchant families in Virginia assisted with the businesses locally when their husbands were absent. In July 1650, William Moseley, a merchant who had emigrated from Rotterdam to Norfolk, left his colonial home temporarily on business. In his absence, Susan Moseley, his wife, opened a letter from Francis Yeardley that came to the house about the exchange of some goods, and she "made bould to answer it." She accepted the offer of five cows and four oxen from Yeardley, which she agreed to accept in exchange for a gold hat band, some rings, and some other pieces of jewelry set with diamonds, sapphires, rubies, and emeralds she had to offer. Mrs. Moseley also told Yeardley the exact value of every piece of jewelry because they had been made for her when she had gone from Rotterdam to the Hague to select them, and she had paid for them herself.[42] When her husband was absent, Susan Moseley stepped in to settle a substantial transaction involving a number of cattle and some imported jewelry. This required her competence to recognize the value of both the jewelry (which she described in terms of Dutch gilders) and of the Virginia cattle. She also had to have confidence in her own ability to make the exchange, and an assurance that her husband would not protest her opening of his mail and making the trade.

Susan Moseley then described the transaction in individual terms, even though the exchange involved goods owned by the couple. She purchased the cattle herself, she said, because of "my greate wante of Cattll." Since the cows and oxen would arguably benefit both Susan and her husband, she could have phrased it in the plural. She further personalized the exchange by writing in her letter to Yeardley that she was willing to part with her jewelry because she would "rayther your Wife . . . weare them then any gentlewoman I yet know in ye country."[43] More than being an impersonal business transaction, selling jewelry for cattle had personal overtones for Mrs. Moseley.

In the eighteenth century, merchant families proposed alliances between their children and the daughters of planters. In 1731 a Mrs. Parke Pepper, the wife of a London merchant, proposed to Daniel Parke that her son marry his daughter. In this instance, the proposed alliance did not take place and Parke claimed, "I do not remember that I expressed anything of matching my daughter to any one." The prospective bride had some say in her own prospective marriage and Parke admitted to Pepper that his daugh-

ter already had been engaged to another man, "much against my inclination, and so near, that the wedding-clothes were made, but it is all over now,
and she protests she will never marry him or any one else."[44]

Other eighteenth-century marriage negotiations succeeded. English
merchant John Norton Sr. married a Virginia bride, Courtenay Walker, in
1743, during his stay in the colony. As a result of his marriage to Walker,
Norton opened an "extensive and useful" network of in-laws in the process.
He maintained these links even after his return to London to direct the family's enterprises from the metropolis.[45] Norton's company, later John Norton
and Sons, eventually grew to include several generations situated on both
sides of the Atlantic. The Nortons accepted tobacco from Virginia planters
and, in return, supplied their customers with the goods they needed and
wanted from England. The Walker-Norton alliance established this family,
and it became significant during the late colonial period and into the war
years. Because extensive letters and records from the Nortons survive, this
family is important to understanding the workings of family firms, it will
thus be discussed in greater detail throughout the rest of this chapter.

Once a man made a successful marriage alliance, men who were starting out in business publicized their new connections. In 1725, Thomas Cabel
of the eastern shore of Virginia attempted to advance his career in transatlantic trade by introducing himself as the husband of Sorrowful Margaret
Custis Kendall, who came from a prominent family. In establishing his credentials, Cabel told John Waple in London that he was willing to accept con-
signments and offered his new in-laws as references to his abilities, informing Waple, "My wife's relations are the greatest Shippers in the Country and
they all aim to have a great respect for me, they at present ship their
Tob[acc]o to Mr. Parry...."[46] By invoking his links to his wife's family he
hoped to benefit from their reputation and influence. The practice of establishing trading links by marriage continued through the middle of the eighteenth century and John Norton's son, John Hatley Norton, followed in his
father's footsteps by marrying a Virginian, the daughter of a prominent official, in 1772. He was congratulated for making an alliance that would be
"very beneficial" to his business.[47]

Marriage among families with trading interests in the colonies allowed
merchants to increase their capital as well as to expand their interests and
strengthen kin-based networks. The full significance of these alliances mattered not only because of the kinship webs they created between buyers and
sellers, but also because merchant women cultivated links in what Jacob
Price has identified as the "intensely personal atmosphere of business in
colonial Virginia."[48]

Women in mercantile families were clearly significant in solidifying family
connections between fathers and sons-in-law, but women's roles in the trad-

ing ventures extended well beyond being passive links for ratifying alliances for extended families; they also negotiated with prospective customers or suppliers to improve business. Women provided their skills and worked to advance the interests of the family businesses by lobbying with acquaintances to create new networks among families. At the simplest level, women in trading families maintained business friendship ties among themselves. Lucy Armistead encouraged her close friend, Marianna Hunter, of the Hunter trading network, to cultivate her alliance with Armistead's "Aunt Norton" from John Norton and Sons while Hunter resided in London on an extended buying trip and visit to her father.[49] Some women were still more active in advancing the careers of men in their families, as is apparent in a 1731 letter describing Jacob Walker's attempts to establish a business relationship with William Beverley of Beverley Park. Anne Walker's dead husband had been the family's link to Mary Latané, a cousin to Beverley, and Anne Walker cultivated that older alliance when she wanted to place her other male relatives within a successful economic network. Jacob wrote directly to William Beverley to offer his proposal for a business connection, while his mother Anne Walker advocated on her son's behalf by writing to Mary Latané who, as a third party, could act as intermediary and put in a good word for Jacob Walker when speaking to William Beverley. Anne Walker, in her letter advancing her son, mostly discussed her own family and their circumstances. The tone suggests that the two women corresponded infrequently, at best. However, in the final paragraph of the letter she lobbied for her son's business prospects, telling Latané that her son would be willing to act as agent for Beverley in Hampton and to "be his customer if they agree." Walker added the warning that if Beverley "stir[red] not" all would be "lost" for her son's business.[50]

Men depended upon family connections to supply them with capital for their businesses. The Blaws-Hansford family provides an example of how a man needed his female relative's backing to make his business succeed. Mr Blaws drew on the financial support of his sister, Miss Blaws (later Mrs. Hansford). In 1749, Mr. Blaws asked his sister for even greater assistance, requesting that he be allowed to bring her "name into the Trade."[51] The full extent of Mrs. Hansford's obligations was contested once Mr. Blaws died, when some of the estate's creditors demanded that Mrs. Hansford pay the debts. Mrs. Hansford's husband insisted that "His Wife has allways denied it [her participation in the partnership] to him before and since their Marriage" and that he would pay the debts only if the creditor could produce a letter from Mrs. Hansford proving that she was a partner. Mr. Hansford claimed that his wife had only lent Mr. Blaws £600 on bond and, in fact, the estate owed the Hansfords money as repayment for that bond.

One Blaws creditor, a Norfolk merchant named Charles Steuart, insisted that Mrs. Hansford should be held accountable for the debt because "It was generally believed that she was concerned in Trade with him."[52] Steuart never mentioned Mrs. Hansford as a possible witness in the case, suggesting that either she had died or her husband had taken over her business entirely. What remained unremarkeable in the dispute was that a sister might back her brother directly in a business or that she could be involved on an even more active level. Steuart seemed confident the sum could be recovered precisely because he had several witnesses, including the Blaw's clerk, who could vouch that the brother and sister were "concerned together in Trade."[53] Business was a family matter drawing on the resources of both women and men to make a success of an enterprise. Mr Blaws appeared to be a ruggedly individualistic capitalist, but he was only able to do so with, at least, a generous loan from a female family member and, at most, his sister's support as a partner in trade.

In the eighteenth century, trading families depended on women to solidify links through personal or written contact with firms' suppliers or customers. Martha Goosley of Yorktown exchanged letters with John Norton's firm during the 1760s and 1770s, promoting the interests of her own son, who was captain of a ship transporting tobacco from Virginia to Britain and trading in the West Indies. Goosley sent gifts of hominy and ham to Courtenay Norton, John Norton's wife, who lived in London. Goosley exchanged a lively set of letters with the Nortons that were laced with humor, and she kept the Nortons up to date on public affairs, Virginia prices, and juicy gossip about Yorktown's residents' foibles. In commenting on a recent May to December marriage in 1769, she facetiously asked, "Pray why may not an old Man afflicted with the Gout have the Pleasure of a fine hand to rub his feet and warm his flannells[.] Comfortable amuesement you will say for a girl of fifteen but She is to have a Chariot and there is to be no Padlock but upon her mind."[54] Despite her acerbic humor (she was more often the butt of her own jokes), her correspondence was intended to advance the economic interests of herself and her son.[55]

London merchants like the Nortons received other recommendations for contacts from women. In 1768, John Norton received a new client, William Burton, by way of a recommendation from a Virginian who assured Norton that the new shipper would be a good risk. The recommender offered as credentials the planters' family relationship—Burton's daughter had married the son of Mrs. Savage, who was kin to the recommender.[56] Norton himself had earlier relied for business on his friends, who were the relatives of a certain Captain Lilly, when shipping tobacco.[57] Even during the uncertainties of 1780, Miss Tucker, a client of the Nortons, recommended merchants as correspondents to her male and female friends. Miss Tucker described herself as a "Bird of Passage" and was confused about where she belonged in the midst of the Revolution, but she still lobbied on behalf of her friends.[58]

Both men and women relied on family connections to improve their business. When Mann Page sent an order to John Norton, he requested that certain goods be purchased from Mrs. Lucy Randolph; "she is a Relation," he explained, "& has solicited that she may be employed." His wife specifically encouraged patronage of Lucy Randolph's business.[59] In this instance, Page drew on family ties, bypassing another, established, pattern of trade. Here, too, family connections benefited women in business by placing them within a network of suppliers and customers.[60]

Young women could receive recommendations this way as well. In 1700, Jane Metcalfe recommended an English woman she described as "of good friends, and well bread yet vere humble and good humered" to work in her widowed daughter-in-law's Virginia home.[61] In 1770, a young girl was recommended for work through a network that included the women of the families. In this instance, Anne Matthews wrote from Virginia on behalf of her motherless granddaughter, who refused to live with her father and stepmother, in hopes that either the merchant or his wife could make contact with family members in England. There, the girl could be employed in one of the "Many prittey traids" deemed suitable for her.[62] For Anne Matthews, the women in the English merchant's family provided a suitable connection for the advancement of children in the next generation. In this instance, the merchant's wife had lived in Virginia and Matthews could name specific common acquaintances who linked Matthews' granddaughter to the merchant family, drawing on personal connections to achieve her goals.[63]

Before leaving England to set up a shop in Virginia, Charlotte Dickson, the mother of an adolescent boy, worked to forge ties with John Norton and Sons and to establish a business she could eventually turn over to her son, Beverley Dickson. Although she planned that her son, would eventually take an active hand in the business, Charlotte Dickson made the initial contact with John Norton in London before she and her son departed England for Virginia. Concerned about Beverley Dickson's present pursuits perhaps as much as his future, Charlotte confided she thought he would "better be in some Busyness than Idly spending" his time in less productive endeavors. In order to house their store, Beverley secured two rooms in a brick house and within a year mother and son had purchased a house on Williamsburg's main street, "near the Capitol the most convenient in Town for the Store." She secured the financing and directed where remaining funds should be invested. She ordered goods and promised future orders if sales were good and indicated which London wholesalers were unacceptable to her business. While Beverley was still a minor his mother remained the head of the firm. Once he came of age, Beverley wrote to the Nortons informing them that he and his mother were now "in partnership." Charlotte Dickson was willing to launch her son in business and give him increasing responsibility in the firm, but, like the Nortons' own arrangement, also chose to retain an active hand in the multigenerational family business.[64]

Virginia women also knew enough about the family businesses to offer testimony in court concerning outstanding debts. In 1751, "Samuel Dyer and Sarah his wife" petitioned the York County Court to recover twenty-nine shillings due by account from Gideon Marr. In this case, Samuel Dyer offered no testimony, but the court called Sarah, who proved the account by her oath alone.[65] In the interest of advancing businesses, families posted individuals, many with power of attorney, at different locations in their trade networks. As a result, some women took over segments of the trade, even managing portions of transatlantic trade networks. The mechanics of creating a successful trade network required drawing on the efforts and expertise of extended families and members of both sexes.

Sisters and mothers of traders, as well as wives in merchant families, could serve as pivot points in transatlantic trade, sending goods from England to provide for Virginia consumers and keeping accounts in the family exchanges. In the 1690s, Jane Metcalfe directed the economic affairs of her children on both sides of the Atlantic from her home base in London. In 1694, she apologized to Richard, her son in Virginia, for her inability to pave his way to export his tobacco to English merchants, but her "acquantance with and Interest in Virginia Traiders" in London had declined with the death of one of her former contacts and her estrangement from another. Metcalfe encouraged her son to consign his tobacco that year to a Bristol merchant and made reference to a particularly good contact who "is as honest a man as leves." Shipping to Bristol had the added advantage, she informed her son, of arriving faster and safer than if the tobacco were shipped to London. She expected to make contacts for her son, and within four years she connected with a London merchant, Micajah Perry, and encouraged her son to consign his tobacco to Perry if the crop proved of high enough quality.[66] In addition to making connections for Richard from her home base, Jane Metcalfe handled bills of exchange her son sent her, though she complained that she could not always raise the money to pay them on demand.[67]

Metcalfe encouraged her daughter, whom she referred to as "thy Sis Talbett," in her business, too. Mrs. Talbett, who lived in England, had been widowed with four children, and the estate she hoped to inherit was tied up in a lawsuit. In the meantime, she set up a business selling "hood carses of all sorts" and hoped to expand into selling fine linen and laces when she had the capital to do so. Nevertheless, she feared she would be unsuccessful, in which case she planned to go to Virginia to purchase her brother's Potomac plantation if he still offered it for sale, promising to pay the same price for it as any stranger would. In the meantime, Jane Metcalfe suggested that her son send a hogshead or two of tobacco to his sister to encourage her in her business. Mrs. Talbett would be "vere Just and Careful" in selling them and providing the return goods according to his order. The Talbetts had managed some of Richard Metcalfe's business before Mr. Talbett died, and Jane Metcalfe was not above snooping in the accounts to find out about tobacco sold previously and the fate of a still sent to Virginia for Metcalfe. The French, unfortunately, captured the still.[68] Thus, while Virginia women in trading families certainly served as "deputy husbands," their roles were not limited to working only with spouses. Virginia men also found their sisters and their mothers and their aunts taking a hand in running affairs.[69]

The records of several other families with transatlantic business interests demonstrate how responsibilities were assigned among various family members and show that women had knowledge about aspects of trade. Between 1712 and 1719, John Opie wrote from Virginia to his sisters Susanna Opie and Eleanor Harte, who lived in Bristol, requesting them to take care of his business in England.[70] A further connection cemented this particular family network because one of the ship captains with whom John Opie traded was Captain Harte. In letters in 1712 John Opie asked Eleanor Harte to balance his accounts and receive payment on a debt owed him. If there was any money left out of the obligations he owed, he wished her to use it to purchase both coarse and fine linen to send him. In another letter several years later, he requested that his sisters send two grades of linen to him in the colony.[71]

Forty years later, Roger Atkinson, who traded on the James River in the 1760s and 1770s relied on his sister in his business. Atkinson himself based his operations in Appomattox and corresponded with his sister, who lived in London, writing to ask for her assistance in several matters. In 1769 he sent her bills of exchange for the sizable sum of £162.1.10 sterling by way of his ship's captain and asked her to make payments out of the receipts. In the context of these financial conditions, having a trustworthy contact in England benefited Atkinson's business. Atkinson described specific debts to be paid to creditors, but also left his sister with discretionary power to pay any other debts "that I cannot recollect, for I am now f[ro]m. home."[72] Atkinson also counted on his sister to maintain the social connections that cemented business associations. In 1770, he forwarded to her fifteen hams for distribution among the people he listed, but added that she could give the hams to others "as you think proper," suggesting he trusted her prudence in allocating the gifts.[73] The following year, he sent flour as well as hams, which he requested her to "present as formerly." At the same time, he sent payments by way of the captain and asked his sister to pay his supplier of felt hats.[74] In the Goosley family during the 1770s a mother and son worked as another transatlantic team. For them, the geography was reversed and the widowed Martha Goosley, based in Yorktown, managed family lawsuits while her son, a ship captain, was en route to or in London.[75]

Once family networks had been established, women maintained the ties that bound cooperating interests together across generations as well as across distance. Family members could work as interchangeable elements within the operations of the firms, allowing men to represent the collective undertaking under most circumstances, but placing women in the position of taking over when necessary. When men left home to pursue their interests, women could handle some of the business, and after the death of a husband a widow could step in, leaving the family trade under the direction of a woman in precisely the same manner Child described in his warning to English trading families. An example of how women moved into the leadership of the transatlantic trade emerges from exchanges between the Durleys of Virginia and their agents in London, the Parkers, during the 1740s.

William Durley traded from Nansemond, Virginia, but traveled to London on business and died there in 1741. This meant his wife was an "economic widow," gaining knowledge about the business even before her husband died. He left no will, but the Prerogative Court of Canterbury granted the administration of the estate to William Parker,[76] attorney of Durley's widow, Mary. A tangled inheritance was further complicated because the Durley family was part of an imperial trade network: William Durley based his operations in Nansemond, Virginia, but his brother had worked out of India. The pivot of the operation was the family agent in London—William Parker—who forwarded news between the brothers. In addition, William Durley had traveled to England to manage the family business.[77] As a result, when Mary Durley's husband died, her responsibilities extended even farther, geographically. Four years earlier, William Durley's brother John had died a bachelor in Calcutta, leaving a will granting his property to William but naming no executor. When William died, the management of both brothers' estates fell to Mary Durley, who remained in Nansemond, Virginia.[78] Mary Durley was left with bills of exchange from India, while her investment portfolio included "India bonds" in the East India Company as well as bank annuities placed out at 4 percent interest.[79] She received help from English attorneys acting on her behalf, and regular information from William Parker on the state of the family's financial condition in England: she regularly asked for accounts from Parker, though she did not always receive them promptly.[80]

Mary Durley corresponded with William Parker, the family's agent in London, and drew substantial sums, in hundreds of pounds sterling, in bills of exchange on Parker. Early in Durley's widowhood, Parker complained about her drawing bills of exchange without granting power of attorney or advising him of it first. Parker maintained a personal as well as a business relationship with the family and enquired about the progress of the Durley children's education.[81] It was Parker who wrote to ask her how to settle her deceased husband's affairs in London, informing her of her husband's debts and making suggestions about what to do with the old furniture he left in his London lodgings at his death.[82] Despite Parker's earlier complaints, he carried on the trade with Mary Durley until his own death.[83]

The issues raised in the settlement of the Durley estates dragged on, and William Parker died leaving his widow, Mary, responsible in England. Mary Parker and Mary Durley continued to corresponded over trade after their husbands died. Mary Parker wrote to Mary Durley in February of 1748 to inform her of William Parker's death and to explain that she had found that accounts left Durley creditor to Parker for the sum of £1251.8.1 In addition, Mary Parker reported that she had paid Mary Durley's bill of exchange to a third party in London. Mary Parker also used her discretion and sold the East India bonds, "thinking it best for your Interest and safety" and applied the £1221 in proceeds toward bank annuities that would provide Mary Durley with the comfortable income of £52 per year. Mary Parker wrote that she would have accounted for the state of another Durley estate at St. Helen's but a continuing lawsuit over that property left the business uncertain. Having accomplished these tasks, Mary Parker launched into an apologetic excuse as to why Mary Durley could no longer depend upon Parker: she had not been well since her husband's death, implying her grief kept her from health. Parker also asked Durley to find another agent, or "friend" in Parker's words, to handle the affairs because she was "to far in Years to be any way serviceable to you."[84] Mary Parker's letter reveals what a London agent's wife or widow might be expected to accomplish for the firm's colonial correspondents: receiving accounts and providing information on the balances, paying off obligations incurred by bills of exchange, and recognizing when and how to buy and sell bonds in global companies or stock in the Bank of England. When Parker requested to be excused from further activities in managing affairs for correspondents, she based her infirmity not on sex but on old age and debilitating grief. Sex, it appears, provided no excuse for shirking obligations to business alliances.

Other merchants seemed to have made similar allowances for grief—but not sex—in dealing with female correspondents in Virginia. Before informing Martha Curtis of the current prices for tobacco sold in England, mechant James Gildart wrote, "[I]f you are pleased to Hon[ou]r. me w[i]th. a Continuance of your Friendship you shall ever find. me Ready to render you the best. Services in my Power," acknowledging her discretionary power to select a new agent with the death of her husband.[85] In 1757, Gildart condoled with Custis on her husband's death and excused her, under the circumstances, for failing to send him a letter with the five hogsheads of tobacco she had shipped him. He attributed her oversight to "the affliction.

you must be under." After she had recovered from her grief, however, Martha Custis's agent expected her to carry on with the business of the tobacco trade. In a similar fashion, John Opie had been willing to make excuses for his English sister's tardy response to his request for her to send him a copy of the accounting of their brother's will and sending the proceeds in the form of a shipment of linen. He had heard she had been ill and this was an adequate reason for her not complying with his request, but he made no excuses for her based on her sex.[86]

Mary Durley's new agents, Tyson and Moore, the men who replaced Mary Parker after she died, used a more blunt tone in corresponding with Durley. They scolded her for not providing Mary Parker with an answer to her request for guidance on how to tie up the loose ends of Durley's accounts.[87] Later, they pointed out that Durley had not sent them a power of attorney yet, and they still paid the bills of exchange totaling £200 drawn on them even though they believed themselves legally exempt from responsibility for the debts.[88] By November 1753, Mary Durley's letter added the names of her son Horatio Durley and son-in-law Matthew Godrich to the signatures when corresponding with James Stockdale, a merchant receiving her orders in Liverpool.[89] She still made payments through Tyson and More, but by adding her son's and son-in-law's names to the letters she may have been preparing to turn the correspondence over to them and gradually introduce them to the workings of transatlantic trade. The closing greeting given in terms of "for my son & son-in-law" indicates she still considered herself the letter's primary author, but the fact that they could sign their own names while she merely made her mark suggests that their skills would allow them to take a more active hand in the complexities of transatlantic trade in the late eighteenth century.

Susanna Minvielle, another widow with trade to Virginia but based in Barbados, waited longer to turn her business over to her son. She conducted trade to Virginia through Charles Steuart, her contact in Norfolk, Virginia.[90] She accepted the responsibility for sizable exchanges in slaves and goods, leaving her son to take over the business singlehandedly only after she died.[91] Minvielle recommended Steuart to associates in Barbados and collectively "Messrs" [sic] Minvielle, Moore, De Piza, and Massiah sent forty-eight slaves to Virginia, selling them for £26 each, according to a letter of July 1751. Steuart assured Susanna Minvielle "& them in Co[mpany]" with her that slaves sold for a high price in Virginia that year because tobacco prices had been high and there had been "but small importations of Negroes," making slaves in great demand.[92]

In the 1751 correspondence, Steuart thanked Minvielle and hoped she would do further business with him before providing her with local prices for corn, pork, tallow, rum, sugar, molasses, and wine—merchandise characteristic of the north- and southbound trade between the Chesapeake area and the Caribbean. Letters to "Madam & Co." in subsequent years advised Susanna and her associates of the state of the markets in Virginia for slaves, foods, sugar, and rum. The greeting "Madam" demonstrates that they publicly acknowledged her as the head of the company. They also kept her informed of the details of trade: in a January 1752 letter to "Mrs. Minvielle & son," Steuart reported that the demand for grain in Madeira and Europe had dropped off, while spices obtained poor returns because of the "great plenty." Slaves, however, remained in demand. He enclosed a list of current commodity prices.[93]

In further letters in 1752 Steuart tried to encourage Susanna Minvielle to ship more slaves. He informed her he had corn, pork "&c" ready to ship south to her and gave her advice on how to deal in the slaves.[94] In his March correspondence, Steuart further encouraged her to ship slaves, informing Minvielle of news from Bristol that Virginians were ordering a large number of slaves directly from Africa, but also claiming that this should not dissuade her from sending her own slaves up from the West Indies because slaves brought directly from Africa tended to arrive in poor health, "being late in the Seas or [subject to] some misfortune" by which less than half the number of slaves "expected or wanted" ever arrived. The brutality of the Middle Passage worked to Minvielle's economic advantage.

Clearly a woman within this trade network could profit directly from the slave trade. Minvielle was unusual in the magnitude of her slave trading, but other women also dealt in slaves. Steuart corresponded with a Mrs. Vinncent about some business, including the sale of a slave, and seemed to expect her to understand the context of the transaction.[95] European-American women benefited from the system of bound labor that allowed themselves and their families to exploit the labor of slaves, and they reaped profits from the sales of slaves to planters.

Slaves seemed to provide a dependable source of income to Minvielle: while they provided a profit, other Barbadian goods fared unevenly on the mainland. The exported rum sold slowly in Virginia; in November 1752, Steuart reported that most of Minvielle's rum remained unsold, leaving her with a total unpaid balance at that point of £100.[96] A month later Steuart reported that the rum still sold slowly.[97] Steuart explained the workings of the credit networks in his letters. When Barbadians reduced their demand for the goods Steuart sold, he explained that he planned to expand his sales of wine to the island. He asked her to send the proceeds from the sales to him in sugar.[98] In later letters concerning the wine sales he asked her to comply with orders from a third party in Barbados. In addition, he requested that she advise two merchants in London of her plans for shipping on various accounts, including his own.[99] As all of this correspondence shows, Mrs. Minvielle was expected to have a wide knowledge of trade in order to succeed in the business.

The firm Steuart called "Madam & Co.," or Mrs. Minvielle and Son, finally came to an end in the middle of 1753 with the death of Susanna Minvielle. Steuart wrote a letter of condolence to Elias Minvielle, but also to express his interest in continuing to trade with the new head of the Minvielle family enterprise and even to "enlarge [Minvielle's] interest here." As usual, Steuart reported the prices of rum and sugar.[100] What is striking about the letter is that Steuart, by pointing out his desire to continue to do business with Elias Minvielle, allowed that Elias might choose to take his business elsewhere now that he was the single Minvielle family member involved in operating the business. This suggests that at least as a formality Steuart acknowledged that the mother and son might have differences of opinion in deciding how to run their business, and only with the death of Mrs. Minvielle could the son expect to have the deciding voice in the company. Until then, Mrs. Minvielle had chosen how to operate the business.

Other widows who carried on family businesses knew enough about the economy in general, and assessing the proper price for the quality of goods offered in particular, to complain when they thought suppliers cheated them. In 1716, Mary Anderson informed her London factors, Micajah and Richard Perry, that her husband, Captain Robert Anderson, had died and that she, along with her two brothers, were responsible for the family's business. For the next two years, the three corresponded with their merchants. Mary Anderson sent tobacco on consignment to the Perrys for the English market. No helpless widow, within two months she began complaining to her English merchants that the goods and servants they sent to Virginia failed to meet her requirements. The "Supposed Taylor" did not know "so much as to handle a Needle much less to Work or Cutt out," leading her to believe he had never worked as a tailor and that sending him was "a trick putt upon you, upon me" and upon the reputed tailor himself. In addition she disapproved of the quality of cloth the Perrys sent and pointed out the printed calico for which she was charged a high price was "realy very Cours" leading her to believe she would never be able to sell it at a profit over the price the Perrys charged for it wholesale. As for the striped holland cloth, she was "positive" she could not sell it for the cost to her. As a result, she hoped they would "abate something" on the prices since they were "very Extortionable." She attempted to be diplomatic about the reasons why she was being sold inferior goods at high prices and pointed out the Perrys must have been unaware that their suppliers sent poor quality cloth and an untrained tailor and that the Perrys themselves were being cheated by a Mr. Mackouall. The letter indicates that slightly over a year after she informed the Perrys that she was taking over the family's business, she knew enough about the quality and prices of goods to be able to report her dissatisfaction and demand a rebate on her accounts.[101] Mary wrote many letters discussing the Anderson tobacco trade to England and had them cosigned by her brothers-in-law David and Matthew Anderson; intriguingly, Mary wrote the letter complaining about the cloth on her own.

In addition to the continuity of a widow taking over a family business, or a female relative operating the business from one terminal on the family's trade web, another pattern of female economic activity within families existed in the eighteenth century. Within established transatlantic mercantile enterprises, women could undertake distinctive tasks that benefited the families' endeavors. Women depended upon family connections, but within family-owned businesses women benefited the companies by bringing special skills, perceived as distinctively female, to the advancement of the enterprises.

For certain kinds of goods, colonists trusted women to make their purchases. Mrs. Scott, a member of the household of Governor John Murray, Earl of Dunmore, instructed Dunmore's London merchant that she wanted a Mrs. Anderson to buy her London goods. Fashion did not seem to be Mrs. Scott's primary concern when acquiring her largely pink-and-white wardrobe, perhaps because of her stout figure. When ordering stays (undergarments similar to corsets) she stated that she didn't mind "the fashion" but wanted them "made easy & full in the Stomick."[102] Instead, she wanted the purchaser and "your Sister" to buy the goods "in the cheepest way for me," suggesting women could be counted upon for frugal as well as fashionable transactions.[103]

In the eighteenth century, women in mercantile families still acted as agents in family businesses when necessary, as they had in the seventeenth century. Increasingly they took on the additional responsibility of conducting specialized transactions, even in local trade within the colony, in order to build the customer base. Mary (Harrison) Gordon usually traveled to the family stores with her husband, and on rarer occasions with her sister-in-law or by herself.[104] Once she went to the store to obtain mourning goods for a bereaved family after she received word from a messenger of a death in the neighborhood;[105] she also traveled to the home of another woman to purchase butter, suggesting her importance to the family in both acquiring and selling goods as well as the significance of her presence in cementing the relationship between herself as representative for the merchant family and women in the consumer families.[106] In much the same way, Courtenay Norton shopped for small items, purchasing goods locally in other Virginia stores for customers of the Norton business when she thought the merchandise would suit them. In addition to selecting goods on her husband's account, Mrs. Norton chose a piece of "fine Irish Linen," measuring twenty-six yards, for Mr. George Walker.[107] The fabric was a fairly expensive item, and Walker may have considered Mrs. Norton a better judge of the fabric's quality than he would have been. As in ordinary keeping, a merchant woman's selection of fabrics was an extension of her domestic activities into a wider world of economic exchanges.

Female members of the leading mercantile houses trading in Virginia acted as buyers of commodities to be shipped from England—an extension of the work of single women who also traded upon their expertise as milliners, advertising the fashionable merchandise available in their establishments. Because popular culture in late-eighteenth-century England linked women with consumption and associated them with elevated taste it is not surprising, then, that colonists depended on women in trading families to select appropriate merchandise for domestic use in Virginia.[108] Women within family businesses acted as arbiters of taste when powerful mercantile houses expanded the choice and increased the quantity of fashionable goods offered to colonists.

Women's roles within businesses are also visible in the correspondence from tobacco planters who shipped crops to their agents, who then sold them in Britain and in turn sent consumer goods back to the Virginians. Profit could be made in acting as agents in England and Scotland. The Scots Cunninghame stores added a markup of 65 to 75 percent to goods sold to Virginians in the 1760s. T. M. Devine observes that "great care was always taken in ensuring that storekeepers procured articles to suit planter preferences" and they suffered reprimands when they submitted vaguely worded requests.[109] Maintaining a successful business required obtaining a good price for tobacco in Britain and sending pleasing merchandise in return. It was in the second half of this equation that women were particularly significant.

The segment of the trade from Britain to America had to be managed carefully for the merchants to succeed. Tobacco exported from the Chesapeake was a bulk product requiring considerable cargo space on ships bound for England, while the return imports to America of cloth and metals were less bulky.[110] Given the fluctuating prices on tobacco, the return portion of the trade might well offer the margin of profitability to the merchant. Here, expertise in selecting goods would be an advantage to the merchants, as Mrs. Anderson's critique of the Perry Company's slipshod selections has already shown us. Robert Bristow of London suggested as much when writing to Thomas Booth in Virginia in 1718 about the business. Bristow commented, "The Buying & sending of Goods being the most troublesome part of ye Virginia business whoever does yt ought to sell your Tobacco" and offered to do both for Booth.[111] Managing the westward exports effectively was a significant, and often burdensome, aspect of commercial success. Textiles and clothing were an important part of the export business. It has been estimated that textile products made up over half of the goods exported from England to the colonies. During the late colonial period, colonists spent about 9 percent of their per capita income on textile products imported from Great Britain and another 1 percent on related haber-dashery items and accessories.[112] Analysis of Virginia country store account books from Southside—the region south of the James River—reveals that fabrics and notions (the thread and goods associated with clothing produc-tion) made up 40 percent of total sales in the 1750s and 65 percent of sales in the 1760s.[113]

The significance of finished goods—and textiles and clothing in particular—provides the context for recognizing the importance of women's participation in family enterprises. Women of merchant families focused much of their attention on acquiring goods—especially clothing—to send to the colonies, and cloth and clothing were significant elements in the colo-nial import trade. In the competition for business in nearby Maryland, James Russell's enterprise succeeded in becoming "the biggest if not the richest trading to the Chesapeake" in the 1760s by operating a store and con-signment house.[114] This he accomplished by cultivating a reputation for sell-ing tobacco at a good price, but also because he sent back good merchan-dise. Russell's English exports were of the latest fashion, in part because of his frequent shipments, allowing for goods in current taste. But Russell also benefited from the skill with which his wife, Ann Lee Russell, selected goods that pleased the colonial customers. An Annapolis shopkeeper wrote that the goods Ann Russell sent became "the Standard of Taste" in Annapolis.[115]

While newspaper advertisements stressed that goods offered for sale were of the latest fashion, Virginians' tastes seemed to have lagged some-what behind those of England. In sending goods to Thomas Booth, his English merchant apologized for not sending "Drugget" curtains as requested, but such curtains were no longer "made or used" now that "ours all...run into printed stuffs...." He then described other suppliers of con-sumer goods as "very well liked in Virg[ini]a."[116]

Female preferences set the fashion in clothing for Virginians. Timeliness was an essential component of fashionability, and milliner Catherine Rathell boasted that she carried "the newest Fashion...and purchased since *July* last, from the eminent Shops." Who selected the goods was as significant as the timeliness of the merchandise; Rathell advertised that "genteel Assortment of MERCERY, MILLINERY, JEWELLERY, &c...being chosen by herself," and her expertise in fashionable goods was a selling point.[117] Occasionally she allowed her supplier to select the goods; for example, in one instance, she merely asked for gentlemen's sleeve buttons "of the Neatest New fashion."[118] But in others she stated what she wanted and the particular merchants in London who would supply the goods: Sword Canes from Mr. Masden in Fleet Street "Such as I had from him" and other goods from Messrs. Wooley & Hamings at No 137 in Cheapside.[119] Even when she wrote to John Norton and Sons to supply her, she gave specific instructions describing exactly what she wanted and who should supply the goods.

FIGURE 6.2 *Frances Norton's Dress.* Silk Gown and Matching Petticoat. "By tradition made in England in 1778 and brought to Virginia by Mrs. Frances Norton, daughter of Courtenay Norton."[125] Reproduced by permission of the Colonial Williamsburg Foundation. Accession G1946–133, 1953–171, 2.

The correspondence between customers and merchants demonstrates the commercial activities of married women who have eluded historians who dwelt excessively on legal status at the expense of understanding actual pursuits. Robert Cary and Company served Daniel Parke Custis and later his widow Martha (Dandridge) Custis (Washington),[120] but a receipt of goods sent to Custis indicates that Mrs. Cary purchased some of the items.[121] Elizabeth Perry made selections and offered advice to a Mrs. Jones on clothing. Perry explained that she bought a more fashionable "Parkey Burdet" instead of the originally requested fabric because she "[th]ought a chery dery had too mean a look," or too down-market an image for her Virginia customer. The substitution was more expensive than the original order. Perry was also unable to find the requested "sprigg'd muslin...there is no such thing."[122] Perry's letter is interesting in that it is directly between the female purchaser and female buyer at a time when much of the correspondence regarding purchases was made through male family members.

Virginia-born English resident Courtenay Norton served as a purchaser of goods for her family's firm, John Norton and Sons. One Virginia woman, when ordering china through the Nortons in 1771, requested specifically that Mrs. Norton choose the dishes.[123] This is significant because during the Revolutionary War era ceramic increasingly replaced pewter for drinking vessels. Ceramic teacups became an increasingly common consumer item even for "middling" level colonists, and fashions and technologies were subject to rapid changes. A range of merchandise, from cheap to expensive (some cups and saucers cost the equivalent of a week's wages of a laborer), was offered to Virginia customers. Even less prosperous Virginians sought to "live in the vogue of the cosmopolitan center of the British empire" by acquiring and using newly available creamware and patterned ceramics.[124] In this context of specialized consumer demand for the latest fashions of goods that displayed a family's social ranking and economic position, a customer could turn to Mrs. Norton's taste in goods available in England. (For some indication of the Norton women's choice in fashion items, see fig. 6.2). The family business benefited from her specialized function within the firm.

Mrs. Norton also acquired supplies at the wholesale level when Charlotte Dickson set up a Williamsburg store with her son Beverley. Then, the Dicksons ordered their goods from the firm of John Norton and Sons and, in thanking the Nortons for supplying them with merchandise that sold quickly, Beverley wrote that they were "oblig'd" to Mrs Norton "for choosing her things so well."[126]

Mrs. Norton occasionally ran into communications difficulties because of the distance between the London and Yorktown bases of operation. After the Dicksons set up their Williamsburg shop they asked Mrs. Norton to get a pair of stays made to the same measurements as those on file with an English supplier. A notation on Dickson's letter indicated that the stay maker had died in the meantime and no measure was available. The following summer the Dicksons sent a new set of measurements and specific instructions to buy from a particular London firm. Courtenay Norton, after receiving complaints in 1773 about the millinery goods she had shipped to her son John Hatley Norton, asked him to be more careful in indicating price, quality, and sizes of goods he ordered. By 1775 she seemed more annoyed about his requests and wrote him "I Must now take the liberty to say you are not Explicit enough in regard to your goods without which it is impossible to execute your orders." Until he forwarded information about where the merchandise should be sent, she was stuck storing it in a closet.[127]

Sometimes Courtenay Norton's efforts amounted to customer relations work. When Rebecca Chamberlayne of New Kent, Virginia, wrote to complain that "the Goods sent this Year are in general bad," she gave instructions that she would be "much obliged to Mrs. Norton if she will be at the trouble of choosing" the suit of worked muslin Chamberlayne listed on an enclosed invoice.[128] A year earlier Chamberlayne had offered her "compliments to Mrs. Norton" and thanks to her "for the trouble she took in the choice of my Petticoat."[129] Mann Page, an elite planter and customer of the Nortons, enclosed with an invoice of new goods to be sent from London that "My Wife desires her compliments to Mrs. Norton and returns her Thanks for the trouble she was at in buying her Things last year," indicating that Courtenay Norton had selected goods for Mary Page, too.[130] The letter also suggests the competition among sellers of fashionable goods, because after thanking Mrs. Norton, Mann Page wrote that despite Norton's work in the past year, his wife had decided to send her business to Lucy Randolph, a "Relation."

Mrs. Norton's taste was further put to use for the family when her son John Hatley Norton, who had been placed in Yorktown to serve in the London-based family network, took a Virginia bride and the London family sent goods to the colony to help the couple set up housekeeping. George Norton wrote to his brother that the goods had been sent and "my Mother has chosen every thing that required her judgement in, to which is added an assortment of grocery."[131] She suggested that John Hatley Norton distribute a new medicine, Dr. Norrice's drops, through one of the Nortons' regular correspondents, Mrs. Martha Goosley, and her network of "patience." Martha Goosley could then report back to Courtenay Norton about the drug's efficacy.[132] This suggests that drugs, too, had a fashionability and were considered part of women's responsibility. This is consistent with "receipts" for home remedies being included in women's cookbooks in the eighteenth century.

Mrs. Norton's eye and expertise benefited John Norton and Sons again in 1772 when Catherine Rathell sought to establish a larger account with the merchant house because of the expansion of her millinery business to a prominent location in Williamsburg. Rathell wrote that she made her decision to buy goods for her shop through the Nortons because of "the very great Character I have had from Many of My Acquaintance of Mrs. Nortons great Carefullness in buying & Sending the Neatest and Cheapest goods in, thats sent to Virginia."[133] Rathell's custom was significant enough to deserve separate mention in a summary of Norton orders, and John Norton wrote that she "draws on [us] largely" for goods.[134] Later that year Rathell wrote that she was disappointed in the cost and quality of goods the Nortons sent her and returned "2 Doz[e]n. T[o]upees" she deemed unsalable. Still, she placed another order and asked for the credit for those toupees to be applied to various types of laces, edgings, and gauze and would once more "Esteem it a very particular favor if Mrs. Norton will make a Choice of them for me."[135]

Women within other merchant families also selected the merchandise for their fashion-conscious colonial customers. Virginian Hannah (Lee) Corbin and her household dealt with several British houses, including those of Archibald Ritchie, William Molleson, and James Russell. Corbin was politically astute and well-connected as a sister of Richard Henry Lee and William Lee, but she was also concerned with maintaining up-to-date tastes. In 1772 she received a "Neat fash[iona]ble. dress'd Baby...in a Box" sent with her goods from William Molleson in London (see figs. 6.3 and 6.4).[136] Fashion dolls such as the one Corbin obtained served eighteenth-century merchants as a means of increasing consumption by manipulating taste and encouraging change for the sake of change. Residents in London as well as those in the colonies studied fashion dolls to learn of newest trends in clothing styles.[137] Corbin was apparently sufficiently interested in knowing the latest fashion when selecting her own attire to order a fashion doll and encouraged her daughter's interest in clothing. When Corbin's relative Lucinda Lee visited Hannah's home, Lucinda noted that her cousin, Hannah's granddaughter, "has a quantity of Cloaths. She has put on every day since I have been here a different dress of muslin, and all handsome." Merchants benefited from their customers' desire to be in vogue. Mrs. Molleson had obtained some of the goods sent to Corbin, and included in the bills Mr. Molleson sent to Corbin was one from Frederick Hahn in Covent Garden indicating that Mrs. Molleson placed an order for Hannah Corbin for "a Checkd Lustring Turnd Negligie and Coat Pinkd,... ferret, and Sleeve lining,... [and] a turned Stomacher and knots."[138]

Dealing across a wide geographic region, Mrs. Molleson also selected goods for Maryland customers. Her husband wrote to Captain Charles Ridgely several times commenting that Mrs. Molleson assisted in the choice of certain articles. Mrs. Molleson also sent a message concerning fashionable trimmings to Rebecca (Dorsey) Ridgely, wife of the captain.[139] One of Molleson's suppliers advertised that he made "the Newest Fashion Mantuas & Coats" and a "variety of Trimmings & Hoops in the Newest Taste," among other goods, emphasizing the timeliness of his merchandise. It is no surprise

FIGURE 6.3 *Doll, Augusta Marianna.* English, 1780. Wood, Gesso, Glass Eyes, Real Hair. Accession Misc. 339–1984. Reproduced by Permission of the Victoria and Albert Museum Picture Library, London.

FIGURE 6.4 *Elizabeth Page Holding a Fashionably Dressed Doll.* Painting of Elizabeth and Mann Page, her brother, by John Wollaston. Elizabeth was born in 1751, the daughter of Mann and Ann (Tayloe) Page of Rosewell, Gloucester County, Virginia. She later married Benjamin Harrison, of Prince George County. Accession 1973.16. Reproduced by permission of the Virginia Historical Society.

that female members of merchant families were sent to shop for the Virginia customers when selecting fashions.

Another woman of a merchant house, Mrs. Russell, also patronized Frederick Hahn's store to obtain goods for the family of Martha Tuberville, Hannah's daughter, according to a receipt dated September 14, 1772.[140] Mrs. Russell continued her efforts to acquire pleasing merchandise for clients of James Russell and spent part of September 19, 1772 buying chintz muslin for the Tubervilles from a London linen draper in Cheapside.[141] It is likely that Mrs. Russell did the additional shopping, because the Tuberville accounts for September 1772 indicate that the family was sent a copy of "Raffhealds Cookery." The bill was first written out to "Mrs. Russell, D[ebto]r to T. Cadell," but "Mrs." was scratched out and replaced with "Mr" Russell. Perhaps one placed the order and the other retrieved the book, or Mrs. Russell posted the purchase to an account under Mr. Russell's name. If the latter was true, there may be other purchases made by Mrs. Russell, and other merchant women as well, but posted under a man's name. It is likely that more, rather than less, business was conducted by women in the eighteenth century.

Even when establishing autonomous businesses, women could and did take advantage of family connections. This is hardly surprising—men also benefited from family networks and their relatives in business. One revealing example of the significance of family alliances in the success of a female-owned business is the enterprise of Williamsburg milliner Catherine Rathell, who kept shops in the 1760s and 1770s. Rathell came to Virginia and established herself in trade in Fredericksburg, adding temporary stops in Williamsburg to her calendar so she could offer goods to visitors to the colony's capital during meetings of the assembly. Ultimately she sold goods for "Ladies and Gentlemen" at a permanent shop in Williamsburg.[142]

In her initial commerce, Rathell stressed the fact she dealt only in cash, because, according to an early *Virginia Gazette* advertisement, she was "but lately come into the country, and her continuance here very uncertain."[143] Her dealings also indicate Rathell was a shrewd businesswoman in other respects and not afraid to demonstrate that fact. In discussing her cash-only policy, her advertisement indicated that this really helped her customers because she was able to sell "at a very low advance" and, additionally, she was "contented to make a reasonable profit" rather than gouging her customers. The cash-only policy would work to the advantage of the customers in one other way: the "fall of the exchange [rate] shall be to their benefit," an important consideration when both seller and customer worked within a transatlantic economy based upon multiple currencies.[144] (The exchange rate was fluctuating wildly during the period Rathell established herself in Williamsburg.[145])

Despite her continuing presence in Virginia, Rathell claimed the cash-only policy stemmed from her plans to return "home" to Britain after the

June court to acquire new goods to sell to customers in town when they attended the October meeting of the General Court.[146] Rathell's limited capital, coupled with lack of access to credit, or fear of indebtedness, required her to restrict the credit she in turn could extend to customers and to demand "ready Money only."[147] Her final series of notices in the *Virginia Gazette* indicate that while she only sold goods for cash she must have extended credit earlier, since she demanded "that all who are indebted to me will pay off their Accounts this Meeting." She offered to pay off local creditors as well because she planned to return to England "as soon as I dispose of my Goods (till the Liberty of Importation is allowed)" and as a result was "under the Necessity of not parting with a single Shilling's Worth without Cash."[148]

Rathell's insistence in cash dealing is significant because other late-eighteenth-century Virginia retailers relied upon credit to generate sales. James Soltow has suggested that Rathell demanded cash because she was recently established in business in Virginia and "may have been trying to impress her creditors,"[149] and her correspondence with potential suppliers does stress her policy for payments. For example, she sought to establish a business relationship with John Norton and Sons of London. In requesting goods of the Nortons, she wrote that she had already discussed the prospect of ordering from them with Norton's son, John Hatley Norton, in Yorktown, who had told her, she noted, that he had said there would be no objection "provided I would be sure to be punctual in My Payments. Which you May depend I shall, and Allways be proud to have Mr. Norton on the Spot to receive the Cash as it coms in."[150] When Rathell established her store at a favorable site in Williamsburg, opposite the Raleigh Tavern and near the capitol, she again wrote to Norton and Sons for goods because she hoped "to do three times the Business I ever did." She gave as a reference of her prompt payment "your friend" Colonel George Mercer, "Who is Not unacquainted with My Method of Dealing, and Who can Inform you I Sell for Nothing but redy Cash, so by giving no Credit, I Can at all times Either Command Goods or Cash."[151] The relationship between Norton and Rathell continued during her residence in Virginia until 1772. Rathell even offered goods wholesale in three advertisements and sent goods on commission, though these were seen as being part of a different enterprise that threatened the success of her regular business. For a woman dealing in trade, dependence on cash may have allowed Rathell greater access to English wholesalers. In marketing her goods, she cited her expertise in clothing construction and her knowledge of the latest taste in fashion, having recently arrived from England. But her correspondence reveals that she needed more than skill to succeed in the colony; she needed connections.

When Rathell needed another supplier for her business, she was successful in obtaining a glowing reference from a relative to aid her cause. Roger Atkinson, the Appomattox merchant who relied on his London sister to help him run his business, wrote a March 1773 letter to his "Brother," a Captain Fearson, to recommend a kinswoman as a dependable wholesale customer for Fearson's house. After Atkinson's discussion of his own difficulty in paying his English suppliers, and before his commenting on his family's health and well-being, Atkinson spoke highly of Catherine Rathell's dependability and business abilities, but also of her family connection to Atkinson: "Mrs. Catharine Rathell, a Relation of my Wife's, has wrote to your house for some Goods—She is in ye Millinery way, & deals only for ready Money—is very industrious & frugal, & proposes to pay ye Money to Mr. Hanson for his bills, as she receives it. I doubt not but that she will be punctual to her Proposals, wch I hope will be agreeable to you."[152] Rathell had been in business six years by the time Atkinson wrote on her behalf, and she returned to London herself on purchasing trips, as well as ordering goods through John Norton and Sons; still, the reference to family connections allowed Rathell to extend her business even farther. While Rathell seems the epitome of the independent, individualistic woman establishing her own business and making it a success, she, like other women, needed the references and support of her family network to allow her to establish her business. In this respect she resembled many of the men of her time.

The high demand for Rathell's merchandise simply may have allowed her to demand cash in an economy otherwise dependent on selling on credit. Her customers were the political and economic elite of the colony, and were people accustomed to being extended credit to make their purchases. But if her cash sales were sufficiently brisk she had no reason to resort to selling extensively on credit, especially since her letters to suppliers reveal a desperation for more goods to sell to an insatiable clientele. In the end, this policy served her well. Other merchants were left holding uncollected planter debts after the credit crisis of the early 1770s while Rathell was able to sell off her business and leave the colony with the coming of the Revolution. Ultimately, Rathell's shrewdness benefited her little. She was drowned on the return journey home to England when the ship she was on sank within sight of Liverpool.[153] In the end, poor timing, with the arrival of the Revolution, and bad luck, triumphed over cautious dealing for Catherine Rathell.

Both women and men contributed to the success of the largest family enterprises, providing capital, connections, and expertise that allowed these businesses to succeed. A few traders, like Rathell, ran businesses of their own while relying on family connections to make their enterprises work. These women clearly constituted a numerical minority of the people undertaking business in their own names. Others, like the women in the Norton family, subsumed their work within the framework of a larger family enterprise.

Their work in providing merchandise to customers to suit colonial tastes made them necessary to the smooth operation of several of the family trade empires. The historical female colonists took their knowledge about consumer goods a step further than Daniel Defoe's fictional Moll Flanders's specifications in purchasing silver-hilted swords and a scarlet cloak for her husband. Where Moll only bought for her own family's consumption, women in trading families might be expected to select goods for customers' families and to encourage customers to keep business in house.

In taking on certain tasks within family businesses, women could maintain the operations themselves, serving as representatives of the family firms at terminal points in the trade webs, especially in the seventeenth century, or as widows operating firms. In these largest, often transatlantic businesses, individualistic economic undertakings were luxuries neither men nor women could afford—the work and contributions of all allowed the businesses to succeed or fail.[154] In addition, the shift to concern for more fashionable goods in the eighteenth century seems to have provided a specialized role within those family businesses for women within mercantile houses.

"ANY THING WILL I AGREE TO FOR THE COMMON GOOD": TOWARD THE REVOLUTION

Researching history is a bit like reading a mystery novel all the while knowing that Colonel Mustard did the murder in the conservatory with the candlestick. Readers will not be surprised to know what happened next: Virginia joined the colonies declaring independence and seized the opportunity to enact laws and formulate a culture to match their own ideals.

This book ends at the period preceding the War of Independence and consequently provides a context for women's wartime activism. Even before the imperial crisis occurred, propertied women had been involved in transatlantic exchanges and become knowledgable about trade, as chapters 5 and 6 demonstrate. During the war these women built on this existing knowledge. Martha Jacquelin, one of Norton and Sons' York River customers, referred to herself as an "associator" who sympathized with the colonists' nonimportation movement and who had earlier renounced tea drinking. Assuming that Courtenay Norton of the Norton and Sons family shared her views, Jacquelin wrote that her actions would give her "great merit" with Mrs. Norton and, as an afterthought, added "not that I doubt Mr. Norton either."[1] Yorktown's Martha Goosely planned to observe all the strict rules she expected the Virginia Associates to propose because "any thing will I agree to for the common good."[2] Historians have acknowledged the ways that women took an interest in public affairs during the Revolution and supported the boycotts that preceded the war. This book traces the colonial antecedents to women's interest in trade, consumption, home production, and boycotts that characterized Revolutionary-era women's public efforts.[3]

The war shaped the consciousness of two other women mentioned in chapter 6, Catherine Rathell and Courtenay Norton. For both, the war had fatal consequences. As a loyalist, Catherine Rathell sold out her stock, gave up her Williamsburg millinery business, and returned "home" to England when hostilities broke out, but was drowned when her ship sank. Virginia-born Courtenay Norton supported the colonists from her home in London from the time of the Stamp Act on, and by 1780 she determined to return home to Virginia.[4] On a stopover in Barbados en route, Norton contracted a fatal illness and was buried at Bridgetown.[5] Nevertheless, her legacy persisted in Virginia and her children and grandchildren carried on the family business.

After the war, white Virginia women's political activism became subsumed in the party politics that provided a space where they could voice their concerns through legislative petitions, voluntary associations, political reports, and various publications, though they were excluded from both holding office and voting.[6] Still other elite women retreated into a private world of domesticity and child rearing, concentrating their efforts, as "republican mothers," on educating the next generation's virtuous (male) citizens to take over.[7] Women's virtue became more narrowly defined as modesty and sexual purity.[8] A new style of homegrown prescriptive literature developed to instruct Anglo-American girls and young women how to behave. While some of the old treatises encouraging obedience persisted, a new form of "conduct fiction" taught young women that they were mistresses of their own fates, though there was only one happy outcome available to them: marriage. Emphasis on contract and consent in family relationships paralleled a rise in the ideal of the "companionate" marriage, which emphasized affection between husband and wife as a basis for relationships that nevertheless remained unequal.[9]

In the generation after the War of Independence, Virginians looked back with awe at the competence of earlier women in legal and economic activities. Littleton Tazewell, himself a lawyer, representative to the Virginia House of Delegates, and ultimately a U.S. senator, celebrated his ancestor, Gertrude (Littleton) Harmanson, as "a very singular character indeed." Tazewell bragged that as a widow, Harmanson managed her estates herself "with as much industry skill and attention as any man could have done." She supervised her estates directly by riding on horseback alone across the eastern shore, and "was reputed there the best manager they had." She acquired additional land during her widowhood and used the courts to protect it according to her own interests. Tazewell reported that according to family tradition, "By some means or other she had picked up some knowledge of the law too, and is said to have prepared not only all her own deeds contracts and other writings, but even to have given written opinions upon legal question[s] submitted to her by her neighbors and friends."[10] Corroborating evidence from the Virginia statutes and from private papers supports Tazewell's claims.[11] Her own records indicate she ordered law books from her agents in England and specified in an invoice exactly which books she wanted.[12] Harmanson's reputation extended beyond the circle of friends and neighbors, and one of the judges of the Virginia Court who had practiced on the eastern shore early in his career "often" reported to Tazewell that "he had seen several of these legal opinions that had been formerly given by Mrs. Harmanson which were even then held there in very high respect, & as he thought were singularly correct. And if the Act of Assembly to which I have refer'd above, or her own will, be either of them her own composition, they unquestionably manifest (and especially the latter) no mean specimen of the legal skill of the day...."[13] By the nineteenth century, Harmanson had become symbolic of the competent female colonist for a descendent, but also for the general court judge who held up Tazewell's female ancestor as a role model to the young male lawyer.[14]

Early-nineteenth-century hagiography celebrated competent female colonists, but tidewater Virginia after the Revolutionary War offered fewer avenues to economic success for planters of either sex. The region became a backwater, as tobacco lands became exhausted while the western portions of the state remained dynamic. Virginia's tidewater region never developed the major urban centers that provided the setting for women's agency in the early republic, and even Williamsburg slipped into decay after Virginia's capital moved to Richmond, causing the year-round urban population to decline precipitously. With the region's decline, Virginians—male and female—sought solace in religion, which provided women with further, albeit very limited, alternative routes to moral authority.[15] More overtly political avenues to power, including suffrage and married women's property rights would only come much later.

This book has dealt with the colonial tidewater, suggesting the "limits of possibility" colonial women faced and the ways they negotiated those limits. The "typical" or statistically described experience of colonial women has been well analyzed in other contexts and this book has not sought to recover that ground; instead, it analyzes the renegotiation of the boundaries that governed women's lives and the ways that women sought to assert their wills when they had the authority and resources to do so. This sort of approach, used by women's historians back to Mary Beard, allows us to see law as a powerful sort of prescriptive literature imposed upon women, but one that propertied women sometimes sought to evade. As Duncan Kennedy has observed, "We assume the legal ground rules are stable, and that what 'counts' is the ability of actors to work within them, 'bend' them, or get good interpretations 'at the margin.' Law as ground rules therefore seems uninteresting as a focus of explanation."[16] The law was not stable and mattered precisely because it established the rules from which people negotiated.[17] Conversely, we only understand what that law meant when we see how it functioned in practice. Coercion and subjectivity work together and may be understood only in relation to each other: "the face becomes the mask; particular male and female subjects are the products of as well as the actors in the bargaining drama."[18] In negotiating the law and in pursuing economic goals, Anglo-American women of property sought to protect their own and their families' interest and did so by negotiating the restrictions imposed upon themselves.

Historians of colonial America have rightly outlined the limitations imposed on women as the necessary first step toward understanding the nature of gender roles, but a first step does not preclude further exploration. With knowledge about women's oppression as a backdrop, this book has reconsidered the limited ways in which propertied women sought, and sometimes gained, subjectivity when they had even limited opportunities and resources at their disposal.

Viewing propertied Anglo-American women exclusively as victims in a patriarchal world, under the control of powerful, independent men, fails to account for the wide range of these women's experiences. In the colonial period, when economic power came more from family ties than individual financial independence, even elite white men depended upon these connections. Many women also benefited from those links; they both exercised a degree of power and suffered substantial subordination within the familial hierarchy. Awareness of the variations in these women's lives allows us a more richly textured analysis of women's, and men's, past. Rather than dividing the "experience" of women in the past from the gendered social structures, this book shows that even while these structures imposed limitations on women, female colonists of means did not always abide by them if they contradicted their best interests. Furthermore, propertied women adapted their strategies to respond to the shifts in the economic, legal, and demographic contexts in which they operated.

Language and power were gendered in colonial Virginia, but action and language also conflicted. Placing the history of gender and the history of propertied women's lives side by side reveals inherent contradictions, and these contradictions demonstrate how both women's lives and the expectations imposed upon them became transformed in the colonial period. The law provided a significant method for ordering society, but not the exclusive means for doing so. Furthermore, women with resources and knowledge used the law as a conduit for their authority when they could. Colonial men acknowledged women's abilities, granting them power of attorney to advance family interests and agreeing to arrangements such as prenuptial gifts and contracts by which women protected the property of the "ghost families" they had formed with previous husbands.

Some of these Anglo-Virginia women took a more aggressive stance than did the grieving widow Susanna Lister, whose plight opened this book. Lister took on economic roles and social responsibilities but still invoked the trope of the helpless widow when it suited her own plans. In colonial

Virginia, individual widows and wives actively protected and advanced their families' interests, sometimes appearing in their own right or as attorneys-in-fact for others in the local law courts. In the test cases put forward by Susanna Cooper and Frances Greenhill, colonial officials even accepted the notion that under certain circumstances, married women should have control over family property without a husband's interference. In more ordinary circumstances, women made and sustained the personal side of business contacts. Despite all of these accomplishments, colonial social norms placed women in a subordinate role. Southern women, like their northern counterparts, acted more like "deputy husbands" than autonomous actors. These women needed to act shrewdly to fulfill these various obligations. Women not only knew about the ideals, they could also invoke the familiar cultural ideals themselves when directing their own business, and use the seemingly restrictive ideals to their own advantage.[19]

By the middle of the eighteenth century, ideals and reality for propertied women seemed to be on a collision course. Prescriptive literature, largely imported from England but embraced by the colonists, enjoined women to silence and submissiveness, yet these same women undertook such a wide range of activities, including economic pursuits, that previous generations of historians were led (or misled) to consider this period a "golden age" for women. Colonial historians were left with the dilemma of explaining how competence and submission coexisted. In the colonial assembly, powerful Virginians embraced women's agency in the passage of the laws Susanna Cooper and Frances Greenhill presented in seeking to be declared femes soles for the purposes of disposing of property (even though these two women were married). Only the British king stood in the way of this momentous change in married women's legal status at midcentury. So, with independence, one might expect to find a bit of legal innovation in married women's property rights. No such luck: the new state of Virginia confirmed most of the colonial restrictions on married women's property, even restricting the dower rights of widows to slaves.[20] Behind-the-scenes maneuvering remained the means for propertied women with political interests to pull strings.[21] Virginia courts after the War of Independence provided rudimentary protection of individual married women's property rights by means of separate estates, but only because listing a family's assets under a woman's name prevented creditors from seizing that property, not because powerful Virginia men developed a feminist consciousness.[22]

The Revolutionary War made the contradiction between gender ideals and women's realities obvious to a few outspoken Virginians. In 1778 Hannah (Lee) Corbin took on the issue explicitly: taxation without representation was as unfair for women as it was for men.[23] Mary Willing Byrd, a wealthy widow, likewise protested her exclusion from the full exercise of citizenship: "I have paid my taxes, and have not been Personally or Virtually represented. My property is taken from me and I have no redress." Although she could and did petition her state's Governor, she could not vote. Nor did Byrd, incensed at losing her "property," see any contradiction between recovering her "property," in this case forty-nine slaves, and Revolutionary ideals, even as she complained at the poor treatment she received as a virtuous female citizen.[24] St. George Tucker, the Virginia jurist who published an annotated version of *Blackstone's Commentaries* to assist lawyers in the new state in 1803, attacked the limitations of women's property rights and access to suffrage under the British common law that Virginians preserved after the Revolution, and enumerated the ways in which English law made unfair legal distinctions between men and women.[25] More systematic attacks on the subordination of women would come later.

As citizens in a state within a newly independent nation, Virginians could now debate the nature of property and the significance of gender under the law without having to worry about the threat of disallowal of laws from the crown. Still, even when Americans had the freedom to enact their own laws without interference, women's rights advanced slowly, and revolutionaries like Corbin, Byrd, and Tucker remained in the minority.[26] As this book has demonstrated, the construction of gender as an ideal and the experience of women in practice had both undergone changes during the colonial period, but ideals and practices still moved in different directions.

STANDARD ABBREVIATIONS

CHS: Chicago Historical Society
CLRO: Corporation of London Record Office
CW: Colonial Williamsburg
DOW: Deeds, Orders, and Wills
FP: Family Papers
HL: Huntington Library, (San Marino, California)
HSP: Historical Society of Pennsylvania (Philadelphia)
JO: Judgments and Orders
LC: Library of Congress
LVA: Library of Virginia, Archives Division, Richmond
OW: Orders and Wills
PRO: [British] Public Record Office, Kew, holds records of the following:
    C: Chancery
    CO: Colonial Office
    PC: Privy Council
SHC: Southern Historical Collection, University of North Carolina
UVA: University of Virginia, Alderman Special Collections
VCRP: Virginia Colonial Records Project. Copies of Survey Reports and microfilms in the Rockefeller Library of Colonial Williamsburg, Library of Virginia (Richmond), Alderman Library at the University of Virginia (Charlotttesville) and the Virginia Historical Society (Richmond)
VHS: Virginia Historical Society (Richmond)
VMHB: *Virginia Magazine of History and Biography*
W&M: College of William and Mary, Special Collections
WMQ: *William and Mary Quarterly*
YC: York County

NOTES ON DATES

Before 1752, England and its colonies followed the Julian (Old Style) calendar. In 1752, both shifted to the Gregorian (New Style) calendar in use in Europe. In the Julian calendar, March 25 was the first day of each year while in the Gregorian Calendar January 1 started the new year. By 1752, the Old Style calendar was also eleven days behind the New Style calendar. When the new calendar was adopted, those eleven days were lost.

In this book, New Style dates appear for the period after January 1, 1752 and Old Style dates appear for references before 1752, generally with one exception: Old Style years for dates between January 1 and March 25 are indicated with both years; for example, February 22, 1670 appears as 1670/1. For more information on this subject, see W. A. Speck, *Stability and Strife: England, 1714–1760* (Cambridge, MA: Harvard University Press, 1977), 254–5.

ACKNOWLEDGMENTS

1. J. Franklin Jameson, preface to *Essays in Colonial History Presented to Charles McLean Andrews by His Students* (1931; reprt. Freeport, NY: Books for Libraries Press, 1966), ix-x.
2. Ibid.

INTRODUCTION

1. Daniel Defoe, *Moll Flanders*, ed. James Sutherland (Boston: Houghton Mifflin, 1959), 291.
2. Timothy Silver, *A New Face on the Countryside: Indians, Colonists, and Slaves in South Atlantic Forests, 1500–1800* (Cambridge: Cambridge University Press, 1990), 154–55.
3. Jack P. Greene, *Pursuits of Happiness: The Social Development of Early Modern British Colonies and the Formation of American Culture* (Chapel Hill: University of North Carolina Press, 1988), 167–68.
4. "Coastal Plain Province: The Geology of Virginia," College of William and Mary Geology Department Website, <http://www.wm.edu/CAS/GEOLOGY/virginia/coastal_plain.html>; The excellent photographs and drawings on the website will help readers visualize the landscape.
5. See, for example, Kevin P. Kelly, "Settlement Patterns in Surry County," in *The Chesapeake in the Seventeenth Century: Essays on Anglo-American Society and Politics*, ed. Thad W. Tate and David Ammerman (New York: Norton, 1979), 196.
6. English women had a better chance than English men of surviving Indian attacks. In the well-known 1622 "uprising" Indians took some English women captive as servants but killed English men immediately. As many as twenty female, but no male, colonists were taken captive in this uprising. At least one redeemed captive owed Dr. Pott, the man who paid her ransom, a term of service to compensate for his payment and claimed her "new servitude [under Pott] ... differeth not from her slavery with the Indians." J. Frederick Fausz, "The Missing Women of Martin's Hundred," *American History* 33 (1998): 56–62.
7. Statistics on longevity are for Middlesex County. See Darrett B. and Anita H. Rutman, "'Now-Wives and Sons-in-Law': Parental Death in a Seventeenth-Century Virginia County," in Tate and Ammermann, eds., *The Chesapeake in the Seventeenth Century*, 157–59. This summary is based on the tremendous flowering of local studies of the Chesapeake in the 1970s and 1980s. Classic works include Tate and Ammerman's, *The Chesapeake in the Seventeenth Century*; Lois Green Carr, Philip D. Morgan, and Jean B. Russo, eds., *Colonial Chesapeake Society* (Chapel Hill: University of North Carolina Press, 1988); Lois Green Carr and Lorena S. Walsh, "The Planter's Wife: The Experience of White Women in Seventeenth-Century Maryland," *WMQ*, 3d ser., 34 (1977): 542–71; Edmund S. Morgan, *American Slavery, American Freedom: The Ordeal of Colonial Virginia* (New York: Norton, 1975); Darrett B. and Anita H. Rutman *A Place in Time: Middlesex County, Virginia, 1650–1750* (New York: Norton, 1984) and the long-running York County Project, based at Colonial Williamsburg, initially under the direction of Peter V. Bergstrom and Kevin P. Kelly. An easily accessible analysis of the York County Project data is Caroline Julia Richter, "A Community and Its Neighborhoods: Charles Parish, York County, Virginia, 1630–1740 (Ph.D. diss., College of William and Mary, 1992). For gender composition of the English emigrants to Virginia, see Suzanne Lebsock, *"A Share of Honour": Virginia Women, 1600–1945* (Richmond: Virginia Women's Cultural History Project, 1984), 18. More recent scholarship has reconsidered the extent to which Chesapeake culture was "distinctive." For an overview, see Karen Ordahl Kupperman, "The Founding Years of Virginia—and the United States," *VMHB* 104 (1996): 103, and Lois Green Carr, Philip D. Morgan, and

Jean B. Russo, *Colonial Chesapeake Society* (Chapel Hill: University of North Carolina Press, 1988), 5; for early women's emigration patterns, see David R. Ransome, "Wives for Virginia, 1621," *WMQ*, 3d ser., 48 (1991), 3–18.

8. In his 1705 history of Virginia, Robert Beverley attributed the Englishmen's reluctance to marry Indian women to the fact that the latter were "pagans," and to English fears that they might conspire with "their own nation" against their husbands. Beverley himself believed that the early colony would have been more peaceful if the colonists had encouraged marriage between "Christians and Indians." Beverley cited the alliance between John Rolfe and Pocahantas as his model. Robert Beverley, *The History and Present State of Virginia,* ed. Louis B. Wright (Chapel Hill: University of North Carolina Press, 1947), 38–39, 287.

9. Women who would have been considered unmarriageable in England, for bearing a child out of wedlock, for example, found no impediments to marriage in the colonial Chesapeake. Irmina Wawrzyczek, *Planting and Loving: Popular Sexual Mores in the Seventeenth-Century Chesapeake* (Lublin: Uniwersytetu Marii Curie-Sklodowskiej, 1998), 73. English men far outnumbered English women throughout the seventeenth century. Debate continues on the numbers and sex ratios of the early settlement, but the fact of an overwhelmingly male population persists in all. Virginia Bernhard, "'Men, Women and Children' at Jamestown: Population and Gender in Early Virginia, 1607–1610," *Journal of Southern History* 58 (1992): 599–618; Thomas M. Camfield, "A Can or Two of Worms: Virginia Bernhard and the Historiography of Early Virginia, 1607–1610," *Journal of Southern History* 60 (1994): 649–62; Virginia Bernhard, "A Response: The Forest and the Trees: Thomas Camfield and the History of Early Virginia," *Journal of Southern History* 60 (1994): 663–70.

10. Morgan, *American Slavery, American Freedom,* 407–8; For 1698, see Kevin P. Kelly, "Demographic Description of Seventeenth-Century York County," unpublished research report, Department of Historical Research, Colonial Williamsburg Foundation, 18.

11. David W. Galenson, *White Servitude in Colonial America: An Economic Analysis* (Cambridge: Cambridge University Press, 1981), 23–25. Beverley, *History of the Present State,* 287. Eighty percent of women who emigrated from England were indentured servants who owed four to seven years of service to a master before they enjoyed their freedom. Lebsock, *"A Share of Honour,"* 17.

12. One author of literature promoting the colony estimated that a good maid might serve at most three months, rather than the common five to seven year term, before some man purchased her remaining time in return for marrying him. Mildred Campbell, "Social Origins of Some Early Americans," *Seventeenth-Century America: Essays in Colonial History,* ed. James Morton Smith (Chapel Hill: University of North Carolina Press, 1959), 74. Some of the colony's respectable settlers complained about the shipment of felons. Walter Hart Blumenthal, *Brides from Bridewell: Female Felons Sent to Colonial America* (Rutland, VT: Charles E. Tuttle, 1962), 17. For an account that stresses the respectable, middling origins of the early women sent for wives to the colony, see Ransome, "Wives for Virginia."

13. David R. Ransome, Introduction to Nicholas Ferrar, *Sir Thomas Smith's Misgovernment of the Virginia Company,* ed. David R. Ransome (Cambridge: Roxburghe Club, 1990), xvi–xvii.

14. Morgan, *American Slavery, American Freedom,* 166; Carr and Walsh, "The Planter's Wife," 542–71.

15. Laurel Thatcher Ulrich, *Good Wives: Image and Reality in the Lives of Women in Northern New England, 1650–1750* (Oxford: Oxford University Press, 1983), 36.

16. Subordinates who ultimately offer a more overt threat are those who are believers in the system who become disillusioned: "The anger born of a sense of betrayal implies

an earlier faith." James C. Scott, *Domination and the Arts of Resistance: Hidden Transcripts* (New Haven: Yale University Press, 1990), 70, 107.

17. Bettina Aptheker, *Tapestries of Life: Women's Work, Women's Consciousness and the Meaning of Daily Experience* (Amherst: University of Massachusetts Press, 1989), 60, 173–75, 187; the final quote from Ricky Sherover-Marcuse, "Liberation Theory: Axioms and Working Assumptions about the Perpetuation of Social Oppression," cited on 168.

18. Ira Berlin, *Many Thousands Gone: The First Two Centuries of Slavery in North America* (Cambridge, MA: Belknap Press, 1998), 4–5; Awareness of the interaction between power and resistance already permeates the historical study of North American slavery. Philip D. Morgan seeks to balance slaves' oppression and ability to shape their own lives in *Slave Counterpoint: Black Culture in the Eighteenth-Century Chesapeake and Lowcountry* (Chapel Hill: University of North Carolina Press, 1998), xxii–xxiv. For white women's power in Caribbean slave societies, see Hilary McD. Beckles, "White Women and Slavery in the Caribbean," *History Workshop* 36 (1993): 66–82.

19. The literature on this subject is extensive, but, for a theoretical overview, see Stanley L. Engerman, "Slavery, Serfdom, and Other Forms of Coerced Labour: Similarities and Differences," in *Serfdom and Slavery: Studies in Legal Bondage*, ed. M. L. Bush (London: Longman, 1996): 18–41. For an analysis of the varieties of slave experiences in North America that takes into consideration both change over time and geographic variations, see Berlin, *Many Thousands Gone*.

20. Elisabeth Anthony Dexter, *Colonial Women of Affairs* (Boston, 1924; rev. ed., Boston: Houghton-Mifflin, 1931), viii. The book was reprinted yet again in 1972. Mary Sumner Benson, in her study of ideas about women, confirmed Dexter's conclusion that "the social and economic code permitted activity for self-support or aid of the family when necessary." *Women in Eighteenth-Century America: A Study of Opinion and Social Usage* (New York: Columbia University Press, 1935), number 405 of the *Columbia University Studies in History, Economics and Public Law*, 241–44.

21. Laurel Ulrich notes that these earlier histories concentrate on the eighteenth century and fail to consider economic and social distinctions among women. "Their insights were not pursued in later works"; Ulrich, *Good Wives*, 277.

22. As a result, Spruill's book has withstood the test of time better than Dexter's. Julia Cherry Spruill, *Women's Life and Work in the Southern Colonies* (1938; reprint, New York: Norton, 1972), 65. Spruill's work was reprinted in 1966, and in 1972, with an introduction by Anne Firor Scott celebrating its "impeccable scholarship" and "keen insight" (vi).

23. Mary Beth Norton, "Eighteenth-Century American Women in Peace and War: The Case of the Loyalists," *WMQ*, 3d ser., 33 (1976): 390. Norton expanded her ideas further in *Liberty's Daughters: The Revolutionary Experience of American Women 1750–1800* (Boston: Little, Brown, 1980), 133–51. Mary Beth Norton, "The Evolution of White Women's Experience in Early America," *American Historical Review* 89 (1984): 593–619. Carol Berkin also has encouraged colonial historians to move beyond the golden age debate to find different lines of analysis in "Clio's Daughters: Southern Colonial Women and Their Historians," in *The Devil's Lane: Sex and Race in the Early South*, ed. Catherine Clinton and Michele Gillespie (New York: Oxford University Press, 1997), 20. Other historians concurred with Norton, so much so that "golden age" fatigue appears to have set in. See, for example, Marylynn Salmon, *Women and the Law of Property in Early America* (Chapel Hill: University of North Carolina Press, 1986). Historians of European women are also trying to keep golden age theories at bay; for an overview see Judith M. Bennett, "'History That Stands Still': Women's Work in the European Past," *Feminist Studies* 14 (1988): 269–83.

24. Carole Shammas, "Early American Women and Control over Capital," in *Women in the Age of the American Revolution*, ed. Ronald Hoffman and Peter J. Albert

(Charlottesville: University Press of Virginia, 1989), 139; see also Carole Shammas, "How Self-Sufficient Was Early America?" *Journal of Interdisciplinary History* 13 (1982): 247–72; Carole Shammas, Marylynn Salmon, Michel Dahlin, *Inheritance in America from Colonial Times to the Present*, (New Brunswick, NJ: Rutgers University Press, 1987), 56–62; and Alice Hanson Jones, "The Wealth of Women, 1774," *Strategic Factors in Nineteenth Century American Economic History: A Volume to Honor Robert W. Fogel*, ed. Claudia Golding and Hugh Rockoff, (Chicago: University of Chicago Press, 1992), 250–51.

25. Kathleen M. Brown, *Good Wives, Nasty Wenches and Anxious Patriarchs* (Chapel Hill: University of North Carolina Press, 1996), 173.

26. Brown, *Good Wives, Nasty Wenches and Anxious Patriarchs*, 173–86. Terri L. Snyder confirms Brown's findings and determines that between 1680 and 1700, Virginians "rehabilitated patriarchy" by enacting laws that confirmed the power of white men within households; Terri L. Snyder, "'Rich Widows are the Best Commodity This Country Affords': Gender Relations and the Rehabilitation of Patriarchy in Virginia, 1660–1700" (Ph.D. diss., University of Iowa, 1992), 286–87. Patriarchy looms large in the history of colonial Virginia, back to the time when the big planters themselves emphasized their resemblance to biblical patriarchs. Subsequent historians have continued to depict these men as such. According to Daniel Blake Smith, beginning in the middle of the eighteenth century Virginians adopted sentimental views of marriage, but "husbands continued to control their wives, insisting on obedience and a pleasing disposition." Men's power outside the household confirmed this, so that law and planter inclination "conspired to limit the economic freedom of wives severely." Daniel Blake Smith, *Inside the Great House: Planter Family Life in Eighteenth-Century Chesapeake Society* (Ithaca: Cornell University Press, 1980), 21–22, 174. According to Smith, planter patriarchs like William Byrd of Westover "presided over the family with unchallenged authority." For the geographic restrictions placed on women, see Rhys Isaac, *The Transformation of Virginia, 1740–1790* (New York: Norton, 1982), 21, 57. Kulikoff claims, however, that colonial patriarchy "asserted that women were legally inferior to men, and separated the economic roles of men and women into distinct spheres, with men responsible for the economic well-being of the family, and for civic participation outside it and women responsible for child nurture and household management"; Allan Kulikoff, *Tobacco and Slaves: The Development of Southern Cultures in the Colonial Chesapeake, 1680–1800* (Chapel Hill: University of North Carolina Press, 1986), 165–204. In his second book Kulikoff highlights the repressive nature of law, concluding that "[u]nder common law, married women had no rights to property"; Allan Kulikoff, *The Agrarian Origins of American Capitalism* (Charlottesville: University Press of Virginia, 1992), 2, 30. For a contrasting view, see Kenneth A. Lockridge, *On the Sources of Patriarchal Rage: The Commonplace Books of William Byrd and Thomas Jefferson and the Gendering of Power in the Eighteenth Century* (New York: New York University Press, 1992).

   Historians whose findings are exceptional in adopting longer term perspectives are Joan R. Gundersen, Gwen Gampel, and Linda Speth. Joan R. Gundersen and Gwen Victor Gampel, "Married Women's Legal Status in Eighteenth-Century New York and Virginia, *WMQ*, 3d ser., 39 (1982): 114–34. Linda Speth, a scholar who studied both the seventeenth and eighteenth centuries, offers an exceptionally nuanced analysis of change over time in Virginia. She determined that the colonial period certainly did not qualify as a golden age in legal terms, but it also did not constitute a "grim patriarchal milieu." Linda E. Speth, "More than Her 'Thirds': Wives and Widows in Colonial Virginia," in *Women, Family, and Community in Colonial America: Two Perspectives* (New York, 1983); Salmon, *Women and the Law of Property*, xii; 197, n. 4; 256.

27. A political theory approach to patriarchy in early British America and its practical application in local communities appears in Mary Beth Norton, *Founding Mothers*

and Fathers: Gendered Power and the Forming of American Society (New York: Knopf, 1996).

28. Joan Wallach Scott, "Gender: A Useful Category of Analysis," in *Feminism and History*, ed. Joan Scott, (Oxford: Oxford University Press, 1996), 167.

29. bell hooks, "Changing Perspectives on Power," in *Feminist Theory from Margin to Center* (Boston: South End Press, 1984), 86–91.

30. hooks has an activist goal in mind and believes that oppression in the present will end only when powerful people recognize the authority they exercise. Ibid, 54–55, 89–90.

31. For the role of Frances Berkeley in seventeenth-century politics, see Linda L. Sturtz, "'Dining Room Politics:' Lady Berkeley of Virginia," Paper presented to the Courts Without Kings Conference, Society for Court Studies, Boston, MA, September 22, 2000.

32. Lebsock, *A Share of Honour*, 23.

33. Carr and Walsh, "The Planter's Wife;" Timothy H. Breen, "Horses and Gentlemen: The Cultural Significance of Gambling among the Gentry of Virginia," *WMQ*, 3d ser., 34 (1977), 239–57; Isaac, *Transformation of Virginia*; Smith, *Inside the Great House*; Kulikoff, *Tobacco and Slaves*.

34. [George Savile, Marquis of Halifax], *The Lady's New-Year's Gift: or Advice to a Daughter* (London: Randal Taylor, 1688), 26, 116. *The Lady's New-Year's Gift* appeared frequently in colonial estate inventories and newspaper advertisements. Spruill, *Women's Life and Work*, 216.

35. Sara Mendelson and Patricia Crawford, *Women in Early Modern England, 1550–1720* (Oxford: Clarendon Press, 1998), 374–75.

36. Linda Pollock, "'Teach Her to Live under Obedience': the Making of Women in the Upper Ranks of Early Modern England," *Continuity and Change* 4 (1989): 231–58. Pollock offers as an example the correspondence of Mary Throckmorton, an English woman who reported of an exchange in 1607, in which Throckmorton had answered a letter "like a woman, very submissively, if that will serve. . . ." in making her request.

37. Margaret Hunt criticizes historians' earlier willingness to take prescriptive literature as normative in English history. Works popular in eighteenth-century England included publications by Joseph Addison and Richard Steele, Lord Halifax's *Advice to a Daughter* (1688), James Fordyce's *Sermons* (1765) and Sarah Fielding's *The Governess* (1749). Margaret R. Hunt, *The Middling Sort: Commerce, Gender and the Family in England, 1680-1780*, (Berkeley and Los Angeles: University of California Press, 1996), 75. One historian who understood the full implications of the advice girls received was Julia Cherry Spruill, who pointed out that advice was "inconsistent" and that reading the contradictions within conduct literature "must have been more confusing than enlightening;" Spruill, *Women's Life and Work*, 217–18. Catherine Kerrison, "By the Book: Advice and Female Behavior in the Eighteenth-Century South," (Ph.D. diss., College of William and Mary, 1999), 53.

38. A pioneer in searching for women's agency within the restrictive structures of colonial America is, ironically, primarily a European historian. See Natalie Zemon Davis, *Women on the Margins: Three Seventeenth-Century Lives* (Cambridge, MA: Belknap, 1995). An opposing perspective asserts that moving beyond "victimization" to focus on "female agency rather than obedience, female subversion rather than submission, female activism rather than passivity" is "tantamount to historical absolution: it lets patriarchy off the hook" and "distorts history." Elaine Forman Crane, *Ebb Tide in New England: Women, Seaports, and Social Change, 1630–1800* (Boston: Northeastern University Press, 1998), 3–4. Crane correctly points out the generational dimension of this debate, with scholars "coming of age" in the 1980s and 1990s seeking agency while the previous generation stressed victimization.

39. Linda Gordon, "On 'Difference,'" *Genders* 10 (1991): 92. "I am arguing that the current women's-studies focus on difference is not the best rubric under which to understand social divisions, for many reasons perhaps the most important of which is that this focus has been, sometimes unconsciously, masking the importance of power differentials and relations." Gordon brings up the specific example of African-American women's lives being comprehensible only within the context of their relationship to whites "including exploitation, domination, fear, and exclusion, for examples" (105-6). For further discussion of the ways white women benefit from racist hierarchies, see Barbara Hilkert Andolsen, *"Daughters of Jefferson, Daughters of Bootblacks": Racism and American Feminism* (Atlanta: Mercer University Press, 1986), 113–15.

40. Norma Basch, *In the Eyes of the Law: Women, Marriage, and Property in Nineteenth-Century New York* (Ithaca: Cornell University Press, 1982), 38.

41. Slave-owning women could be self-deluded about the nature of the relationship between mistress and slave, assuming a cordial relationship with a slave—especially a house slave with whom she shared daily life. For example, Williamsburg resident Betty Randolph expressed surprise when, during the War of Independence, Randolph's slave Eve, left the Randolph household and joined the British Army to secure her own freedom from slavery. When Randolph recovered Eve at the end of the war, her decision to sell "indicates that she took greater offense" at Eve's attempt to seek her freedom than she did at other slaves' similar efforts. Caroline Julia Richter, "The Randolph House," Colonial Williamsburg Research Report, 11, 13, 15.

42. Linda L. Sturtz, "'Madam and Co.': Women, Property and Power in Colonial Virginia" (Ph.D. diss., Washington University, 1994), 206–76. Much of the debate over the extent to which "mistresses and slaves shared the bonds of oppression" in the south concentrates on the nineteenth century. For the colonial period, see Joan R. Gundersen, "The Double Bonds of Race and Sex: Black and White Women in a Colonial Virginia Parish," *Journal of Southern History* 52 (1986): 351–72. For an overview of the nineteenth-century literature, see Gail S. Terry, "Sustaining the Bonds of Kinship in a Trans-Appalachian Migration, 1790–1811," *VMHB* 102 (1994): 455–76. Gundersen argues that colonists created a community of women "but not a community of equals" (351), and Terry concludes that even in a "best case" scenario, in the early national period, slaves and mistresses could cooperate to achieve a common goal, but they were in no sense equals. (472–73, 476.))

43. Gundersen and Gampel, "Married Women's Legal Status," 115, 130. Historians of the other colonies have traced a decline in women's legal rights at the middle of the eighteenth century. For other mainland English colonies, see Cornelia Hughes Dayton, *Women before the Bar: Gender, Law, and Society in Connecticut, 1639–1789* (Chapel Hill: University of North Carolina Press, 1995); Deborah A. Rosen, *Courts and Commerce: Gender, Law and the Market Economy in Colonial New York* (Columbus: Ohio State University, 1997), 95–110, 125; A. G. Roeber, "'The Origin of Whatever Is Not English among Us': The Dutch-Speaking and the German-Speaking Peoples of Colonial British America," in *Strangers within the Realm*, ed. Bernard Bailyn and Philip Morgan (Chapel Hill: University of North Carolina Press, 1991), 220–83.

    For works finding no declension or compensation for decline by gains in other areas, see Joan M. Jensen, *Loosening the Bonds: Mid-Atlantic Farm Women, 1750–1850* (New Haven: Yale University Press, 1986), 18–27; and Elizabeth Marie Pruden, "Family, Community, Economy: Women's Activity in South Carolina, 1670–1770" (Ph.D.diss., University of Minnesota, 1996), 197. The legal role of women in Maryland remains inconclusive. See Carr and Walsh, "Planter's Wife"; Gwen Victor Gampel, "The Planter's Wife Revisited: Women, Equity Law, and the Chancery Court in Seventeenth-Century Maryland," in *Women and the Structure of Society: Selected Research from the Fifth Berkshire Conference on the History of Women* ed. Barbara J.

Harris and Jo Ann K. McNamara (Durham: Duke University Press, 1984), 20–35. Vivan Bruce Conger, "If Widow, Both Housewife and Husband May Be," in *Women and Freedom in Early America*, ed. Larry D. Eldridge (New York: New York University Press, 1997), 258–59.

The classic treatment of "Anglicization" is John M. Murrin's "Anglicizing an American Colony: The Transformation of Provincial Massachusetts" (Ph.D. diss., Yale University, 1966). For the interplay between anglicization and creolization in the Chesapeake colonies, see Greene, *Pursuits of Happiness*, 93–94.

44. Olwen Hufton discusses the "limits of possibility" in her analysis of women in western Europe between 1500 and 1800. Her warning about the "erection of the theoretical or 'generic' woman and man, ... at the expense of what was, as far as one can discern, the experience of real people" is equally appropriate for the Virginia setting. Like Hufton's work, this present volume seeks to analyze the interaction between practice and belief. Olwen Hufton, *The Prospect before Her: A History of Women in Western Europe*, vol. 1 (1500–1800), (New York: Knopf, 1996), 1, 7.

45. Gayatri Chakravorty Spivak, cited in Catherine Hall, "Gender Politics: Rethinking the Histories of Empire," in *Engendering History*, ed. Verene Shepherd, Bridget Brereton, and Barbara Bailey (Kingston, Jamaica: Ian Randle, 1995), 51. For a fictional treatment of the privilege of white women in Britain's second empire, see E. M. Forster's *A Passage to India* (1924).

46. Tim Stretton summarizes the recent historical literature on English women under the law in the early modern period, pointing out that women played an increasingly active role in law suits in the late sixteenth and early seventeenth centuries, but warns against excessive optimism about women's agency. Stretton, *Women Waging Law in Elizabethan England* (Cambridge: Cambridge University Press, 1998), 216–18.

47. Verene Shepherd poses a succinct description of the "revisionist" strand in Caribbean gender history in Caribbean plantation colonies in her review of *Slave Cultures and the Cultures of Slavery*, ed. Stephan Palmie (Knoxville: University of Tennessee Press, 1995) in *WMQ*, 3d ser., 54 (1997): 257–58. For a sustained analysis, see Hilary McD. Beckles, *Centering Woman: Gender Discourses in Caribbean Slave Society* (Kingston, Jamaica: Ian Randle, 1998); The pathbreaking work on this topic is Lucille Mathurin [Mair], "A Historical Study of Women in Jamaica from 1655 to 1844" (Ph.D. diss., University of the West Indies, Mona, 1974), 120–21, 158–94; Barbara Bush, "White 'Ladies', Coloured 'Favourites' and Black 'Wenches': Some Considerations of Sex, Race and Class Factors in Social Relations in White Creole Society in the British Caribbean," *Slavery and Abolition*, 2 (1981): 245–62. Catherine Hall, *White, Male and Middle Class: Explorations in Feminism and History* (New York: Routledge, 1992), 208. Verena Martinez-Alier, *Marriage, Class and Colour in Nineteenth-Century Cuba* (1974, reprt. Ann Arbor: University of Michigan, 1989). Trevor Burnard, "Family Continuity and Female Independence in Jamaica, 1665–1734," *Continuity and Change* 7 (1992): 194; Burnard addresses the problem of white women's victimhood and argues that white women "were relegated to irrelevancy in early Jamaica, making slaves on sugar plantations the 'real victims.'" Linda L. Sturtz, "The 'Dim Duke' and Duchess Chandos," *Revista/Review Interamericana* 29 (1999), http://www.sg. inter.edu/revisa-ciscla/>. Caribbean scholars have also examined the property ownership of black and "colored" women in the eighteenth century. See, for example, Susan M. Socolow, "Economic Roles of the Free Women of Color of Cap Français," in *More Than Chattel: Black Women and Slavery in the Americas*, ed. David Barry Gaspar and Darlene Clark Hine (Bloomington: Indiana University Press, 1996), 279–97. For a larger framework for interpreting imperialism, see Ann Laura Stoler, *Race and the Education of Desire* (Durham: Duke University Press, 1996).

48. Mendelson and Crawford, *Women in Early Modern England, 1550–1720*, 17.

49. Lister Papers, Virginia Colonial Records Project, microfilm reel 854. The papers were deposited in a local collection in England, first at the Shibden Hall Folk Museum and then in the Archives Department of the Halifax Central Library, and are currently in the Calderdale District Archives, West Yorkshire. They were microfilmed as part of the massive Virginia Colonial Records Project (VCRP), meant to preserve records pertaining to Virginia history housed in British and European collections. I am grateful to John Kneebone, Brent Tarter, and John M. Hemphill II for explaining how the VCRP material worked in the days before on-line finding aids. Copies of the VCRP survey reports and microfilmed manuscripts are available at Colonial Williamsburg's Rockefeller Library, University of Virginia's Alderman Library, the Library of Virginia, and the Virginia Historical Society.

50. The brothers bought a share of a sloop and assured their brother that "we have a good deal of Business every day if please God our undertakings do but answer according to our expectations. . . ." The Listers put personal comfort aside and decided that "where there is Money to be got ye. unpleasantness of ye. countery must not be taken notice of" despite the fact that Virginia "is a very hot countrey in the sumertime & very cold in ye. winter." June 25, 1735. Thomas and Jeremy Lister in Virginia to Samuel Lister at Shibden, Lister papers, VCRP microfilm.

51. Susanna Lister to Samuel Lister, October 20, 1744, Lister Papers, VCRP. Three brothers, Jeremy (1713–1788), William (1712–1743), and Thomas (1708–1740) emigrated to Virginia, though Jeremy later returned to Halifax. Another brother, Japhet (1715–1782), remained in England and for a short time served as an agent operating out of London and Halifax on behalf of the American brothers while Samuel (1706–1766) participated in the cloth trade from England and later became involved in the family business. Genealogical information from D. W. Ockelton, introduction to "The Fawcett and Lister Papers from the Shibden Hall Folk Museum" (later the Archives Department, Halifax Central Library, now the West Yorkshire Archive Service—Calderdale District Archives), VCRP microfilm reel 854. A fuller genealogy exists in a volume discussing another strong Lister woman—Anne Lister, Susanna's great niece: see Jill Liddington, *Female Fortune: Land, Gender and Authority. The Anne Lister Diaries and Other Writings 1833–36* (London: Rivers Oram Press, 1998), 4–8. Ockelton's introduction to the collection reports the sum that Susanna Lister owed.

52. Susanna Lister to Samuel Lister, December 1, 1745, Lister Papers, VCRP.

53. Susanna Lister to Samuel Lister, December 1, 1745 and September 15, 1746, Lister Papers, VCRP. Murray proved a difficult challenge to the family as a whole, not just to Susanna. The Listers continued to face difficulties in dealing with Murray into the 1750s. The English side of the family finally resorted to contacting Charles Steuart of Norfolk to collect debts Murray owed to William's estate and to William Bowden, the family's London merchant. Samuel Lister, in Yorkshire, criticized Murray's manner of doing business: "I am sorry you have given me so much occasion to suspect that your principles are not such as I formerly esteemed them, and I must own it is pity to see a person capable of writing in such honorable and acceptable terms and of sincerity or due regard to his word and promises." (Samuel Lister to James Murray, March 10, 1755). Steuart chased Murray to Williamsburg in 1755 to try to obtain repayment of the balance, but finally resorted to bringing a suit in General Court in 1757. By then, the debt existed as both obligations to Samuel Lister, directly, and to William Bowden, who had issued a bill of exchange. (See note 55 for description of bills of exchange). At the General Court, Steuart's lawyer finally received a judgment, though Murray threatened to delay the suit, and could have "kept the suit depend[in]g these 3 years" if Steuart had not compromised. This case is traced in various letters: Steuart to Mr. Lister [presumably Samuel] August 7, 1755; Samuel Lister, in Halifax, Yorkshire, to James Murray, August 10, 1755; Charles Steuart, in Portsmouth, to James Murray,

August 20, 1755; Charles Steuart, in Portsmouth, to William Bowden, December 25, 1756; and Charles Steuart to Samuel Lister May 10, 1757, all in the Charles Steuart Letter Books, 1751–1763, Historical Society of Pennsylvania.

54. Lewis began the letter by saying his daughter had instigated the correspondence by writing to him to complain of Murray. John Lewis, Virginia, to Samuel Lister, Halifax, March 29, 1747, Lister Papers, VCRP.

55. Bills of exchange allowed transatlantic trade to proceed despite colonists' inadequate access to coinage. In this system, Lister, like other colonists who exported commodities, built up credit in their English merchants' hands. When colonial exporters needed to make a payment, they drew on this credit through bills of exchange—a "written order from one person to another to pay a third party a certain sum in money at [a] specified time." This form of payment was necessary because English law prevented export of sterling coins or bullion from the mother country. Without a mint and before the introduction of paper money in 1755, "Virginia currency was only a money of account." Historian John M. Hemphill II has pointed out that "the bill of exchange, although technically and legally of different origin, served the colonial planter much like a modern check, with the English merchant occupying the role of the present-day banker (...often covering overdrafts)." Bills of exchange were negotiable and could be endorsed to others. The definition of bills of exchange is from Sir James Murray, *A New English Dictionary on Historical Principles* [the Oxford English Dictionary], cited by John M. Hemphill II, *Virginia and the English Commercial System, 1689–1733: Studies in the Development and Fluctuations of a Colonial Economy under Imperial Control* (New York: Garland, 1985), 128–29. John McCusker also sees the check as the closest analogy to a bill of exchange because a check is a bill of exchange drawn on a bank. Bills of exchange were particularly useful in paying obligations in a distant location. John J. McCusker, *Money and Exchange in Europe and America, 1600–1775: A Handbook* (Chapel Hill: University of North Carolina Press, 1977), 19.

56. Susanna Lister to Samuel Lister, October 20, 1744, VCRP.

57. Mary Beth Norton has found that recently widowed women of the 1790s and 1800s, sometimes suffering from depression, genuinely believed in their own helplessness: "A husband's death thrust a woman abruptly into a world with which she had had little previous contact, precisely at a time when she was ill prepared to adjust to new responsibilities." Norton, *Liberty's Daughters*, 133.

58. He suggested William Bowden, in Seething Lane, London, as a correspondent. Samuel Lister to Susanna Lister, August 30, 1745, Lister Papers, VCRP.

58. The emigre brothers, Thomas and William, married two Virginia sisters, Anne and Susanna Lewis, daughters of Thomas Lewis of Virginia. Thomas and Anne married in 1733, the same year that Thomas migrated. William came to Virginia in 1736, married Susanna in 1738, and eventually the couple moved on to New Bern, North Carolina, where he engaged in the slave trade. Thomas and William remained in America until their deaths in 1740 and 1743, respectively, whereupon the two sisters became responsible for the family finances. A letter from Phebe Lister to Rev. John Lister dated September 22, 1737, indicates that their brother William had arrived safely at York Town in Virginia. Lister Papers, VCRP.

60. Anne Lister to Rev. John Lister, Halifax, June 9, 1752, Lister Papers, VCRP. From this and other correspondence in the collection, we know that William was sent to his uncle's school and had plans to study for the ministry, but was considered too old to begin his preparations and was later apprenticed to another brother in England. According to D. W. Ockelton, William Lister Jr., (1734–1789) never returned to Virginia, but married Margaret Lewis of Lonhorne, South Wales and settled there.

61. Anne Lister to Rev. John Lister, June 9, 1753, Lister Papers, VCRP.
62. The classic definition of "creole society" in Anglo-America is Edward Kamau Brathwaite's: creole society is "the result of a complex situation where a colonial polity reacts, as a whole to external metropolitan pressures and at the same time to internal adjustments made necessary by the juxtaposion of master and slave, elite and labourer, in a culturally heterogeneous relationship." Edward Kamau Brathwaite, *The Development of Creole Society in Jamaica, 1770–1820* (Oxford: Clarendon Press, 1971), xvi.

CHAPTER 1

1. Our understanding of the demographic framework for this history greatly improved with the impressive statistical analyses historians undertook during the 1970s and 1980s. Darrett B. and Anita H. Rutman, *A Place in Time: Middlesex County, Virgina, 1650–1750* (New York: Norton, 1984), 114; Sarah Jane Weatherwax, "The Importance of Family in the Community of New Poquoson Parish, York County, Virginia, in the Late Seventeenth Century" (M.A. thesis, College of William and Mary, 1984), 36.
2. Edmund Morgan estimates that for 1625, Virginia had a sex ratio of 333 white men for each 100 white women. By 1698, Kevin Kelly calculated that the more established York County had 487 men compared to 390 women, certainly closer to parity, but the unbalance persisted to the end of the seventeenth century. Edward S. Morgan, *American Slavery, American Freedom: The Ordeal of Colonial Virginia* (New York: Norton, 1975), 407. Kevin P. Kelly, "Demographic Description of Seventeenth-Century York County," unpublished research report, Department of Historical Research, Colonial Williamsburg Foundation, 18.
3. The articles collected in Tate and Ammerman's classic book paint this picture of the Chesapeake in the seventeenth century. See the essays by Carville V. Earle, Lorena S. Walsh, and Darrett B. and Anita H. Rutman. Carville V. Earle, "Environment, Disease, and Mortality in Early Virginia," 96–125; Lorena S. Walsh, "'Till Death Us Do Part': Marriage and Family in Seventeenth-Century Maryland," 126–52; and Darrett B. and Anita H. Rutman, "'Now-Wives and Sons-in-Law:' Parental Death in a Seventeenth-Century Virginia County," 153–82, in *The Chesapeake in the Seventeenth Century*, ed. Thad W. Tate and David Ammerman (New York: Norton, 1979), 153–82.
4. In the English context, Susan Staves suggests that women's interests were often "integral and necessary parts of the 'family'" rather than simply competing with kin concerns. Expectations about how to manage collective family assets changed in England during the early modern period where, increasingly, English widows gained only "temporary custody" over property and men specifically excluded their widows from property ownership if they remarried. For a succinct summary of the "strict settlement" debate, see Susan Staves, *Married Women's Separate Property in England, 1660–1833* (Cambridge, MA: Harvard University Press, 1990), 199–205. In the sixteenth century, half of the widows in Abingdon, England, remarried, but by the first half of the seventeenth century, only 37.5 percent of the widows remarried. One reason for the shift included a trend of male testators imposing a penalty on their widows if they remarried. Another reason was that a widow would lose her legal identity, control over her property, and autonomy in managing her children's estates if she remarried. Barbara J. Todd, "The Remarrying Widow: A Stereotype Reconsidered," in *Women in Tudor-Stuart England*, ed. Mary Prior (New York: Methuen, 1986), 54–92, esp. 73, 76–77. For the experience of remarrying widows in the colonies, see Vivian Bruce Conger, "'Being Weak of Body but Firm of Mind and Memory': Widowhood in Colonial America, 1630–1750" (Ph.D. diss., Cornell University, 1994), 34–148. Conger

points out that "it would have been impossible for any one widow to adhere to all of the rights and responsibilities she acquired at the death of her husband for one simple reason: they were too complex and too ambiguous" (147).

5. William Blackstone, *Commentaries on the Laws of England, 1765* (Oxford, 1765–1769), 1:430; *The Lawes Resolution of Women's Rights; or, The Laws Provision for Women...* (London, 1632), reprinted in *New World, New Roles: A Documentary History of Women in Pre-Industrial America*, ed. Sylvia R. Frey and Marian J. Morton (New York: Greenwood, 1986), 92–94; also cited in Julia Cherry Spruill, *Women's Life and Work in the Southern Colonies* (1938; reprt. New York: Norton, 1972), 340. Amy Louise Erickson, *Women and Property in Early Modern England* (London: Routledge, 1993). Historians of English law lead the way in demonstrating how women manipulated this tradition to their own advantage when they could.

6. The widow received one-third of the real estate for her use during her lifetime. The share of personal property the wife could claim depended upon the number of children born to the marriage. The widow was guaranteed a third of the personal estate if the couple had fewer than three children. If the couple had three or more children, the husband could limit his widow to a child's share of the personal estate, though he could leave her more. William Waller Hening, ed., *The Statutes at Large: Being A Collection of All the Laws of Virginia, from the First Session of the Legislature, in the Year 1619*, 13 vols. (Richmond and Philadelphia: printed for the editor, 1809–1823), vol. 2, 303.

7. In 1705, Virginia enacted a law stating a widow could petition to have a husband's will declared "null and void" if it provided her with less than her proper share. In 1727, the assembly "clarified" the law, stating that slaves were to be included in the portion a widow could claim as her dower, but that widows gained only a life right to dower slaves. The 1727 act required the widow to renounce her husband's will within nine months of his death. Hening, *Statutes at Large*: October 1673, vol. 2, 303; October 1705, vol. 3, 373; February 1727, vol. 4, 220; October, 1748, vol. 5, 447–48.

   If the wife predeceased her husband, he received all of her property for life as "curtesy." S. F. C. Milsom, *Historical Foundations of the Common Law* (Toronto: Butterworths, 1981), 167–69.

8. The further legal workings of women in merchant families will be discussed in greater detail in chapters 3 and 6.

9. By the seventeenth century, puritans and some other English legal reformers feared that equity circumvented justice rather than preserving it. As a result, New England colonies did not import equity in their legal systems, though both Chesapeake colonies, South Carolina, and New York did. Milsom, *Historical Foundations of the Common Law*, 82–85, 91; Erickson, *Women and Property*, 26; Marylynn Salmon, *Women and the Law of Property in Early America* (Chapel Hill: University of North Carolina Press, 1986), 120–21; Suzanne Lebsock, *Free Women of Petersburg: Status and Culture in a Southern Town, 1784–1860* (New York: Norton, 1984), 53–55; Hening, *Statutes at Large*, vol. 1, 303. There is an extensive literature on women's oppression under common law and its mitigation through equity. For additional information, see Mary Ritter Beard, *Woman as Force in History: A Study in Traditions and Reality* (New York: Macmillan, 1946); Spruill, *Women's Life and Work in the Southern Colonies*; Mary Beth Norton, *Liberty's Daughters; The Revolutionary Experience of American Women 1750–1800* (Boston: Little, Brown, 1980); and Linda K. Kerber, *Women of the Republic: Intellect and Ideology in Revolutionary America* (Chapel Hill: University of North Carolina Press, 1980). For a history that considers English women's frequent use of the Court of Requests, which functioned as an equity jurisdiction, see Tim Stretton, *Women Waging Law in Elizabethan England* (Cambridge: Cambridge University Press, 1998). Stretton found that thousands of women per year were involved in civil litigation in this forum in the early seventeenth century. For the

summary of early-nineteenth-century critics of separate estates as undermining common law protection of women, see Hendrick Hartog, "Wives as Favorites," in *Law as Culture and Culture as Law*, ed. Hendrick Hartog and William E. Nelson (Madison, WI: Madison House Publishers, 2000), 292–321. For a parallel treatment of Victorian England that suggests that men's physical control of their wives (and the potential for violence) mattered more than legal authority in restricting married women, see Maeve E. Doggett, *Marriage, Wife-Beating and the Law in Victorian England* (London: Weidenfeld and Nicolson, 1992), 35.

10. Susie M. Ames, ed., *County Court Records of Accomack-Northampton, Virginia, 1640–1645* (Charlottesville: University Press of Virginia, 1973), 433. Salmon, *Women and the Law of Property*, 89.

11. Margaret R. Hunt, *The Middling Sort: Commerce, Gender and the Family in England, 1640–1780* (Berkeley and Los Angeles: University of California Press, 1996), 158; Erickson, *Women and Property*, 104, 158–59. For a succinct summary of the "strict settlement" debate, see Staves, *Married Women's Separate Property in England*, 199–205.

12. Rutman and Rutman, "Now-Wives and Sons-in-Law," 171–73.

13. Lois Green Carr, "Inheritance in the Colonial Chesapeake," in *Women in the Age of the American Revolution*, ed. Ronald Hoffman and Peter Albert (Charlottesville: University Press of Virginia, 1989), 174; Linda Speth, "More than Her 'Thirds': Wives and Widows in Colonial Virginia," in *Women, Family, and Community in Colonial America: Two Perspectives* (New York: Institute for Research in History and the Haworth Press, 1983) 17–19.

14. English conduct manuals in the sixteenth and seventeenth centuries warned step-parents how to behave morally toward their stepchildren and refrain from "robbing" the children. Stepparents "got little gratitude or respect" for their endeavors. Stephen Collins, "'Reason, Nature and Order': the Stepfamily in English Renaissance Thought," *Renaissance Studies* 13 (1999): 312–23.

15. Sarah Thorowgood Gookin later married again and became Mrs. Yeardley; July 13, 1647, *Book "B" Lower Norfolk County, Virginia, 2 November 1646–15 January 1651/2* transcribed by Alice Granbery Walter, (n.p.: published by Alice Granbery Walter, 1978), 47, 48r.

16. Morgan, *American Slavery, American Freedom*, 169. Rutman and Rutman, *A Place in Time*, 117.

17. For example, Mildred Smith's husband made her sole executor of his estate and granted her some land and a share in the family mill equivalent to that which his sons received, but only as long as she remained a widow. If Mildred Smith remarried, she not only lost her share in the mill but was required to give security for the children's portions of the estate. For Smith, see York County: Orders, Wills, Inventories (here-after cited as York OWI) book 18, will written March 11, 1736/7, recorded March 19, 1738: 487–88, LVA. For other wills with similar provisions, see Richard Garvis's 1741 will declaring that his wife should enjoy the possession and profits of the land "so long as she continued a widow." York County Wills and Inventories (hereafter cited as York Wills and Inventories) book 9, March 16, 1741: 697–88, nuncupative (spoken) will of Richard Garvis, LVA. A similar impulse shaped the will of Edward Coffey in Essex County. Coffey gave his wife Ann livestock for her lifetime unless she remarried, in which case the stock was to be divided among the children. Essex County [loose] suit papers, Will of Edward Coffey, written February 14, 1715/6, recorded November 20, 1716, LVA. Lisa Wilson points out that "the specter of a second husband, not the widow's competence or reliability, was the focus of these testators' concerns" when limiting a remarrying widow's power over property in Pennsylvania. Lisa Wilson, *Life after Death: Widows in Pennsylvania, 1750–1850* (Philadelphia: Temple University Press, 1992), 55.

18. Biographical information about the Yeardleys and Francis West appears in the documents produced in a court case heard after Temperance's death. Throughout those records she appears as Dame Temperance Yeardley despite her marriage to West. The case was heard in 1630 as *Ralph Yeardley c. Francis West*. PRO, C 24/562/131 (Chancery—town depositions) for depositions by William Claiborne (also spelled Claybourne), Susan Hill, George Minifie, and Tobias Algate. Ralph Yeardley's replication is in C 2 (Charles I) Y7/34, VCRP microfilm 949; Court of chancery bills and answers, series 1, Charles I, undated (c. 1630). Other materials related to this case are in PRO C 33/160.

19. William Claiborne remembered Sir George's death as occurring in November 1627, Temperance's death in October or November 1628, and the length of Temperance's life after marriage to West as eight months. May 14, 1630, Deposition of William Claiborne, 28, of Jamestown. *Yeardley c. West*, PRO C 24/562/131 (town depositions). A later source pushes her death ahead to December 1628. Temperance Yeardley's date of birth is unknown, but she was probably no younger than thirty-one and no older than forty-eight at the time of her death. Her older sister was christened in July, 1579, so Temperance could not have been born before 1580. Assuming she was at least seventeen by the time her first child was born, she was born by 1597. John Frederick Dorman, *Adventurers of Purse and Person: Virginia 1607–1624/5*, ed. Virginia M. Meyer (Alexandria VA: Order of First Families of Virginia, 1987), 723–26. William Thorndale argues that Temperance had married as her first husband Richard Barrow in 1609. William Thorndale, "Flowerdew and Rossingham," *Virginia Genealogist* 34 (1990): 205–6. Thorndale also provides the christening date of Temperance's older sister.

20. One witness testified that she sent 40,000 "weight" of tobacco to him in two shipments. She sent a further hundred hogsheads containing an estimated 18,000 "weight" to a different merchant in Southampton. The number of barrels is based on the calculation that one hogshead equaled 180 weight. Replication of Ralph Yeardley brought to the answer of Francis West, Esq, defendant. PRO C 2 Y7/34, Court of Chancery Bills and Answers, series 1, Charles I (undated, c. 1630), VCRP microfilm 949. William Claiborne had become a powerful "merchant-planter-councilor" with significant political connections. Thus, he was a useful agent for Yeardley's purposes. Robert Brenner, *Merchants and Revolution: Commercial Change, Political Conflict, and London's Overseas Traders, 1550–1653* (Cambridge: Cambridge University Press, 1993), 120–24.

21. John West became a member of the House of Burgesses in 1628, the same year as his marriage to Temperance, and eventually served on the Council (1631–1659) as justice of the peace for York County (1634), as acting governor (1635), and as muster-master for the colony beginning in 1641. Dorman, *Adventurers of Purse and Person*, 657.

22. Interrogatory no. 3 and answers to that question, British PRO, C 24/562/131 (Chancery—town depositions).

23. Extracts from the dispute between Francis West and Ralph Yardley over Temperance's estate. *Genealogies of Virginia Families from Tyler's Quarterly Historical and Genealogical Magazine* (Baltimore: Genealogical Publishing, 1981), 541–43.

24. Interrogatory no. 6, especially deposition of Claiborne, May 14, 1630, PRO, C 24/562/131 (Chancery—town depositions).

25. Interrogatory no. 3, British PRO, C 24/562/131 (Chancery—town depositions).

26. Claiborne's deposition, response to interrogatory no. 3, British PRO, C 24/562/131 (Chancery—town depositions).

27. Ralph Yeardley of London, bill dated February 1, 1629/30, Chancery Proceedings Charles I. W. 63. No. 42. Francis West, complainant, abstracted in *Genealogies of Virginia Families*, 541. Salmon, *Women and the Law of Property*, 81–82.

28. "Reading the banns," or publicly announcing the upcoming marriage in church occurred on three consecutive Sundays before the wedding took place. Parishioners

were asked to state if they knew of any reason why the couple could not be married. An alternative to obtaining a license, reading the banns provided official recognition that neither prospective marriage partner already had a living spouse. In the early years of the colony, only the governor could issue a marriage license. Hening, *Statutes at Large*, February 1631, vol. 1, 156. Essex County (Old Rappahannock County) Deeds and Wills (1677–1682), August 15, 1679, recorded November 5, 1679: 242–43, LVA. The records of Old Rappahannock County are now included in the Essex County Court records.

29. Essex County Deeds 26, written March 9, 1752, recorded July 21, 1752: 95–96, LVA.

30. Morgan, *American Slavery, American Freedom*, 165; Like Virginia widows, Maryland widows who resorted to prenuptial agreements showed "far greater concern for their children's welfare than they did for themselves." Gwen Victor Gampel, "Planter's Wife Revisited: Women, Equity Law, and the Chancery Court in Seventeenth-Century Maryland," in *Women and the Structure of Society*, ed. Barbara Harris and Jo Ann McNamara (Durham: Duke University Press, 1984), 26. Neither sex ratios nor "frontier" conditions alone determined inheritance practices in the colonies. For the provisions for widows in settings where women were in the majority of the population, see Gloria L. Main, "Widows in Rural Massachusetts on the Eve of the Revolution," *Women in the Age of the American Revolution*, ed. Ronald Hoffman and Peter J. Albert (Charlottesville: University Press of Virginia, 1989), 84. In frontier areas of the Chesapeake in the eighteenth century, widows received larger proportions of their husbands' estate, but were increasingly limited to these benefits during widowhood alone and lost them during a subsequent marriage. On the eighteenth-century frontier, fewer immigrants arrived as servants and settlers were less affected by the high mortality rates of the seventeenth-century settlements. Carr, "Inheritance in the Colonial Chesapeake," 177–79.

31. Gwen Gampel attributes the lack of Maryland women's resort to equity in terms of the population's lower-class origins, the lack of kin who could negotiate on behalf of brides, and Maryland's hostility to enforcing agreements. In contrast to Virginia practice, Maryland resisted recognizing femes coverts as independent actors even further by not allowing husbands to appoint wives as representatives in court during their absences. Gampel, "The Planter's Wife Revisited: Women, Equity Law, and the Chancery Court in Seventeenth-Century Maryland," 28.

32. For such an interpretation, see Mary Beth Norton's discussion of Elizabeth Murray Campbell Smith Inman, who lived in the eighteenth century and negotiated agreements with each of her husbands so that she could maintain control over her resources for her own economic pursuits. Norton, *Liberty's Daughters*, 147–51.

33. Her full name would have been Mary (Foliott) Power Seale Collier Whitby Stark.

34. Will of Henry Power, York County Deeds, Orders, and Wills (hereafter York DOW), book 9, written August 1, 1692, recorded September 26, 1692: 176, LVA.

35. The agreement established a trust setting aside property for the "use and behalf of the said Mary Seal" during her lifetime, and after her death designating the property would descend to her children according to her will. Indenture from John Seale to Thomas Barber and Charles Hansford. Deed of Jointure, York DOW book 9, written May 18, 1693 with John Seale, recorded May 24, 1693: 220, 229–30. Mary Whitby and Thomas Whitby, York Deeds and Bonds book 2, December 24, 1706: 218–19, LVA. Indenture from William Stark "gent" to J[onathan] Power planter and Henry Power planter, York DOW 14, document dated May 14, 1714: 333.

36. Richard Parker to Mary Perkins. Recorded September 5, 1656, document dated July 1656. Beverley Fleet, *Virginia Colonial Abstracts: Charles City County, 1655–1658*, v. 10 (Baltimore: Genealogical Publishing, 1961), 48.

37. York DOW 4, April 19, 1669: 246.

38. York DOW 5, February 27, 1672: 7.

39. York DOW 1, April 3, 1651: 96.

40. Norfolk County Deeds 4, October 16, 1683, f. 164, 151r, microfilm, LVA.

41. Essex County (Old Rappahannock) Deeds and Wills (1677–1682), November 14, 1679, recorded November 3, 1680: 289–90. John Rice agreed to a bond for performance of this agreement on November 5, 1680. The couple also recorded an extensive inventory of the goods and chattels in her possession, including debts owed to her; see 290–94.

42. March 10, 1652, recorded April 5, 1653. Surry County "Deeds, Etc. No. 1 1652–1672," [DOW] 1652–72; Surry County LVA microfilm, 27. Trustees were Colonel George Ludlowe, Captain George Jordan, and William Browne.

43. Robert Jones established the trust for Mary after they married. He granted a bed, bed furniture, fabrics, horses and cattle. York DOW 3, October 25, 1662: 179.

44. York DOW 4, January 26, 1669: 224.

45. York DOW 3: 173; York DOW 1, April 3, 1651: 96; Mary Beth Norton, *Founding Mothers and Fathers: Gendered Power and the Forming of American Society* (New York: Knopf, 1996), 155–56, discusses gifts made prior to remarriage.

46. Eve Williams, of Farnham Parish, Rappahannock County. Essex County Deeds and Wills (1677–1682), written March 9, 1681, recorded November 1, 1682: 369–70, LVA.

47. Mary Day and John Billington to her son John Day. Essex (Old Rappahanock) Deeds, book 7, made April 20, 1683, recorded June 8, 1683: 47–48a, LVA microfilm.

48. The children were Joseph Toppin, William Anderson, Elizabeth Anderson and John Anderson; The first child may have been from yet another marriage. Deed of gift, York DOW 12, written July 24, 1702, Peter Vines's mark recorded August 24, 1702: 13, 17.

49. Essex County [Loose] Suit Papers, September 20, 1687, LVA.

50. York DOW 8, dated May 3, 1687, recorded September 24, 1690: 484–5.

51. York DOW 8, December 18, 1689: 351.

52. For additional examples of widows making gifts to their children immediately prior to a subsequent marriage, see Elizabeth Cole and John Tavernor, Essex County (Old Rappahannock) Deeds and Wills (1677–1682), November 26, 1678, 210, LVA; Ann Goodrich to her son, "reserving the use" of the land "for my Naturall life." Essex County (Old Rappahannock) Deeds and Wills (1677–1682), written April 30, 1680, recorded May 7, 1680, LVA. Mary Day to son John Day, with consent of John Billington "with whom I am this day to intermarry," Essex County (Old Rappahannock) Deeds (1682–1686), April 20, 1683, recorded June 6, 1683: 47–48 LVA.

53. Katherine Smith, "now Wife" of George Smith to her daughter Katherine Hopkins. Essex County (Old Rappahannock) Deeds and Wills (1677–1682), November 1, 1682: 370.

54. Since seventeenth-century Virginians used "daughter-in-law" to refer interchangeably to either a stepdaughter or a son's wife, Jane must have been a stepdaughter. York DOW 3, June 24, 1659: 56. The will also designated that the decedent's wife and son-in-law were to provide Jane with a different calf if the first died.

55. I have found similar incidents of eighteenth-century Jamaican women granting valuable and encumbered property to their daughters and granddaughters.

56. Norfolk Deeds 4, October 16, 1683: 151r [listed as 151a in book], 164.

57. The contract also outlined provisions for the property if the couple remained childless. If Mary died first the property was divided among Mary's kin and Porter. If Porter died first, Mary retained half of the property and Porter's kin received half.

58. Speth, "More Than Her 'Thirds,'" 17; Carr, "Inheritance in the Colonial Chesapeake," 173.

59. Daniel Blake Smith, *Inside the Great House: Planter Life in Eighteenth-Century Chesapeake Society* (Ithaca: Cornell University Press, 1980), 177; Suzanne Lebsock, *"A Share of Honour": Virginia Women, 1600–1945* (Richmond: Virginia Women's Cultural History Project, 1984), 49; Carr, "Inheritance in the Colonial Chesapeake," 171–72,

174, 187, 194; Gail S. Terry, "Women, Property, and Authority in Colonial Baltimore County: Evidence from the Probate Records, 1660–1759" (paper presented at the Forty-fifth Conference on Early American History, Baltimore, 1984). I am grateful to Professor Terry for sharing this paper with me; James P. P. Horn, *Adapting to A New World: English Society in the Seventeenth-Century Chesapeake* (Chapel Hill: University of North Carolina Press, 1994), 227–28.

60. In the early years of the colony the secretary of the colony certified and sealed administrations, but the colony later shifted the burden of administering estates to the county courts. Hening, *Statutes at Large*, November 1645, vol. 1, 303.

61. York Orders and Wills 16, November 20, 1721: 86. Lucinda Smith and her husband Lawrence overseeing the estate of Alexander Atkinson.

62. York Orders and Wills 16, January 15, 1721/2: 102. She was administrator of the estate of Elizabeth Moody and executor of her father, Philip Moody. See a related phenomenon in the grants of power of attorney to married women to allow them to act in court.

63. Case heard in April Court, 1739. He borrowed a total of £261.0.10 sterling and £77.4.6 1/2 current money between July 1729 and January 1731. Barradall's reports, in *Virginia Colonial Decisions: The Reports by Sir John Randolph and by Edward Barradall of Decisions of The General Court of Virginia, 1728–1741*, ed. R. T. Barton (Boston: Boston Book Company, 1909), B294.

64. The defendants claimed the date had been cut out of the bond, "with Design I suppose to impose it for a Thing of later Date than it really is."

65. *Virginia Colonial Decisions*, B297.

66. Ibid., B304.

67. The name is spelled both as Blackerby and Blackersby. Two depositions give a marriage date of July 1746; one indicates a 1747 date.

68. Carpenter v. Stott, Lancaster County Court, Chancery file 1764-5, LVA.

69. Deposition of Thomas Stott, deposition of John Carpenter, *Carpenter v. Stott*, Lancaster County Court, Chancery file 1764–1765, LVA.

70. Jane Metcalfe to "Dear Child" [Richard Metcalfe], January 5, 1697, Metcalfe Family Papers, Chicago Historical Society. A longer discussion of the Metcalfe family appears later in this book. I am grateful to James C. Robertson for bringing this collection to my attention.

71. This case established an important enough model, in the eyes of jurist John Randolph, that he included it his collection of law reports. Sir John Randolph, an English-trained lawyer, collected notes from significant cases heard before the Virginia court. Mrs. Cooper may have been married previously, but this is the first marriage mentioned in the suit and for the purposes of this case will be considered the first marriage. This case is reported in Randolph's reports, *Virginia Colonial Decisions*, R59.

72. The mother, Mrs. Cooper at the time of the trial, had been previously married to a Bushrod at the time of the birth of her daughters. She then married an Allerton and finally married Cooper. See Randolph's reports in *Virginia Colonial Decisions*, R57–59. She is referred to as Mrs. Cooper in this discussion for the sake of convenience; Her daughter is referred to as Mrs. Berryman because that was her name at the time of trial.

73. *Virginia Colonial Decisions*, R59.

74. York Judgments and Orders 16, March 16, 1761: 218.

75. Jack P. Greene, ed., *The Diary of Colonel Landon Carter of Sabine Hall, 1752–1778* (Charlottesville: Virginia Historical Society, 1965), vol. 2, 965–66. Lucy Carter, later Colson, displays the behavior nineteenth-century American legal theorists posited as the reason why coverture benefited women: men's marital power was "prelegal" leav-

ing the law in the position of "mopping up the mess that the social world or testosterone had left behind." Hendrick Hartog, "Wives as Favorites," 298.

76. See, for example, the will of Richard Miars, Norfolk Wills and Deeds (1742–1749), February 15, 1745, 125–27, microfilm, LVA.

77. York Wills and Inventories 18, document dated May 16, 1739, recorded December 17, 1739: 537. Received Yorktown lot 75 outright and claim of the land next to the lot.

78. York Orders (1765–1768), April 18, 1768: 489. Trust left in hands of David Jameson. One of the witnesses to the will was Martha Goosley, another Yorktown resident from a family with trading interests extending beyond the colony.

79. Anna Catherine Moore, Virginia, to John Norton, London, 28 September 1771; Bernard Moore, Virginia, to John Norton, London, September 28, 1771. Norton Papers, CW, microfilm 1485.2, ff. 45–47.

    In nineteenth-century Virginia, separate estates granting married women independent ownership of land could be manipulated to benefit men in danger of losing all to bankruptcy. See Lebsock, *The Free Women of Petersburg*, 65–67.

80. In antebellum Virginia, the earlier type of trust, arising from marriage contract, was rare. Ibid., 61, 72.

81. See 1753, Account Book of John Tayloe, VHS.

82. Deposition of Thomas Dunston, York DOW 9, February 24, 1691/2: 101.

83. *Virginia Colonial Decisions*, B15.

84. She may have been his stepmother, because she is referred to as Ralph Green's wife, but never as Robert Green's mother.

85. Mary Anne Latané, also known as Marianne and Molly, married Dr. John Clements (also Clement) and was still living at the time her mother made her will. The couple did have surviving children. Lucy Temple Latané, *Parson Latané, 1672–1732* (Charlottesville: The Michie Company, 1936), 93–94.

86. Papers of the Latané and related Waring, Allen, Temple, Roane and Dix families [hereafter Latané FP] box 1, folder 6, 1852–1891 and n.d. items (eighteenth century), UVA.

87. In England, the differences of age "did not cancel out those of class and sex, but they still did a great deal to determine how people were treated, how they were expected to behave, and what degree of authority they enjoyed." Keith L. Thomas, "Age and Authority in Early Modern England," *Proceedings of the British Academy* 62 (1976), 206–48; for a contrasting view of the American situation, see Carol F. Karlsen, *Devil in the Shape of a Woman: Witchcraft in Colonial New England* (New York: Norton, 1987), 75–76, 113–16.

88. Her full name was Elizabeth "Betty" (Lewis) Littlepage Holladay. Will of James Littlepage, October 25, 1766, recorded December 4, 1766, Holladay Family Papers (hereafter Holladay FP), items b333–336, VHS. The accounting indicated James Littlepage left 4212 acres in Hanover and Orange Counties, a mill, and a large quantity of tobacco and corn which exceeded the value of the tracts of land in Orange County. Part of the land was sold, according to the terms of the will, and Elizabeth received a cash settlement for that land. Recorded May 5, 1768, Holladay FP; b333–36 VHS. This family engaged in extensive legal wrangling. This chapter addresses only the materials related to prenuptial agreements in the eighteenth-century letter from John Lewis to Elizabeth (Lewis) Littlepage, November 16, 1766, Holladay FP, items a900–903, VHS; renunciation of will dated December 4, 1766, Hanover County Court, Holladay FP, VHS, items b350–53.

89. Demurrer of Holladay and Elizabeth Holladay, in answer to suit of Robert Spilsby Coleman and Mary his wife, Holladay FP, items b265–66 VHS. Littlepage provided for children by a previous marriage but not for his children by Elizabeth.

90. Information on Betty Holladay's estate in: Deposition of Robert Spilsby Coleman and Mary his wife, November 5, 1789, item b264; Answer of Benjamin Lewis, Holladay FP,

items b270, 271, 274, 275–6, 278, 282, VHS. Benjamin Lewis's deposition states that the indenture establishing the trust was made March 14, 1774 and recorded in the general court December 9, 1783. Corroborating evidence of Betty Holladay's purchases in widowhood: an indenture of April 16, 1773, Ben Lewis and Martha his wife sold land to Betty Littlepage. The land was 484 acres in Spotsylvania county, devised by Zachary Lewis, deceased, to Ben Lewis. Holladay FP, item b352, VHJ.

91. Ibid.

92. Demurrer and answer of Lewis Holladay and Betty his wife, Bill in Chancery, Holladay FP, item b 264, VHS.

93. Affection and property were intertwined in marriage considerations, even in the late eighteenth century, demonstrating the continuity of old ideas and suggesting the confusion facing those who misunderstood the changing conventions. For popular fiction's treatment of these linked considerations in the Early Republic, see Cathy Davidson, *Revolution and the Word: The Rise of the Novel in America* (New York: Oxford University Press, 1986).

94. Robert Coleman, December 2, 1782, Holladay FP, items b337–40, VHS.

95. High Court of Chancery, May 25, 1790: dismissed; Virginia Court of Appeals June 24, 1811; *Lewis Holladay and Betty his wife v. Robert Spilsby Coleman and Nancy his wife* [sic, see letter to Lewis Holladay from James Rawlings September 10, 1811 concerning erroneous inclusion of Nancy rather than Mary]—reports on decision of Supreme Court of Chancery May 28, 1805: decision that the deed of settlement made in 1774 was fraudulent, appeal is dismissed, slaves claimed by appellees under will of Zachary Lewis, court discovers no ground to appeal; Lewis Holladay to give bond for delivery of slaves after death of Betty Holladay. Decree aforesaid be reversed and annulled. All in Holladay FP items b150–55, VHS.

96. Opinion of Waller Holladay concerning Elizabeth (Lewis) Littlepage Holladay's deed of trust. Holladay FP, items a1595, opinion: 1, 10–12, VHS.

97. Richard Coleman to Elizabeth Holladay, July 13, 1783, Holladay FP, items b337–40, VHS.

98. Demurrer of Betty and Lewis Holladay, Holladay FP, items b265–66, VHS.

99. Deposition of Mary Coleman, aged 37 years, Holladay FP, items b270–82, VHS.

100. For a discussion of the social meaning of property see David T. Konig, "The Virgin and the Virgin's Sister: Virginia, Massachusetts, and the Contested Legacy of Colonial Law," *The History of the Law in Massachusetts: the Supreme Judicial Court, 1692–1992* (Boston: Supreme Judicial Court Historical Society, 1992), 95–96. For conflicting notions about what property in land meant in America see William Cronon, *Changes in the Land* (New York: Hill and Wang, 1983).

CHAPTER 2

1. Historians have studied transfer of English law to the English colonies to determine the impact on women's status before the law and in society at large. Local variations existed between colonies, as local practice varied in localities the colonists left in England. See, for example: Marylynn Salmon, *Women and the Law of Property in Early America* (Chapel Hill: University of North Carolina Press, 1986); Julius Goebel Jr., "King's Law and Local Custom in Seventeenth-Century New England," *Columbia Law Review* 31 (1931): 444; George L. Haskins, "Reception of the Common Law in Seventeenth-century Massachusetts," in *Law and Authority in Colonial America Selected Essays*, ed. George A. Billias (Barre, MA: Barre Publishers, 1965); 24, Lyle Koehler, *A Search for Power: The "Weaker Sex" in Seventeenth-Century New England* (Urbana: University of Illinois Press, 1980), 50–51; Julia Cherry Spruill, *Women's Life and Work in the Southern Colonies* (1938; reprint, New York: Norton, 1972), 340; and Roger Thompson, *Women in Stuart England and America: A Comparative Study*

(Boston: Routledge and Kegan Paul, 1974). Variations existed within England, as well. For this period, see Barbara J. Todd, "Free Bench and Free Enterprise: Widows and Their Property in Two Berkshire Villages," in *English Rural Society 1500–1800*, ed. John Chartres and David Hey (Cambridge: Cambridge University Press, 1990), 175–200, which demonstrates localized legal and customary differences even within an English county.

2. In his classic study of "anglicization" John Murrin argues that Massachusetts law "anglicized" in the late seventeenth century. John M. Murrin, "Anglicizing an American Colony: The Transformation of Provincial Massachusetts," (Ph.D. diss., Yale University, 1966). For a discussion of transfer and innovation in the colonial law more generally, see Lawrence M. Friedman, *A History of American Law* (New York: Touchstone, 1973), 29–90. Friedman briefly describes the development of law concerning ownership of slaves in Virginia, but focuses on the intent behind the 1705 statute rather than the application of the law. (74–75). David T. Konig determined that Massachusetts and Virginia law shared a "legal culture" that "used the law as a tool to conserve real property holding and preserve the family unit." Residents in both colonies shared family values relative to property, though they might rely on different legal mechanisms to provide the means of achieving their goals. Konig invokes the Virginia amendments to slave law as indicative of the way the colony fell behind Massachusetts economically in part because of the lack of liquidity of their primary form of wealth, slaves, despite Virginia's advantageous development of bills of exchange as a means of creating a fluid economy. David T. Konig, "The Virgin and the Virgin's Sister: Virginia, Massachusetts, and the Contested Legacy of Colonial Law," *The History of the Law in Massachusetts: The Supreme Judicial Court, 1692–1992* (Boston: Supreme Judicial Court Historical Society, 1992) 96. For anglicization of procedure in other colonies see Cornelia Hughes Dayton, *Women before the Bar: Gender, Law, and Society in Connecticut, 1639–1789* (Chapel Hill: University of North Carolina Press, 1995), 44–47. For an analysis that highlights the role of commercialization in dividing women's and men's activities in New York and Pennsylvania, see Deborah A. Rosen, *Courts and Commerce: Gender, Law, and the Market Economy in Colonial New York* (Columbus: Ohio State University Press, 1997), 130–31; and Karin A. Wulf, *Not All Wives: Women of Colonial Philadelphia* (Ithaca: Cornell University Press, 2000), 187–91. P. J. Marshall, drawing on the work of John Murrin, suggests that the colonies developed stronger ties to Britain in the years immediately preceding the Revolution, but that the colonies and Britain were "drifting apart" in one "notable exception"—politics. P. J. Marshall, "Britain and the World in the Eighteenth Century II: Britons and Americans," *Transactions of the Royal Historical Society*, 6th ser., 9 (1999), 1–16.

3. November 19, 1745, Privy Council Register (March 5, 1744/5 to July 23,1746) PRO PC 2/99, f. 252. Report that Privy Council sent Frances Greenhill's bill to the King's Attorney and Solicitor General for an opinion. For the negative impact of legal anglicization on women's property rights in the Middle Colonies, see William M. Offutt Jr., "The Limits of Authority: Courts, Ethnicity, and Gender in the Middle Colonies, 1670–1710," in *The Many Legalities of Early America*, ed. Christopher L. Tomlins and Bruce H. Mann (Chapel Hill: University of North Carolina Press, 2001), 384.

4. See chapter 1 for a discussion of femes coverts and coverture.

5. Carole Shammas, "Early American Women and Control over Capital," in *Women in the Age of the American Revolution*, ed. Ronald Hoffman and Peter J. Albert (Charlottesville: University Press of Virginia, 1989), 135.

6. For a widow's exchange of her dower rights in land for an annuity to be paid in tobacco, see Mary Paget to James Munday Senior, October 5, 1751, Essex County Deeds, (26) 97. For negotiation in which a woman exchanged her dower rights for absolute control of a steady supply of cattle, including the right to will them away, see

William Thornton to Elizabeth Thornton, November 4, 1679, Essex County (Old Rappahannock) Deeds and Wills, 1677–1682, 238. Jack Goody, "Inheritance, Property, and Women: Some Comparative Considerations," in *Family and Inheritance: Rural Society in Western Europe 1200–1800*, ed. Jack Goody, Joan Thirsk, and E. P. Thompson (Cambridge: Cambridge University Press, 1976), 11.

7. In seventeenth-century Middlesex County, poor relief recipients tended to be single individuals without kin in the colony to help them. By the 1720s and 1730s, adult women became the more frequent recipients. Darrett B. Rutman and Anita H. Rutman, *A Place in Time: Middlesex County, Virginia, 1650–1750* (New York: Norton, 1984), 197.

8. A jury divided up the property among the heirs. For a 1655 example, see William Waller Hening, *Statutes at Large: Being A Collection of All the Laws of Virginia, from the first Session of the Legislature, in the year 1619* (Richmond and Philadelphia: Printed for the Editor, 1809–1823), vol. 1, 405. In 1664, the legislature explained that, after the property had been divided into thirds, the widow had first choice as to which property she wanted. Hening, *Statutes at Large*, vol. 2, 212.

9. Lucy Payne, widow of William, claimed her dower in land her late husband had sold to Abraham White. White began building on the land before she relinquished her dower. Her husband died shortly thereafter, leaving the purchaser to negotiate with Payne and, in 1770, to sue in equity to claim the dower share. The suit concluded with him paying costs. *White v. Payne et al.*, 1770–71, Lancaster County Chancery Records, Archives Division, LVA. Common law allowed widows a life right to a third of the real estate. Frederick Pollock and Frederic Maitland, *The History of English Law* (Cambridge: Cambridge University Press, 1923), vol. 2, 418–28. This sum was adopted in Virginia statutes. Hening, *Statutes at Large*, vol. 2, 212, vol. 3, 303. Salmon, *Women and the Law of Property*, 151–52.

10. Attorneys acting on behalf of the Tyson family warned Mrs. Tyson, whose husband placed family land up for sale in 1767 after encountering financial difficulty, that she needed to convey her right of dower because if she would not her refusal to do so would "injure the sale." According to two deponents, Mrs. Tyson "express'd some reluctance to pass her right but finally agreed to convey her right." Whether or not she actually renounced her claim became the focal point of a later lawsuit when she attempted to seize dower in the sold lands. The county sheriff told Mrs Tyson she was not obliged to make over her dower to the purchasers and he reported that upon hearing this "Mrs. Tyson declared she would not make over her Dower" so he ousted the purchaser. Joint answer of John Bowdoin and Wather Hyslop, defendants to a Bill of Complaint of Jacob Nottingham and others; deposition of John Wilkins, Sr., Sheriff, dispute heard August 1771, Northampton County Court Records, loose papers, bundle 75.

11. The Virginia precedent adopting bargain and sale was established in a case involving Lady Frances Berkeley's agreement to Governor William Berkeley's sale of land. Hening, *Statutes at Large*, vol. 2, 324. These two types of conveyancing are described in Salmon, *Women and the Law of Property*, 17–18. By 1748, legislation indicated that a wife could acknowledge her assent to a land transaction outside of court if court officials went to her home and examined her apart from her husband and recorded this fact. Hening, *Statutes at Large*, vol. 4, 411.

12. Deposition of Elizabeth Osborne, September 2, 1685, MCD (Mayor's Court Depositions) 39, Corporation of London Records Office. Extracts from the mayor's court records in the Corporation of London Records Office appear by permission of the Corporation of London.

13. One early, very public transaction included proper examination. In 1674, Frances and William Berkeley's sale of land to William Cole listed the examinations of Dame Frances by both the general court and by "some gentlemen" of the House of Burgesses suggesting that Cole wished to close all potential loopholes in the transaction. Hening,

Statutes at Large, vol. 2, 321–24. The Berkeleys were selling 1350 acres of land. The 1705 revision required that even a person who died with a will was bound to the rule that the widow must receive at least one-third of the property. If a husband died leaving her less than her third, the widow could petition to have the will declared null and void and be "impowered" to sue for her full share. Hening, *Statutes at Large,* vol. 3, 373.

14. Marylynn Salmon finds that "after an initial period of confusion," in colonial history, in which husbands sold land without their wives' consent, legal authorities adopted bargain and sale with private examination as the proper means for land sales. Salmon, *Women and the Law of Property,* 17–18.

15. For example, see York DOW 8, February 24, 1687: 24.

16. This use of "dowry" appeared several times in the Old Rappahannock—later called Essex—County court records and may indicate a "folklore" of legal knowledge passed down among the court officials in the county. See, for example, the following: Esther Dirke discharged her stepson from her claims to "all dowry of Land thirds of the Estate," and other obligations April 11, 1679, Essex County (Old Rappahannock), May 7 or 15, 1679; Elizabeth Burgess acknowledged "my part of Dowry or thirds of six hundred Acres," date of sale: January 30, 1690, recorded acknowledgement, November 22, 1690; both the Dirke and Burgess acknowledgments recorded in Essex County [loose] suit papers, LVA. Margett Taliaferro, "Relinquish my wright of Dowry," Essex County Court, misc. box 1677-1845, 7 August 1711, folder 1710-12, LVA. A 1701 bond for a marriage agreement in York County, likewise, referred to a Sarah Sanders Atkinson's "Dowry or Thirds," but this is unusual usage in York County. York Deeds and Bonds, 2: 338–40.

17. York DOW 1657–1662, January 26, 1657, November 8, 1651 (*sic*), February 7, 1659; Actual power of attorney granted from Anne Crumpe to William Crumpe recorded May 24, 1660, f. 82.

18. York DOW 4, recorded January 10, 1671, 311.

19. York Deeds and Bonds 2 (1701–1713), recorded March 2, 1695: 35.

20. York DOW 4, January 24, 1670: 338; York DOW 6, January 25, 1679: 71.

21. For examples, see James and Elizabeth Blaxton to William Wise, York Deeds and Bonds 1 (1701–1713), February 21, 1701: 1–6; Elias and Mary Wills to Thomas Vines, November 24, 1701, 7–12; Thomas and Hester Sessions to Robert Snead, January 24, 1701: 15–20; and Robert and Mary Reade to William Allin, 24 May 1703: 63-5.

22. Henry Hartwell, James Blair, and Edward Chilton, *The Present State of Virginia, and the College,* ed. Hunter Dickinson Farish (Charlottesville: University Press of Virginia, 1964), 45.

23. This transformation led to the county courtroom becoming more of "a male preserve." Dayton, *Women before the Bar,* 87.

24. Even the deeds for land sold by residents of other counties but recorded in York are worded more carefully than the York deeds of comparable dates.

25. Indenture with marks of both John and Elizabeth Rhodes, York Deeds and Bonds 2, 18 May 1702: 54; release with John Rhodes's personal acknowledgment to the land and the addition of Elizabeth Rhodes's acknowledgment, York Deeds and Bonds 2, both on August 24, 1702: 58–59.

26. York Deeds and Bonds 1 (1694–1701), May 24, 1701: 303–4.

27. On Fouace, see "Colonial Letters: Ludwell," *VMHB* 5 (1897–98): 45 and "Letters of Rev. Stephen Fouace," *WMQ,* 1st ser., 12 (1903–4): 134; On Lewis Burwell, see "Council Papers, 1698–1701," *VMHB* 23 (1915): 38, and "Wiatt Family," *WMQ,* 1st ser., 7 (1898–99): 43. "Major" Lewis Burwell died in 1710, His son, also Lewis, was still a student at the College of William and Mary in 1718.

28. Edward and Mary Athy to Jonathan Doswell, York Deeds and Bonds 3 (1713–1729): 3-4.

29. She won the case. Pole also maintained forms for writs and indentures for reference. Folder of Godfrey Pole Papers from Gloucester County, 1717–1724 and n.d; Northampton County Court House, Eastville, Virginia.
30. York Deeds and Bonds 3 (1713–1729), July 14 and 18, 1720: 336–37.
31. Hening, *Statutes at Large*, vol. 2, 324.
32. Ibid., vol. 3, 319–22.
33. I am grateful to John M. Hemphill II for this information; David T. Konig, "Country Justice: The Rural Roots of Constitutionalism in Colonial Virginia," in *An Uncertain Tradition: Constitutionalism and the History of the South*, ed. James Ely and Kermit Hall (Athens: University of Georgia Press, 1989), 71.
34. Konig, "Country Justice" 70–71.
35. Hening, *Statutes at Large*, vol. 3, 159.
36. Ibid., vol. 4, 401; vol. 5, 411.
37. William Porter and his wife Jane sold a total of 499 acres in Middlesex County to Thomas and Roger Jones in 1703 and 1704, but the Porters' son Francis attempted an ejectment to recover the land because his mother had never privately acknowledged the deed. Francis Porter died before his case was completed, but the Jones decedents wished to remedy the defect and brought this case in Chancery against Francis Porter's heirs. *Jones &c. v. Porter* (Chancery) [April 1740], Thomas Jefferson, *Reports of Cases Determined in the General Court of Virginia from 1730 to 1740; and from 1768 to 1772* (Buffalo: W. S. Hein, 1981), 62–67.
38. Ibid., 62.
39. Northampton County Court Records, bundle 56: March 1764 Finished Causes.
40. St. George Tucker, *Blackstone's Commentaries with Notes of Reference to the Constitution and Law of the Federal Government of the United States and of the Commonwealth of Virginia*, 5 vols., (Philadelphia: William Young Birch and Abraham Small,1803), 138.
41. Salmon, *Women's Property Rights*, 38. Mary Beth Norton cited Salmon's earlier work in *Liberty's Daughters: The Revolutionary Experience of American Women, 1750–1800* (Boston: Little, Brown, 1980), 46.
42. Peter V. Bergstrom, "A Stop Along the Way," a paper presented to the Philadelphia Center for Early American Studies at the University of Pennsylvania, October 17, 1986, discusses settlement patterns in tidewater Virginia.
43. The relative abundance of land and the effect on property distribution was noted even as late as 1803. St. George Tucker commented on the link between availability of land and legal practice concerning women's property, writing, "Jointures are very rare in Virginia, consequently the right of dower occurs in almost every case when a man leaves a widow in this country, where land is so abundant, that very few men of any substance are wholly without some property therein, of which the wife may be endowed." St. George Tucker, *Blackstone's Commentaries*, 136.
44. On factors limiting availability of western land to Anglo-Americans, see Woody Holton, *Forced Founders: Indians, Debtors, Slaves and the Making of the American Revolution in Virginia* (Chapel Hill: University of North Carolina Press, 1999), 3–38.
45. Carole Shammas, Marylynn Salmon, and Michel Dahlin, *Inheritance in America from Colonial Times to the Present* (New Brunswick, N.J., 1987), 55. Allan Kulikoff, *Tobacco and Slaves: The Development of Southern Cultures in the Colonial Chesapeake, 1680–1800* (Chapel Hill: University of North Carolina Press, 1986), 51.
46. There are numerous examples of these. See, for example, York Deeds 6, January 19, 1778: 2–3; July 20, 1778: 4–6.
47. The increase in numbers and status of lawyers facilitated the efforts. A. G. Roeber, *Faithful Magistrates and Republican Lawyers: Creators of Virginia Legal Culture, 1680–1810* (Chapel Hill: University of North Carolina Press, 1981); Jack P. Greene,

Pursuits of Happiness: The Social Development of Early Modern British Colonies and the Formation of American Culture (Chapel Hill: University of North Carolina Press, 1988), 89–93.

48. Ira Berlin, *Many Thousands Gone: The First Two Centuries of Slavery in North America* (Cambridge, MA: Belknap Press, 1998), 8.

49. Lois Green Carr, "Inheritance in the Colonial Chesapeake," *Women in the Age of the American Revolution,* ed. Ronald Hoffman and Peter Albert (Charlottesville: University Press of Virginia, 1989), 159, 168–69, 175. Jean Butenhoff Lee, "Land and Labor: Parental Bequest Practices in Charles County, Maryland, 1732–1783," in *Colonial Chesapeake Society,* ed. Lois Green Carr, Philip D. Morgan, and Jean B. Russo (Chapel Hill: University of North Carolina Press, 1988), 333. For the literature on the tendency toward gender specific devolution of personalty and slaves to daughters and land to sons, see, for Maryland, Gail S. Terry, "Women, Property, and Authority in Colonial Baltimore County, Evidence from the Probate Records, 1660–1759," paper presented to the Forty-fifth Conference on Early American History, Baltimore, 1984. Maryland" and, for Virginia, see C. Ray Keim, "Primogeniture and Entail in Colonial Virginia," WMQ, 3d ser., 25 (1968): 553, 557–58. Virginians also entailed slaves on sons. The Burwell family provides a significant example of this. Lorena S. Walsh, *From Calabar to Carter's Grove: The History of a Virginia Slave Community* (Charlottesville: University Press of Virginia, 1997), 223. For a reconsideration of the gendered nature of personality and real estate among parental bequests, see Wayne Graham, "For Generations: Wills, Inventories, and Wealth in Colonial Virginia" (M.A., thesis, College of William and Mary, 2001).

50. Russell R. Menard, "From Servants to Slaves: The Transformation of the Chesapeake Labor System," *Southern Studies* 16 (1977): 355–90. Alan Kulikoff refers to seventeenth-century planters' "insatiable demand" for labor; Kulikoff, *Tobacco and Slaves,* 33. Kulikoff describes land scarcity at the root of social crisis in the Chesapeake by the eighteenth century, (428). In this setting, widows who inherited slaves could lease them out to neighbors for income.

51. *Herndon et al. v. Carr,* in Jefferson, *Reports,* 135.

52. A. Leon Higginbotham Jr., *In The Matter of Color: Race and the American Legal Process in the Colonial Period* (New York: Oxford University Press, 1978), 50.

53. Black's Law Dictionary defines the terms as follows:

> A chattel is an article of personal property not freehold or fee in land.
> Personal chattels refer to movable things.
> Real chattels are "such as concern, or savor of realty, such as leasehold estates; interests issuing out of, or annexed to real estate." Chattel interests that devolve as real estate.
> Chattel Real: all interests in real estate of lesser dignity than a freehold estate... descended under the rules for devolution of personal property, not as freehold or fee simple estates.

Henry Campbell Black, *Black's Law Dictionary* (St. Paul: West Publishing, 1990), 236.

54. Hening, *Statutes at Large,* vol. 3, 333. Higginbotham discusses this law in *In the Matter of Color,* 50–53, though he amends the wording of the law itself. Virginia's slave law evolved to meet not only the desires of slave-owning legislators and their constituents, but also in response to merchants' demands for liquid assets they could seize from planters with debts. In most colonies and states the law considered slaves to be held as a form of chattel property, but, as Jefferson's interest demonstrated, Virginia's slave law was distinctive and the categories of property changed over time. The 1705 law provided various loopholes that in practice allowed property in slaves to continue to be more like personal and chattel property. For example, the law deemed unsold slaves in a merchant's or factor's possession exempt from designation as real estate and considered these particular slaves to be personal estate "in the

same condition they should have been in, if this act had never been made." Owners of property in slaves could not base their claim to voting privileges solely on their ownership of slaves; the law continued to require freehold ownership of real estate in land for this purpose. Slaves also continued to be liable to claims for payment of debts and were not subject to escheat. Slaves remained similar to chattels or personal estate in these respects.

55. Joan R. Gundersen and Gwen Victor Gampel, "Married Women's Legal Status in Eighteenth-Century New York and Virginia," *WMQ*, 3d ser., 39 (1982): 121. For an alternative view, see Carole Shammas, Marylynn Salmon, and Michael Dahlin's focus on the reduced monetary value to widows of slaves held for life only, as was the case when slaves were redefined as real estate. Shammas, Salmon, and Dahlin, *Inheritance in America*, 35; Salmon, *Women and the Law of Property*; see also Terri L. Snyder, "Legal History of the Colonial South," *WMQ*, 3d ser., 50 (1993): 24–25.

56. Widows had the first choice of which thirds of the property they wanted; September, 1664, Hening, *Statutes at Large*, vol. 2, 212. Widows could sue out writs of partition and dower to regain slaves after 1705. Hening, *Statutes at Large*, vol. 3, 334. For intestacy, see October 1705; Hening, *Statutes at Large*, vol. 3, 371–76. Personal estate remaining after debts had been paid was divided into thirds, with the widow taking one-third and the children sharing the remainder. The widow received more property if there were no children, or only one child was born to the marriage. Hening, *Statutes at Large*, vol. 3, 373. Exceptions existed for women who had obtained jointures to the bar of dower. Hening, *Statutes at Large*, vol. 3, 374.

57. Women benefitted from slave ownership in indirect as well as direct ways. In old age widows who no longer managed their own plantations could lease slaves out for cash. David Goldfield believes that urban slave hiring probably began with the development of southern cities, and seemed to be in place in Charleston by 1712. David R. Goldfield, "Black Life in Old South Cities," in *Before Freedom Came: African-American Life in the Antebellum South*, ed. Edward Campbell and Kym Rice (Richmond: Museum of the Confederacy and University Press of Virginia, 1991), 130. For the implications of the "dangerous and lucrative system" of hiring out slaves in post-Revolutionary Virginia, see Douglas R. Egerton's discussion on the background of Gabriel's Rebellion of 1800. Egerton points out that many of the rebels had a "rough form of freedom" because of their being hired out, and suggests that this status, combined with the fact that their owners were often women and children, left them with a "tenuous tie in a society built upon patriarchalism" when the more typical slave lived under the more direct control of a master. Douglas R. Egerton, *Gabriel's Rebellion: The Virginia Slave Conspiracies of 1800 and 1802* (Chapel Hill: University of North Carolina Press, 1993), 23–25. For a discussion of the leasing of Monticello slaves, and of parents ultimately able to purchase freedom for their children, see Lucia C. Stanton, "'Those Who Labor for My Happiness': Thomas Jefferson and His Slaves," in *Jeffersonian Legacies*, ed. Peter S. Onuf (Charlottesville: University Press of Virginia, 1993), 170–71.

58. "Under Maryland law chattel could not be entailed, although the probate court recognized such bequests in a restricted manner." Lee, "Land and Labor" 310–11, 336.

59. Hening, *Statutes at Large*, vol. 4, 222–28.

60. This is outlined in the 1727 "Act to explain and amend" the 1705 act. Hening, *Statutes at Large*, vol. 4, 227. The only restriction on a widow's claim of dower rights to slaves in 1705 was that she could only claim those rights so long as neither she nor her future husband(s) sent the slaves out of the colony. Hening, *Statutes at Large*, vol. 3, 334–35. If the husband of the widow sent the slaves out of the colony the person who held the rights in reversion gained possession of the slaves only during the husband's life.

61. An entailed estate passed unchanged from generation to generation, though entails could be broken through private legislation.

62. Hening, *Statutes at Large*, vol. 4, 227. It was explained in an address by a joint committee of the governor and council and the House of Burgesses, April 15, 1752: "wives' slaves were vested in their husbands; they were only to be given or bequeathed as chattels, and no remainder of them was to be limited otherwise than as a chattel personal by the rules of common law" (vol. 5, 440; Hening's transcript of the address).

63. Brewer proposes that entailing slaves annexed to land allowed for feudalism to be "redeveloped in a new form in Virginia." Holly Brewer, "Entailing Aristocracy in Colonial Virginia: 'Ancient Feudal Restraints' and Revolutionary Reform," *WMQ*, 3d ser., 54 (1997): 338–40. Wayne Graham found that entails of land persisted even after post-Revolutionary prohibitions. Graham, "For Generations." For subsequent disputes about whether slaves needed to be "annexed" to land for the entail on them to take effect, see David T. Konig, "Legal Fictions and the Rule(s) of Law: The Jeffersonian Critique of Common-Law Adjudication," in *The Many Legalities of Early America*, ed. Christopher L. Tomlins and Bruce H. Mann (Chapel Hill: University of North Carolina Press, 2001), 111–13. While English landowners could dock entails after 1540 by the process of fine and recovery, Virginians had more difficulty breaking them after legislation in 1705 and could only do so by legislative action. Keim, "Primogeniture and Entail," 540.

64. Keim, "Primogeniture and Entail," 562. Holly Brewer reveals the flaws in Keim's conclusion that entailing was uncommon in colonial Virginia by demonstrating the cumulative effect of colonists' using entail to remove land from circulation. She estimates that "a very high percentage of land—a full 78 percent—would have been entailed" by the Revolutionary War generation. Brewer, "Entailing Aristocracy in Colonial Virginia," 321, 343. No comparable figures exist on the proportion of Virginia slaves entailed over the colonial period. Although more work needs to be done to estimate the proportion of slaves entailed in Virginia, Lorena Walsh determined that it would be "virtually impossible" to tell how many slaves were entailed. Lorena S. Walsh, *From Calabar to Carter's Grove*, 276, n. 68. Keim pointed out the need for more work on the extent of slave entails in his 1968 article; Keim, "Primogeniture and Entail," 584.

65. Konig, "Legal Fictions and the Rule(s) of Law," 111–12. Keim, "Primogeniture and Entail," 540, n. 4; Hening, *Statutes at Large*, vol. 4, 225.

66. Gooch also expressed concern that creditors, "especially British Merchants," would be defrauded when they discovered their debtors' slaves were settled in tail. Governor's letters to the Board of Trade, received June 30, 1728, PRO CO, 5/1321, f. 41.

67. As late as October 1722, the general court determined that slaves did not pass as personal estate in a will. *Smith v. Griffin*, in Jefferson, *Reports*, 132.

68. Salmon, *Women and the Law of Property*, 154.

69. The colonists protested the king's action and in a statement outlined some of their concerns about the way in which slaves were categorized as a type of property. Confusion was part of the colonists' stated concern, since the 1705 shift of slaves from personal to real property "destroyed old titles, and created new" and was "productive of many suits": changing the law meant that slaves "might not at the same time be real estate in some respects, personal in others, and both in others," a situation sure to create stated confusion. Hening, *Statutes at Large*, vol. 5, 432–43. In their appeal the colonists claimed that they were concerned about creditors seizing their slaves for debt, a task made difficult by the debtors' slaves being entailed. This, according to the petitioners, was dangerous to the credit of the country, "And should credit be destroyed in a trading country, as ours may be properly called, the consequence might be fatal." Hening, *Statutes at Large*, vol. 5, 442, note.

70. "Sir William Gooch's Observations upon Several Acts passed at Virginia," received May 7, 1750, read May 10, 1750, PRO CO 5/1327, f. 72v.

71. The king disallowed the law in October 1751, but that did not stop an energetic appeal from the colonists for reconsideration. Disallowed, October 31, 1751, PRO CO 5/1327, part 1, f. 159. William Robinson and W[illiam?] Fairfax wrote to the king in late 1751 explaining why the act should pass and asking that slaves be returned to their "natural Condition" as personal estate. December 21, 1752. W. Fairfax and John Robinson to Council. PRO CO 5/1327, part 2, f. 236–38. Despite the long plea from the colonists, the law remained disallowed.

72. Hening, *Statues at Large*, vol. 5, 448, n; see also PRO CO 5/1327, f. 238.

73. Edward Barradall studied in England, served as legal advisor to Lord Fairfax on his Northern Neck lands, and became mayor of Williamsburg within a year of his marriage to Sarah Fitzhugh, a member of a prominent Virginia family. The mayoralty was only the first of the public offices he held in the colony. Barradall often faced Randolph in the courtroom; his notes continue to 1741. R. Earl Nance, "Edward Barradall," *The Virginia Law Reporters before 1880*, ed. W. Hamilton Bryson (Charlottesville: University Press of Virginia, 1977), 71-74. *Jones v. Langhorne, Virginia Colonial Decisions: The Reports by Sir John Randolph and by Edward Barradall of Decisions in the General Court of Virginia, 1728–1741*, ed. R. T. Barton (Boston: Boston Book Company, 1909), B55.

74. Richard Lee (Williamsburg) to Landon Carter (Richmond), November 26, 1776, Lee Family Papers, VHS.

75. Revisal of the Laws, 1776–1786, reprinted in *The Papers of Thomas Jefferson*, ed. Julian P. Boyd et. al. (Princeton: Princeton University Press, 1958), vol. 2, 398.

76. Salmon, *Women and the Law of Property*, 155; Although Holly Brewer primarily focused on entailed lands in her study, she, too, postulates that "Revolutionary reforms may also have adversely affected the status and wealth of elite women" so that "perhaps some elite women had more power and wealth under the patriarchal system than the early republican." Brewer, "Entailing Aristocracy in Virginia," 343–44.

77. Slave families probably benefited from being annexed to entailed land because they faced less fear of being separated from any family and community members who were also attached to the land. Brewer, "Entailing Aristocracy in Virginia," 340.

78. Britain abolished slavery in its colonies through the 1833 Abolition of Slavery Act, which went into effect on August 1, 1834, though a period of "apprenticeship" kept former slaves in continuing bondage. Transcript of *Somerset v. Stewart* as cited by David Brion Davis, *The Problem of Slavery in the Age of Revolution, 1770–1823* (Ithaca: Cornell University Press, 1975), 486. At the time of the case, there were thousands of slaves in England. Robin Blackburn, *The Overthrow of Colonial Slavery, 1776–1848* (London: Verso, 1988), 99–101. For earlier cases on slavery in England and the failure of villeinage to serve as a precedent, see Davis, *The Problem of Slavery*, 472–89.

79. Nance, "Edward Barradall," 71–74. *Blackwell v. Wilkinson* (October 1768) in Jefferson, Reports of Cases, 76. *Jones v. Langhorne,* cited in both Barradall's and Randolph's reports, *Virginia Colonial Decisions*, B53-55, R109–11.

80. R. Earl Nance, "Sir John Randolph," in *The Virginia Law Reporters before 1880*, ed. W. Hamilton Bryson (Charlottesville: University Press of Virginia, 1977), 68.

81. In addition, the details recorded in the arguments reveal the culture's assumptions about gender, women's claim to property, and the gender-specific power potentially accompanying property in the colonial period. The arguments are discussed in greater detail in Linda L. Sturtz, "'Madam and Co.': Women, Property, and Power in Colonial Virginia" (Ph.D. diss., Washington University, 1994), 206–76.

82. Three sets of reports, including Thomas Jefferson's, on cases heard in the general court of the colony reveal the complications caused by the evolution of slave law during the eighteenth century. Although no judges' opinions exist on the general court cases, the reports still demonstrate the tremendous significance of the cases to peo-

ple at the time. In addition to Jefferson's reports, the notes of two other Virginia lawyers, Edward Barradall and Sir John Randolph, survive. Randolph, educated at the College of William and Mary and admitted to Gray's Inn, London, practiced law in Virginia, and recorded notes on his arguments and those of his opponents on cases heard by the general court; his surviving notes span the years from 1729 to 1732. Later in the eighteenth century, Thomas Jefferson made his own collection of cases, subsequently published in 1829—three years after his death. Jefferson probably began collecting cases during the time he practiced in the general court, and some of the earlier cases were related to cases he prepared. These cases included a selection of thirty cases from the earlier Randolph and Barradall notes, as well as one case taken from the now lost reports made by William Hopkins. To these Jefferson added his own reports made from cases heard between 1768 and 1772. George M. Curtis, "Thomas Jefferson," in *The Virginia Law Reporters before 1880*, ed. W. Hamilton Bryson (Charlottesville: University Press of Virginia, 1977), 75–84. The chronological range of Jefferson's reports also suggests the persistence of the problems with slave law since the reports include cases tried before Jefferson was born and then remained significant enough into the early nineteenth century for a descendant to publish this collection.

83. Colonists with legal training thought slaves resembled villeins, unfree persons born to their servility, though villeinage had died out in England so the parallel did not shape the development of slave law in Virginia. Christopher Dyer, "Memories of Freedom: Attitudes towards Serfdom in England, 1200–1350," in *Serfdom and Slavery: Studies in Legal Bondage*, ed. M. L. Bush (London: Longman, 1996), 278–79. The classic study of racism and the cultural dimension of its root of the development of slavery in America is Winthrop Jordan, *White over Black: American Attitudes toward the Negro, 1550–1812* (Chapel Hill: University of North Carolina Press, 1968). For a brief overview of the development of slave law see Friedman, *A History of American Law*, 73–76.

84. In addition, Lamb picked up on the legalistic point that the act had no suspending clause, a necessary element in new legislation by the 1749 date of the law. PRO CO 5/1327, part 1, f. 139.

85. By the time of the Revolution, "American divorce already diverged dramatically from its principal English roots," and late colonial attempts to enact divorces in Pennsylvania, New Hampshire, and New Jersey met with Privy Council disallowance. In 1773, English authorities instructed colonial governors to prevent all future divorces within the colonies. Norma Basch, "From the Bonds of Empire to the Bonds of Matrimony," in *Devising Liberty: Preserving and Creating Freedom in the New American Republic*, ed. David T. Konig (Stanford: Stanford University Press, 1995), 220.

86. An abandoned or unsupported woman could sue for alimony from her husband's estate. The (Old) Rappahannock County court ordered Elizabeth Hanslip to take possession of all the couple's property in the county "as Alimony & towards her future support & maintenance." Essex County (Old Rappahannock) Orders (1683–1685), March 5, 1685: 79. In another case, a county court protected a woman's right to alimony while it halted Rawleigh Chinn's efforts in 1722 to defraud his wife, Easter, by conveying away the property intended as her alimony. This arose from a case of cruelty: "Chinn her caveat ag[ains]t. Chinn" Lancaster County, Chancery 1722-folder 01, September 12, 1722, LVA. In the post–Revolutionary War period, law reporter David Watson recorded in his notes for the case of *James and Elizabeth Martin v. John Thomson* that, despite St. George Tucker's conclusion that no suits for alimony could be made in the Virginia courts, *Martin v. Thomson* and "common practice of the county courts" demonstrate that "suits for alimony may be brought in our courts." Watson left the case undated in his notes, but the cases he included come from 1799

to 1809. W. Hamilton Bryson, *Miscellaneous Virginia Law Reports, 1784–1809* (Dobbs Ferry, NY: Oceana Publications, 1992), 78–79.

87. April 24, 1704, *Legislative Journals of the Council of Colonial Virginia*, ed. H. R. McIlwaine, 2d ed. (Richmond: Virginia State Library, 1979), 390.

88. April 24, and May 8, 1704, *Journals of the House of Burgesses of Virginia, 1702/3–1705; 1705–1706; 1710–1712*, ed. H. R. McIlwaine (Richmond: The Colonial Press, E. Waddey Company, 1912), vol. 4, 48, 74.

89. The Greenfeild case differed slightly from the later Cooper and Greenhill cases because it began in the Council (the upper house) rather than the House of Burgesses.

90. "An Act, to enable Frances Greenhill, to sell and dispose of her lands, and other estate, by deed or will, notwithstanding her husband Joseph Greenhill shall happen to be living; and for other purposes therein mentioned", Chapter 33, May 1742, Hening, *Statutes at Large*, vol. 5, 216–17. The bill described land in her birthplace of Prince George County as well as her land in Surry County. Other documents place all of the land in Surry. PRO CO 5/1326, ff. 23-24.

91. June 23, 1730, *Journal of the House of Burgesses, 1727–1734, 1736–1740*, ed. H. R. McIlwaine (Richmond: The Colonial Press, E. Waddey Company, 1910), vol. 6, 86.

92. James Oldham, *The Mansfield Manuscripts and the Growth of English Law in the Eighteenth Century* (Chapel Hill: University of North Carolina Press, 1993), 1245–51, 1275–76, 1292, 1296–99, 1302–3, 1311. Note the significance of the empire, especially the West Indies and Ireland, in several of these cases on marriage, 1272–75 and 1311, for example.

93. This Paschall Greenhill may have been Frances's father-in-law. A Joseph Greenhill, son of Paschall, was listed as being a merchant of Bristol, Rhode Island and a son of Paschall Greenhill. The Amelia County, Virginia records indicate that the merchant Joseph Greenhill had a son, David. If this Joseph Greenhill was Frances's husband, Frances Greenhill had a stepson. The court may have expected Paschall Greenhill to protect his grandson's rights against Frances's claims. The Rhode Island business would help explain Joseph's prolonged absence. Gibson Jefferson McConnaughey, *Unrecorded Deeds and Other Documents, Amelia County, Virginia* (Amelia, VA: Mid-South Publishing, 1994), 16.

94. It is possible that further records were lost in the 1734–36 gap. June 30, 1730, *Journal of the House of Burgesses, 1727–1734, 1736–1740*, ed. McIlwaine, vol. 6, 86.

95. Basch argues that the community petitions suggest a "bottom-up" explanation of cultural diffusion. Virginians' support of Greenhill demonstrates a pre-Revolutionary version of this. Norma Basch, "The Bonds of Matrimony," 239; Brewer, "Entailing Aristocracy," 326; May 1, 1742, "Advertisement," Governor's Correspondence (enclosures), PRO CO 5/1325, f. 103r. William Fawne and Joseph Carter, "Clearks" of the churches in Marchants Brandon Parish, signed that they had published the notes and that "several of the parishioners … took notice of and read" the note. Affidavits of Joseph Carter and Williams Fawne before W. Harrison, June 8, 1742, PRO CO 5/1325, ff. 110r, 111r. In 1816, when Robert Wright petitioned for divorce, over fifty neighbors petitioned the legislature on his behalf. Thomas E. Buckley, S. J., "Unfixing Race: Class, Power, and Identity in an Interracial Family," *VMHB* 102 (1994): 350, 366.

96. May 24, 1742 and June 11–12, 1742, *Legislative Journals of the Council*, ed. McIlwaine, 913, 919–20, 921.

97. Hening, *Statutes at Large*, vol. 5, 218–19.

98. William Gooch to Board of Trade, Governor's Correspondence, August 11, 1742, PRO CO 5/1325, f. 107v.

99. PRO CO 5/1366, f. 357.

100. Francis Fane to The Lords Commissioners for Trade and Plantations, January 31, 1743, PRO CO 5/1326, ff. 23r–24v.

101. Greenhill sent Mr. Athawes, a Virginia merchant, to speak as her representative in the case, a logical choice since he would travel back and forth between the colony and London. Progress of the bill recorded on the wrapper, PRO CO 5/1326 f. 24. Postponement in *Journal of the Commissioners for Trade and Plantations from January 1741/2 to December 1749 Preserved in the Public Record Office* (London: His Majesty's Stationery Office, 1931), 101.

102. *Journal of the Commissioners for Trade and Plantations 1741/2 to 1749*, 157, 239.

103. Listed as R. Plumer, J. Pitt, Mondon, M. Bladen.

104. March 22, 1744/5, "Virginia Correspondence—Original, Board of Trade," PRO CO 5/1326, f. 187.

105. King in Council at Court in Kensington, July 23, 1746, PRO CO 5/1326, f. 225. Progress recorded on wrapper, f. 228v: Order of Council, July 23, 1746, reappeal; received February 24, 1746/7; read March 25, 1746/7.

106. She also claimed that her business contacts refused to perform contracts and agreements they had made with her and trespassed on her tenements. "An Act, to enable Susannah Cooper, to sell and dispose of her personal estate, by deed or will, notwithstanding her husband, Isles Cooper, shall happen to be living; and for other purposes therein mentioned"; Chapter 41, September 1744, Hening, *Statutes at Large*, vol. 5, 294–96.

107. Colonel Gooch to the Board of Trade, December 21, 1744, "Trade," PRO CO 5/1326, ff. 53–54. Progress of bill from wrapper: received March 11, 1744/5 from Mr. Athawes, read March 19, 1744/5, "Abson."

108. Gooch to the Board of Trade, 21 December 1744, PRO CO 5/1326, ff. 53–54.

109. Ibid., PRO CO 5/1326, ff. 53–54r.

110. Gooch cited in Greene, *Peripheries and Center*, 27.

111. Board of Trade to Gooch, June 27, 1745, PRO CO 5/1366, ff. 376–78.

112. For a recent treatment of Cooper's case that assumed that it succeeded despite the lack of the bill's return to the colony see Kathleen M. Brown, *Good Wives, Nasty Wenches, and Anxious Patriarchs: Gender, Race, and Power in Colonial Virginia* (Chapel Hill: Univeristy of North Carolina Press, 1996), 337. In contrast, Marylynn Salmon points out that Cooper's bill died in the Board of Trade because it contained a suspending clause that killed it unless the board approved of the Virginia Legislature's act. Salmon, *Women and the Law of Property*, 55, 208–9, n. 61.

113. July 3, 1745, PRO CO 5/1366, f. 388.

114. Sent to Matthew Lamb, March 18, 1746/7, PRO CO 5/1366, f. 402.

115. Mr. Lamb, Lincoln's Inn, to the Commissions for Trade and Plantations, February 3, 1754. According to the wrapper, this was received February 5, 1754 and read April 5, 1754. PRO CO 5/1328, ff. 81r-v.

116. Board of Trade to Governor Gooch, June 27, 1745, PRO CO 5/1366, ff. 376-8.

117. See chapter 4 for more on female ordinary keepers.

118. "Virginia Gazette Day Book 1750–1752, and 1764–1766," ed. Paul P. Hoffman (Charlottesville: Microfilm Publications of the University of Virginia, 1967), no. 5: 16, 20. She also purchased both a set of cups and saucers for beverage service and a number of corks, presumably for use in storing drinks. Francis Jerdone Senior Journal, May 1, 1749–July 10, 1755, f. 85, LVA; Francis Jerdone Senior Journals, September 15, 1750–June 2, 1760, ff. 25, 81, 110, LVA; Ledger of Unknown Hanover County, Virginia, merchant 1750–1751, February 19, 1750 or 1751, (photostat), LVA. Her credits in the account books of other Virginians show that she provided board for an employee and a slave of a local planter. Account for boarding Benjamin Haselwood and "my [Wlilliam Bassett's] negro Minney." The cost of boarding Minney was half the charges for Benjamin Haselwood. William Bassett Account Book 1728–1755, August 20, 1740, VHS.

119. William Bassett incurred a large debt of £27.0.3 to Cooper for "my Expences at the Election." William Bassett Account Book 1728–1755, n.d. (late 1773), VHS.

120. Bills of exchange substituted for metallic currency for remittances from the colonies for several reasons. Losses due to transportation disasters, such as a sinking ship, could be minimized, and bills of exchange served as a form of credit during the time before the bills were cashed through a predictable and legal form of, effectively, bill "kiting." Discounts on the face value of the bill accounted for the lapse of time—often thirty, sixty or ninety days—for which the bill extended credit. For a thorough description of how bills of exchange functioned in the transatlantic economy see Jacob M. Price, "Transaction Costs: A Note on Merchant Credit and the Organization of Private Trade," in *The Political Economy of Merchant Empires*, ed. James D. Tracy (Cambridge: Cambridge University Press, 1991), 283–88.

121. William Bassett Account Book 1728–1755, f. 56, VHS. Bassett dealt with Cooper so frequently that he paid a debt to a third party through his account with her.

122. Jerdone allowed her to incur a debt of £9.19.9. Jerdone Account Book 1751–52, microfilm, 4, CW. For more on Jerdone, see chapter 5.

123. Two separate casks of beer to Mrs. Greenhill, William Bassett Account Book 1728–1755, August 25, 1739, VHS. Other men and women purchased casks of beer at this time.

124. Amy Louise Erickson, *Women and Property in Early Modern England* (London: Routledge, 1993), 30, 136.

125. Salmon, *Women and the Law of Property*, 70.

126. Oldham, *Mansfield Manuscripts*, 1246–47.

127. Manuscript opinion of Ringsted v. Lady Lanesborough, cited in Oldham, *Mansfield Manuscripts*, 1245.

128. Mansfield, cited in Oldham, *Mansfield Manuscripts*, 1247.

129. Lawrence Stone, *Road to Divorce: England 1530–1987* (Oxford: Oxford University Press, 1990), 155.

130. Ibid., 325.

131. Susan Staves, "Chattel Property Rules and the Construction of Englishness, 1660-1800," *Law and History Review* 12 (1994), 123–53.

132. The gendered nature of encumbered property mattered more to the imperial authorities than the conception that real property was somehow sacrosanct. What made the Greenhill and Cooper bills distinctive was the way they sought relief from the gender-specific obstructions to disposal of property suffered by femes coverts.

133. Virginians who "docked" entails often used the proceeds of the sale to purchase property to be protected under a substitute entail. For example, a tract of land could be sold to acquire more conveniently situated land, a portion of entailed land might be sold to purchase slaves to be annexed to land, or entailed slaves sold to buy land. Brewer, "Entailing Aristocracy in Virginia," 327; Oldham, *Mansfield Manuscripts*, 1245.

134. Report that Privy Council sent Frances Greenhill's bill to the King's Attorney and Solicitor General for an opinion, November 19, 1745, Privy Council Register (March 5, 1744/5 to 23 July 1746) PRO PC 2/99, f. 252.

135. Francis Fane to The Lords Commissioners for Trade and Plantations, January 31, 1743, PRO CO 5/1326, ff. 23r–24v.

136. Joan Hoff points out the irony that the War of Independence reduced wifely independence in terms of equity remedies, the source of limited legal power that Mary Beard discussed in her analysis of American women. Joan Hoff, *Law, Gender, and Injustice: A Legal History of U.S. Women* (New York: New York University Press, 1991), 127–30. For persistence of women's subordination after the revolution, see Linda K. Kerber, *Toward an Intellectual History of Women* (Chapel Hill: University of North Carolina

Press, 1997), 177–78, 261–302. Ironically, while the colonists pressed the limits of laws regarding coverture in the Greenhill and Cooper test cases, the Revolutionary generation and their immediate descendants delayed in shifting toward providing women with contractual independence and more autonomous control over their property while they generally freed property from encumbrances. James Willard Hurst, *Law and the Conditions of Freedom in the Nineteenth-Century United States* (Madison: University of Wisconsin Press, 1956), 14–16.

137. Suzanne Lebsock, *The Free Women of Petersburg: Status and Culture in a Southern Town, 1784–1860* (New York: Norton, 1985), 85.

138. For one attempt to adapt the theories of post-colonial studies to gender systems in Britain's American empire see Kenneth A. Lockridge, *On the Sources of Patriarchal Rage: The Commonplace Books of William Byrd and Thomas Jefferson and the Gendering of Power in the Eighteenth Century* (New York: New York University Press, 1992). Margaret Strobel points out the position of European women within the second British empire: they enjoyed "opportunities not found in Europe," but, simultaneously, they were expected to guard "social boundaries." Margaret Strobel, *European Women and the Second British Empire* (Bloomington: Indiana University Press, 1991), xi, xiii, 9. For discussions of the complexity of gender and race in colonial cultures and the ways that white women benefited, see: Vron Ware, *Beyond the Pale: White Women, Racism and History* (London: Verso, 1992); Catherine Hall, "Gender Politics and Imperial Politics: Rethinking the Histories of Empire," in *Engendering History: Caribbean Women in Historical Perspective*, ed. Verene Shepherd, Bridget Brereton, and Barbara Bailey, (Kingston, Jamaica: Ian Randle, 1995); and Ashis Nandy, *The Intimate Enemy: Loss and Recovery of Self under Colonialism* (Delhi: Oxford University Press, 1983).

139. Transcribed in Frank L. Dewey, *Thomas Jefferson: Lawyer* (Charlottesville: University Press of Virginia, 1986), 57–72.

CHAPTER 3

1. William planned to leave the colony, and granted those powers for as long as he was absent. January 4, 1715/[6]; recorded September 18, 1716, LVA, Essex County (Old Rappahannock County) Misc. Recs. 1677–1845, folder 1713–1716. For widowhood and legal responsibilities, see Lois Green Carr and Lorena S. Walsh, "The Planter's Wife: Experience of White Women in Seventeenth-Century Maryland," *WMQ*, 3d ser. 34 (1977): 542–71. Daniel Blake Smith, *Inside the Great House: Planter Life in Eighteenth-Century Chesapeake Society* (Ithaca: Cornell University Press, 1980).

2. See Act 7, November 1645, in Hening, *Statutes at Large*, vol. 1, 302. See Peter Charles Hoffer, *Law and People in Colonial America* (Baltimore: Johns Hopkins University Press, 1992): 40–42.

3. Women were far more likely to be grantors of powers of attorney than recipients. When acknowledging alienation of their dower rights to land, women often appointed attorneys to act on their behalf so that they could avoid traveling to court. Examples of women appointing attorneys in this circumstance appear throughout the runs of court records in the colonial tidewater counties. For a collected run of power of attorney, however, see Essex County, Misc. Box 1677–1845, LVA.

4. Linda Kerber points out that these grants of power of attorney demonstrate the resilience of coverture and the desire of men as well as women to navigate the system of coverture to their own advantage. Linda K. Kerber, Concluding Comments, Many Legalities Conference, Williamsburg, Virginia, November 1996. The classic discussion of how men benefited from women's separate control of property in antebellum Virginia is Suzanne Lebsock, *The Free Women of Petersburg: Status and Culture in a Southern Town, 1784–1860* New York: Norton, 1985).

5. The best overview on the "diversity" of colonial law relating to economically active women and, specifically, to feme sole trader provisions, is Marylynn Salmon's book. Salmon also highlights the significance of husbands' written or tacit consent in the courts' acceptance of women's economic agency. Marylynn Salmon, *Women and the Law of Property in Early America* (Chapel Hill: University of North Carolina Press, 1986), xiii, 5, 44–57, 68–70, 76, 86, 104–8, 189, 192, 207. Husband-to-wife powers of attorney certainly fits this definition.

6. Salmon, *Women and the Law of Property*, 44-9, 55-7; Laurel Thatcher Ulrich, *Good Wives: Image and Reality in the Lives of Women in Northern New England, 1650–1750* (Oxford: Oxford University Press, 1983), 36.

7. York County DOW book 4, 10 April 1667: 129. For the Henshaw power of attorney see Essex County, Misc. Box 1677–1845, Powers of Attorney, folder 1706–1708, LVA. Philip Lacke and Thomas Griffin were the defendants in the cases. Lacke was also listed as the purchaser of the tract of land.

8. York DOW 9, March 24, 1692/3: 215. In his power of attorney he recorded "I doe hereby ratify & confirme what my sd attor shall act or doe in my behalfe" It is not clear if Margrett was literate, but her husband made his mark to the document, suggesting that he was not.

9. James R. Perry, *The Formation of a Society on Virginia's Eastern Shore* 1615–1658 (Chapel Hill: University of North Carolina Press), 81; York DOW 2, October 26? 1647: 287; York DOW 2, December 16, 1647: 312. Both were cases of Smith confessing judgement, a procedure by which a debtor gives "direction for entry of judgment against him in the event he shall default in payment." Henry Campbell Black, *Black's Law Dictionary* (St. Paul: West Publishing, 1990), 259–60. Elizabeth Alvis confessed judgment on behalf of her husband Emanuell Alvis to Richard Young, attorney of William Allin, for 302 pounds of tobacco and cask. See previous chapter for a discussion of the growing formalization of law in Virginia, with particular reference to women's property rights. York DOW 3, November 12, 1660: 94.

10. Confessed judgment before Captain Thomas Barber, justice of the peace, with Robert Bee and John Young acting as securities. York DOW 12, November 19, 1702: 58. See Cope Doyley's estate inventory, York DOW 12, November 10, 1702: 59–65. George Martin was listed as purchasing two parcels. One was valued at £3.1.0 for two new muslin "Night rails", two handkerchiefs, two "laced Heads and Ruffles," yards of gold striped ribbon, "one suit of Black knots." The second parcel contained more ribbon, a "black Lute String hood," white gauze, "a large Ivory comb," a "suite of musling Head Cloaths laced," more ruffles, a pair of gloves, 3 "cramp" necklaces, some thread, some "tape for lace," and a fan.

11. For Weeks's power of attorney, see DOW 4, February 26, 1665/6:56; for her confessing judgment to Peter White, see DOW 4, January 24, 1667/8:164; For Bryan's power of attorney, see York DOW 4, July 25, 1670: 299. Anne Clopton got into more trouble when after an unfavorable decision in the court, she told her son John Dennett, "if thy father had been as rich a man as Capt. Archer, he had had justice done him as well as Capt. Archer, but he being a poor man there was none for him." She and her husband were fined two-hundred pounds of tobacco for their "words tending to the contempt of his Maj[esty]'s government. See York DOW 6, April 24, 1683: 493, 497.

12. For the Wilkins power of attorney, see Susie M. Ames, ed., *County Court Records of Accomack-Northampton, Virginia, 1640–1645* (Charlottesville: University Press of Virginia, 1973), 326. For Horsmonden's power of attorney, see October 4, 1656, Beverley Fleet, abstr., *Virginia Colonial Abstracts: Charles City Co. 1655-8* (Baltimore: Genealogical Publishing, 1961), v. 10, 48-9. For the Yeardley power of attorney, see Norfolk County Wills and Deeds C 1651–1656, microfilm reel 44, p. 64, LVA. Yeardley granted extensive authority, including the right to collect and record levies and record debts appearing to be due to Colonel Yeardley by bill or account, to sue and

"arrest imprison or impleade out of prison, as occasion shall require." Document written November 12, 1653, recorded December 15, 1653. Francis Yeardley was the son of a former Governor of Virginia, and Sarah was a wealthy widow at least thirty-six years old when twenty-three-year-old Francis married her in 1647. Edmund S. Morgan, *American Slavery, American Freedom: The Ordeal of Colonial Virginia* (New York: Norton, 1975), 167. This age calculation assumes she was at least sixteen years old at the time of her first marriage.

13. Power of attorney granted York DOW 5, September 19, 1672: 24. She signed her document with an *X*. The case was recorded York DOW 5: 21. Anne Littleton acted as attorney for her husband and agent for her father in the nearby Northampton County Court, but appointed an attorney of her own when a case went across the Chesapeake Bay to Jamestown for hearing by the colony-level court. *County Court Records of Accomack-Northampton, Virginia, 1640–1645*, 316, 377, 385.

14. York DOW 8, November 7, 1689, March 24, 1689/90: 327, 410. Jane Mountfort was involved in other suits, both with her husband and individually.

15. York DOW 9, recorded March 24, 1692/3, document signed August 26, 1691: 214–15.

16. York DOW 11, recorded September 26, 1698, document signed June 13, 1698: 104–5. He also indicated she could assign someone else to be her substitute if she preferred. Although Gloucester residents, they had the power of attorney recorded in York County.

17. York DOW 11, February 24, 1701: 573–74. The letter was witnessed by two women, Hester Sessions and Mary Curtis.

18. Eastern shore historian Susie Ames described Littleton as one of the "foremost planters on the Eastern Shore." *County Court Records of Accomack-Northampton, 1640–1645*, xi; Nathaniell was in England in the early 1640s. (363). Cases concerned disputed accounts for trade in commodities, including tobacco, beaver fur, and corn. At least once Anne Littleton successfully petitioned for a case to go to jury trial (January 1644/5, 365.) One case listed as her own, not her husband's, involved one of her employees "engaged" to her who had absconded across the bay; she sued the man who provided the servant's passage. She sent this case to the colony-level quarter court at the capital in Jamestown, appointing an attorney of her own, as did the other party in the suit. (316, 377, 385). For references to her appearances on behalf of her husband, see 309, 315, 365, 387. In one instance, the same day that she appeared on behalf of her husband she also obtained a certificate the court granted in right of her father for his transportation of twenty-four people to the colony, saving him a trip to the court. (309).

There may have been a "bystander phenomenon" for women attending courts. David T. Konig has discussed the ways that courts appointed "bystanding" men visiting county courts to juries. David T. Konig, comment on session of Early American Law, meeting of the American Historical Association, Atlanta, 1996. Mary Seale, who appeared at the York County Court to serve as attorney for her husband to prosecute a complaint in chancery, appeared that same day along with three other women as a witness against Elizabeth Babb, widow who was suspected of murdering her newborn child. Perhaps only coincidence brought Seale to court for two cases heard on the same day, but it is possible that Seale either took care of the family's legal chores having already been summoned to answer in the Babb case or, conversely, that the court identified Seale, already at the court on her own business, as a reliable witness to report "news" on a neighborhood infanticide case. Seale would not necessarily have been an eyewitness in the case since the courts heard witnesses who could provide neighborhood "received wisdom" (glorified gossip) to the court. York DOW 10, March 24, 1696/7: 370–71. Rhys Isaac, *The Transformation of Virginia 1740–1790* (New York: Norton, 1982), 91.

19. Spanish Town, Jamaica, Island Records Office, Deeds, liber 1, Old Series, f. 15, September 17, 1665: Margary Dogg, attorney for her husband, Edward Dogg; f. 33, February 16, 1664/5: Sarah Barker for her husband Thomas Barker. For a woman serving for someone other than her husband, see Spanish Town, Jamaica Archives Office, 1B/11/1/1, Patents liber 1661–1665, f. 33v: Margery Pullon for Michael Peterson to collect debts from Zachary (Dolinquet?) for a half a share in ship *Bridget* May 26, 1663. York DOW 3, April 24, 1658: 26. York DOW 3, June 24, 1658: 27. York DOW 3, December 20, 1660: 100.

20. York DOW 3, December 20, 1660, January 25, 1660/1, February 25, 1660/1: 100, 104, 110.

21. York DOW 3, February 25, 1660/1: 112. Purchases made of Robert Aldred totaling £4.16.6 included liquor, cinnamon, bread, tailor's work, a coffin for her son, and maintenance work on a saw. She paid £1.10.0 and left the rest on account owed to Aldred.

22. York DOW 3, October 31, 1661, December 20, 1661, December 21, 1661, January 25, 1661/2: 134, 137–38, 142–43, 145. For case initiated against Whiskins, see York DOW 3, April 24, 1662: 162. For reference to Jones's debt to John Whiskins for four days attendance as a witness in the case, see York DOW 3, March 10, 1661/2, April 24, 1662: 152, 162.

23. English historians Leonore Davidoff and Catherine Hall use the term *establishment* to mean the "combined enterprise and family/household" that incorporated women and men into English enterprises, albeit in radically different positions. They refer to women in family businesses as a "hidden investment" in these firms. Davidoff and Hall focus on the period between 1780 and 1850. Leonore Davidoff and Catherine Hall, *Family Fortunes: Men and Women of the English Middle Class, 1780–1850* (London: Hutchinson, 1987), 198, 272. Margaret R. Hunt, who has studied England in the period between 1680 and 1780, found more potential for tension and outright conflict of men's and women's interests in family-based firms. Margaret R. Hunt *The Middling Sort: Commerce, Gender and the Family in England, 1680–1780* (Berkeley and Los Angeles: University of California Press, 1996), 7. Catherine Hall took up the theme of challenges in her essay, "Strains in the 'Firm of Wife, Children and Friends,'" in *White, Male, and Middle Class: Explorations in Feminism and History* (New York: Routledge, 1992), 172–202.

24. York DOW 3, March 10, 1661/2, April 24, 1662: 151, 161.

25. Jacob M. Price, "One Family's Empire: The Russell-Lee-Clerk Connection In Maryland, Britain, and India, 1707–1857," *Maryland Historical Magazine* 72 (1977): 176; Robert Vaulx married Elizabeth Burwell, sister of Lewis Burwell. "Kenner Family," WMQ, 1st Ser., 14 (1905–1906): 178. He owned Vaulx's Hall plantation on the west side of Queen's Creek. His brothers Humphrey, Thomas, and James also immigrated to the colony. James Vaulx's son, Robert, settled in Dorchester County, Maryland, and Robert's son Robert settled in Westmoreland County. WMQ, 1st Ser., 3 (1894-1895): 14. For bond for tobacco shipped to London and Holland, see York DOW 2, February 5, 1646/7: 219. For Robert's owning a share of a ship, see York DOW(2) 377, [25 May 1648.] One of the brothers, Humphrey Vaulx of New Kent County, Virginia, served as Robert's attorney in some York cases after Elizabeth Vaulx died. York DOW 9, July 24, 1691: 44–45. For a description of the Queen's Creek plantation, see deed of sale to Peter Temple, York DOW 7, October 17, 1685: 169; York DOW 3, May 9, 1659: 55.

26. Power of attorney written September 6, 1656, by Robert Vaulx in London, her "Ever honrd. and Deare husband," and recorded as part of her own grant of power of attorney to Robert Bournes in York DOW 3, document date May 6, 1659, recorded May 9, 1659: 55. For record of tobacco shipped to Robert Vaulx in London, see York DOW 3, June 24, 1661: 119. For Elizabeth Vaulx in York County courts, see York DOW 3, February 25, 1657/8, May 9, 1659: 17, 50, 56.

27. See York DOW 3, December 21, 1657: 9, for certificate granted to Elizabeth Vaulx for four-hundred acres for transportation of eight people. Robert received two-thousand acres in Westmoreland, November 16, 1657, Patent Book 4: 172 cited in Nell Marion Nugent, *Cavaliers and Pioneers: Abstracts of Virginia Land Patents and Grants* (Richmond: Virginia State Library and Archives, 1992), 1: 366. Robert received a land certificate for 3100 acres in return for the importation of sixty-two people. DOW 3, April 4, 1659:51.

    In 1657, by a conveyance authorized by her husband, Robert Vaulx, "gent.," she sold four-hundred acres of land to her "well beloved kin" John and Charles Woodington. This was part of a tract of six-thousand acres that was sold on the provision that John and Charles seat the land. York DOW 3, document dated October 6, 1657, recorded October 26, 1657: 4. By this means Elizabeth's strategy of settling reliable relatives on adjacent land to watch over the owners' land is in keeping with the practice of other women who were absentee landlords of large tracts of land under speculation. A similar pattern of land management emerges from a 1653 letter from Anna Bernard, a woman writing to preserve her holdings. Anna's letter reveals that distance could be as great a barrier to a woman's direct supervision of her business affairs as her gender. Anna Bernard wrote to Walter Brodhurst thanking him for his care in seeing that her land was settled to prevent escheat. She was unable to come to Potomac until the ships returned, but offered one-hundred acres to "any honest man" to seat the land. She asked that the settler be a good neighbor and that he not settle the land between her plantation and the river because she wanted to avoid trespass against her neighbor and vice versa. (Anna Bernard to Mr. Walter Brodhurst, letter proved February 20, 1653, in "Extracts from Northumberland County Records," *WMQ*, 1st Ser. 4 (1894–1895): 77–78. Elizabeth Vaulx accomplished the same task by granting her "kin" small parcels of her lands. On the trip to England, see York DOW 3, May 9, 1659: 56; York DOW 4, August 24, 1665, April 24, 1666, June 25, 1666, August 24, 1666: 29, 30, 60, 69–70, 98.

28. Westmoreland County Deeds and Wills book 1, July 10, 1655: 37, LVA; For description of land sale, see deposition of John Quisenberry, aged eighty years, about the event that took place "about fifty years ago," January 31, 1707/8, in John Frederick Dorman, abstr., *Westmoreland County, Virginia, Deeds, Patents, Etc., 1665–1677 To Which is Appended Westmoreland County, Virginia, Deeds and Wills Number 4, 1707–1709* (Washington, D.C.,: n.p., 1975), part 4: 75–76. There are several references to Vaulx in Lancaster County. See Beverley Fleet, ed., *Lancaster County Record Book, #2, 1654–1666* (Richmond: n.p. [1937]), April 27, 1659, 185 and June 1, 1663 (recorded June 22, 1663), 265. For Vaulx's death, see Bruton Parish Death Register in York County Project, Master Biographical File, Colonial Williamsburg, October 5, 1666.

29. For a more extensive treatment of women's roles in family business in this mid- to late eighteenth-century frontier, see Gail S. Terry, "Family Empires: A Frontier Elite in Virginia and Kentucky, 1740–1815" (Ph.D. diss., College of William and Mary, 1992).

30. The Cabell family name was also recorded under different spellings, among them Cabbell and Cabel. These are from a small packet of waxed paper entitled "signatures of Mrs. Elizabeth Cabell," file entitled "Scraps and fragments, August 24, 1741 to January 16, 1772," in box 1, Papers of the Cabell Family, [hereafter Cabell FP] Special Collections Department, University of Virginia Library. The fragments, no more than one inch by three inches in size, all include Elizabeth Cabell's signature and are clipped to exclude the rest of the letter. The cited text comes from the obverse of fragment 2a.

31. For Cabell's business in Pennsylvania see folder 1745; for business in Great Britain see folder "c. 1745," rough draft in *Cabell v. Mayo*; William Cabell, Warminster, to "Loving Wife," January 19, 1736, folder "William Cabell 3 letters. 1736-7." Cabell also asked her to "keep My poore children close to their books." All in box 1, Cabell FP, UVA.

32. Box 1, folder c. 1745, Cabell FP, Rough draft in *Cabell v. Mayo*, box 1, folder 1731–1768, Cabell FP, UVA. The power of attorney was dated August 27, 1735.

33. She spelled his name "Barradil" and her own name as "Cabbell." Elizabeth Cabell, Goochland, to Edward Barradall, Williamsburg, October 15, 1739 and March 20, 1744, both in box 1, Cabell FP, UVA.

34. Elizabeth Cabell, Goochland, to Edward Barradall, Williamsburg, October 15, 1739, box 1, and March 20, 1744, box 1, both in Cabell FP, UVA. On October 31, 1745, the general court, sitting in chancery, completed a subsequent final reckoning including the fees and determined that Cabell owed £34.15.3 plus costs, and Carrington gave a receipt for payment on May 20, 1746. For subsequent disputes, see decision of the Cumberland Court, June 23, 1767, in folder date June 23, 1767, box 1, Cabell FP, UVA.

35. Mary Beth Norton describes the temporary widows, capable women who increasingly took over family business over the course of the War for Independence in *Liberty's Daughters*.

36. York DOW 4, November 14, 1666, recorded December 20, 1666: 123; York DOW 3, May 31, 1658, recorded June 24, 1658: 31; debt to Richard Awborne York DOW 5, April 26, 1675: 110. John Woods was dead by February 24, 1670/1, York DOW 4: 312. For married women's separate ownership of specific types of minor property (paraphernalia and pin money) in English history, see Susan Staves, *Married Women's Separate Property in England, 1660–1833* (Cambridge, MA: Harvard University Press, 1990), 147–49. For references to paraphernalia in Virginia, see Elizabeth Smyth's order, October 11, 1684, Essex County (Old Rappahannock) Court Orders, 1683–1685, 110.

37. York DOW 3, November 12, 1660: 94. This is the same case mentioned earlier in this chapter.

38. Vergett confessed judgment to John Cooper for 1293 pounds of tobacco and cask. York DOW 4, June 24, 1668, March 10, 1668/9: 186, 227, 251. York DOW 5, September 19, 1672, November 25, 1672: 30, 32.

39. York DOW 6, February 24, 1679/80: 205. York DOW 1, March 5, 1679, recorded 24 January 1694: 518. The ninety-nine year lease was for five-thousand pounds of tobacco and payment of the annual quitrent.

40. For other historians' work on collective family interests in property, see Shammas, "Early American Women and Control over Capital," Carole Shammas, Marylynn Salmon, and Michel Dahlin, *Inheritance in America from Colonial Times to the Present* (New Brunswick, NJ: Rutgers University Press, 1987), 56–62, and Alice Hanson Jones, "The Wealth of Women, 1774," in *Strategic Factors in Nineteenth-Century American Economic History: A Volume to Honor Robert W. Fogel*, ed. Claudia Golding and Hugh Rockoff (Chicago: University of Chicago Press, 1992), 250–51.

41. For discussion of separation in England see Amy Louise Erickson, *Women and Property in Early Modern England* (London: Routledge, 1993, 124–28. In *Road to Divorce: England 1530–1987*, Lawrence Stone discusses the exceptional and expensive nature of English parliamentary divorce. Jane (Ludwell) Lee appears to have been the younger stepsister of Lewis Burwell Jr., making Lewis Burwell stepbrother-in-law to Daniel Parke. This would make Elizabeth Vaulx, sister of Lewis Burwell, Sr., the stepaunt of Jane Parke. Based on information in Archibald Bolling Shepperson, *John Paradise and Lucy Ludwell* (Richmond: Dietz Press, 1942), 450. Jane (Ludwell) Parke's father, Philip Ludwell, married Frances Berkeley, Governor William Berkeley's widow, after Jane's mother died, making Jane stepdaughter to Frances Berkeley (who did not take the name Ludwell after her remarriage.) Jane Parke's relatives included some of the wealthiest, most powerful members of Virginia society.

42. York DOW 8, December 13, 1688, July 24, 1689, September 24, 1689: 184, 188, 307, 311 (against James Whaley); York DOW 8, November 7, 1689, December 18, 1689, January 24, 1689/90, February 24, 1689/90: 324, 352, 371, 389 (against Thomas Ballard and John Weyman).

43. York DOW 8, September 24, 1690: 485. York DOW 10, September 24, 1697, October 11, 1697: 462, 470. The servant was Elizabeth Burnell. The fine, paid to the parish, allowed Burnell to be exempt from whipping. York DOW 11, written April 27, 1697, recorded March 24, 1698: 23–24. She called on another woman, Elizabeth Archer, to be one of the four witnesses to the power of attorney.

44. York DOW 11, December 24, 1700: 379. Jane Parke's action of debt against Isabell Peling and Mary White was not prosecuted and was dismissed. York DOW 11, February 25, 1700/1: 387. Robert Cobbs assigned as plaintiff against Use Gibson for debt; not prosecuted, dismissed. York DOW 12, March 24, 1704/5: 321. Jane Parke recorded as defendant in ejectment firme, a legal action for recovering or trying titles to land. See entries for "ejectment" and "ejectione firmae" in Black, *Black's Law Dictionary*, 516–17. York DOW 12, February 25, 1702/3, January 24, 1703/4: 96, 163; William Gibbs, by his attorney Orlando Jones, confessed judgment to Jane Parke, attorney to Daniel Parke, for the sum of 637 pounds of sweet-scented tobacco and cask.

45. Cattle in seventeenth-century York County produced no more than half the number of calves that English cattle did in the same era. Lois Green Carr, Russell R. Menard, and Lorena S. Walsh, *Robert Cole's World: Agriculture and Society in Early Maryland* (Chapel Hill: University of North Carolina Press, 1991), 45–50; 291, n. 47; York DOW 11, March 25, 1700: 236; York DOW 13, January 8, 1706/7, March 24, 1707/8, May 24, 1708: 33, 125, 141. York DOW 12, March 9, 1705/6, May 24, 1706: 394, 408. The plaintiff in the slave case summoned two witnesses who were paid for eight days' attendance at the court as witnesses against Jane Parke.

46. James Ming countered by appealing to the General Court. Unfortunately, we have no way of knowing what happened at the colony court level because the records have been destroyed.

47. Jane Parke's death recorded in Bruton Parish Death Register, 1708, in York County Project, Master Biographical File, Colonial Williamsburg: York DOW 11, January 25, 1699/1700: 282–83. Edward Greenfield estimates that Parke was born in 1668, was married by 1686. Edward Greenfield, "Some New Aspects of the Life of Daniel Parke," *VMHB* 54 (1946): 306–15; this information appears on 307. Both of Parke's daughters died young, as well.

48. Several generations of women in this family might have learned to be independent and justifiably suspicious of their husbands, since all seem to have sired parallel families. Daniel Parke openly provided for his mistress, Katherine Chester, and her daughter, Lucy. It is possible Daniel Parke was merely following his father's example in starting a parallel family. (York DOW 8, document dated September 28, 1687, recorded March 25, 1689: 239.) In the third generation, Daniel's white son-in-law John Custis freed Jack, whom he identified as "my Negro boy" born of "my Negro Wench Young Alice." "Father to Son: Letters from John Custis IV to Daniel Parke Custis," ed. Jo Zuppan, *VMHB* 98 (1990): 81–100. The father's close ties to his son are apparent in his will, where he mentioned a portrait made of his son. The Parke-Custis families found ways to evade legal constrictions defining race as well as gender.

49. It is interesting to note that the Parkes' daughter, Frances Custis, resorted to an informal agreement during one of the many disputes she had with her own husband. These seem to be elite colonists' versions of the "self-divorce" and for Daniel Parke, "pseudo-remarriage" that Norma Basch discovered in Revolutionary and post-Revolutionary America. The daughter's agreement was not recorded as a power of attorney, but as an enumerated list of each party's obligations. "Fragment of an Agreement between John Custis and Frances (Parke) Custis" [June] 1714: Box 1, Packet 1, loose papers, Northampton County Clerk's Office. Norma Basch, "From the Bonds of Empire to the Bonds of Matrimony," 217–18.

50. York DOW 11, March 24, 1697/8: 23–24. More on this family can be found in the Hardwicke Papers, vol. 869, Printed Cases, British Library, Add. Mss. 36,217, ff.161r–171r. From 1733 to 1754 a dispute raged between Parke's Virginia descendants and his heirs in the Leeward Islands. See VCRP Survey Report 11408. The state of the family dispute at midcentury appears in the printed version of the case of Charles Dunbar of Antigua, son of Thomas Dunbar Parke, appellant, v. Daniel Parke Custis, son and heir, also sole executor of John Custis, "To Be heard before the Lords of the Committee of His Majesty's Privy Council for Plantation Affairs on 24 June 1757." The copy in the collection of the Virginia Historical Society includes annotations.

51. Jane Parke's July 12, 1705 letter was printed in Greenfield, "Some New Aspects of the Life of Daniel Parke," 313.

52. Philip Ludwell [Sr.], London to Philip Ludwell of "Green Spring," December 20, 1707, James City County, Virginia, Lee Family Papers, VHS.

53. This took place on December 7, 1710. The mob then looted his house. Even Lothrop Withington, who thought historians overdid their criticism of Parke's character, admitted that he "violently" dragged Mrs. Blair out of her pew during church services, horsewhipped Francis Nicholson, then governor of Maryland, and, in 1692 seduced a married English woman called alternately "Mistress Berry" or, in Parke's own words, "Cousin Brown." Berry-Brown bore a son, Julius Caesar Parke, whom Daniel Parke named in his will as "godson." Parke named his "godson" residual heir to Parke's Leeward Island estate and to his coat of arms if Katherine Chester, his acknowledged daughter born out of wedlock, refused to change her name to Parke and to accept Daniel's estate and coat of arms. Lothrop Withington, "Virginia Gleanings in England," *VMHB* 20 (1912): 372–81.

54. Essex [loose] suit papers January 4, 1715[/6], recorded September 18, 1716, LVA. For Hethersall's power of attorney and subsequent litigation, see York DOW 6, February 26, 1682/3, February 4, 1683/4: 470, 560. Note the terms of the marriage agreement Rebecca Hethersall made on behalf of her daughter, Rebecca Wythe, when Wythe married John Tiplady (York DOW 8, July 24, 1690: 471.) For Croshaw, see York DOW 4, June 24, 1668: 196. For Duke, see December 4, 1722 transcript in Jane Morris, *The Duke-Symes Family* (Philadelphia: Dorrance 1940), 62.

55. William Blackstone, *Commentaries on the Laws of England* (Oxford: Clarendon Press, 1765–1769) vol. 1, 430–33. Does this make the wife "deputy lord" rather than "deputy husband"?

56. In 1752, Benjamin Smith of Essex County "for divers Consideration" appointed his wife Margaret and his friend James Webb attorneys with broad powers over his Virginia business. Essex County, Misc. Box 1677–1845, folder "Powers of Attorney 1752–1806, 1845," subfolder 1752–3 and subfolder 1732–4, LVA. Robert Hockley appointed his "trusty and well beloved wife" his attorney on August 15, 1732 (recorded September 19, 1732). He granted "sole & full power & authority" to arrest or recover debts from, or "any person," among a long list of other rights. The Essex County collection of powers of attorney provides a long-term view of who served under such a power.

57. For North Carolina women, see Linda L. Angle, "Women in the North Carolina Colonial Courts, 1670–1739" (M.A. thesis, University of North Carolina, 1975), 48–65. For West Jersey, see Hoffer, *Law and People in Colonial America*, 63–64.

58. Susan Staves, "Chattel Property Rules and the Construction of Englishness, 1660–1800," *Law and History Review* 12 (1994): 123–53; James Oldham, *The Mansfield Manuscripts and the Growth of English Law in the Eighteenth Century* (Chapel Hill: University of North Carolina Press, 1993), 1245–1251. Erickson, *Women and Property in Early Modern England*, 30, 136; Stone, *Road to Divorce*, 155; The imperial reaction to developments in colonial Virginia appears in chapter 2 of this volume.

59. St. George Tucker, ed., *Blackstone's Commentaries: With Notes of Reference, to the Constitution and Laws, of the Federal Government of the United States; and of the Commonwealth of Virginia*, 5 vols., (Philadelphia: William Young Birch and Abraham Small, 1803), vol. 2, 445; note that two pages are numbered 445. For post-Revolutionary, antifeminist attempts among Virginians to create separate estates for women, see Lebsock, *Free Women of Petersburg*, 54–86; Lebsock found that the number of separate estates "mushroomed" in the antebellum period, but that women did not obtain unrestricted control over property.

60. Through other procedures, including marriage agreements, women and men tried to find ways to counter coverture. Their attempts sometimes failed, but even failed efforts reveal that women were willing to seek out greater autonomy and improved material conditions, and that some men believed they would benefit from this situation, as well. See Linda L. Sturtz, "Innovation and Tradition in an Imperial-Colonial Contest," paper presented to the International Seminar on the History of the Atlantic World, 1500–1800, Harvard University, Cambridge, MA, 1997.

61. Significant articles that deal with married women's property in colonial Virginia include Linda E. Speth, "More Than Her 'Thirds': Wives and Widows in Colonial Virginia," *Women and History* 4 (1983): 5–42; For the region of Virginia situated south of the James River, see Joan R. Gundersen and Gwen Victor Gampel, "Married Women's Legal Status in Eighteenth-Century New York and Virginia," *WMQ*, 3d ser., 39 (1982): 114–34.

CHAPTER 4

1. Carl R. Lounsbury, ed., *An Illustrated Glossary of Early Southern Architecture and Landscape* (Charlottesville: University Press of Virginia, 1999), 249, 369.

2. Court records of crimes against single white women may be disproportionately large compared to traces of crimes against white women in families. The latter could be underreported if white men "refused to admit in public that they had failed to protect themselves and their families against their bondsmen." Philip J. Schwarz, *Twice Condemned: Slaves and the Criminal Laws of Virginia, 1705–1865* (Baton Rouge: Louisiana State University Press, 1988), 84.

3. Carol F. Karlsen, *Devil in the Shape of a Woman: Witchcraft in Colonial New England* (New York: Norton, 1987), 83.

4. See Lawrence Friedman's *The Republic of Choice* for a discussion of how authority has been transferred from a more personalized patriarchal structure to a more bureaucratized system of authority in government institutions over the course of American history. Lawrence M. Friedman, *The Republic of Choice: Law, Authority, and Culture* (Cambridge, MA: Harvard University Press, 1990). From these cases it appears that women turned to bureaucratic authority earlier to uphold their place in the larger society.

5. Elizabeth Marie Pruden, "Family, Community, Economy: Women's Activity in South Carolina, 1670–1770" (Ph.D. diss., University of Minnesota, 1996), 283.

6. James Hunter Jr. and Roe Latimer and Company Account, transaction date August 1777, folder "July 18, 1778," box 5, Hunter-Garrett Collection, UVA.

7. Account with receipt on reverse, folder 1769-1772, box 17, Papers of the Webb-Prentice Families and others, UVA. Another woman, Marian Blair, who dealt with a Mr. Marse, used guilt, instead, to encourage payment from him for her mending of ten shirts and five stocks. She received payment of £1.10.0 on August 6, 1772. Folder 1769-1772, box 17, Webb-Prentice Collection, UVA.

8. Carter Burwell Account Books (1738–1755) and Ledgers (1736–1746, 1773–1779, 1764–1776, 1779–1786), CW, microfilm. Pagination is often omitted in these, but see,

for example, n.p [p. 36] for Mrs. Pattison's purchases of almost two-thousand pounds of pork in 1745. 1755, Account Book 1747–1764, William Lightfoot papers, 1740–1764, f. 130, CW Microfilm-1555.

9. *Virginia Gazette*, September 12, 1771, as cited in Julia Cherry Spruill, *Women's Life and Work in the Southern Colonies* (Chapel Hill: University of North Carolina Press, 1938; reprint, New York: Norton, 1972), 300.

10. Many establishments went unlicensed, either permanently or occasionally, so this is only a record of the legal businesses operating in the county, not an absolute measure of all ordinaries. In addition, women kept "lodging houses" that did not have to be licensed. Patricia Gibbs has traced the Williamsburg lodging houses through the *Virginia Gazette* and other sources. Throughout the colonies, lodging houses in the second half of the eighteenth century were less expensive and provided more privacy and peace than the taverns, where patrons shared rooms, and even beds, with strangers. Patricia A. Gibbs, "Taverns in Tidewater Virginia, 1700–1774," (M.A. thesis, College of William and Mary, 1968), 132–206. March 1660, William Waller Hening, ed. *The Statues at Large: Being A Collection of All Laws of Virginia, from the First Session of the Legislature, in 1619*, (Richmond and Philadelphia: Printed for the Editor, 1809–1823) vol. 2, 19. Kym S. Rice, *Early American Taverns: For the Entertainment of Friends and Strangers* (Chicago: Regnery Gateway, 1983), 42, 85–124.

11. We can determine the history of only half of the Williamsburg taverns because the town existed in two counties, James City County and York County, and most of the James City County records have been destroyed.

12. Hening, *Statutes at Large*, September 1668, vol. 2, 268. This seems to contrast with the English pattern of harsher regulation of alehouses originating with the Puritans and being imposed during the interregnum. In the late seventeenth and early eighteenth centuries, the trend in England was toward taxing rather than closing the alehouses. By the 1730s, excise on drink provided a quarter of the national tax revenues. Peter A. Clark, *The English Alehouse: A Social History, 1200–1830* (London: Longman, 1983), 166–80, 185.

13. York Orders and Wills 16, January 16, 1721, March 20, 1721: 13.

14. York DOW 13, July 25, 1709: 236. Elizabeth Moody later married Powers. Because another ordinary keeper in York, operating at the same time, was also named Elizabeth Powers, Elizabeth Moody Powers will be called "Elizabeth Moody" in this chapter.

15. York DOW 10, 54–55.

16. Hening, *Statutes at Large*, October 1705, vol. 3, 396.

17. Ibid., October 1644, vol. 1, 287.

18. Ibid., November 1645, vol. 1, 300; March 1659, vol. 1, 521–22.

19. Only "middling" and "best" quality drinks were listed. "Roger's best Virga." Ale sold for the same cost as Pennsylvania "Bear." York Orders and Wills, 14 (1709–1716), March 19, 1710/1: 6, 71.

20. On the role of women in earning income through hospitality and ordinary keeping elsewhere in the British Empire, see John Demos, *A Little Commonwealth: Family Life in Plymouth Colony* (New York: Oxford University Press, 1970), 89–90; and Paulette A. Kerr, "Victims or Strategists? Female Lodging-House Keepers in Jamaica," in *Engendering History: Caribbean Women in Historical Perspective*, ed. Verene Shepherd, Bridget Brereton, and Barbara Bailey (Kingston, Jamaica: Ian Randle, 1995), 197–212. Spruill, *Women's Life and Work*, 293-303.

21. Documenting these sorts of businesses, even in the present, is problematic enough because many of the owners wish to keep their profits private to prevent government regulation, including tax collection. It should not be surprising that finding records of these businesses in the past proves doubly difficult. For a few examples of contemporary women marketing food, drink, and lodging, see Lesley McKay, "Women's

Contribution to Tourism in Negril, Jamaica," 278–79, 282; Jean Besson, "Reputation & Respectability Reconsidered: A New Perspective on Afro-Caribbean Peasant Women," 25–27; and Riva Berleant-Schiller and William M. Maurer, "Women's Place is Every Place: Merging Domains and Women's Roles in Barbuda & Dominica," 76; in *Women and Change in the Caribbean: A Pan-Caribbean Perspective*, ed. Janet Momsen (Kingston, Jamaica: Ian Randle, 1993); Erna Brodber's study delves back into the eighteenth and nineteenth centuries to discuss the sale of lodging and storage space in cities, especially for transients with business in town. Erna Brodber, *A Study of Yards in the City of Kingston* (Mona, Jamaica: Institute of Social and Economic Research, University of the West Indies, 1975), 4–9.

22. Patricia Gibbs stresses the domestic elements of tavern keeping while Kierner points out the more public elements of such businesses. Gibbs, "Taverns," 44; Cynthia A. Kierner, *Beyond the Household: Women's Place in the Early South, 1700–1835* (Ithaca: Cornell University Press, 1998), 2, 37. For the gendering of public and private spaces, see Jessica Kross, "Mansions, Men, Women and the Creation of Multiple Publics in Eighteenth-Century British North America," *Journal of Social History* 33 (1999): 385–408; Linda L. Sturtz, "'Dining Room Politics': Lady Berkeley of Virginia," paper presented to the Courts Without Kings Conference, Boston, MA, September 22, 2000.

23. Although women's share of the tavern business declined, their proportion of the boardinghouses increased in both Charleston and Boston. Rice, *Early American Taverns*, 42.

24. Suzanne Lebsock, *The Free Women of Petersburg: Status and Culture in a Southern Town, 1784–1860* (New York: Norton, 1985), 177–78; Barbara Carson traces the rise of hotels and "commercialized leisure" in contrast to traveling motivated for business purposes during a period of prosperity after 1763. Barbara G. Carson, "Early American Tourists and the Commercialization of Leisure," in *Of Consuming Interests: The Style of Life in the Eighteenth Century*, ed. Cary Carson, Ronald Hoffman, and Peter J. Albert (Charlottesville: University Press of Virginia, 1994), 374.

25. This includes licenses issued in the first decade of each year in the York County Court. Taken from the York County Court records, LVA microfilm and Colonial Williamsburg York County Project transcripts.

26. York DOW 9, August 24, 1693: 240; bond against future illegal sales, York DOW 9, March 26, 1694: 314.

27. Caroline Julia Richter, "A Community and Its Neighborhoods: Charles Parish, York County, Virginia, 1630–1740," (Ph.D. diss., College of William and Mary, 1992), 309–10.

28. York DOW 13, August 24, 1708: 158.

29. November 22, 1727, Essex County Orders (1725–[17]29), 193, LVA microfilm reel 68.

30. Lebsock, *Free Women of Petersburg*, 177–78.

31. Essex Orders (1725–1729), 193, LVA microfilm reel 68, recorded November 21, 1727.

32. Proving husband's will (sole executor and legatee), York DOW 14, February 19, 1711: 55; Purchased York Town Lot, York Deeds and Bonds 2, August 20, 1711: 380-1; Ordinary license, York DOW 14, August 20, 1711: 104; Ordinary license, August 18, 1712.

33. She sued for payment of £5.9.10 1/2 due on balance of accounts for "ordinary expenses" racked up by Arthur Tillyard and calculated after Tillyard's death. Both she and her bookkeeper "Lewis" made oath to the account, and the court ordered the debt be paid to Booth. York DOW 14, March 1713: 238.

34. York DOW 14, October 13, 1711: 116.

35. York DOW 14, January 21, 1712: 124.

36. York Orders and Wills 16, March 20, 1720[/1]: 27.

37. For ten thousand pounds tobacco, York Orders and Wills 16, bond dated March 20, 1720[/1]: 33.

38. Godfrey Pole, Accounts and Other Papers, June 9, 1722, Northampton County Court House, Eastville, Virginia. The Pole papers were notes and documents taken by Godfrey Pole, the English-trained clerk of court on the eastern shore in the eighteenth century. The documents are from other counties, but Pole acted as a lawyer outside the county and apparently brought them back to the eastern shore.
39. Peter Clark discusses alehouses as family businesses in late eighteenth-century England. Clark, *The English Alehouse*, 287–88.
40. York DOW 12, September 24, 1705: 353; York DOW 13, January 25, 1708/9: 187, as cited in Richter, "A Community and Its Neighborhoods," 309–10.
41. Peter Clark describes this pattern for seventeenth-century England. Clark, *The English Alehouse*, 83. Patricia Gibbs described the likelihood that Anne Sullivant's husband Timothy, worked outside the ordinary, perhaps in stonecutting. With her experience maintaining an ordinary in her first marriage, she easily could have run the business herself. Gibbs, "Taverns," 198–99.
42. Gibbs, "Taverns," 149–51, 193–94, 204–5.
43. York Orders and Wills 15: 220; York DOW 16: 75, 238, 306. This couple married within months of Jean Marot's death. In 1718 they took on the administration of Jean Marot's estate and obtained an ordinary license on the same day. She appears to have maintained the ordinary herself because beginning in 1721, the county issued the license in her name, though her new husband lived until about 1730. Gibbs, "Taverns," 199.
44. She left the business by 1783 once tavern-keeping was in deep decline due to the removal of the capital to Richmond. Gibbs, "Taverns," 153–54.
45. Gabriel Marot had York County licenses from 1714 until 1718. York DOW 14: 83, 353; York DOW 14: 384, 550. His widow then operated the tavern between 1719 and 1723. York DOW 15: 550; York DOW 16: 137, 195. After she married Thomas Crease, they continued the ordinary. Gibbs, "Taverns," 182–83, 164. For women learning families' businesses before widowhood in Pennsylvania, see Lisa Wilson, *Life after Death: Widows in Pennsylvania, 1750–1850* (Philadelphia: Temple University Press, 1992), 115.
46. Emma L. Powers, "Landladies and Women Tenants in Williamsburg and Yorktown: 1700–1770," *Common People and Their Material World: Free Men and Women in the Chesapeake, 1700–1830*, ed. David Harvey and Gregory Brown (Richmond: Colonial Williamsburg Foundation, 1995), 19.
47. October 24, 1701, York DOW 11: 513. Her full name is Elizabeth (née Spencer) Leightonhouse Somerwell Powers. She will be referred to as Elizabeth Leightonhouse throughout this chapter to distinguish her from Elizabeth Moody Powers.
48. Anonymous, "French Traveller in the Colonies, 1765," *AHR* 26 (1921):741–42.
49. Surry County Deeds, Wills, Etc. 2 (1671–1684), February 25, 1681/2: 302–3, microfilm, LVA.
50. York DOW 6, February 24, 1680: 206.
51. Betty Leviner, "Patrons and Rituals in an Eighteenth-Century Tavern," *Common People and Their Material World: Free Men and Women in the Chesapeake, 1700–1830*. ed. David Harvey and Gregory Brown (Richmond: Colonial Williamsburg Foundation, 1995), 95–96.
52. Hening, *Statutes at Large*, vol. 2, 269, 361.
53. Carl R. Lounsbury, "Order in the Court: Recommendations for the Restoration of the James City County/Williamsburg Courthouse" (Williamsburg: Colonial Williamsburg Architectural History Department, October, 1985), 9.
54. Gibbs, "Taverns," 97, 99, 107, 117. Rice, *Early American Taverns*, 85–124.
55. In an eerie parallel to more recent cases, Burt found herself accused of defamation after she reported the incident to a local official in order to have the accused attacker

arrested. The official answered "Fie, Betty as soon as you are out of 1 troublesumm business to go into another what is the matter w/ you & John Eaton." York DOW 9, September 26, 1692: 173–76.

56. In Yorktown, sixteen women and fifty-one men received licenses. This assumes that Damarias Brewer and Damarias Butterworth are the same person. For the significance of ordinaries in Yorktown and a list of all ordinary licenses grated there, see Edward M. Riley, "The Ordinaries of Colonial Yorktown," *WMQ*, 2nd. ser., 23 (1943): 8–26. The prime spot for an ordinary in Lancaster seemed to be at the courthouse. Lancaster County Ordinary Bonds, box 7, folder 5 (1721–1850), LVA.

57. York Orders and Wills 14, October 13, 1711: 116; Allen in York DOW 14, October 13, 1711: 113.

58. Leviner, "Patrons and Rituals," 97. Gibbs, "Taverns," 123.

59. York Orders and Wills 14, October 5, 1710: 38.

60. York DOW 14, October 13, 1711: 115.

61. In 1768, Mrs. Gault was "jailer at Williamsburg" and Mary Lindsey and Elizabeth Daniels served as jailers in Henrico and Middlesex Counties, respectively. Their willingness to profit from the lodging of captured runaway slaves demonstrates their complicity with the slave system. Spruill, *Women's Life and Work in the Southern Colonies*, 304.

62. Essex County Orders (1725–1729), November 21, 1727: 171, microfilm, LVA. At the same court, Elizabeth Anderson received two-thousand pounds tobacco for keeping the Piscataway Ferry. This payment was the second largest sum in that account of official expenditures.

63. York Orders and Wills 14, January 21, 1711/12: 123; Other references (as Elizabeth Moody) for sweeping and/or cleaning: York Orders and Wills 14, December 16, 1712: 209, 210; Orders and Wills 15, December 29, 1720: 684–85; York Wills 16, December 7, 1722: 164; York Orders and Wills 16, November 18, 1723: 237.

64. Disputes did not always go to court over men's misbehavior at women's establishments. Susanna Allen suffered a riot at her ordinary in 1712. Louis B. Wright and Marion Tinling, eds., *The Secret Diary of William Byrd of Westover, 1709–1712* (Richmond: Dietz Press, 1941), 517. At Sarah (Taliaferro) Brooke's ordinary, Brooke's Bank, a clergyman threw out an obnoxious fellow lodger. She probably suffered retaliation from this offender, described only as "a Caroline Man," because the following day her dairy mysteriously burned. The clergyman, Robert Rose, often sojourned at taverns when making his circuit to assigned congregations. Ralph Fall, ed., *The Diary of Robert Rose* (Verona, VA: McClure Press, 1977), February 18–19, 1747: 26, 121, 201.

65. Case ended in nonsuit, "no cause of actions shown"; York DOW 5, August 24, 1675: 122; Charges dropped at October 25, 1675 court when Toope did not appear. York DOW 5: 126.

66. The damage amounted to £5 sterling, or one-hundred pounds of tobacco, York DOW 5, August 24, 1675: 122.

67. York DOW 5, October 25, 1675: 126.

68. According to the *Oxford English Dictionary*, the late-eighteenth-century definition of mirkin was "counterfeit hair for women's privy parts" (1796); York DOW 3, October 26, 1658: 38.

69. Performance bond in which John Woods indebted for "one seat of land which the s[ai]d. Eliz[abeth]. now possesses" and all the land and cattle to her children by Robert Frith. If the children die before coming of age, the obligation was to be void and "left to the disposing of Elizabeth Frith." York DOW 3, May 31, 1658: 31.

70. A study of European women in the Caribbean points out that while historians of slavery have avoided the pitfall of seeing women as socially homogeneous, most recent work has focused on slavery from the perspective of black women. White males have been the basis for understanding the colonial enterprise, focusing on "the politics

and entrepreneurship of the white male in shaping the Caribbean world, and sug-gest[ing] the insignificance of ideological, social and economic inputs from white women." Hilary McD. Beckles, "White Women and Slavery in the Caribbean," *History Workshop* 36 (1993), 66.

71. County court personnel sat on oyer and terminer cases, though on different days from their meetings to hear regular county matters, and the county clerk recorded these cases with other county documents. Thad W. Tate, *The Negro in Eighteenth-Century Williamsburg* (Williamsburg: Colonial Williamsburg, 1965), 93. Hugh F. Rankin, *Criminal Trial Proceedings in the General Court of Colonial Williamsburg* (Williamsburg: Colonial Williamsburg, 1965), 46. Schwarz, *Twice Condemned*, 66–77.

72. Hening, *Statutes at Large*, vol. 1, 397–98.

73. Schwarz, *Twice Condemned*, 17. Hening, *Statutes at Large*, vol. 3, 102–3.

74. Schwarz, *Twice Condemned*, 80.

75. Recorded in York Judgments and Orders (hereafter JO), 1746–1752, March 7, 1750[/1]: 398–400[-a].

76. York JO, 1746–1752: 399.

77. York JO, 1746–1752: 400[-a].

78. York JO, 1746–1752: 400-a.

79. York JO, 1746–1752: 400.

80. York JO, 1746–1752: 400-a.

81. William Offutt poses a methodology for assessing the law's protection of white women's property rights and physical well-being, particularly in New England and the middle colonies, and concludes that with growing anglicization in the eighteenth century, the courts provided less protection and relied, instead, on "privatized" jus-tice, including gossip, to supervise women's interests. In Delaware, however, women continued to participate in court cases "on issues concerning body and soul," includ-ing personal safety. William M. Offutt, "The Limits of Authority: Courts, Ethnicity, and Gender in the Middle Colonies," in *The Many Legalities of Early America*, ed. Christopher L. Tomlins and Bruce H. Mann (Chapel Hill: University of North Carolina Press, 2001), 381–84. Virginia court oversight of cases concerning Black women and men's attacks on white women seem consistent with the latter situation.

82. There is a long literature of the significance of the term *Christian* to designate white-ness (and conformity to whiteness) in the seventeenth-century Anglo-American colonies.

83. York Orders and Wills 14: 40, 42. Additional material on Susanna Allen's activities before the court appears in the Roger Jones Family Papers, Library of Congress.

84. York Orders and Wills 14: 49, 84, 84, 113, 115, 118, 119, 121–22, 126–27, 142, 153, 155, 167–70, 172–73, 181, 187, ff.

85. Case brought November 19, 1711, York Orders and Wills 14, December 17, 1711: 118; York Orders and Wills 14: 121–22.

86. Cases (including continued cases) are counted once in this table even if there were multiple hearings of each. Each case is counted as a new case in the following year, even if it continued from the previous year.

87. Number of witnesses paid included four for Smith and three for Allen. Witnesses were paid for travel expenses as well as periods of attendance, ranging from one to eight days in the suit. York Orders and Wills 14: 168–69. Evidences for Smith: Christopher Smith of James City County, William Flintoff of James City County, Henry Sicks, paid for travel from James City County, and James Morris. Evidence for Susanna Allen included William Taylor, John Jarrett, and a second William Taylor.

88. York Orders and Wills 14, June 16, 1712: 167.

89. York Orders and Wills 14: 169.

90. York Orders and Wills 14: 172–73.

91. Ady Booth, York Orders and Wills 14, December 17, 1711, January 22, 1711/12: 121, 126. She also had two suits continued or dismissed in 1713, York Orders and Wills 14, January 20, 1712/3: 221, 216.

92. York Orders and Wills 14, September 21, 1714: 357; Debt suit: "due by bill & acc[oun]t find to the pl[an]tiff 3-19-4 1/2 to be paid in beaf at 12/6 per cent."

93. [Godfrey] Pole papers, loose documents, November 1716 and July 1717, Northampton County Court House.

94. York Orders and Wills 14, May 18, 1713: 247.

95. York Orders and Wills 14, February 16, 1712/3: 228.

96. A "tradition" that persisted into twentieth-century Williamsburg held that Allen kept a brothel, but Patricia Gibbs argues that there is no evidence to support this claim. While Allen's establishment probably was not a "brothel" per se, there is a strong likelihood that sex for money was among the services offered at taverns, including Allen's. Gibbs, "Taverns," 36. Other York County women with disorderly houses were Jone Clark and the suspiciously named Rachael Rodewell, both of whom were presented to the court on November 16, 1741, York DOW: 60. More direct evidence appears for the British Caribbean, where slave masters and mistresses profited by essentially serving as madams and pimps to enslaved women. Hilary McD. Beckles, *Centering Woman: Gender Discourses in Caribbean Slave Society* (Kingston, Jamaica: Ian Randle, 1998). In England, the use of the alehouse for courtship or a location for prostitution declined in the late seventeenth century, perhaps paving the way for "respectable" establishments to operate in the eighteenth. Clark, *The English Alehouse*, 235.

97. York Orders and Wills 14, June 15, 1713, 260; York Orders and Wills 14, July 20, 1713: 268. Jan Lewis has determined from a study of Orange County Court records between 1734 and 1741 that Virginians had little interest in regulating the sexual behavior of their neighbors. Jan Lewis, *The Pursuit of Happiness: Family and Values in Jefferson's Virginia* (Cambridge: Cambridge University Press, 1985), 18–21. Kathleen M. Brown, *Good Wives, Nasty Wenches, Anxious Patriarchs: Gender, Race, and Power in Colonial Virginia* (Chapel Hill: University of North Carolina Press 1996), 196-201.

98. Cunningham signed with an *X* while Allen signed her name. York Orders and Wills 14, February 16, 1712/3: 234. His occupation was listed in his will, York DOW 16: 563.

99. It is possible that these are their children, but there is no evidence to prove it.

100. York Orders and Wills 15: 563. Cunningham made his will on January 13, 1719/20 and his will was probated on February 15, of that year.

101. Lois Green Carr and Lorena S. Walsh, "Changing Lifestyles and Consumer Behavior in the Colonial Chesapeake," in *Of Consuming Interests: The Style of Life in the Eighteenth Century,* ed. Cary Carson, Ronald Hoffman, and Peter J. Albert (Charlottesville: University Press of Virginia, 1994), 63.

102. I am not certain if she sought to retain control over the Aggys because they provided her with a labor source or because she fostered close ties with them. I suspect the former, because they were sold away in Cunningham's will. Mary Aggy had an illustrious legal career of her own. With patronage in high places, she sought "benefit of clergy," a legal privilege accorded to white men and women. John M. Hemphill II, "Mary Aggy," *Dictionary of Virginia Biography*, ed. John T. Kneebone, J. Jefferson Looney, Brent Tarter, and Sandra Gioia Treadway (Richmond: Library of Virginia, 1999), v. 1, 42–43.

103. She is listed as "spinster of Williamsburg" in this document, so I believe she never married formally. [Godfrey] Pole Papers, "York County 1717" file, Northampton County Courthouse.

104. York Orders and Wills 14, November 15, 1714: 367. Allen had reason to take the estate because she had suits with Timberlake at the time of his death. Allen posted bond with Francis Sharp and David Cunningham, recorded on the same day (371).

105. The appraisers took the inventory of the goods "brought before us by Mrs. Susanna Allan." The goods, valued at £23.6.3 included dishes, wine, furniture, clothes, and a saddle. Allen presented the inventory "in open court" on December 10, 1714; recorded December 20, 1714. Further accounts presented June 20, 1715, York Orders and Wills 14, 428-9. Total credits equaled £50:17:07; total debts equaled £180:09:09; Timberlake had taken out an ordinary license before his death.

106. York Orders and Wills 14, December 20, 1714: 375.

107. Ibid., November 15, 1714: 367. Christopher Jackson to take the estate, Susanna Allen to make oath to the inventory.

108. Requests from William Edins to Pole to prosecute Allen for debt, June 13, 1718 and July 15, 1718. [Godfrey] Pole papers, York Folder 1718–1720, Northampton County Court House.

109. In Connecticut, "book debt was in many respects analogous" to assumpsit. Virginia women's account book debts will be discussed in greater detail in chapter 5. Bruce Mann, *Neighbors and Strangers: Law and Community in Early Connecticut* (Chapel Hill: University of North Carolina Press, 1987), 14.

110. Susanna Allen to Mr. Stoner, n.d., York Folder 1718–10, [Godfrey] Pole papers, Northampton County Court House. Pole's notes on outside of letter: "Mr Stoner brought this L[ett]re to me July the 30th 1716."

111. York Orders and Wills 15, will dated March 2, 1719/20, probated May 16, 1720: 600.

112. Jury trials were rare enough that the first references to a jury sitting in a court room appear in 1709 and 1710. Before, petit juries simply stood near a magistrate's trial when they were needed. Lounsbury, "Order in the Court," 68.

113. This license, granted by the court as a charity measure, is discussed earlier in the chapter. York DOW 10: 54–55. "Innholder" in York Deeds and Bonds 1, September 25, 1699: 216–18. Payment for prisoners, York DOW 11, March 24, 1700: 428–29. Leightonhouse also kept school and had young male and female indentured servants living in his home. York DOW 10, March 2, 1696: 259; Indentures of Ann Wilson, orphan, to learn to read, sew, knit and spin, York DOW 10, November 24, 1697: 487; James Manders's complaints about working in the tobacco fields to the neglect of his learning, and contrary to the terms of his articles of agreement. York DOW 9, September 24, 1691: 62. Other cases relating to administration of the Leightonhouse estate: York DOW 11: 481, 482, 486, 492, 514, 517–18, 540, 541, 551, 560–61, 572; York DOW 12: 7–8, 38, 39, 81, 90, 115, 116, 129, 130–31, 144, 169, 184, 260, 208, 234, 239, 245, 249, and 293.

114. York DOW 11, September 24, 1701, July 24, 1701: 492, 486. Some of these cases continued after her subsequent marriage to Mungo Somerwell. York DOW 12, 24 November 1704: 260. Even after her third marriage, she continued to take an active hand in her lawsuits. She and her third husband Edward Powers "came personally into Court" to confess judgment on £60.4.0 1/2 due their merchants, Alexander Gordon and John Cook. York DOW 14, September 25, 1710: 34.

115. York DOW 11, October 24, 1701: 513.

116. York DOW 11, March, 24 1701, February 24, 1702: 446–47, 551; Mungo Somerwell agreed to pay Captain Thomas Mountfort the debt his new wife owed Mountfort on March 24, 1702. The newlyweds and John Haley sued and countersued over protested bills of exchange. York DOW 12, September 25, 1702: 7.

117. York DOW 13, February 24, 1707: 37. The attorney, "having their papers," failed to attend court once when he was sick. York DOW 12, September 24, 1704: 249. At least one of the protested bills of exchange disputes was sent to auditors to settle in March, 1704. York DOW 12: 293.

118. York DOW 13, February 25, 1707: 52. Somerwell's credits (£368.11.2 1/2) exceeded what he owed (£82.9.7). The couple also regained a lot in Yorktown that her first hus-

band had forfeited and constructed several buildings there. November 1707, accounting, York DOW 13: 85; Deeds and Bonds 2: 233–4.

119. York DOW 13, June 25, 1707, August 5, 1707, March 25, 1708, 77, 86, 128.
120. York DOW 14, August 24, 1701: 28. This was a case over a protested bill of exchange made with London merchants.
121. York Wills and Inventories 18, September 15, 1733: 70.
122. York DOW 9, February 26, 1693/4: 298; York Deeds and Bonds 1, November 24, 169: 97–99; York DOW 10, November 24, 1696: 339; York DOW 11, December 24, 1700: 408; York DOW 13, June 24, 1707, will probated February 24, 1707/8: 72, 122.
123. York DOW 13, August 24, 1708: 158.
124. York DOW 13, January 25, 1708/9: 186. This is the first reference I have seen in the records to her having an ordinary in York County, despite the language of "renewing" the license.
125. York DOW 13, July 25, 1709, August 24, 1709: 236, 246.
126. She had a case against Samuel Smith in 1709, settled an account with William Wamsey, and initiated a case against Michael Archer.
127. York DOW 13, February 24, 1710: 268; York DOW 14, February 19, 1711, March 17, 1712, March 16, 1713, March 15, 1714: 47, 138, 237, 312.
128. York Orders and Wills 15, June 15, 1719, June 20, 1720, : 438, 446, 622; York Orders and Wills 16, July 17, 1721, March 18, 1723, August 17, 1724, May 17, 1725, June 20, 1726, July 17, 1727, May 20 and 21, 1728, July 17, 1728, and June 16, 1729: 60, 63, 196, 297–98, 333, 337; 388, 392, 466, 472, 512, 610.
129. References for claims against the county for Elizabeth Moody Powers keeping the courthouse: for 1711 services, account of January 21, 1712, York DOW 14: 123. Later references: York DOW 14, December 16, 1712: 209–10; York Orders and Wills 15, November 17, 1710, December 29, 1720: 505, 684–85; York Orders and Wills 16, December 7, 1722, November 18, 1723: 164, 237.
130. Some evidence of his generosity to the children from her first marriage is evident in his will. He left her the house and lot in Yorktown unless she remarried. If she married again (and she did not) the property was to be managed for the benefit of the Moody children, Elizabeth and Ishmael. He may have worried that a new stepfather would be less generous or he may have thought his wife should be more properly submissive to a new husband and not managing the Powers estate after remarrying. Will recorded May 12, 1719, York DOW 15: 452.
131. Administrator, with Robert Ballard and John Moody, for the estate of James Simmons, York Orders and Wills 17, March 16, 1730: 59. Suit of trespass on the case between Elizabeth Powers and William Adams, she to recover after he had claimed pauper status to obtain legal representation against her. York Orders and Wills 17, May 18, 1730, August 17, 1730: 64, 88. In a similar case in which she was a defendant, the case had to wait until one of the deponents came back to Virginia "to clear his ship." She lost this second case shortly before her death. York Orders and Wills 17, June 21, 1731, July 19, 1731: 182, 194.
132. York Orders and Wills 16, September 17, 1722: 156–57.
133. York Orders and Wills, 16, December 16, 1723, May 18, 1724, June 15, 1724: 240, 268, 283.
134. Made attorney in 1692, DOW(1) 433. Had a case before the court as attorney and, the same, subpoenaed to appear in the case of Elizabeth Babb. The child disappeared shortly after birth. York DOW 10, March 24, 1697: 371–72.

CHAPTER 5

1. Bernard Capp has argued that in the early modern period, English men expressed the precariousness of their domestic authority in ballads, jest books, pamphlets, and

plays filled with jokes about assertive and shrewish wives. According to Capp, "ordinary women in early modern England were not the helpless, passive victims of male authority, despite the barrage of patriarchal teaching fired at them." Instead, the debates over gender roles suggest uncertainty about women's and men's proper places in society. Bernard Capp, "Separate Domains? Women and Authority in Early Modern England," in *The Experience of Authority in Early Modern England*, ed. Paul Griffiths, Adam Fox, and Steve Hindle (London: Macmillan, 1996), 117–45, esp. 119, 139. D. E. Underdown has described the harsh popular response to women's increasingly threatening power to male household authority in the early modern period. D. E. Underdown, "The Taming of the Scold: the Enforcement of Patriarchal Authority in Early Modern England," in *Order and Disorder in Early Modern England* ed. Anthony Fletcher and John Stevenson, (Cambridge: Cambridge University Press, 1985), 116–36. For an overview of early modern women's work in Europe, see Merry E. Wiesner, *Women and Gender in Early Modern Europe* (Cambridge: Cambridge University Press, 1993), 82–114. For the significance of economic roles in constructing manhood as well as womanhood, see Susan Dwyer Amussen, "'The Part of a Christian Man: The Cultural Politics of Manhood in Early Modern England," in *Political Culture and Cultural Politics in Early Modern England*, ed. Susan Dwyer Amussen and Mark A. Kishlansky (Manchester: Manchester University Press, 1995), 213–33.

2. *Dialog between Honest John and Loving Kate with Their Contrivance for Marriage and Way to Get a Livelyhood, part 2* (Bow Churchyard, London, n.d.), part of the British Library collection of early-eighteenth-century chapbooks.

3. Laurel Thatcher Ulrich, *Good Wives: Image and Reality in the Lives of Women in Northern New England, 1650–1750* (Oxford: Oxford University Press, 1983), 36–37.

4. For a succinct overview of how the accounting system worked, see James O'Mara, *An Historical Geography of Urban System Development: Tidewater Virginia in the Eighteenth Century* (Ontario: York University Geographical Monographs, 1983), 295–99. The workings of the accounting system of credits and debits Christopher Clark found at work in Massachusetts seem similar to those at work in Virginia stores. Christopher Clark, *The Roots of Rural Capitalism: Western Massachusetts, 1780–1860* (Ithaca: Cornell University Press, 1993).

5. Laurel Thatcher Ulrich, "Martha Ballard and Her Girls: Women's Work in Eighteenth-Century Maine," in *Work and Labor in Early America*, ed. Stephen Innes (Chapel Hill: University of North Carolina Press, 1988), 71–73; Laurel Thatcher Ulrich, *A Midwife's Tale: The Life of Martha Ballard Based on Her Diary, 1785–1812* (New York: Knopf, 1990), 80.

6. Laurel Thatcher Ulrich, "Martha Ballard and Her Girls: Women's Work in Eighteenth-Century Maine," in *Work and Labor in Early America*, ed. Stephen Innes (Chapel Hill: University of North Carolina Press, 1988), 80-1. Ulrich cites Nancy Osterud's work on rural New England.

7. This is a complicated journal and account book included in a pocketbook. Multiple members of the Granbery family used it over the course of several centuries. Sarah Granbery is poorly documented, and could be either the wife or mother of John Granbery Jr., who is listed as owning the book by 1708. Abigail (Langley) Granbery Hargroves Journal, pp. 52, 54, VHS. Additional information on the family in Granbery Papers, section 8, VHS.

8. Ulrich, *Good Wives*, 38.

9. Discussions of how markets developed has drawn heated attention, but has focused primarily on New England, especially in the post-Revolutionary War period. Gordon S. Wood, "Inventing American Capitalism," *New York Review of Books*, June 9, 1994, 44–48. Most of the discussion omits any gender analysis, which makes terms like *moral economy* ring hollow when assuming a unity of family desires: "The economy

that resulted, these historians say, was inevitably a moral one. Household interests and communal values overrode the acquisitive instincts of individuals" (45).

10. Sarah Lush made her mark to a receipt dated June 30, 1765 from Neil Jamieson for the sum of £1.3.6. Neil Jamieson (Norfolk; partner in John Glassford and Company Papers) 1105–6, microfilm exposure 608, LC.

11. Susie M. Ames, ed., *County Court Records of Accomack-Northampton, Virginia 1640–1645* (Charlottesville: University Press of Virginia, 1973), 12.

12. Bassett (1709-43) was a merchant in New Kent County. See "1736 Aug[ust] 1 To your balance in my Wifes Book," in William Bassett Account Book for 1728–55, f. 9, VHS.

13. Rebecca married John Coles in 1769 when she was nineteen years old. She records quantities of poultry and hogs raised as well as spinning, weaving, and harness making at the plantation through 1824, when she died. The account books have been mistakenly attributed to her husband, but comparing the handwriting and internal evidence in the books, it is clear she "recycled" an account book he barely used and began writing her own accounts in 1774. First account book in folder listed as "1774–1780 Col. John Coles of Enniscorthy–account book–hogs, bacon, turkeys, chickens" Carter-Smith letters UVA. The short, upside-down, reverse portion of the book is John Coles's account of "seasoning his mares" and can be compared to his handwriting in the letters he writes to his wife—for example, the letter he wrote her on August 26, 1775, in the same collection. The writing in the account books misattributed to him matches her handwriting in other letters. She also records purchasing "gown for self" in April 1777 and "shifts Mr Coles & self" that same year. In May 1778, she acquired "gowns for mamma & self" and shirts for "Mr. Coles." For a sample of her handwriting, see the 1780 letter from Rebecca Elizabeth Coles, "Your truly affectionate wife." This matches the handwriting in the accounts. The account books cover 1774–80, 1801–09, 1810-11 (apparently clothes for plantation consumption), and 1810–25, with a different handwriting for the final portion of this last book.

14. See "chicken account" for the year 1776 for payments to Syrus, Old Kate, Solomon, John, Charles, and Joe, for example. [Rebecca Coles and] "Col. John Coles" Account Book, Carter-Smith Papers, UVA. Near Lynchburg, Virginia, slaves brought yarn, fabric, quilts, eggs, and chickens to market and, in the early nineteenth century purchased goods at a local store. Ann Smart Martin, "Sukey's Mirror: Consumption, Commodities and Cultural Identity in Eighteenth-Century Virginia," paper presented at the Berkshire Conference on the History of Women, Chapel; Hill, NC, 1996, 11.

15. See page beginning "Cotton made in 1773" for these references; 1774–1780, "Col. John Coles" Account Book, Carter-Smith Papers, UVA.

16. Dorothy Henry's account lists a balance in Bassett's wife's account, but no particulars. William Bassett Account Book, f. 9, VHS.

17. A fine imposed in Northampton County demonstrates how a local court acknowledged women's participation in a barter economy. In 1641, "the widow Taylor" called "Goodwife" Custis names when Taylor disapproved of Custis's manner of milking the cow. Rather than being levied a cash fine as punishment for her scolding, Mrs. Taylor was ordered to pay Mr. Custis one pot of milk a day for the rest of that summer. Susie M. Ames, *Studies of the Virginia Eastern Shore in the Seventeenth Century* (Richmond: Dietz Press, 1940), 194.

18. Accounts of Mildred Gregory and others mention the "chicken book." "Merchant. King and Queen County," [hereafter "Merchant, King and Queen County], f. 107, Business Papers, LVA.

19. For other women's exchanges see Mildred Gregory, Elizabeth Hall, and Anne Gregory in "Merchant, King and Queen County," 107, 126, 131.

20. "Merchant, King and Queen County," 110. Ann Martin has found an instance of a woman supplying a storekeeper with chickens in return for a pewter dish in 1772. Martin, "Sukey's Mirror," 9–10.

21. Account Book 1738–1755, f. 19 (1742), Burwell Papers, microfilm, CW. Another cash seller of poultry was a man named "Potter's Bob," probably a slave.

22. "Merchant, King and Queen County" 131.

23. Ibid., 180.

24. Ibid., 126.

25. Ibid., 171.

26. Ann Martin refines the classification of women's participation in trade, looking at three elements in their market activity: "agency," defined as "who controlled access to resources and initiated purchase choice, action (who physically moved about the landscape to acquire goods)," and "authority (who was the final arbiter of consumption decisions)." Martin, "Sukey's Mirror," 2.

27. *Calendar of Virginia State Papers and Other Manuscripts . . . Preserved in the Capitol at Richmond*, 11 vols., ed. William Pitt Palmer (Richmond: Commonwealth of Virginia, 1875–1893), vol. 1 (1652-1781), 228.

28. During the Revolutionary War period, women supplied another important animal product, tallow. William Williams received credit for various goods and services, but specific notation indicates the tallow supplied twice in 1777 came from "your Wife." Edward Taylor's Ledger, Commenced January 18, 1775: 7, microfilm no. 532, LVA.

     In 1780, James Hunter Jr., a merchant based in Fredericksburg, purchased tallow from a Mrs. Thurston but was disappointed when supplies were shorter than expected, because she "was Deceiv'd in the Quantity that she had to spare." The women of the Hunter and Thurston families also exchanged cotton, finished cloth, and sugar. William P. Thurston to James Hunter Jr., February 5, 1780, Hunter-Hitchcock-Coit Papers, personal papers, LVA.

29. Robert Carter to Mrs. Smith, August 27, 1774, Robert Carter Letter Book 2 (microfilm), CW, as cited in Joan R. Gundersen and Gwen Victor Gampel, "Married Women's Legal Status in Eighteenth-Century New York and Virginia," *WMQ*, 3d ser., 39 (1982), 131. Gundersen and Gampel claim the transaction involved Mrs. Smith because Anglican clergymen were prevented from doing manual labor, but a wife of a clergyman was permitted to conduct the trade. Other examples of women not married to clergymen marketing family produce suggests that the occupation of the husband was not the determining factor in whether women sold these goods.

30. December 16, 1773, *Journal and Letters of Philip Vickers Fithian 1773-1774: A Plantation Tutor of the Old Dominion*, ed. Hunter Dickinson Farish, (Williamsburg: Colonial Williamsburg, 1957), 32.

31. Ester Boserup, *Woman's Role in Economic Development* (New York: St. Martin's, 1970), 15–51, 94–95.

32. Ulrich, "Martha Ballard and Her Girls," 82, n. 26.

33. Department of International Economic and Social Affairs, Statistical Office and International Research and Training Institute for the Advancement of Women, *Methods of Measuring Women's Participation and Production in the Informal Sector*, Studies in Methods Series F, no. 46 (New York: United Nations, 1990), 104, 106.

34. Folder: Business Papers 1769–1772, Box 17, Webb-Prentis Collection, UVA.

35. Mary P. Ryan, *Women in Public: Between Banners and Ballots, 1825–1880* (Baltimore: Johns Hopkins University Press, 1990) discusses women's changing access to public spaces in the nineteenth century. Laurel Thatcher Ulrich, "Of Pens and Needles," *Journal of American History* 77 (1990): 200–207.

36. In England, writers increasingly associated shopping with women in the late eighteenth century. Elizabeth Kowaleski-Wallace, *Consuming Subjects: Women, Shopping, and Business in the Eighteenth Century* (New York: Columbia University Press, 1997), 84. Rhys Isaac, *The Transformation of Virginia: 1740–1790* (New York: Norton, 1982), 57; Daniel B. Thorpe, "Doing Business in the Backcountry: Retail Trade in Colonial Rowan County, North Carolina," *WMQ*, 3d ser., 48 (1991): 398; Darrett B. Rutman and

Anita H. Rutman, *A Place in Time, Middlesex County, Virginia, 1650–1750* (New York: Norton, 1984), 230.

37. In her analysis of the customers visiting John Hook's store near Lynchburg, Virginia, Ann Martin finds that women enjoyed "a sense of pleasure" in their visits to the stores in the late eighteenth- and early nineteenth centuries, and that older teenagers and unmarried women traveled to stores on sociable outings. Parallel to the Rutmans' conclusions for the 1650–1750 period, Martin has determined that women made their own choices in selecting merchandise, particularly fabrics, sewing tools, and "fashion" items, including feather plumes. She believes that many of the women shopped on household accounts under their husbands' or fathers' names rather than purchasing goods with independent funds. Ann Smart Martin, "The Black Box of Household Consumption: Women and the Retail Trade in Virginia, 1750–1820," paper presented to the Triangle Early American History Group, Chapel Hill, March 23, 2001, 26; Martin, "Sukey's Mirror," 6–8.

38. Thorpe, "Doing Business in the Backcountry," 391. When undertaking studies of economies from the past, one should remember that well into the twentieth century women's limited access to consumer and commercial credit remained a feminist issue.

39. See discussion of the Bassett Account Books, above. Ann Martin has detected a pattern that points to women's purchases being concealed under the cash columns in account books. In backcountry Virginia, goods acquired by cash (rather than credit) included a large proportion of the same textiles and sewing items women bought on credit or by exchange. Thus, the anonymous cash entries point to the "missing women" shopping in Virginia stores. Martin, "The Black Box of Household Consumption," 18–19.

40. Jerdone Account Book [daybook] 1750–1752, Jerdone Papers, W&M.

41. Jerdone Account Book [daybook] 1750–1752, November 16, 1750: Mrs. Mild [red] Lightfoot scratched out and transferred to cash; December 19, 1751, "Mrs Jenny Ansell pr. her self Dr" crossed out and replaced with "cash;" Two entries, one on February 2, 1752 and one on February 13, 1752: Mrs Jean Ansell again crossed out and replaced with cash. Ansell used credit and cash on various other transactions, and in one, of March 31, 1752, "cash" was crossed out and replaced with a reference to a ledger entry. November 29, 1751, December 19, 1751, February 2, 1752, February 12, 1751, May 15, 1751; Jerdone Papers, W&M.

42. Mrs. Rebeckah Hudson, Mrs. Elizabeth Hendley, "by cash received of you," Thomas Partridge Account Book, ff. 16, 60, VHS.

43. Mrs. Grace Roland, Thomas Partridge Account Book, f. 21, VHS.

44. Mrs. Elizabeth Joyner, by John Joyner, perhaps a son, Thomas Partridge Account Book, f. 32, VHS.

45. Mary Winson, Mary Mask, Margaret Hundley, Sarah Anderson, Alice Butler in Hanover County Merchant Ledger 1750–1751: 4, 77, 83, 86–87, photocopy, LVA.

46. Unity Dandridge, Susannah Cooper, Ann Rice, Elizabeth Prosser, Elizabeth Vaughan, Mrs. Else Taylor, Mrs. Arnott, Charity Anderson in Hanover County Merchant Ledger, 1750–1751: 63, 73, 81, LVA.

47. Mary Winson (used both forms of payment), Mary Burnett, Ann Cluverius, Hanover County Merchant Ledger 1750–1751: 4, 65, 87, 90, LVA.

48. Mordecai Booth Account Book c. 1746–1752, January 5, 1746, f. 63, Baylor Family Papers, VHS.

49. Account Book [daybook] Yorktown, 1750–52, Jerdone Papers, W&M. Entries for 1750: October 20; for 1751: March 21, March 29, August 15, August 23, September 4, November 19, December 19; for 1752: January 3, February 2, February 13, March 10, March 26, March 31, June 23, May 15.

50. Mrs. Norton purchased fabric for George Walker, and James Mitchell's daughter, Peggy, purchased six packs of the "best playing cards" on her father's account. (September 21 and 30, 1751). For women charging to husbands' and fathers' accounts, see Jerdone Account Book [daybook], October 4, 1750, December 10, 1750, February 14 and 25, 1750/1, W&M. For other women's purchases and methods of payment in the Jerdone Account Book, see [April] 23, 1751, May 1 and 27, 1751, June 18, 1751, July 19, 1751, August 23, 1751, September 11, 1751, November 3, 1751, October 14, 1751, December 11, 1751, February 19, 1751/2, April 3, 1752, April 6, 1752, and April 3, 1752.

51. Recorded as "Mr. Benjamin Moss D[ebt]or P[e]r. his wife"; June 24, 1752, Jerdone Account Book [daybook] 1750–1752, W&M.

52. Jerdone Account Book [daybook], June 17, 1751, June 20, 1751, W&M. John Norton was also charged for "fine hatt band Crape" for Mrs. Frances Nelson on June 24, 1751. The *Virginia Gazette* reported the death of the Prince of Wales in its issue for May 24, 1751.

53. Ledgers, Edward Dixon Papers 1743–1808, container 1: ff. 27, 37,60, 88, 100, 104, 135, 142, 172, 175, 186, 187, 204, 213, 216, 217, 220; container 2: ff. 25, 80; LC. For similar accounting systems worked for antebellum slave families in the sugar producing regions of Louisiana, see Roderick McDonald: "The debiting systems and the purchasing patterns thus indicate that the slave accounts were family accounts to which the family of the account-holder had access." Roderick A. McDonald, "Independent Economic Production by Slaves on Antebellum Louisiana Sugar Plantations," in *The Slaves' Economy: Independent Production by Slaves in the Americas*, ed. Ira Berlin and Philip D. Morgan, (London: Frank Cass, 1991), 202–3.

54. See the entries for Mrs. Sarah Blalock, February 13, 1752, and Susannah Cooper, November 3, 1751, for example. Jerdone Account Book [daybook], W&M.

55. The purchases are listed under the masters' names, but as "pr." (by) the women by name or "negro girl." The concentration of small purchases in January may reveal some post-Christmas shopping for the women's own consumption, though the large quantities of sugar and molasses were probably for larger household use. Jerdone Account Book [daybook], March 21, 1750/1, March, 1751, April 23, 1751, September 30, 1751, December 19, 1751 (two references), January 12, 1752, January 14, 1752, January 23, 1752, January 30, 1752, February 2, 1752, February 15, 1752, March 23, 1752, April 6, 1752, April 3, 1752, October 9, 1752, February 28, 1752, W&M.

56. One of the most striking examples of an "own-account" African-American man's purchase is that of "Negro George belonging to G. Halloway," who paid two shillings cash for a Bible and had the rest paid for by one Thomas Grayson. It was George's only purchase in this ledger and suggests his determination in acquiring the book that he made this purchase while enslaved. Ledger 1751–52, Unknown Merchant, King and Queen County, January 18, 1752: 47, Business Papers 28893, LVA.

57. This topic is discussed in greater detail in chapter 6.

58. York DOW 12, May 24, 1703: 112.

59. Abigail (Langley) Granbery Hargroves Journal, August 27, 1716: 52, 54, VHS. Additional information on the family in Granbery Papers, section 8, VHS. Because of the wide range of material in this book, it might be more properly called a "commonplace book." Gail S. Terry, *Documenting Women's Lives: A User's Guide to Manuscripts at the Virginia Historical Society* (Richmond: Virginia Historical Society, 1996), 164.

60. Ledger 1751–52, Merchant, King and Queen County: 221, 224, LVA.

61. James Ritchie and Company Account Book, accounts for William Burk, Brown Berryman, and George Brabner, LC. The names appear in approximate alphabetical order in the Account Book.

62. Ritchie Account Book, accounts of Elizabeth Harrison and Elizabeth McCormack, LC.

63. Ritchie Account Book, account of William Pickett, LC.

64. Ledgers, Edward Dixon Papers 1743–1808, container 1: ff. 26, 103; container 2: f. 54, LC.

65. "Liability on book debts turned—at least potentially—far more on the facts of the dispute than on any fixed conception of the law." Bruce H. Mann, *Neighbors and Strangers: Law and Community in Early Connecticut* (Chapel Hill: University of North Carolina Press, 1987), 23. In litigating, a creditor in a book account needed to state that a debtor owed a sum on account and had never paid. Either side could present evidence and rules for recovery were less strict than in debt suits, in terms of stating the exact sum to be recovered, for example. This section draws on Bruce Mann's extensive discussion of book debt in Connecticut in the colonial period. (11–22).

66. Cornelia Hughes Dayton, *Women before the Bar: Gender, Law, and Society in Connecticut, 1639–1789* (Chapel Hill: University of North Carolina Press, 1995), 78–87.

67. Answer of James Gordon, 1764, *Ball v. Gordon*, Lancaster County, Chancery, LVA. Case began in common law in 1755, in chancery in 1759.

68. Merchant, King and Queen County, 200, 213–14.

69. The accounts of Sarah Masters, Mary Turner, George Brabner, Thomas Sullivan and Thomas Gibbons, Ritchie Account Book, LC.

70. Accounts of John Molier, Samuel Sale, George Turner, Richard Conquest, and Jessiephron Clark, Ritchie Account Book, LC.

71. Martha Ballard was both a midwife and cloth producer, allowing her a foot in the exchange economy. Ulrich, *A Midwife's Tale*, 71–82.

72. Account Book 1747–1764, f. 92, William Lightfoot papers, 1740–64; M-1555, CW I encountered a similar version of being a "captive audience" in Jamaica, where resourceful vendors of food set up for business on the highways at railway crossings. Once the driver slowed her vehicle to navigate the crossing, she could, without much trouble, come to a complete stop to purchase cashews, citrus, or the other local road goods. Airport stores similarly play to this captive audience in selling overpriced goods to bored passengers in transit.

73. She seems to be the same "Mrs. Blacley" who had an account at a tavern in Williamsburg. There she was able to purchase oranges when the winter crop arrived. Anne Pattison Account, February 19, 1747/8, f. 150, VHS. This is covered in Linda L. Sturtz, "Catherine Blaikley," *Dictionary of Virginia Biography*, ed. John T. Kneebone, J. Jefferson Looney, Brent Tarter, and Sandra Gioia Treadway (Richmond: Library of Virginia, 1999), vol. 1, 534–35.

74. *Virginia Gazette* (Rind), 10 August 1769.

75. She also received payment from Carter Burwell under "Household Expenses," December 15, 1739, in the amount of £1.02.06. [Carter] Burwell Account Book 1738–65, f. 101, transcript, CW; also microfilm m-1462.

76. *Virginia Gazette* (Purdie & Dixon), October 24, 1771.

77. John Mercer Ledger 1741–1750, account for 1750, book 1: 148, microfilm, CW.

78. Edward Taylor Ledger, Commenced January 18, 1775: 48, 56, 85, 90, 159, microfilm 532, LVA.

79. Dixon Papers, container 1: f. 104, account of Samuel Skinker, f. 204, LC.

80. Dixon Papers, container 1: ff. 104, 108; container 2, f. 36, LC.

81. Jerdone Account Book [daybook], ff. 198, 203, 248, W&M.

82. Jerdone Account Book, 1750–1772, f. 203, MsV 6b, W&M. By contrast, when planter Carter Burwell paid Mary Roberts for midwifery or Elizabeth Hansford for nursing his own daughter and for "looking after my Negroes in the Small pox," he paid cash to settle debts. Carter Burwell Account Book, 1738–1755, microfilm reel 1, f. 35, VHS.

83. *Ball v. Gordon*, 1764, Lancaster County, Chancery, LVA. The orators, Richard and William Ball, described purchases from James Gordon, merchant, made on behalf of Richard Ball between 1749 and 1753, while Ball was underage.

84. Anne Pattison Account Book, entries for April 14 and 30, 1747/8, ff. 153, 156, VHS.
85. Carter Burwell, in his records, reports paying the "Oyster Woman" in cash. April 17, 1740, Carter Burwell Ledger 1738–1756, CW.
86. Cynthia A. Kierner, *Southern Women in Revolution, 1776–1800: Personal and Political Narratives* (Columbia: University of South Carolina Press, 1998), 152–53.
87. Cynthia A. Kierner, *Beyond the Household: Women's Place in the Early South, 1700–1835* (Ithaca: Cornell University Press, 1998), 76.
88. Edward Taylor Ledger, microfilm 532, LVA. Thomas Randolph to Frances Bland Randolph Tucker, Mattoax, November 16, 1776, Tucker-Coleman Papers, W&M. On the link between home-spun cloth consumption and devotion to nonimportation, see Martha Jacquelin to John Norton, August 14, 1769, *John Norton and Sons, Merchants of London and Virginia, Being the Papers from Their Counting House for the Years 1750 to 1795*, ed. Frances Norton Mason (New York: August Kelley, 1968), 103. For a pre-Revolutionary example of a woman exchanging woven yards of cloth for consumer items, see Martin, "Sukey's Mirror," 10.
89. Abigail (Langley) Granbery Hargroves Journal, p. 57 [inside cover], VHS.
90. The Randolph plantations in Charlotte County included seven slave women involved in tasks of cloth production from spinning to sewing by 1775. York Wills and Inventories 22: 337–41, and estate papers of Peyton Randolph, LC, as cited by C. Julia Richter, "The Randolph House," Colonial Williamsburg Research Report, 8, CW.
91. Account Book of Elizabeth (Lewis) Littlepage Holladay, 1-2, Holladay Family Papers, section 69, VHS.
92. Elizabeth Littlepage Account Book, 11–13, VHS.
93. The Jerdones recorded cloth totals in October of each year. Jerdone Account Book, 1750–1772, f. 198, W&M.
94. May 29, 1761, December 22, 1761, November 22, 1763, Jerdone Account Book, 1750–1772, f. 198, W&M.
95. Their daughters Margaret and Mary inherited other land and slaves. Judy's husband named her coexecutor, along with Belsches's brother James and Francis Jerdone. The will was copied into the Francis Jerdone Account Book, folder 6, ff. 8–9, Jerdone Family Papers, LVA. Patrick Belsches's will was recorded in Louisa Wills 1, written December 29, 1763 and proved April 10, 1764: 53–56, LVA. She relinquished dower after her husband was dead; Louisa County Order Book, April 10, 1764: 76–77, LVA. By 1769 Judy Belsches had died and her will was recorded. Louisa County Will Book 2 (1767–1783): 18–21, photostat volume, LVA. She named her brother-in-law Francis Jerdone as her executor.
96. One of the accounts in the book running from 1766 to 1768 describes transactions with Nathan Talley, the overseer, whose wife received a legacy in Judy Belsches's will. A separate booklet has been stitched into this book, beginning on f. 25. The Talley account appears on ff. 6–7. A 1768 reference on f. 6 includes Nathan Talley's receipt for a sum from Francis Jerdone as executor for Judy Belsches, deceased, for the "balance due to me this day." "Jerdone" Account Book, Jerdone Family Papers 1762–1866, LVA.
97. Jerdone Account Book, 1750–1772, f. 196, W&M. The sales book seems to be the Library of Virginia ledger, which includes an account for "Miss Mary Macon of New Kent County." Jerdone Account Book, ff. 16, 27, LVA.
98. Further evidence that this is Belsches's book is the inclusion of an overseer's agreement with Nathan Talley, describing Talley's shares in the corn and tobacco crops as credits and debiting his account for rum, cotton, wool, and sugar, when Talley worked as an overseer for Belsches. Talley purchased a bed with its "furniture" and wool at the estate sale. "Jerdone" Account Book, f. 6, LVA. The Jerdones probably obtained the book when they took over the business upon Belsches's death, in their capacity as coexecutors of the estate. The Belsches family seemed to maintain contact with the Jerdones, and a "Miss Belsches" was mentioned in the Journal of

Alexander Macaulay, who married Francis's daughter Elizabeth. In 1783, Alexander and Elizabeth (Jerdone) Macaulay met with Miss Belsches and taught her a new dance step. "Journal of Alexander Macaulay," *WMQ*, 1st ser., 11 (1903): 181.

99. "Jerdone" Account Book, ff. 26–27, LVA.

100. The cost was usually four to five pence a yard for each type of cloth, though curtains and "counterpins" were eight pence a yard.

101. "The Inventory of the Deceased July Belsches Estate, March 29, 176[8?]," Jerdone Account Book, ff. 11–12, LVA. The shoemaking tools probably were used by John Jones, whose account credits were all in shoemaking in return for board for six months, Virginia cloth, and some clothing (f. 2).

102. [torn] 15, 1762, October 17, 1766, "Jerdone" Account Book, f. 25, LVA.

103. The two other women who wove for her were Mary Macon and Margery Ellyson. "Jerdone" Account Book, f. 4, LVA.

104. Mr. Robert Bain's account (1764), "Jerdone" Account Book, f. 1, LVA.

105. Mrs. Mary Yance (1766-1767), "Jerdone" Account Book, f. 6, LVA.

106. "Jerdone" Account Book, f. 5, LVA.

107. Cloth production by women for trade occurred in the south under a putting-out system before female labor staffed northern factories. For women's and girl's work in the Lowell Mills in the nineteenth century, Thomas Dublin, *Women at Work: The Transformation of Work and Community in Lowell, Massachusetts, 1826–1860* (New York: Columbia University Press, 1979) offers an interesting contrast.

108. In 1812, Thomas Jefferson contacted E. I. Dupont for information on finishing the wool from the Monticello sheep. Jefferson wrote, "I have understood you are concerned in a manufactory of cloth, and will recieve [*sic*] one's wool, have it spun, wove & dyed for an equivalent in the wool." Presumably Dupont had a more automated system for finishing these steps by 1812, but Jefferson's letter demonstrates that he continued the in-kind exchanges and use of an outsider for finishing the products rather than selling raw materials for finished goods. Jefferson's later account, and much fuller description, gives an overview of how cloth production tasks could be delegated on a plantation. Spinning may have been a year-round task on the largest plantations. Jefferson estimated that spinners had nine hours a day for work in January and December and up to fourteen hours a day in June and July, suggesting he expected spinners to be at work throughout the year. Jefferson directed that children of both sexes were to "serve as nurses" until the age of ten. Between the ages of ten and sixteen, boys made nails. Jefferson to E. I. Dupont, Monticello, April 30, 1812, in *The Garden and Farm Books of Thomas Jefferson*, ed. Robert C. Baron (Golden, Colorado: Fulcrum, 1987), 200, 327, 370. Lucia Stanton discusses Jefferson's textile factory within the context of his attempts to maximize the productivity of his work force: "The textile factory 'only employs a few women, children and invalids who could do little in the farm.'" Lucia Stanton, "'Those Who Labor for My Happiness': Thomas Jefferson and His Slaves" in *Jeffersonian Legacies*, ed. Peter Onuf (Charlottesville: University Press of Virginia), 155.

109. William Lee to Cary Wilkinson, Green Spring, May 22, 1771, Lee Family Papers, VHS.

110. Declaration, Paul Phaben engaged as overseer to Benjamin Stratton in 1762, *Stratton v. Phaban*, Northampton County Ended Causes, bundle 57, Eastville, Virginia. Fil'ed June 12, 1764; continued July (time to plead), September (non assumpsit and issue); November, verdict and judgment for plaintiff.

111. Weavers may have had enough work to keep them busy in all but the most hectic months of the agricultural cycle and did not need to wait for the winter months to proceed. "Jerdone" Account Book, LVA.

112. Patricia Cleary, "She Merchants of Colonial America: Women and Commerce on the Eve of the Revolution," (Ph.D. diss., Northwestern University, 1984); Timothy H.

Breen, "The Meanings of Things: Interpreting the Consumer Economy in the Eighteenth Century," in *Consumption and the World of Goods*, ed. John Brewer and Roy Porter (New York: Routledge, 1993), 249–60.

113. Breen, "The Meaning of Things," 257.

114. For English comparisons, see Margaret Rose Hunt, who describes how this ambiguity of status of women made them unstable debtors in eighteenth-century England. Even married women who acted as feme sole traders faced the threat of having their assets confiscated to pay their husbands' creditors. Margaret R. Hunt, *The Middling Sort: Commerce, Gender and the Family in England, 1680–1780* (Berkeley and Los Angeles: University of California Press, 1996), 139–42. For the process of colonial society becoming a consumer culture, see Ann Smart Martin, "Makers, Buyers, and Users: Consumerism and a Material Culture Framework," *Winterthur Portfolio* 28 (1993): 141–57.

CHAPTER 6

1. *The Fortunes and Misfortunes of Moll Flanders . . . At Last Grew Rich, Lived Honest, and Died Penitent* [A Chapbook] (London: Printed in Aldermary Churchyard, n.d. [c. 1750]), 23. British Library no. 1079.i.13(21). It is interesting that this passage remained virtually intact in the translation of Defoe's novel into the brief chapbook form. Much of the rest of the story needed to be edited down, but the process of goods making Moll's husband a "gentleman" remained a central feature. For the comparable passage, see Daniel Defoe, *Moll Flanders*, ed. James Sutherland (Boston: Houghton Mifflin, 1959), 295.

2. At the beginning of the boom in 1619, the best tobacco sold for three shillings (or thirty-six pence) per pound. By 1629, the price had dropped precipitously to one penny per pound, and official attempts to sustain even that low price failed in the 1630s. Merchants who sold to settlers offered goods and liquor directly from the ships, so that one settler saw the vessels as moving taverns. Edmund S. Morgan, *American Slavery, American Freedom: The Ordeal of Colonial Virginia* (New York: Norton, 1975), 108–113, 134.

3. The tenants on the governor's land possessed rare and valuable Chinese porcelains at a time when the China trade to Europe had begun to flourish. Only one bowl unearthed at the site showed any wear, suggesting the display function of these goods. Colonists in the boom period spent lavishly on foods, clothing, gaming, and "all manner of such superfluity." Archaeologists conclude that many of the artifacts were portable forms of wealth and that tenants accumulated these goods for use at a later time when they could leave their seven-year obligatory tenancy and establish themselves elsewhere. Alain Charles Outlaw, *Governor's Land: Archaeology of Early Seventeenth-Century Virginia Settlements* (Charlottesville: University Press of Virginia, 1990), 51, 81, 175. This author believes that the purring cat was an essential resident in homesick settlers' households, not only for her role in vermin control.

4. James P. P. Horn, *Adapting to a New World: English Society in the Seventeenth-Century Chesapeake* (Chapel Hill: University of North Carolina Press, 1994), 301–28, 331–32; quotation on 326.

5. An extensive literature on changes in colonial material culture is emerging. For an early article concentrating on the 1700–1719 period discussing expanding consumption in the prosperous and "middle classes" see James W. Deen Jr., "Patterns of Testation: Four Tidewater Counties in Colonial Virginia," *American Journal of Legal History* 16 (1972): 163–64. Lois Green Carr and Lorena S. Walsh, "Changing Lifestyles and Consumer Behavior in the Colonial Chesapeake," *Of Consuming Interests: The Style of Life in the Eighteenth Century*, ed. Cary Carson, Ronald Hoffman, and Peter J.

Albert (Charlottesville: University Press of Virginia, 1994), 81. For the consumer revolution, see also the other essays in *Of Consuming Interests*.

6. I am not certain if women did this sort of merchandise selection earlier. The seventeenth-century records I have read offer no evidence of this sort of undertaking. This may be attributable to poor record keeping and document preservation in the seventeenth century, or from less emphasis on the fashionability of goods in the earlier period.

7. Richard Bushman makes this distinction in describing George Washington's shopping habits for Mount Vernon. Richard Bushman, "Shopping and Advertising in Colonial America," in *Of Consuming Interests: The Style of Life in the Eighteenth Century*, ed. Cary Carson, Ronald Hoffman and Peter J. Albert (Charlottesville: University Press of Virginia, 1994), 243.

8. John E. Crowley, "The Sensibility of Comfort," *American Historical Review* 104 (1999), 780.

9. For the consumption side of the discussion, see Neil McKendrick, John Brewer, and J. H. Plumb, *The Birth of a Consumer Society: The Commercialization of Eighteenth-Century England* (London: Hutchinson, 1982); For a case study see Amanda Vickery, "Women and the World of Goods: A Lancashire Consumer and Her Possessions, 1751–81," in *Consumption and the World of Goods*, ed. John Brewer and Roy Porter (New York: Routledge, 1993), 274–301; Timothy H. Breen, "'Baubles of Britain': The American and Consumer Revolutions of the Eighteenth Century," *Past and Present* 119 (1988): 73–104; Patricia Cleary discusses women's businesses in her dissertation, but stresses New York, Boston, and Philadelphia. Patricia Cleary, "'She Merchants' of Colonial America: Women and Commerce on the Eve of the Revolution," (Ph.D. diss., Northwestern University, 1984). Regional variations in commerce prevent extrapolating from Northern experience when discussing Southern attitudes toward trade. Ian K. Steele reaffirmes the need for further studies on the consumer revolution in Virginia in "Empire of Migrants and Consumers: Some Current Atlantic Approaches to the History of Colonial Virginia," *VMHB* 99 (1991): 489–512.

10. Jacob M. Price, *France and the Chesapeake* (Ann Arbor: University of Michigan Press, 1973), vol. 1, xiii–xiv.

11. For reconsideration, see Linda K. Kerber, "Separate Spheres, Female Worlds, and Women's Place: The Rhetoric of Women's History," *Journal of American History* 75 (1988): 9–39. Catherine Hall, "Gender Divisions and Class Formation in the Birmingham Middle Class," and "Strains in the 'Firm of Wife, Children and Friends': Middle-Class Women and Employment in Nineteenth-Century England," both in Catherine Hall, *White, Male, and Middle Class: Explorations in Feminism and History* (New York: Routledge, 1992), 94–107 and 172–202. Jacob M. Price, "Notes and Documents: Who Was John Norton? A Note on the Historical Character of Some Eighteenth-Century London Virginia Firms," *WMQ*, 3d. ser., 19 (1962): 407, and Price, *France and the Chesapeake*, vol. 1, xiv.

12. James Henretta and James Lemon debated this point. Henretta claimed family needs, rather than maximizing profit motivated economic endeavors. Southern farms, by contrast to those in Pennsylvania, were "fully capitalistic slave-holding farms." Lemon believed that in rural Pennsylvania colonists placed "individual freedom and material gain over public interest." James Henretta, "Families and Farms: Mentalité in Pre-industrial America," *WMQ*, 3d ser., 35 (1978): 13–15; and James T. Lemon, *The Best Poor Man's Country: A Geographic Study of Early Southeastern Pennsylvania* (Baltimore: Johns Hopkins University Press, 1972), xiii-xv, 105.

13. The many volumes and essays by Jacob Price have delineated family trade webs. See, as simply one example, *France and the Chesapeake*, vol. 1, xiv. For the Glasgow-based tobacco merchants, see T. M. Devine, *The Tobacco Lords: A Study of the Tobacco*

Merchants of Glasgow and their Trading Activities, c. 1740–90 (Edinburgh: Edinburgh University Press, 1975), 3, 12, 92. For parallels with New England, see Bernard Bailyn, *The New England Merchants in the Seventeenth Century* (Cambridge: Harvard University Press, 1955), 136–37. For a study of circles of associates who alternately embraced and eschewed family connections, see David Hancock, *Citizens of the World: London Merchants and the Integration of the British Atlantic Community, 1735–1785* (Cambridge: Cambridge University Press, 1995), 56, 65. For the significance of marriage in cementing partnerships and in capitalizing family firms in England and overseas during a slightly later period, see Leonore Davidoff and Catherine Hall, *Family Fortunes: Men and Women of the English Middle Class, 1780–1850* (London: Hutchinson, 1987), 215, 218.

14. G. Barker-Benfield, *The Culture of Sensibility: Sex and Society in Eighteenth-Century Britain* (Chicago: University of Chicago Press, 1992), 205.

15. Marylynn Salmon points out the significance of the law in reinforcing disproportionate gender division of power over family resources in Marylynn Salmon, *Women and the Law of Property in Early America* (Chapel Hill: University of North Carolina Press, 1986). The link between economic production and social power forms the basis for Joan Jensen's study on Pennsylvania women in which she points out women directed their labor toward maintaining patriarchal families in Joan M. Jensen, *Loosening the Bonds: Mid-Atlantic Farm Women, 1750–1850* (New Haven: Yale University Press, 1986), 35. Laurel Ulrich's studies of gendered division of labor accompanied by temporary overlap of sex roles when expedient cast a different light over the question of competence. Analyzing "roles" requires determining the "attitudes, values and behavior" ascribed to persons and takes into account "normative and behavior dimensions." Ulrich discussed how unwritten codes could be "as effective in determining behavior as legal and economic systems" and that cracking these codes requires paying attention to what women thought they *should* do as well as what they *actually* did. Laurel Thatcher Ulrich, *Good Wives: Image and Reality in the Lives of Women in Northern New England, 1650–1750* (Oxford: Oxford University Press, 1983), 5-6. Ulrich's *A Midwife's Tale* stresses the greater separation between the sexes in this later period. Laurel Thatcher Ulirch, *A Midwife's Tale: The Life of Martha Ballard Based on Her Diary, 1785–1812* (New York: Knopf, 1990).

16. Daniel Defoe, *The Complete English Tradesman in Familiar Letters... To Which is Added a Supplement,* 2d ed. (London: Charles Rivington, 1727; reprt. New York: Augustus M. Kelley, 1969), vol. 1, 287–303.

17. Lawrence Stone and Jean Fawtier Stone, *An Open Elite? England, 1540–1880* (Oxford: Clarendon Press, 1984), 18. [Sir Josiah] Child, *A New Discourse of Trade* (London: n.p., 1693), 5.

18. Jane Metcalfe, London, to "Dear Child" [Richard Metcalfe], Letter fragment, (n.d., but similar wording and information as a complete letter dated January 5, 1697, so probably written at about that time), Metcalfe Family Papers (hereafter Metcalfe FP), Chicago Historical Society (hereafter CHS). Through her letters, Jane Metcalfe appeared to be a doting, if somewhat pontificating, mother and mother-in-law. She was sharp-tongued in railing against her enemies, such as the "wreched wile[y] and wicked Cap. P" and the "proud Imperious woman" responsible for the Metcalfes' legal difficulties, or when she urged her son to turn out a freeloading relative, though she cautioned, "I would not have thee carri it Towards any unchristan like" manner. She offered to come over to Virginia to push this man out or to give him a gift (bribe) to leave her son's family alone. She expressed concern in another letter for her son's rapidly growing family and resorted to religious language to remind him of his "duty" to provide for his family. Even in her bossy way, she encouraged the couple to be kind and loving to each other in practical ways, and continued to fuss over her daughter-in-

law after her son died. She also maintained some ties to her daughter-in-law's parents. She was not above using guilt to get her son to send her the money he owed her.

Metcalfe was widowed herself at the time she wrote the letters. It is quite likely she was widow or daughter-in-law to Gilbert Metcalfe (also spelled Medcalfe), "London, Merchant," who took up over eight-hundred acres of land at the Piankatank River in Gloucester County, Virginia in the seventeenth century. Richard Metcalfe's son was named Gilbert, too, and may well have been named for his grandfather or great-grandfather, the London merchant. Jane Metcalfe possessed Piankatank land she planned to give to her granddaughter. Nell Marion Nugent, *Cavaliers and Pioneers: Abstracts of Virginia Land Patents and Grants* (Richmond: Virginia State Library and Archives, 1992), vol. 1:368, 523. More on the Metcalfe family is in "Metcalfe Families," *WMQ*, 1st ser., 5 (1897–98): 10–12.

19. Jane Metcalfe to "Dear Child" [Richard Metcalfe], January 5, 1697, Metcalfe FP, CHS; Elizabeth Vaulx's supervision of family business occurred while her husband handled legal business in England.

20. Administration of the estate of Richard Metcalfe granted to Anne Metcalfe, November 3, 1698, in Richmond County Court. Robert Headley, *Wills of Richmond County 1699–1800* (Baltimore: Genealogical Publishing, 1983), 5, citing Richmond County Orders 2: 405. A subsequent lawsuit settled in June 1712 between Edward Barrow (Jane's daughter-in-law's next husband) and Gilbert Metcalfe (her grandson), over family slaves demonstrates that she was justified in worrying about the division of property in the family. The parties consented to let Robert Carter settle the case. Carter cited Jane Metcalfe's letters as evidence in his decision and this may account for their preservation. "Award of Robert Carter" reprinted in "Metcalfe Families," 11.

21. Linda Colley, *Britons: Forging the Nation, 1707–1837,* (New Haven: Yale University, 1992), 238.

22. Linda K. Kerber, *Women of the Republic: Intellect and Ideology in Revolutionary America* (Chapel Hill: University of North Carolina Press, 1980); Benjamin Rush, *Thoughts Upon Female Education Accommodated to the Present State of Society, Manners and Government in the United States of America* (1787), reprinted in *Essays on Education in the Early Republic*, ed. Frederick Rudolph (Cambridge, MA: Belknap Press, 1965), 28–29.

23. [Thomas Anburey], *Travels through the Interior Parts of America; in a Series of Letters. By An Officer,* (1789, reprt. New York: New York Times, 1969), 362. The passage is discussed in greater detail in Linda L. Sturtz, "The Ladies and the Lottery: Elite Women's Gambling in Eighteenth-Century Virginia," *VMHB* 104 (1996): 181.

24. Timothy H. Breen, *Tobacco Culture: The Mentality of the Great Tidewater Planters on the Eve of the Revolution* (Princeton: Princeton University Press, 1985), 65.

25. Lydia Jones shipped her tobacco on September 17, 1773, under the mark LI (*I* often being the equivalent initial for names beginning with *J* in shipping marks); Eliza Kennore shipped two barrels with a design mark of her initials EK inside a diamond, July 8, 1774; and Eliza Fitzhugh sent several barrels under the mark EF. Lydia Jones consigned her tobacco to John Norton and Sons; Eliza Kennore consigned to John Backhouse; Eliza Fitzhugh also consigned to John Backhouse. State Records, Auditor of Public Accounts (RG 48), James River Naval Office Records, 1773-1789, APA 301 (Miscellaneous Reel 257), 67, 180, 339; Archives Research Services, LVA.

26. The law listed Elizabeth Wanghop's tobacco under EW, Rebecca Beacham's under RB, and Sarah Hulett's under SH. March 1756 (29 George II) "A SCHEDULE of the Tobacco burnt in Coan Warehouse, to which this Act refers," in William Waller, Hening, ed., *Statutes at Large: Being A Collection of All the Laws of Virginia, from the First Session of the Legislature, in the Year 1619* (Richmond and Philadelphia: Printed for the Editor, 1809–1823), vol. 7, 51–52.

27. Thomas Cabel, "Cherry:Stone" on the Eastern Shore, to Micajah Perry, June 10, 1727. Thomas Cabel Letter Book and Account Book 1722–1757, f. 36., Maryland Historical Society.

28. The account also notes that she had the tobacco inspected at Todd's Warehouse. Virginians exchanged receipts of tobacco inspected and accepted at official warehouses. May 29, 1752, [Unknown] Merchant, King and Queen County, Ledger 1751–52, 231, Business Papers LVA.

29. Account of Eliza Vaughan and Edw[ar]d Lovell, December 7, 1749, William Beverley Account Book kept at Blandfield, Essex County, Virginia, f. 1, entered under heading "Rents due Nov[embe]r. 27, 1749," 1749–1750, VHS.

30. William Beverley Account Book, ff. 7, 15, VHS.

31. Robert Bristow to Thomas Booth, October 1, 1718, Robert Bristow Letter Book, misc. reel 348, LVA.

32. The case concerned the terms of a jointure, a debt incurred by a man and a woman who later married, and the degree to which the woman's taking dower in her dead husband's estate and provisions from its produce canceled her claims for repayment of the antenuptial debt. *Scarbury & Anna Maria [Timson] c. Barber Extor. Barber* (Chancery), April Court 1739, in *Virginia Colonial Decisions: The Reports by Sir John Randolph and by Edward Barradall of the Decisions of the General Court of Virginia, 1728–1741*, ed. R. T. Barton (Boston: Boston Book Company, 1909), B302.

33. Chancery—town depositions, 1728, part 1, 1–3, PRO C 24/1452.

34. Deposition of John Moore, April 20, 1728, *Thomas Colemore, Charles Colemore, Richard Burbyage and Samuel Woodlaw c. Ann Colemore et al.*, PRO C 24/1452, part 1, 1–3.

35. Deposition of John Moore, 20 April 1728, Thomas Colemore, Charles Colemore, Richard Burbyage and Samuel Woodlaw c. Ann Colemore et. al., PRO C 24/1452 part 1, pp. 1-3.

36. Consolidation of economic power through judicious marriages in agricultural settings is known. For example, economic considerations seemed to be at stake when, on the eastern shore of Virginia widowers married widows who held adjacent parcels of land, allowing them to consolidate the properties. James R. Perry, *The Formation of A Society on Virginia's Eastern Shore, 1615–1658* (Chapel Hill: University of North Carolina Press, 1990), 83. Perry's thesis is that a interpersonal and institutional network formed the basis of "the societal network, or web-provided cohesion," and that this cohesion existed on the eastern shore before 1660, allowing him to stress the significance of community over individualism relatively early in Chesapeake history.

37. Jacob M. Price, "One Family's Empire: The Russell-Lee-Clerk Connection in Maryland, Britain, and India, 1707–1857," *Maryland Historical Magazine*, 72 (1997)165–225. Jacob M. Price, *Perry of London: A Family and A Firm on the Seaborne Frontier, 1615–1753* (Cambridge, MA: Harvard University Press, 1992). J. M. Sosin, "English Colonial and Overseas Commerce: The Nexus of Kinship and Trade," *English America and the Restoration Monarchy of Charles II: Transatlantic Politics, Commerce, and Kinship* (Lincoln: University of Nebraska Press, 1980).

38. This case became complicated because the store's account book burned in the Great Fire of London in 1666. Deposition of John Meredith, October 24, 1667, *Meredith v. Middleton*, Mayor's Court Depositions, box 17, CLRO.

39. Deposition of Lucretia Laneare, July 10, 1643, Mayor's Court Depositions 1641–46, MCD 1/86, CLRO. In 1690, one merchant engaged in transatlantic trade provided an informal character reference for a man he described as "soft [and] unthinking," because he believed the business would succeed as a result of the wife who was "notable" and "stirring" and who "by her diligence hath put him in a way to live." Thomas Knight to Thomas Brailsford, April 24, 1690, PRO C 110/152, *Brailsford v. Peers and Tooke*, as cited by Nuala Zahedieh, "Making Mercantilism Work: London

Merchants and the Atlantic Trade in the Seventeenth Century," *Transactions of the Royal Historical Society*, 6th ser., 9 (1999):153.

40. See chapter above on women with power of attorney. English trade with Ireland may also have worked on this basis of women assisting from one terminus of that trade network. See, for example, the depositions of John Messenger and Robert Whitehead, weavers of London, concerning the purchases of Katherine Garland, who subscribed her name to an account for £64.7.1 worth of goods in 1677. The deponents described her husband, Patrick Garland, as a merchant of Dublin. Mayor's Court Depositions, box 33, CLRO.

41. There are numerous examples of seventeenth-century Virginia men authorizing their wives to have power of attorney in their absences; see chapter 3.

42. Susan Moseley, Elizabeth River, to "Worthy Sir" Letter written July 1650, recorded November 10, 1652, Norfolk County Wills and Deeds 8 (1651-6): ff. 24–125, microfilm, LVA.

43. Susan Moseley "Worthy Sir", recorded November 10, 1652, Norfolk County Wills and Deeds C, 24–25.

44. Daniel Parke to Mrs. Parke Pepper, 1731, quoted in *Recollections and Private Memoirs of Washington by his Adopted Son, George Washington Parke Custis, with a Memoir of the Author by His Daughter [Mrs. R. E. Lee]*, (New York: Derby and Jackson, 1860), 18–19.

45. Price, "Notes and Documents," 406.

46. Thomas Cabel, Cherry Stone, Eastern Shore, to John Waple, Royal African House, London, July 16, 1725, Thomas Cabel Letter and Account Book 1722–1757, f. 26, Maryland Historical Society.

47. Captain Goosley, Putney, England, to John Hatley Norton, Virginia, September 29, 1772, in *John Norton and Sons, Merchants of London and Virginia, Being the Papers from Their Counting House for the Years 1750 to 1795*, ed. Frances Norton Mason, (New York: Augustus M. Kelley, 1968), 277.

48. Price, "Notes and Documents," 407.

49. Lucy Armistead to Marianna Hunter, September 4, 1774, Hunter-Garnett Collection, box 2, UVA.

50. Ann Walker, Hampton, to Mary Latané, July 23, 1731, Latané Family Papers, UVA.

51. Steuart had moved his operations to Portsmouth by 1754. [Charles Steuart] to Mr. [James] Buchanan, September 2, 1754, Charles Steuart Letter Books, Norfolk, VA 1751–1763, Historical Society of Pennsylvania (hereafter HSP).

52. Ibid.

53. [Charles Steuart] to [James] Buchanan, November 16, 1754, Charles Steuart Letter Book, Norfolk, VA 1751–1763, HSP.

54. Martha Goosley to John Norton, August 15, 1769, in Mason, ed., *John Norton and Sons*, 102.

55. See September 1, 1770, for example, on having "all my Boys settled" but most of the letters deal with her son's trade in tobacco in Mason, ed., *John Norton and Sons*, 145.

56. Nathaniel Littleton Savage to John Norton, August 24, 1768, Norton-Savage I Correspondence and Documents, box 18, Brock Collection, HL.

57. John Norton to John Hatley Norton, May 25, 1767, microfilm, CW.

58. Miss Tucker (Barbados en route from England) to Mr. Withers, June 9, 1780, in Mason, ed., *John Norton and Sons*, 438.

59. February 22, 1770, in Mason, ed., *John Norton and Sons*, 124.

60. For a late-seventeenth-century example of a mother lobbying to advance her son's career, see Dorothea Torway's letter to B. Harrison Jr. of Williamsburg from January 18, 1699 in which Torway, living in London, hoped to draw on Harrison's connections

to the governor of the colony to secure a post for her son. Letters of January 18, 1699 and February 23, 1702 from Harrison, reproduced in *Executive Journals of the Council of Colonial Virginia*, ed. H. R. McIlwaine (Richmond: Virginia State Library, 1923), vol. 2, 370–73. For a description of how similar connections could work in an elaborate system of "society" women creating political and economic ties to advance their families' position in Victorian Britain, see Leonore Davidoff, *The Best Circles* (1973, reprt. London: Cresset, 1986).

61. Jane Metcalfe, London, to Ann Metcalfe, Rappahannock River, September 27, 1700, Metcalfe Family Papers (hereafter Metcalfe FP), CHS.
62. Anne Matthews to John Norton, July 20, 1770, in Mason, ed., *John Norton and Sons*, 138–39.
63. Matthews reminded Mrs. Norton of her old acquaintanceship to Matthews's daughter, who was the mother of the girl whose interests were being advanced.
64. Charlotte Dickson to John Norton, December 29, 1770; Beverley Dickson to John Norton, October 16, 1771 and May 21, 1772, Norton-Savage I Correspondence and Documents, box 18, Brock Collection, HL.
65. York DOW, December 16, 1751, 504.
66. Jane Metcalfe to Richard Metcalfe, November 29, 1694 and January 5, 1697/8, Metcalfe FP, CHS.
67. Jane Metcalfe to Richard Metcalfe, January 5, 1697, Metcalfe FP, CHS.
68. Ibid.
69. With apologies to Sir Joseph's "sisters, cousins, and aunts" on Gilbert and Sullivan's H.M.S. Pinafore; I am sure there were female cousins involved in shipboard business, but I found these groups of female relatives more overtly working in family businesses—Sister Talbett, Mother Jane Metcalfe, and Aunt Norton.
70. John uses phonetic spelling throughout the letters, writing Susanna as "Shushanner" and Eleanor as "Elenner." Opie Papers, Bristol Records Office 206(16)n. 1–5, VCRP microfilm reel 768.
71. John Opie to Elenner [*sic*] Horte, November 5, 1712; John Opie to "Sisters," May 17, 1716, Opie Papers, Bristol Records Office, 206(16)r, 206(16)s; VCRP microfilm reel 768.
72. November 10, 1769, Roger Atkinson Letter Book 1769–1773 and 1776, f. 16, Business Papers, LVA.
73. Atkinson Letter Book, n.d., but in a group written in Williamsburg June 16, 1770, f. 26, LVA.
74. Atkinson Letter Book, n.d. (between 1771 and 1772 in the letter book), f. 58, LVA.
75. Martha Goosley to John Norton, October 18, 1771, in Mason, ed., *John Norton and Sons*, 200.
76. One task of this court was to oversee wills concerning individuals with interests extending beyond a single jurisdiction.
77. Hubbald wrote to tell Durley that he needed to come to England himself if he wished to resolve the lawsuit concerning his interest in the St. Helen's estate. Durley eventually died in London. After William's death, his wife Mary, was left with the management of the estates, with the help of the family's contact in England. Edward Hubbald, "kinsman," London, to William Durley, on Nansemond River, 18 January 1732, Durley Family Papers (hereafter Durley FP), VHS.
78. Power of Attorney from Mary Durley to James Stockdale of Liverpool, Durley FP, Item 14, VHS.
79. Account of Mrs. Mary Durley 1741 to 1749, item 13; William Parker to Mary Durley, December 13, 1741 both in Durley FP, VHS.
80. W. Parker, London, to Ms Mary Durley Nansemond, March 25, 1745, item 11, Durley VHS. She is, indeed, addressed as "Ms"!

81. William Parker to Ms Mary Durley, March 31, 1744, item 11, Durley FP, VHS.
82. William Parker to Mary Durley, item 1, Durley FP; Account of William Durley's debts in London, item 13, both in Durley FP, VHS.
83. William Parker to Mary Durley, March 31, 1744, item 11; William Parker to Mary Durley, March, 10, 1743/4, item 10, both in Durley FP, VHS.
84. Mary Parker to Mary Durley, February 23, 1747/8, item 6, Durley FP, VHS.
85. James Gildart, Liverpool, to Martha Custis, December 6, 1757, Custis Family Papers (hereafter Custis FP), 1683–1858, items 163–64, VHS.
86. John Opie in "Virginiar" to his Sisters, May 17, 1716, Opie Papers, Bristol Records Office, 206(16)s, VCRP, microfilm 768.
87. W. Tyson and Charles Moore to Mary Durley, November 30, 1751, items 4–5, Durley FP, VHS.
88. W. Tyson and Charles Moore, London, to Mary Durley, 22 June 1753, Durley FP, VHS.
89. Horatio Durley, Matthew Godrich, and Mary Durley to James Stockdale, Merchant, Liverpool, November 17, 1753, item 3, Durley FP, VHS.
90. Charles Steuart Letter Books, Norfolk, VA 1751-1763, HSP. This includes only the outgoing letters from Steuart, so Minvielle's actions must be deduced from his side of the correspondence.
91. There are various spellings of this name in the records. I have standardized it as Minvielle.
92. Two letters dated July 5, 1751 from Charles Steuart, one to Minvielle, William Moore, Isaac De Piza, and Benjamin Massiah, the second to Susanna Minvielle "& Co." Charles Steuart Letter Books, Norfolk, VA 1751-1763, HSP. A receipt sent from Steuart to George Campbell of Liverpool requested that £512.2.3 1/2 sterling in bills be applied to the account of Mrs. Susanna & Elias Minvielle, and Messrs. Moore, de Piza, and Massiah "merchts in Barbados" for the proceeds for the slaves.
93. Charles Steuart to "Madam & Co.," addressed to Mrs. Minvielle and Son, January 9, 1752, Charles Steuart Letter Books, Norfolk, VA 1751–1763, HSP.
94. Charles Steuart to Mrs. Minvielle and Company, March 26, 1752, Charles Steuart Letter Books, Norfolk, VA 1751–1763, HSP.
95. [Charles Steuart] to Mrs. Vinncent, May 24, 1753, Charles Steuart Letter Books, Norfolk, VA 1751–1763, HSP.
96. [Charles Steuart] to Mrs. Susanna & Elias Minvielle, November 20, 1752, Charles Steuart Letter Books, Norfolk, VA 1751–1763, HSP.
97. [Charles Steuart] to Mrs. Susanna and Elias Minvielle, December 29, 1752, Charles Steuart Letter Books, Norfolk, VA 1751–1763, HSP.
98. [Charles Steuart] to Mrs. Minvielle and Company, March 26, 1752, Charles Steuart Letter Books, Norfolk, VA 1751–1763, HSP.
99. [Charles Steuart] to Madam and Company, April 8, 1752, November 20, 1752, and December 29, 1752, Charles Steuart Letter Books, Norfolk, VA 1751–1763, HSP.
100. [Charles Steuart] to Mrs. Minvielle, July 1, 1753, Charles Steuart Letter Books, Norfolk, VA 1751–1763, HSP.
101. Mary Anderson to Messrs. Micajah and Richard Perry, March 23, 1715/6; Mary Anderson to Cuthbert Jones, March 3, and April 30, 1716; Mary Anderson to Messrs Micajah and Richard Perry, May 2, 1716, Robert Anderson Tobacco Letter Book 1698–1717, UVA.
102. James Minzies to John Norton, June 12, 1773, Letter and attached invoice with Mrs. Scott's annotation, in Mason, ed., *John Norton and Sons*, 328–31.
103. Invoice, ibid., 331.
104. "Journal of Col. James Gordon," *WMQ*, 1st ser., 11 (1903); this particular example is on page 197, but there are plenty of others.
105. "Journal of Col. James Gordon," 205.

106. "Journal of Col. James Gordon," 108. See chapter 5 for a discussion of gender overlaps in the Virginia local economies.
107. George Walker account, September 21, 1751, Jerdone Account Book [daybook], W&M.
108. Barker-Benfield, *The Culture of Sensibility*, 206.
109. Devine, *The Tobacco Lords*, 87.
110. Jacob M. Price, "Summation: The American Panorama of Atlantic Port Cities,"in *Atlantic Port Cities: Economy, Culture, and Society in the Atlantic World, 1650–1850,* ed. Franklin W. Knight and Peggy K. Liss (Knoxville: University of Tennessee Press, 1991), 269.
111. Robert Bristow Letter Book, microfilm, LVA. Booth was also manager of Bristow's lands in Gloucester County. Conley L. Edwards, *A Guide to the Business Records in the Archives Branch, Virginia State Library* (Richmond: Virginia State Library, 1983), 24.
112. Carole Shammas, *The Pre-industrial Consumer in England and America* (Oxford: Oxford University Press, 1990), 65.
113. Charles J. Farmer, *In the Absence of Towns: Settlement and Country Trade in Southside Virginia, 1730–1800* (Latham, MD: Rowman and Littlefield, 1993), 164.
114. Jacob M. Price, "One Family's Empire: The Russell-Lee-Clerk Connection in Maryland, Britain, and India, 1707–1857," *Maryland Historical Magazine* 72 (1977): 176.
115. N. Maccubbin to Mrs. Ann Russell, September 8, 1774, Russell Papers, Coutts and Co., London, as cited in Price, "One Family's Empire," 177.
116. Robert Bristow to Thomas Booth, October 1, 1718, Robert Bristow Letterbook, microfilm, LVA.
117. *Virginia Gazette* (Purdie and Dixon), October 10, 1771.
118. Enclosure—list of goods to be sent to Rathell, in Catherine Rathell, Williamsburg, to John Norton, London, December 29, 1771,in Mason, ed., *John Norton and Sons*, 212.
119. Catherine Rathell, Williamsburg, to John Norton, London, November 16, 1771, in Mason, ed. *John Norton and Sons*, 206.
120. Martha Custis to Robert Cary and Company, London, August 20, 1757, #172–77, Custis FP 1683–1858, VHS.
121. Printed bill: "Bot of Nath: Woodrooffe Hosier at the Unicorn near the corner of Friday Street Cheapside," January 17, 1758, Custis FP, VHS.
122. Elizabeth Perry to Mrs. Jones, 30 November 1737, Roger Jones Family Papers. f. 557, LC.
123. Hart and Marshall, Hanover Town, to John Norton, 4 October 1771, John Norton and Sons Papers, microfilm, CW.
124. Ann Smart Martin, "'Fashionable Sugar Dishes, Latest Fashion Ware': The Creamware Revolution in the Eighteenth-Century Chesapeake," in *Historical Archaeology of the Chesapeake*, ed. Paul A. Shackel and Barbara J. Little (Washington, D.C.: Smithsonian Institution, 1994), 180–83.
125. Linda Baumgarten, *Eighteenth-Century Clothing at Williamsburg*, (Williamsburg: The Colonial Williamsburg Foundation, 1986), 13.
126. Beverley Dickson to John Norton, January 3, 1772, Norton-Savage Correspondence and Documents I, box 18, Brock Collection, HL.
127. Courtenay Norton, London, to John Hatley Norton, Yorktown, December 3, 1773; Courtenay Norton, London, to John Hatley Norton, Yorktown, August 30, 1775, in Mason, ed., *John Norton and Sons*, 364, 373.
128. Mrs. Chamberlayne also wanted a copy of the state of her account. Rebecca Chamberlayne, New Kent, to John Norton, London, July 13, 1771, in Mason, ed., *John Norton and Sons*, 166.
129. Rebecca Chamberlayne, Virginia to John Norton, July 28, 1770, John Norton and Sons Papers, 1750–1902, microfilm, CW.

130. Mann Page, Virginia, to John Norton, London, February 22, 1770, in Mason, ed., *John Norton and Sons*, 124.

131. George F. Norton, London, to John Hatley Norton, Yorktown, July 8, 1772, in Mason, ed., *John Norton and Sons*, 252.

132. Courtenay Norton to John Hatley Norton, March 20, 1771, box 19, Brock Collection, HL.

133. John Norton to John Hatley Norton, Yorktown, January 31, 1772, in Mason, ed., *John Norton and Sons*, 217.

134. John Norton, London, to John Hatley Norton, Yorktown, March 10, 1772, in Mason, ed., *John Norton and Sons*, 225.

135. Catherine Rathell, Williamsburg, to John Norton and Sons, London, July 22, 1772, in Mason, ed., *John Norton and Sons*, 258.

136. Peckatone Papers A, section 13, VHS.

137. Neil McKendrick, "The Commercialization of Fashion," in *The Birth of a Consumer Society*, ed. Neil McKendrick, John Brewer, and J. H. Plumb, eds. (London: Hutchinson, 1982), 43–45.

138. Hannah Corbin's daughter was also Hannah, and cousin to Lucinda Lee, daughter of the elder Hannah's brother Thomas Ludwell Lee. Entry for October 23, 1787, *Lucinda Lee, Journal of a Young Lady of Virginia, 1787*, ed. Emily V. Mason (Richmond: Whittet and Shepperson, 1976), 41; Bills in Peckatone Papers A, section 13, VHS.

139. Peckatone Papers A, section 13, VHS. Captain Ridgely, the master of ships trading to Britain, acted as general agent in Maryland for the firm of Russell and Molleson and ultimately built an estate in Baltimore County. William D. Hoyt, "Captain Ridgely's London Commerce, 1757 to 1774," *Americana* 37 (1943): 331, 333, 335.

140. Peckatone Papers A, VHS.

141. Receipt from John Beyer, Linen Draper No. 3 facing Cheapside, Peckatone Papers A, VHS.

142. Mason, ed., *John Norton and Sons*, 518.

143. *Virginia Gazette*, (Purdie), April 18, 1766.

144. *Virginia Gazette*, (Purdie), April 18, 1766 and April 25, 1766. In these advertisements she claimed she had recently arrived, did not know how long she would stay in the colony, and that she had selected the goods herself.

145. In May, 1765, it took £164.17 in Virginia currency to purchase £100 sterling while, a year later, the rate had dropped to £123.74 Virginia currency to £100 sterling, lower than the exchange rate had been in a decade. Gambling that the value of pounds sterling would increase in relation to Virginia currency was reasonable, though it remained relatively stable in the period after the French and Indian War. John J. McCusker, *Money and Exchange in Europe and America, 1600–1775: A Handbook* (Chapel Hill: University of North Carolina Press, 1977), 221-2.

146. *Virginia Gazette*, (Rind) April 13, 1769. Rathell described these goods as "the most fashionable assortment she ever had."

147. *Virginia Gazette*, (Purdie & Dixon) October 10, 1771.

148. *Virginia Gazette*, (Dixon and Hunter) April 22, 1775; *Virginia Gazette*, April 20, 1775.

149. James H. Soltow, *The Economic Role of Williamsburg* (Williamsburg: Colonial Williamsburg, 1965), 131. However, Soltow erroneously claimed that Rathell had only been established in Virginia for a year in 1772. Rathell may have been trying to impress her creditors at this juncture, but not because of her recent arrival in Virginia.

150. Catherine Rathell, Williamsburg, to John Norton, London, November 16, 1771, Williamsburg, in Mason, ed. *John Norton and Sons*, 205.

151. Catherine Rathell, Williamsburg, to John Norton, London, 31 January 1772, Williamsburg, in Mason, ed., *John Norton and Sons*, 217.

152. Roger Atkinson, "Appamx-James River," Virginia, to Beissor Fearson, March 1, 1773, Roger Atkinson Letter Book 1769–1773 and 1776; f. 76, LVA.
153. Mason, ed., *John Norton and Sons*, 518. *Virginia Gazette* (Dixon), February 17, 1776.
154. For a thorough treatment of the workings, rise and subsequent fall of a single family firm trading from Britain to the colonies over several generations, see Price, *Perry of London.*

CONCLUSION

1. Jacquelin reported that she planned to display her political loyalties by dressing in Virginia cloth and moccasins soon. Martha Jacquelin, Virginia [to John Norton, London], August 14, 1769, in Frances Norton Mason, ed., *John Norton and Sons, Merchants of London and Virginia, Being the Papers from Their Counting House for the Years 1750–1795* (New York: August Kelley, 968) 103. Woody Holton, *Forced Founders: Indians, Debtors, Slaves, and the Making of the American Revolution in Virginia* (Chapel Hill: University of North Carolina Press, 1999), 77.
2. Martha Goosley, Yorktown, to John Norton, 13 June 1770, in Mason, ed., *John Norton and Sons*, 136.
3. Linda K. Kerber, *Women of the Republic: Intellect and Ideology in Revolutionary America* (Chapel Hill: University of North Carolina Press, 1980), 48; Mary Beth Norton, *Liberty's Daughters: The Revolutionary Experience of American Women, 1750–1800* (Boston: Little, Brown, 1980), 157–61; Cynthia Kierner argues that prior to the war, southern women's contributions to cloth making went unrecognized. Image caught up to reality with the war. Cynthia A. Kierner, *Beyond the Household: Women's Place in the Early South, 1700–1835* (Ithaca: Cornell University Press, 1998), 72–81.
4. William Nelson, Virginia, to John Norton, London, 25 July 1766, in Mason, ed., *John Norton and Sons*, 14.
5. George F. Norton, Barbados, to James Withers, London, September 19, 1780, in Mason, ed., *John Norton and Sons*, 439–41.
6. Slavery complicated southern white women's relationship to moral reform movements in the antebellum period. Elizabeth R. Varon, *We Mean to Be Counted: White Women and Politics in the Antebellum South* (Chapel Hill: University of North Carolina Press, 1998), 1–2, 38–40.
7. Kerber, *Women of the Republic*, 283–85.
8. Ruth H. Bloch, "The Gendered Meanings of Virtue in Revolutionary America," *Signs* 13 (1987): 37–58; see especially 52.
9. The classic description of companionate marriage is Suzanne Lebsock's: it was "rather like the companionship between a seven-year-old and a ten-year-old: They may have the best of times together, but everyone knows who is in charge....The wife, for her part, had to let her wishes be known, while taking care not to trespass on male prerogatives." Suzanne Lebsock, *The Free Women of Petersburg Status and Culture in a Southern Town, 1784–1860* (New York: Norton, 1985), 32. Catherine Kerrison, "By the Book: Advice and Female Behavior in the Eighteenth-Century South," (Ph.D. diss., College of William and Mary 1999) 186-228; Sarah Emily Newton, "Wise and Foolish Virgins: 'Usable Fiction' and the Early American Conduct Tradition," *Early American Literature* 25 (1990), 141–45.
10. Tazewell was born December 17, 1774 in Williamsburg and studied with George Wythe from 1786 to 1789. He was delegate from James City County to the Virginia House of Delegates from 1798 to 1800 and later a U.S. senator. "Littleton Waller Tazewell's Sketch of his Own Family... 1823: Transcribed and Edited" ed. Lynda Rees Heaton (M.A. thesis, College of William and Mary, 1967), 51.

11. Tazewell's history is corroborated by records of her legal maneuvers in the two private bills presented to the Virginia legislature. William Waller Hening, ed., *Statutes at Large: Being a Collection of All the Laws of Virginia, from the First Session of the Legislature, in the Year 1619* (Richmond and Philadelphia: Printed for the Editor, 1809–1823), vol. 4, 377. *The Laws of Virginia Being a Supplement to Hening's The Statutes at Large, 1700–1750,* ed. Waverly K. Winfree (Richmond: Virginia State Library, 1971), 369–71. Similar stories circulate about South Carolinian Eliza Pinckney offering legal advice to her neighbors.

12. Unfortunately, the invoice of book does not survive. Thomas Cabel, "Cherry:Stone" on the eastern shore, to Micajah Perry, June 10, 1727, Thomas Cabel Letter Book and Account Book 1722–1757, f. 36, Maryland Historical Society. Gertrude Harmanson was the widow of Henry Harmanson; she died in 1732.

13. Tazewell's "Sketch," 51–52. Tazewell reported hearing this from the Hon. James Henry.

14. On interpreting family history as a means to understanding larger historical trends, see Elizabeth Stone, *Black Sheep and Kissing Cousins: How Our Family Stories Shape Us* (New York: Penguin, 1988). Gail Terry discusses the development of family stories in Virginia. Gail S. Terry, "Family Empires: A Frontier Elite in Virginia and Kentucky, 1740–1815," (Ph.D. diss., College of William and Mary, 1992). The Washington-Lee family had similar stories about their ancestor, Mary (Ball) Washington riding horseback over the fields to manage her estates and demanding obedience from her employees. *Recollections and Private Memoirs of Washington by his Adopted Son George Washington Parke Custis, with a Memoir of the Author by His Daughter [Mrs. R. E. Lee]* (New York: Derby and Jackson, 1860), 131, 140.

15. Jan Lewis, *The Pursuit of Happiness: Family and Values in Jefferson's Virginia* (Cambridge: Cambridge University Press, 1985), 41–68.

16. Duncan Kennedy, "The Stakes of Law, or Hale and Foucault!" *Legal Studies Forum* 15 (1991): 345.

17. Ibid., 361.

18. Ibid., 362.

19. See the introduction for the example of Susanna Lister.

20. Revisal of the Laws, 1776–1786, reprinted in Julian P. Boyd et. al., eds., *The Papers of Thomas Jefferson* (Princeton: Princeton University Press, 1950-), vol. 2, 398.

21. John G. Kolp and Terri L. Snyder, "Women and Electoral Culture in Revolutionary Virginia," paper presented at the Fifth Southern Conference on Women's History, Richmond, June 15, 2000. Gail S. Terry, "An Old Family Confronts New Politics: The Preston-Trigg Congressional Contest of the 1790s," in *Diversity and Accommodation: Essays on the Cultural Composition of the Virginia Frontier*, ed. Michael J. Puglisi (Knoxville: University of Tennessee Press, 1997), 233–41.

22. Suzanne Lebsock makes the important point that the status of women could improve without overt feminist motivation, but the results were often limited. In her analysis racism provided the "single greatest barrier" to southern feminism in the period between 1784 and 1860. Lebsock, *Free Women of Petersburg*, 56–67, 240–41.

23. Richard Henry Lee, Hannah's brother and a member of the Continental Congress, responded to his sister's now lost March 1778 letter. The contents of her letter are apparent from his reply. Louise Belote Dawe and Sandra Gioia Treadway, "Hannah Lee Corbin: The Forgotten Lee," *Virginia Cavalcade* 29 (1979): 70–77.

24. Revolutionaries suspected Byrd of harboring loyalist sympathies. Mary Willing Byrd [to Governor Thomas Nelson?] August 10, 1781, and Mary Willing Byrd to Baron Steuben, February 23, 1781, in Boyd et al., ed., *The Papers of Thomas Jefferson* vol. 5, 703–4, 689–90; see also Kierner, *Beyond the Household*, 119–20, 150–51.

25. Tucker, *Blackstone's Commentaries: with Notes of Reference to the Consitution and Law of the Federal Government of the United States and of the Commonwealth of Virginia* (Philadelphia: William Young Birch and Abraham Small, 1803), vol. 2, 445. For Tucker's changing views, see Philip Hamilton, "Revolutionary Principles and Family Loyalties: Slavery's Transformation in the St. George Tucker Household of Early National Virginia," *WMQ*, 3d ser., 55 (1998): 531–56. St. George Tucker insisted on a prenuptial agreement for the marriage of Beverley Tucker and Polly Coalter because he would "by no means consent that Polly shall be left to the Vicissitudes of Life, of Virginia Laws, & Virginia Adjudications in Cases of *widows*." St. George Tucker to John Coalter, December 4, 1808, cited in Norton, *Liberty's Daughters*, 135. Norton also points out that young brides failed to see the utility of the protection their elder relatives offered through the prenuptial arrangements.

26. Virginia did not ratify the Nineteenth Amendment to the Constitution, and the state's women gained the vote "courtesy of Uncle Sam" through the effects of national rather than state suffrage laws. Marjorie Spruill Wheeler, *New Women of the Old South: The Leaders of the Woman Suffrage Movement in the Southern States* (New York: Oxford University Press, 1993), 172–73. The Virginia legislature finally ratified the Nineteenth Amendment as a symbolic gesture in 1952. Suzanne Lebsock, *"A Share of Honour": Virginia Women 1600–1945* (Richmond: Virginia Women's Cultural History Project, 1984), 155.

SELECTED BIBLIOGRAPHY

PRIMARY SOURCES

MANUSCRIPTS

Bristol Records Office
Opie Papers. Microfilm.

British Public Record Office, Kew
C 2 Charles I Y7/34: Chancery, Bills and Answers, Series 1, Charles I, undated (c. 1630).
C 24/562/131: Chancery, Town Depositions.
C 24/1452: part 1, Chancery, Town Depositions 1728.
C 33/160: Chancery.
C 41/11: Chancery, Register of Affidavits. July 25, 1638. Trinity B.
CO 1/47: Colonial Office, Letters and Papers Concerning American Plantations.
CO 5/28: Colonial Office, Original Correspondence—Secretary of State 1773, Orders in Council.
CO 1325–28: Colonial Office, Virginia Correspondence—Original, Board of Trade.
CO 5/1366, 1371: Colonial Office, Commissions, Instructions, Board of Trade Correspondence.
PC 2/99: Privy Council Register.

British Library
Hardwicke Papers, vol. 869. Printed Cases. Add. Mss. 36,217.

Chester Historical Society, West Chester, PA
Mercer, John. Ledger and Travel Journal.

Chicago Historical Society
Metcalfe Family Papers.

College of William and Mary, Swem Special Collections
Jerdone Papers.
Tucker-Coleman Papers.

Colonial Williamsburg
Burwell, Carter. Account Books (1738–55) and Ledgers (1736–1746, 1773–1779, 1764–1776, 1779–1786). Microfilm.
Carter, Robert. Letter Book. Microfilm.
Jerdone Account Book 1751–52. Microfilm.

Lightfoot, William. Papers. Microfilm.
Norton, John and Sons Papers. Microfilm.
York County Project Master Biographical File. Research Department.

Corporation of London Records Office
Mayor's Court Depositions.
Mayor's Court Original Bills.

Historical Society of Pennsylvania, Philadelphia
Steuart, Charles. Letterbooks 11 and 12, 1751–1763. Microfilm.

Huntington Library, San Marino, CA
Norton-Savage Correspondence and Documents. Brock Collection.

Jamaican Records, Spanish Town, Jamaica
Deeds. Liber 1. Old Series. Island Records Office.
Patents Liber 1661–1665. 1B/11/1/1. Jamaica Archives Office.

Library of Congress
Dixon, Edward, 1743–1808. Papers and Ledgers.
Jamieson, Neil. (Norfolk) Papers. Microfilm.
Jones, Roger. Family Papers.
Ritchie, James and Company Account Book. Records, Essex County 1761–1813.

Library of Virginia: Archives Research Services, Richmond, Virginia
Ambler, Mary (Cary). Journal, 1763–1770. Personal Papers Collection.
Atkinson, Roger. Letterbook 1769–1774. Business Records Collection.
Bristow, Robert. Records, 1688–1750. Letterbook 1705–1737; 1746–1750. Business Records
    Collection.
Hunter-Hitchcock-Coit Papers, 1765–1925. Personal Papers Collection.
Jerdone Family Papers, 1762–1866. Personal Papers Collection.
Jerdone, Francis (Senior). Journal and Accounts, May 1, 1749–July 10, 1755, 1836–1845,
    1873. Business Records Collection.
Jerdone, Francis (Senior). Journal, September 15, 1750–June 2, 1760. Business Records
    Collection.
Merchant, Hanover County. Ledger, 1750–1751. Business Records Collection.
Merchant, King and Queen County. Business Ledger, 1751–1752. Business Records
    Collection.
State Records, Auditor of Public Accounts (RG 48), James River Naval Office Records,
    1773–1789, APA 301 (Miscellaneous Reel 257), Archives Research Services.
Taylor, Edward. Ledger 1775–1789. Business Records Collection.

Maryland Historical Society
Cabel, Thomas. Letterbook and Account Book 1722–1757.

Northampton County Courthouse
[Godfrey] Pole papers, loose documents.
See also unpublished county records, below.

University of North Carolina
Dabney, Charles W. Papers #1412. Southern Historical Collection, Wilson Library,
    University of North Carolina at Chapel Hill.

University of Virginia Library, Special Collections Department
Ambler, Elizabeth. Ambler Family Papers
Anderson, Robert. Tobacco Letterbook 1698–1717.
Papers of the Cabell Family.
Carter-Smith Letters.
Hunter-Garnett Collection.
Papers of the Latané and related Waring, Allen, Temple, Roane and Dix Families.
Papers of the Webb-Prentice Families and others.

Virginia Historical Society (VHS)
Bassett, William. Account Book, 1728–1755 and Loose Accounts.
Baylor Family Papers, Mordecai Booth Ledger, 1746–1752.
Beverley, William, Account Book Kept at Blandfield, Essex County.
Custis Family Papers. 1683–1858.
Durley Family Papers.
Granbery Papers.
Hargroves, Abigail (Langley) Granbery. Journal.
Holladay Family Papers.
Lee Family Papers.
Partridge, Thomas. Account Book (Hanover County), 1734–1745.
Peckatone Papers.
Pattison, Anne. Account.

West Yorkshire Archive Service, Calderdale District Archives
Lister Papers, Archives Department.

UNPUBLISHED COUNTY RECORDS
Albemarle County Court Papers 1773–1780, 1782–173. Local Records Collection. Archives
    Research Services. Library of Virginia.
Essex County Court Records. Includes Old Rappahannock County. Local Records
    Collection. Archives Research Services. Library of Virginia.
    Deeds.
    Miscellaneous Box, 1677–1845. [Loose] Suit Papers.
Lancaster County Court. Local Records Collection. Archives Research Services. Library of
    Virginia.
    Chancery.
    Ordinary Bonds.
Louisa County. Local Records Collection. Archives Research Services. Library of Virginia.
    Order Books.
    Will Books. Photostat.
Lower Norfolk County and Municipal Court Records. Microfilm. Local Records Collection.
    Archives Research Services. Library of Virginia.
    Deeds.
    Wills & Deeds.
    Order Books.
Norfolk County. Microfilm. Local Records Collection. Archives Research Services. Library
    of Virginia.
    Deeds.
    Orders.
    Wills.
    Wills and Deeds.

Northampton County. Northampton County Courthouse.
  Bound Eighteenth-Century Executors' and Administrators' Bonds.
  Ended Causes and Loose Papers.
Surry County. Local Records Collection. Archives Research Services. Library of Virginia.
  Deeds, Etc. [Deeds, Orders and Wills]. Microfilm.
Westmoreland County Deeds and Wills. Microfilm. Local Records Collection. Archives
  Research Services. Library of Virginia.
York County Court Records. Microfilm. Local Records Collection. Archives Research
  Services. Library of Virginia.
  Deeds, Orders and Wills.
  Orders.
  Orders, Wills.
  Orders, Wills and Inventories.
  Judgments and Orders.
  Wills, [Orders], and Deeds.

PUBLISHED SOURCES

Ames, Susie, ed. *County Court Records of Accomack-Northampton, Virginia, 1640–1645.*
  Charlottesville: University Press of Virginia, 1973.
[Anbury, Thomas]. *Travels through the Interior Parts of America; in a Series of Letters. By An
  Officer.* (1789, reprt. New York: New York Times, 1969).
Anonymous. "French Traveller in the Colonies, 1765." *American Historical Review* 26
  (1921), 726–47.
Beverley, Robert. *The History and Present State of Virginia.* Edited by Louis B. Wright.
  Chapel Hill: University of North Carolina Press, 1947.
Blackstone, William. *Commentaries on the Laws of England, 1765.* Oxford: Clarendon Press,
  1765–1769.
Book "B," Lower Norfolk County, Virginia, 2 November 1646 –15 January 1651/2. Transcribed
  by Alice Granbery Walter. N.p.: Alice Granbery Walter, 1978.
Boyd, Julian P. et. al., eds. *The Papers of Thomas Jefferson.* Princeton: Princeton University
  Press, 1950- .
Bryson, W. Hamilton. *Miscellaneous Virginia Law Reports, 1784–1809.* Dobbs Ferry, NY:
  Oceana Publications, 1992.
*Calendar of Virginia State Papers and Other Manuscripts... Preserved in the Capitol at
  Richmond.* 11 vols. Edited by William Pitt Palmer. Richmond: Commonwealth of
  Virginia, 1875–1893.
Carter, Landon. *The Diary of Colonel Landon Carter of Sabine Hall, 1752–1778.* 2 vols.
  Edited by Jack P. Greene. Charlottesville: Virginia Historical Society, 1965.
Child, [Sir Josiah]. *A New Discourse of Trade.* London, 1693.
"Council Papers, 1698–1701," *Virginia Magazine of History and Biography,* 23 (1915):
  34–46.
[Custis, George Washington]. *Recollections and Private Memoirs of Washington by his
  Adopted Son, George Washington Parke Custis, with a Memoir of the Author by His
  Daughter [Mrs. R. E. Lee].* New York: Derby and Jackson, 1860.
Defoe, Daniel. *The Complete English Tradesman in Familiar Letters... To Which is Added a
  Supplement.* 2d. ed. London: Charles Rivington, 1727; reprt. New York: Augustus M.
  Kelley, 1969.
———. *The Fortunes and Misfortunes of Moll Flanders... At Last Grew Rich, Lived Honest,
  and Died Penitent* [A Chapbook]. London: Printed in Aldermary Churchyard, [c.
  1750], 23. British Library #1079.i.13(21).

———. *Moll Flanders*. Edited by James Sutherland. Boston: Houghton Mifflin, 1959.

———. *Dialog between Honest John and Loving Kate with Their Contrivance for Marriage and Way to Get a Livelyhood, Part 2*. London: Printed in Bow Churchyard, n.d.

Dorman, John Frederick, abstr. *Westmoreland County, Virginia, Deeds, Patents, Etc., 1665–1677 To Which is Appended Westmoreland County, Virginia, Deeds and Wills Number 4, 1707–1709*. Part IV. Washington, D.C.: n.p. 1975.

"Extracts from Northumberland County Records." *William and Mary Quarterly*, 1st Ser., 4 (1894–1895): 77–78.

Fithian, Philip. *Journal and Letters of Philip Vickers Fithian 1773–1774: A Plantation Tutor of the Old Dominion*. Edited by Hunter Dickinson Farish. Williamsburg: Colonial Williamsburg, 1957.

Fleet, Beverley, abstr. *Virginia Colonial Abstracts: Charles City County, 1655–1658*. vol. 10. Baltimore: Genealogical Publishing, 1961.

———, ed. *Lancaster County Record Book, #2, 1654–1666*. Richmond: n.p. [1937].

Fordyce, James. *Sermons to Young Women*. 3rd ed. London: A. Millar and T. Cadell, 1766.

Fouace, Stephen. "Letters of Rev. Stephen Fouace." *William and Mary Quarterly*, 1st. ser. 12 (1903–4): 134–37.

Hartwell, Henry, James Blair, and Edward Chilton. *The Present State of Virginia, and the College*. Edited by Hunter Dickinson Farish. Charlottesville: University Press of Virginia, 1964.

Headley, Robert. *Wills of Richmond County, 1699–1800*. Baltimore: Genealogical Publishing, 1983.

Heaton, Lynda Rees, ed. "Littleton Waller Tazewell's Sketch of His Own Family. 1823: Transcribed and Edited." M.A. thesis, College of William and Mary, 1967.

Hening, William Waller ed. *The Statutes at Large: Being A Collection of All the Laws of Virginia, from the First Session of the Legislature, in the Year 1619*. 13 vols. Richmond and Philadelphia: Printed for the Editor, 1809–1823.

Jefferson, Thomas. *The Garden and Farm Books of Thomas Jefferson*. Edited by Robert C. Baron. Golden, CO: Fulcrum, 1987.

———. *Reports of Cases Determined in the General Court of Virginia from 1730 to 1740; and from 1768 to 1772*. Buffalo: W. S. Hein, 1981.

John Norton and Sons, Merchants of London and Virginia, Being the Papers from Their Counting House for the Years 1750 to 1795. Edited by Frances Norton Mason. New York: Augustus M. Kelley, 1968.

Journal of the Commissioners for Trade and Plantations from January 1741/2 to December 1749 Preserved in the Public Record Office. London: His Majesty's Stationery Office, 1931.

Lee, Lucinda. *Lucinda Lee, Journal of a Young Lady of Virginia, 1787*. Edited by Emily V. Mason. Richmond: Whittet and Shepperson, 1976.

Macaulay, Alexander. "Journal of Alexander Macaulay." *William and Mary Quarterly*, 1st ser., 11 (1903): 180–90.

McConnaughey, Gibson Jefferson. *Unrecorded Deeds and Other Documents, Amelia County, Virginia*. Amelia, VA: Mid-South Publishing, 1994.

Oldham, James. *The Mansfield Manuscripts and the Growth of English Law in the Eighteenth Century*. Chapel Hill: University of North Carolina Press, 1993.

Rose, Robert. *Diary of Robert Rose*. Edited by Ralph Fall. Verona, VA: McClure Press, 1977.

Rush, Benjamin. *Thoughts on Female Education Accomodated to the Present State of Society, Manners and Government in the United States of America*. (1787), reprinted in *Essays on Education in the Early Republic*. Edited by Frederick Rudolph. Cambridge MA: Belknap Press, 1965.

[Savile, George, Marquis of Halifax]. *The Lady's New-Year's Gift: or Advice to a Daughter*. London: Randal Taylor, 1688.

Tinling, Marion, ed. *The Correspondence of The Three William Byrds of Westover, Virginia 1684–1776*. 2 vols. Charlottesville: University Press of Virginia, 1977.

Tucker, St. George. *Blackstone's Commentaries with Notes of Reference to the Constitution and Law of the Federal Government of the United States and of the Commonwealth of Virginia*. 5 vols. Philadelphia: William Young Birch and Abraham Small, 1803.

Virginia Colonial Decisions: The Reports by Sir John Randolph and by Edward Barradall of Decisions of the General Court of Virginia, 1728-1741. Edited by R. T. Barton. Boston: Boston Book Company, 1909.

Virginia Colony. *Executive Journals of the Council of Colonial Virginia*. Edited by H. R. McIlwaine. Richmond: Virginia State Library, 1923.

———. *Journals of the House of Burgesses of Virginia*. Edited by H. R. McIlwaine and John Pendleton Kennedy. Reprt. Richmond:[The Colonial Press, E. Waddey Company], 1905–1915.

———. *Minutes of the Council and General Court of Colonial Virginia*. Edited by H. R. McIlwaine. Richmond: Virginia State Library, 1924.

Virginia Gazette, various publishers, various issues, September 10, 1736 to February 17, 1776.

Virginia Gazette Day Book 1750-1752, and 1764-1766, edited by Paul P. Hoffman. Charlottesville: Microfilm Publications of the University of Virginia, 1967.

Virginia Gazette of Williamsburg 1736–1780. (Williamsburg: Institute for Early American History and Culture, 1950, microfilm). Includes the *Virginia Gazettes* published by Dixon and Hunter; Parks; Pinckney; Purdie; Purdie and Dixon; and Rind.

Winfree, Waverly K., ed. *The Laws of Virginia Being a Supplement to Hening's The Statutes at Large, 1700–1750*. Richmond: Virginia State Library, 1971.

Wright, Louis B. and Marion Tinling, eds. *The Secret Diary of William Byrd of Westover, 1709–1712*. Richmond: The Dietz Press, 1941.

Zuppan, Jo. "Father to Son: Letters from John Custis IV to Daniel Parke Custis." *Virginia Magazine of History and Biography* 98 (1990): 81–100.

SECONDARY SOURCES

Ames, Susie M. *Studies of the Virginia Eastern Shore in the Seventeenth Century*. Richmond: Dietz Press, 1940.

Amussen, Susan Dwyer. "'The Part of a Christian Man: The Cultural Politics of Manhood in Early Modern England." In *Political Culture and Cultural Politics in Early Modern England*, edited by Susan Dwyer Amussen and Mark A. Kishlansky, 213–33. Manchester: Manchester University Press, 1995.

Andolsen, Barbara Hilkert. *"Daughters of Jefferson, Daughters of Bootblacks": Racism and American Feminism*. Atlanta: Mercer University Press, 1986.

Angle, Linda L. "Women in the North Carolina Colonial Courts, 1670–1739." M.A. thesis, University of North Carolina, 1975.

Aptheker, Bettina. *Tapestries of Life: Women's Work, Women's Consciousness and the Meaning of Daily Experience*. Amherst: University of Massachusetts Press, 1989.

Bailyn, Bernard. *The New England Merchants in the Seventeenth Century*. Cambridge, MA: Harvard University Press, 1955.

Barker-Benfield, G. J. *The Culture of Sensibility: Sex and Society in Eighteenth-Century Britain*. Chicago: University of Chicago Press, 1992.

Basch, Norma. "From the Bonds of Empire to the Bonds of Matrimony." In *Devising Liberty: Preserving and Creating Freedom in the New American Republic*, edited by David T. Konig, 217–42. Stanford: Stanford University Press, 1995.

———. *In the Eyes of the Law: Women, Marriage, and Property in Nineteenth-Century New York*. Ithaca: Cornell University Press, 1982.

Baumgarten, Linda. *Eighteenth-Century Clothing at Colonial Williamsburg.* Williamsburg, VA: Colonial Williamsburg, 1986.

Beard, Mary Ritter. *Woman As Force in History: A Study in Traditions and Reality.* New York: MacMillan, 1946.

Beckles, Hilary McD. *Centering Woman: Gender Discourses in Caribbean Slave Society.* Kingston, Jamaica: Ian Randle, 1998.

———. "White Women and Slavery in the Caribbean." *History Workshop* 36 (1993): 66–82.

Bennett, Judith M. "'History That Stands Still': Women's Work in the European Past." *Feminist Studies* 14 (1988): 269–283.

Benson, Mary Sumner. *Women in Eighteenth-Century America: A Study of Opinion and Social Usage.* Columbia University Studies in History, Economics and Public Law, no. 405. New York: Columbia University Press, 1935.

Bergstrom, Peter V. "A Stop Along the Way." Paper presented at the Philadelphia Center for Early American Studies at the University of Pennsylvania, October 17, 1986.

Berkin, Carol. "Clio's Daughters: Southern Colonial Women and Their Historians." In *The Devil's Lane: Sex and Race in the Early South,* edited by Catherine Clinton and Michele Gillespie. New York: Oxford University Press, 1997.

Berlin, Ira. *Many Thousands Gone: The First Two Centuries of Slavery in North America.* Cambridge, MA: Belknap Press, 1998.

Bernhard, Virginia. "'Men, Women and Children' at Jamestown: Population and Gender in Early Virginia, 1607–1610." *Journal of Southern History* 58 (1992): 599–618.

———. "A Response: The Forest and the Trees: Thomas Camfield and the History of Early Virginia." *Journal of Southern History* 60 (1994): 663–70.

Black, Henry Campbell. *Black's Law Dictionary.* St. Paul: West Publishing, 1990.

Blackburn, Robin. *The Overthrow of Colonial Slavery, 1776–1848.* London: Verso, 1988.

Bloch, Ruth H. "The Gendered Meanings of Virtue in Revolutionary America." *Signs* 13 (1987): 37–58.

Blumenthal, Walter Hart. *Brides from Bridewell: Female Felons Sent to Colonial America.* Rutland, VT: Charles E. Tuttle, 1962.

Boserup, Ester. *Woman's Role in Economic Development.* New York: St. Martin's, 1970.

Bowler, Clara Ann. "Carted Whores and White Shrouded Apologies: Slander in the County Courts of Seventeenth-Century Virginia." *Virginia Magazine of History and Biography* 85 (1977): 411–26.

Brathwaite, Edward Kamau *The Development of Creole Society in Jamaica, 1770–1820.* Oxford: Clarendon Press, 1971.

Breen, Timothy H. "'Baubles of Britain': The American and Consumer Revolutions of the Eighteenth Century." *Past and Present* 119 (1988): 73–104.

———. "Horses and Gentlemen: The Cultural Significance of Gambling among the Gentry of Virginia," *William and Mary Quarterly,* 3d ser., 34 (1977): 239–57.

———. "The Meanings of Things: Interpreting the Consumer Economy in the Eighteenth Century." In *Consumption and the World of Goods,* edited by John Brewer and Roy Porter, 249–60. New York: Routledge, 1993.

———. *Tobacco Culture: The Mentality of the Great Tidewater Planters on the Eve of the Revolution.* Princeton: Princeton University Press, 1985.

Brenner, Robert. *Merchants and Revolution: Commercial Change, Political Conflict, and London's Overseas Traders, 1550–1653.* Cambridge: Cambridge University Press, 1993.

Brewer, Holly. "Entailing Aristocracy in Colonial Virginia: 'Ancient Feudal Restraints' and Revolutionary Reform." *William and Mary Quarterly,* 3d ser., 54 (1997): 307–46.

Brodber, Erna. *A Study of Yards in the City of Kingston.* Mona, Jamaica: Institute of Social and Economic Research, University of the West Indies, 1975.

Brown, Kathleen M. *Good Wives, Nasty Wenches and Anxious Patriarchs: Gender, Race, and Power in Colonial Virginia.* Chapel Hill: University of North Carolina Press, 1996.

Buckley, Thomas E., S.J. "Unfixing Race: Class, Power, and Identity in an Interracial Family." *Virginia Magazine of History and Biography* 102 (1994): 349–80.

Burnard, Trevor. "Family Continuity and Female Independence in Jamaica, 1665–1734." *Continuity and Change* 7 (1992): 181–98.

Bush, Barbara. "White 'Ladies,' Coloured 'Favourites' and Black 'Wenches': Some Considerations of Sex, Race and Class Factors in Social Relations in White Creole Society in the British Caribbean." *Slavery and Abolition* 2 (1981): 245–62.

Bushman, Richard. "Shopping and Advertising in Colonial America." In *Of Consuming Interests: The Style of Life in the Eighteenth Century*, edited by Cary Carson, Ronald Hoffman, and Peter J. Albert, 233–51. Charlottesville: University Press of Virginia, 1994.

———. *The Refinement of America: Persons, Houses, Cities.* New York: Knopf, 1992.

Camfield, Thomas M. "A Can or Two of Worms: Virginia Bernhard and the Historiography of Early Virginia, 1607–1610." *Journal of Southern History* 60 (1994): 649–62.

Campbell, Mildred. "Social Origins of Some Early Americans." In *Seventeenth-Century America: Essays in Colonial History*, edited by James Morton Smith, 63–89. Chapel Hill: University of North Carolina Press, 1959.

Capp, Bernard. "Separate Domains? Women and Authority in Early Modern England." In *The Experience of Authority in Early Modern England*, edited by Paul Griffiths, Adam Fox, and Steve Hindle, 117–45. London: Macmillan, 1996.

Carr, Lois Green. "Inheritance in the Colonial Chesapeake." In *Women in the Age of the American Revolution*, edited by Ronald Hoffman and Peter J. Albert, 155–208. Charlottesville: University Press of Virginia, 1989.

Carr, Lois Green and Lorena S. Walsh. "Changing Lifestyles and Consumer Behavior in the Colonial Chesapeake." In *Of Consuming Interests: The Style of Life in the Eighteenth Century*, edited by Cary Carson, Ronald Hoffman, and Peter J. Albert, 59–166. Charlottesville: University Press of Virginia, 1994.

———. "The Planter's Wife: The Experience of White Women in Seventeenth-Century Maryland." *William and Mary Quarterly*, 3d ser., 34 (1977): 542–71.

Carr, Lois Green, Russell R. Menard, and Lorena S. Walsh. *Robert Cole's World: Agriculture and Society in Early Maryland.* Chapel Hill: University of North Carolina Press, 1991.

Carr, Lois Green, Philip D. Morgan, and Jean B. Russo, eds. *Colonial Chesapeake Society.* Chapel Hill: University of North Carolina Press, 1988.

Carson, Barbara G. "Early American Tourists and the Commercialization of Leisure." In *Of Consuming Interests: The Style of Life in the Eighteenth Century*, edited by Cary Carson, Ronald Hoffman, and Peter J. Albert, 373–405. Charlottesville: University of Virginia Press, 1994.

Clark, Christopher. *The Roots of Rural Capitalism: Western Massachusetts, 1780–1860.* Ithaca: Cornell University Press, 1993.

Clark, Peter P.. *The English Alehouse: A Social History, 1200–1830.* London: Longman, 1983.

Cleary, Patricia. "She Merchants of Colonial America: Women and Commerce on the Eve of the Revolution." Ph.D. diss., Northwestern University, 1984.

"Coastal Plain Province: The Geology of Virginia," College of William and Mary Geology Department Website, <http://www.wm.edu/CAS/GEOLOGY/virginia/coastal_plain.html>.

Colley, Linda. *Britons: Forging the Nation, 1707–1837.* New Haven: Yale University Press, 1992.

Collins, Stephen. "'Reason, Nature and Order': the Stepfamily in English Renaissance Thought." *Renaissance Studies* 13 (1999): 312–23.

"Colonial Letters: Ludwell," *Virginia Magazine of History and Biography* 5 (1897–98): 42–53.

Conger, Vivian Bruce. "'Being Weak of Body but Firm of Mind and Memory': Widowhood in Colonial America, 1630–1750." Ph.D. diss., Cornell University, 1994.

———. "If Widow, Both Housewife and Husband May Be." In *Women and Freedom in Early America*, edited by Larry D. Eldridge. New York: New York University Press, 1997.

Crane, Elaine Forman. *Ebb Tide in New England: Women, Seaports, and Social Change, 1630–1800*. Boston: Northeastern University Press, 1998.

Cronon, William. *Changes in the Land*. New York: Hill and Wang, 1983.

Crowley, John E. "The Sensibility of Comfort." *American Historical Review* 104 (1999): 749–82.

Curtis, George M. "Thomas Jefferson." *The Virginia Law Reporters before 1880*, edited by W. Hamilton Bryson, 75–84. Charlottesville: University Press of Virginia, 1977.

Davidoff, Leonore. *The Best Circles*. 1973; reprt. London: Cresset, 1986.

Davidoff, Leonore and Catherine Hall. *Family Fortunes: Men and Women of the English Middle Class, 1780–1850*. London: Hutchinson, 1987.

Davidson, Cathy. *Revolution and the Word: The Rise of the Novel in America*. New York: Oxford University Press, 1986.

Davis, David Brion. *The Problem of Slavery in the Age of Revolution, 1770–1823*. Ithaca: Cornell University Press, 1975.

Davis, Natalie Zemon. *Women on the Margins: Three Seventeenth-Century Lives*. Cambridge, MA: Belknap, 1995.

Dawe, Louise Belote and Sandra Gioia Treadway. "Hannah Lee Corbin: The Forgotten Lee," *Virginia Cavalcade* 29 (1979): 70–77.

Dayton, Cornelia Hughes. *Women before the Bar: Gender, Law, and Society in Connecticut, 1639–1789*. Chapel Hill: University of North Carolina Press, 1995.

Deen, James W. Jr. "Patterns of Testation: Four Tidewater Counties in Colonial Virginia." *American Journal of Legal History* 16 (1972): 154–76.

Demos, John. *A Little Commonwealth: Family Life in Plymouth Colony*. New York: Oxford University Press, 1970.

Devine, T. M. *The Tobacco Lords: A Study of the Tobacco Merchants of Glasgow and Their Trading Activities, c. 1740–90*. Edinburgh: Edinburgh University Press, 1975.

Dewey, Frank L. *Thomas Jefferson: Lawyer*. Charlottesville: University of Virginia Press, 1986.

Dexter, Elisabeth Anthony. *Colonial Women of Affairs* Boston, 1924; revised Edition, Boston: Houghton-Mifflin, 1931.

Doggett, Maeve E. *Marriage, Wife-Beating and the Law in Victorian England*. London: Weidenfeld & Nicolson, 1992.

Dorman, John Frederick. *Adventurers of Purse and Person: Virginia 1607–1624/5*, ed. Virginia M. Meyer. Alexandria, VA: Order of First Families of Virginia, 1987.

Dublin, Thomas. *Women at Work: The Transformation of Work and Community in Lowell, Massachusetts, 1826–1860*. New York: Columbia University Press, 1979.

Dyer, Christopher. "Memories of Freedom: Attitudes towards Serfdom in England, 1200–1350." In *Serfdom and Slavery: Studies in Legal Bondage*, edited by M. L. Bush, 277–95. London: Longman, 1996.

Earle, Carville V. "Environment, Disease, and Mortality in Early Virginia." In *Chesapeake in the Seventeenth Century: Essays on Anglo-American Society and Politics*, edited by Thad W. Tate and David Ammerman, 96–125. New York: Norton, 1979.

Edwards, Conley L. *A Guide to the Business Records in the Archives Branch, Virginia State Library*. Richmond: Virginia State Library, 1983.

Egerton, Douglas R. *Gabriel's Rebellion: The Virginia Slave Conspiracies of 1800 and 1802*. Chapel Hill: University of North Carolina Press, 1993.

Engerman, Stanley L. "Slavery, Serfdom, and Other Forms of Coerced Labour: Similarities and Differences." In *Serfdom and Slavery: Studies in Legal Bondage*, edited by M. L. Bush, 18–41. London: Longman, 1996.

Erickson, Amy Louise. *Women and Property in Early Modern England*. London: Routledge, 1993.

Farmer, Charles J. *In the Absence of Towns: Settlement and Country Trade in Southside Virginia, 1730–1800*. Latham, MD: Rowman and Littlefield, 1993.

Fausz, J. Frederick. "The Missing Women of Martin's Hundred." *American History* 33 (1998): 56–62.

Frey, Sylvia R. and Marian J. Morton, *New World, New Roles: A Documentary History of Women in Pre-Industrial America*. New York: Greenwood, 1986.

Friedman, Lawrence M. *A History of American Law*. New York: Touchstone, 1973.

———. *The Republic of Choice: Law, Authority, and Culture*. Cambridge, MA: Harvard University Press, 1990.

Galenson, David W. *White Servitude in Colonial America: An Economic Analysis*. Cambridge: Cambridge University Press, 1981.

Gampel, Gwen Victor. "The Planter's Wife Revisited: Women, Equity Law, and the Chancery Court in Seventeenth-Century Maryland." In *Women and the Structure of Society: Selected Research from the Fifth Berkshire Conference on the History of Women*, edited by Barbara J. Harris and Jo Ann K. McNamara. Durham: Duke University Press, 1984.

Genealogies of Virginia Families from Tyler's Quarterly Historical and Genealogical Magazine. Baltimore: Genealogical Publishing, 1981.

Gibbs, Patricia A. "Taverns in Tidewater Virginia, 1700–1774." M.A. thesis, College of William and Mary, 1968.

Goebel, Julius Jr. "King's Law and Local Custom in Seventeenth-Century New England." *Columbia Law Review* 31 (1931): 416–48.

Goldfield, David R. "Black Life in Old South Cities." In *Before Freedom Came: African-American Life in the Antebellum South*, edited by Edward Campbell and Kym Rice. Richmond: The Museum of the Confederacy and the University Press of Virginia, 1991.

Goody, Jack. "Inheritance, Property, and Women: Some Comparative Considerations." In *Family and Inheritance: Rural Society in Western Europe 1200–1800*, edited by Jack Goody, Joan Thirsk, and E. P. Thompson, 10–36. Cambridge: Cambridge University Press, 1976.

Gordon, Linda. "On 'Difference.'" *Genders* number 10, (Spring 1991): 9–111.

Graham, Wayne. "For Generations: Wills, Inventories, and Wealth in Colonial Virginia." M.A. thesis, College of William and Mary, 2001.

Greene, Jack P. *Pursuits of Happiness: The Social Development of Early Modern British Colonies and the Formation of American Culture*. Chapel Hill: University of North Carolina Press, 1988.

Greenfield, Edward. "Some New Aspects of the Life of Daniel Parke." *Virginia Magazine of History and Biography* 54 (1946): 306–15.

Gundersen, Joan R. "The Double Bonds of Race and Sex: Black and White Women in a Colonial Virginia Parish." *Journal of Southern History* 52 (1986): 351–72.

Gundersen, Joan R. and Gwen Victor Gampel. "Married Women's Legal Status in Eighteenth-Century New York and Virginia." *William and Mary Quarerly*, 3d ser., 39 (1982): 114–34.

Hall, Catherine. "Gender Politics and Imperial Politics: Rethinking the Histories of Empire." In *Engendering History: Caribbean Women in Historical Perspective*, edited by Verene Shepherd, Bridget Brereton, and Barbara Bailey, 48–59. Kingston, Jamaica: Ian Randle, 1995.

———. *White, Male and Middle Class: Explorations in Feminism and History*. New York: Routledge, 1992.

Hamilton, Philip. "Revolutionary Principles and Family Loyalties: Slavery's Transformation in the St. George Tucker Household of Early National Virginia." *William and Mary Quarterly*, 3d ser., 55 (1998): 531–56.

Hancock, David. *Citizens of the World: London Merchants and the Integration of the British Atlantic Community, 1735–1785.* Cambridge: Cambridge University Press, 1995.

Hartog, Hendrick. "Wives as Favorites." In *Law as Culture and Culture as Law,* edited by Hendrick Hartog and William E. Nelson, 292–321. Madison, WI: Madison House Publishers, 2000.

Haskins, George L. "Reception of the Common Law in Seventeenth-Century Massachusetts." In *Law and Authority in Colonial America Selected Essays,* edited by George A. Billias, 17–31. Barre, MA: Barre Publishers, 1965.

Hemphill, John M. II. "Mary Aggy." In *Dictionary of Virginia Biography* edited by John T. Kneebone, J. Jefferson Looney, Brent Tarter, and Sandra Gioia Treadway, 42–43. Vol. 1. Richmond: Library of Virginia, 1999.

———. *Virginia and the English Commercial System, 1689–1733: Studies in the Development and Fluctuations of a Colonial Economy under Imperial Control.* New York: Garland, 1985.

Henretta, James. "Families and Farms: Mentalité in Pre-industrial America." *William and Mary Quarterly,* 3d ser., 35 (1978): 3–32.

Higginbotham, A. Leon, Jr. *In The Matter of Color: Race and the American Legal Process in the Colonial Period.* New York: Oxford University Press, 1978.

Hine, Darlene Clark. "Rape and the Inner Lives of Black Women in the Middle West: Preliminary Thoughts on the Culture of Dissemblance." *Signs* 14 (1989): 912–20.

Hoff, Joan. *Law, Gender, and Injustice: A Legal History of U.S. Women.* New York: New York University Press, 1991.

Hoffer, Peter Charles. *Law and People in Colonial America.* Baltimore: Johns Hopkins University Press, 1992.

Holton, Woody. *Forced Founders: Indians, Debtors, Slaves and the Making of the American Revolution in Virginia.* Chapel Hill: University of North Carolina Press, 1999.

hooks, bell. *Feminist Theory from Margin to Center.* Boston: South End Press, 1984.

Horn, James P. P. *Adapting to A New World: English Society in the Seventeenth-Century Chesapeake.* Chapel Hill: University of North Carolina Press, 1994.

Hoyt, William D. "Captain Ridgely's London Commerce, 1757 to 1774." *Americana* 37 (1943): 326–70.

Hudak, Leona M. *Early American Women Printers and Publishers, 1639–1820.* Metuchen, NJ: Scarecrow Press, 1978.

Hufton, Olwen. *The Prospect Before Her: A History of Women in Western Europe* (1500-1800). New York: Knopf, 1996.

Hunt, Margaret R. *The Middling Sort: Commerce, Gender and the Family in England, 1680–1780.* Berkeley and Los Angeles: University of California Press, 1996.

Hurst, James Willard. *Law and the Conditions of Freedom in the Nineteenth-Century United States.* Madison: University of Wisconsin Press, 1956.

Isaac, Rhys. *The Transformation of Virginia, 1740–1790.* New York: Norton, 1982.

Jameson, J. Franklin. *Essays in Colonial History Presented to Charles McLean Andrews by His Students.* 1931; reprt. Freeport, NY: Books for Libraries Press, 1966.

Jensen, Joan M. *Loosening the Bonds: Mid-Atlantic Farm Women, 1750–1850.* New Haven: Yale University Press, 1986.

Jones, Alice Hanson. "The Wealth of Women, 1774." In *Strategic Factors in Nineteenth Century American Economic History: A Volume to Honor Robert W. Fogel,* edited by Claudia Golding and Hugh Rockoff. Chicago: University of Chicago Press, 1992.

Jordan, Winthrop. *White over Black: American Attitudes toward the Negro, 1550–1812.* Chapel Hill: University of North Carolina Press, 1968.

Karlsen, Carol F. *Devil in the Shape of a Woman: Witchcraft in Colonial New England.* New York: Norton, 1987.

Keim, C. Ray. "Primogeniture and Entail in Colonial Virginia." *William and Mary Quarterly*, 3d ser., 25 (1968): 545–86.

Kelly, Kevin P. "Demographic Description of Seventeenth-Century York County." Unpublished research report, Department of Historical Research, Colonial Williamsburg Foundation.

———. "Settlement Patterns in Surry County." In *Chesapeake in the Seventeenth Century: Essays on Anglo-American Society and Politics*, edited by Thad W. Tate and David Ammerman, 183–205. New York: Norton, 1979.

Kennedy, Duncan. "The Stakes of Law, or Hale and Foucault!" *Legal Studies Forum* 15 (1991): 327–65.

"Kenner Family." *William and Mary Quarterly*, 1st. ser. 14 (1905–6): 173–81.

Kerber, Linda K. "Separate Spheres, Female Worlds, and Women's Place: The Rhetoric of Women's History." *Journal of American History* 75 (1988): 9–39.

———. *Toward an Intellectual History of Women*. Chapel Hill: University of North Carolina Press, 1997.

———. *Women of the Republic: Intellect and Ideology in Revolutionary America*. Chapel Hill: University of North Carolina Press, 1980.

Kerr, Paulette A. "Victims or Strategists? Female Lodging-House Keepers in Jamaica." In *Engendering History: Caribbean Women in Historical Perspective*, ed. Verene Shepherd, Bridget Brereton and Barbara Bailey, 197-212. Kingston, Jamaica: Ian Randle, 1995.

Kerrison, Catherine. "By the Book: Advice and Female Behavior in the Eighteenth-Century South." Ph.D. diss., College of William and Mary, 1999.

———. "By the Book: Eliza Ambler Carrington and Conduct Literature in Late Eighteenth-Century Virginia." *Virginia Magazine of History and Biography* 105 (1997): 27–52.

Kierner, Cynthia A. *Beyond the Household: Women's Place in the Early South, 1700–1835*. Ithaca: Cornell University Press, 1998.

———. *Southern Women in Revolution, 1776–1800: Personal and Political Narratives*. Columbia: University of South Carolina Press, 1998.

Kolp, John G. and Terri L. Snyder, "Women and Electoral Culture in Revolutionary Virginia." Paper presented at the Fifth Southern Conference on Women's History, Richmond, Virginia, June 15, 2000.

Konig, David T. "Country Justice: The Rural Roots of Constitutionalism in Colonial Virginia." In *An Uncertain Tradition. Constitutionalism and the History of the South*, edited by James Ely and Kermit Hall. Athens: University of Georgia Press, 1989.

———. "Legal Fictions and the Rule(s) of Law: The Jeffersonian Critique of Common-Law Adjudication." In *The Many Legalities of Early America*, edited by Christopher L. Tomlins and Bruce H. Mann, 97–121. Chapel Hill: University of North Carolina Press, 2001.

———. "The Virgin and the Virgin's Sister: Virginia, Massachusetts, and the Contested Legacy of Colonial Law." *The History of the Law in Massachusetts: the Supreme Judicial Court, 1692–1992*. Boston: Supreme Judicial Court Historical Society, 1992.

Kowaleski-Wallace, Elizabeth. *Consuming Subjects: Women, Shopping, and Business in the Eighteenth Century*. New York: Columbia University Press, 1997.

Kross, Jessica. "Mansions, Men, Women and the Creation of Multiple Publics in Eighteenth-Century British North America." *Journal of Social History* 33 (1999), 385–408.

Kulikoff, Allan. *The Agrarian Origins of American Capitalism*. Charlottesville: University Press of Virginia, 1992.

———. *Tobacco and Slaves: The Development of Southern Cultures in the Colonial Chesapeake, 1680–1800*. Chapel Hill: University of North Carolina Press, 1986.

Kupperman, Karen Ordahl. "The Founding Years of Virginia—And the United States." *Virginia Magazine of History and Biography* 104 (1996): 103–12.

Latané, Lucy Temple. *Parson Latané, 1672–1732.* Charlottesville: Michie, 1936.

Lebsock, Suzanne. *The Free Women of Petersburg: Status and Culture in a Southern Town, 1784–1860.* New York: Norton, 1985.

———. *"A Share of Honour": Virginia Women, 1600–1945.* Richmond: Virginia Women's Cultural History Project, 1984.

Lee, Jean Butenhoff. "Land and Labor: Parental Bequest Practices in Charles County, Maryland, 1732–1783." In *Colonial Chesapeake Society,* edited by Lois Green Carr, Philip D. Morgan, and Jean B. Russo, 306–341. Chapel Hill: University of North Carolina Press, 1988.

Lemon, James T. *The Best Poor Man's Country: A Geographic Study of Early Southeastern Pennsylvania.* Baltimore: Johns Hopkins University Press, 1972.

Leviner, Betty. "Patrons and Rituals in an Eighteenth-Century Tavern," *Common People and Their Material World: Free Men and Women in the Chesapeake, 1700–1830,* edited by David Harvey and Gregory Brown. Richmond: Colonial Williamsburg Foundation, 1995.

Lewis, Jan. *The Pursuit of Happiness: Family and Values in Jefferson's Virginia.* Cambridge: Cambridge University Press, 1985.

Liddington, Jill. *Female Fortune: Land, Gender and Authority. The Anne Lister Diaries and Other Writings 1833–36.* London: Rivers Oram Press, 1998.

Lockridge, Kenneth A. *On the Sources of Patriarchal Rage: The Commonplace Books of William Byrd and Thomas Jefferson and the Gendering of Power in the Eighteenth Century.* New York: New York University Press, 1992.

Lounsbury, Carl R. "Order in the Court: Recommendations for the Restoration of the James City County/Williamsburg Courthouse." Williamsburg: Colonial Williamsburg Architectural History Department, 1985.

Lounsbury, Carl R., ed., *An Illustrated Glossary of Early Southern Architecture and Landscape.* Charlottesville: University Press of Virginia, 1999.

McCusker, John J. *Money and Exchange in Europe and America, 1600–1775: A Handbook.* Chapel Hill: University of North Carolina Press, 1977.

McDonald, Roderick A. "Independent Economic Production by Slaves on Antebellum Louisiana Sugar Plantations." In *The Slaves' Economy: Independent Production by Slaves in the Americas,* edited by Ira Berlin and Philip D. Morgan. London: Frank Cass, 1991.

McKendrick, Neil, John Brewer, and J. H. Plumb. *The Birth of a Consumer Society: The Commercialization of Eighteenth-Century England.* London: Hutchinson, 1982.

Main, Gloria L. "Widows in Rural Massachusetts on the Eve of the Revolution." In *Women in the Age of the American Revolution,* edited by Ronald Hoffman and Peter J. Albert, 67–90. Charlottesville: University Press of Virginia, 1989.

Mann, Bruce H. *Neighbors and Strangers: Law and Community in Early Connecticut.* Chapel Hill: University of North Carolina Press, 1987.

Marshall, P. J. "Britain and the World in the Eighteenth Century II: Britons and Americans." *Transactions of the Royal Historical Society,* 6th ser., 9 (1999): 1-16.

Martin, Ann Smart. "The Black Box of Household Consumption: Women and the Retail Trade in Virginia, 1750–1820." Paper presented to the Triangle Early American History Group, Chapel Hill, NC, March 23, 2001.

———. "'Fashionable Sugar Dishes, Latest Fashion Ware': The Creamware Revolution in the Eighteenth-Century Chesapeake." In *Historical Archaeology of the Chesapeake,* edited by Paul A. Shackel and Barbara J. Little, 169–83. Washington, D.C.: Smithsonian, 1994.

———. "Makers, Buyers, and Users: Consumerism and a Material Culture Framework." *Winterthur Portfolio* 28 (1993): 141–57.

———. "Sukey's Mirror: Consumption, Commodities and Cultural Identity in Eighteenth-Century Virginia." Paper presented at the Berkshire Conference on the History of Women, Chapel Hill, NC, 1996.

Martinez-Alier, Verena. *Marriage, Class and Colour in Nineteenth-Century Cuba.* 1974; reprt. Ann Arbor: University of Michigan Press, 1989.

Mathurin [Mair], Lucille. "A Historical Study of Women in Jamaica from 1655 to 1844." Ph.D. diss., University of the West Indies—Mona, 1974.

Menard, Russell R. "From Servants to Slaves: The Transformation of the Chesapeake Labor System." *Southern Studies* 16 (1977): 355–90.

Mendelson, Sara and Patricia Crawford. *Women in Early Modern England, 1550–1720.* Oxford: Clarendon Press, 1998.

"Metcalfe Families." *William and Mary Quarterly,* 1st ser., 5 (1897–98): 10–12.

Milsom, S. F. C. *Historical Foundations of the Common Law.* Toronto: Butterworths, 1981.

Momsen, Janet, ed. *Women and Change in the Caribbean: A Pan-Caribbean Perspective.* Kingston, Jamaica: Ian Randle, 1993.

Morgan, Edmund S. *American Slavery, American Freedom: The Ordeal of Colonial Virginia.* New York: Norton, 1975.

Morgan, Philip D. *Slave Counterpoint: Black Culture in the Eighteenth-Century Chesapeake and Lowcountry.* Chapel Hill: University of North Carolina Press, 1998.

Morris, Jane. *The Duke-Symes Family.* Philadelphia: Dorrance, 1940.

Murrin, John M. "Anglicizing an American Colony: The Transformation of Provincial Massachusetts." Ph.D. diss., Yale University, 1966.

Nance, R. Earl. "Edward Barradall." In *The Virginia Law Reporters before 1880,* edited by W. Hamilton Bryson, 71–74. Charlottesville: University Press of Virginia, 1977.

———. "Sir John Randolph." In *The Virginia Law Reporters before 1880,* edited by W. Hamilton Bryson. Charlottesville: University Press of Virginia, 1977.

Nandy, Ashis. *The Intimate Enemy: Loss and Recovery of Self under Colonialism.* Delhi: Oxford University Press, 1983.

Newton, Sarah Emily. "Wise and Foolish Virgins: 'Usable Fiction' and the Early American Conduct Tradition." *Early American Literature* 25 (1990): 139–67.

Norton, Mary Beth. "Eighteenth-Century American Women in Peace and War: The Case of the Loyalists." *William and Mary Quarterly,* 3d ser., 33 (1976): 386–405.

———. "The Evolution of White Women's Experience in Early America." *American Historical Review* 89 (1984): 593–619.

———. *Founding Mothers and Fathers: Gendered Power and the Forming of American Society.* New York: Knopf, 1996.

———. "Gender and Defamation in Seventeenth-Century Maryland." *William and Mary Quarterly,* 3d ser., 44 (1987): 3–39.

———. *Liberty's Daughters: The Revolutionary Experience of American Women, 1750–1800.* Boston: Little, Brown, 1980.

Nugent, Nell Marion. *Cavaliers and Pioneers: Abstracts of Virginia Land Patents and Grants.* Vol. 1. Richmond: Virginia State Library and Archives, 1992.

Ockelton, D. W. Introduction to "The Fawcett and Lister Papers from the Shibden Hall Folk Museum." In Virginia Colonial Records Project, microfilm reel 854.

Offutt, William M. Jr. "The Limits of Authority: Courts, Ethnicity, and Gender in the Middle Colonies, 1670–1710." In *The Many Legalities of Early America,* edited by Christopher L. Tomlins and Bruce H. Mann, 357–387. Chapel Hill: University of North Carolina Press, 2001.

O'Mara, James. *An Historical Geography of Urban System Development: Tidewater Virginia in the Eighteenth Century.* Ontario: York University Geographical Monographs, 1983.

Outlaw, Alain Charles. *Governor's Land: Archaeology of Early Seventeenth-Century Virginia Settlements.* Charlottesville: University Press of Virginia, 1990.

Pares, Richard. "A London West India Merchant House, 1740–69." *The Historian's Business and Other Essays*. 1961, reprt., Westport, CT: Greenwood Press, 1974.

Perry, James R. *The Formation of a Society on Virginia's Eastern Shore 1615–1658*. Chapel Hill: University of North Carolina Press, 1990.

Pollock, Frederick and Frederic Maitland. *The History of English Law*. Cambridge: Cambridge University Press, 1923.

Pollock, Linda. "'Teach Her to Live under Obedience': The Making of Women in the Upper Ranks of Early Modern England." *Continuity and Change* 4 (1989): 231–58.

Powers, Emma L. "Landladies and Women Tenants in Williamsburg and Yorktown: 1700–1770." In *Common People and Their Material World: Free Men and Women in the Chesapeake, 1700–1830*, edited by David Harvey and Gregory Brown. Richmond: Colonial Williamsburg Foundation, 1995.

Price, Jacob M. *France and the Chesapeake*. 2 vols. Ann Arbor: University of Michigan Press, 1973.

———. "Notes and Documents: Who Was John Norton? A Note on the Historical Character of Some Eighteenth-Century London Virginia Firms." *William and Mary Quarterly*, 3d ser., 19 (1962): 400–407.

———. "One Family's Empire: The Russell-Lee-Clerk Connection in Maryland, Britain, and India, 1707–1857." *Maryland Historical Magazine* 72 (1977): 165–225.

———. *Perry of London: A Family and A Firm on the Seaborne Frontier, 1615–1753*. Cambridge, MA: Harvard University Press, 1992.

———. "Summation: The American Panorama of Atlantic Port Cities." In *Atlantic Port Cities: Economy, Culture, and Society in the Atlantic World, 1650–1850*, edited by Franklin W. Knight and Peggy K. Liss, 262–76. Knoxville: University of Tennessee Press, 1991.

———. "Transaction Costs: A Note on Merchant Credit and the Organization of Private Trade." In *The Political Economy of Merchant Empires*, edited by James D. Tracy, 276–97. Cambridge: Cambridge University Press, 1991.

Pruden, Elizabeth Marie. "Family, Community, Economy: Women's Activity in South Carolina, 1670–1770." Ph.D. diss., University of Minnesota, 1996.

Rankin, Hugh F. *Criminal Trial Proceedings in the General Court of Colonial Williamsburg*. Williamsburg: Colonial Williamsburg, 1965,

Ransome, David R., ed. "Introduction." *Sir Thomas Smith's Misgovernment of the Virginia Company by Nicholas Ferrar*. Cambridge: Roxburghe Club, 1990.

Ransome, David R. "Wives for Virginia, 1621." *William and Mary Quarterly*, 3d ser., 48 (1991): 3–18.

Rice, Kym S. *Early American Taverns: For the Entertainment of Friends and Strangers*. Chicago: Regnery Gateway, 1983.

Rich, Adrienne. *On Lies, Secrets, and Silence*. New York: Norton, 1979.

Richter, Caroline Julia. "A Community and Its Neighborhoods: Charles Parish, York County, Virginia, 1630–1740." Ph.D. diss., William and Mary College, 1992.

———. "The Randolph House." Colonial Williamsburg Research Report.

Riley, Edward M. "The Ordinaries of Colonial Yorktown." *William and Mary Quarterly*, 2nd ser., 23 (1943): 8–26.

Roeber, A. G. *Faithful Magistrates and Republican Lawyers: Creators of Virginia Legal Culture, 1680–1810*. Chapel Hill: University of North Carolina Press, 1981.

———. "'The Origin of Whatever Is Not English among Us': The Dutch-Speaking and the German-Speaking Peoples of Colonial British America." In *Strangers in within the Realm*, edited by Bernard Bailyn and Philip Morgan. Chapel Hill: University of North Carolina Press, 1991.

Rosen, Deborah A. *Courts and Commerce: Gender, Law and the Market Economy in Colonial New York*. Columbus: Ohio State University Press, 1997.

Rutman, Darrett B. and Anita H. "'Now-Wives and Sons-in-Law': Parental Death in a Seventeenth-Century Virginia County." In *Chesapeake in the Seventeenth Century*, edited by Thad W. Tate and David Ammerman, 153–82. New York: Norton, 1979.

———. and Anita H. *A Place in Time: Middlesex County, Virginia, 1650–1750*. New York: Norton, 1984.

Ryan, Mary P. *Women in Public: Between Banners and Ballots, 1825-1880*. Baltimore: Johns Hopkins University Press, 1990.

Salmon, Marylynn. *Women and the Law of Property in Early America*, Chapel Hill: University of North Carolina Press, 1986.

Schwarz, Philip J. *Twice Condemned: Slaves and the Criminal Laws of Virginia, 1705–1865*. Baton Rouge: Louisiana State University Press, 1988.

Scott, James C. *Domination and the Arts of Resistance: Hidden Transcripts*. New Haven: Yale University Press, 1990.

Scott, Joan Wallach. "Gender: A Useful Category of Analysis." In *Feminism and History*, edited by Joan Wallach Scott, 152–180. Oxford: Oxford University Press, 1996.

Shammas, Carole. "Early American Women and Control over Capital." In *Women in the Age of the American Revolution*, edited by Ronald Hoffman and Peter J. Albert, 134–54. Charlottesville: University Press of Virginia, 1989.

———. "How Self-Sufficient Was Early America?" *Journal of Interdisciplinary History* 13 (1982): 247–72.

———. *The Pre-Industrial Consumer in England and America*. Oxford: Oxford University Press, 1990.

Shammas, Carole, Marylynn Salmon, and Michel Dahlin. *Inheritance in America from Colonial Times to the Present*. New Brunswick, N.J.: Rutgers University Press, 1987.

Shepherd, Verene. Review of *Slave Cultures and the Cultures of Slavery*, edited by Stephan Palmie (Knoxville: University of Tennessee Press, 1995). *William and Mary Quarterly*, 3d ser., 54 (1997): 257–58.

Shepperson, Archibald Bolling. *John Paradise and Lucy Ludwell*. Richmond: Dietz Press, 1942.

Silver, Timothy. *A New Face on the Countryside: Indians, Colonists, and Slaves in South Atlantic Forests, 1500–1800*. Cambridge: Cambridge University Press, 1990.

Smith, Daniel Blake. *Inside the Great House: Planter Family Life in Eighteenth-Century Chesapeake Society*. Ithaca: Cornell University Press, 1980.

Snyder, Terri L. "Legal History of the Colonial South." *William and Mary Quarterly*, 3d ser., 50 (1993): 18-27.

———. "'Rich Widows are the Best Commodity This Country Affords': Gender Relations and the Rehabilitation of Patriarchy in Virginia, 1660–1700." Ph.D. diss., University of Iowa, 1992.

Socolow, Susan M. "Economic Roles of the Free Women of Color of Cap Français." In *More Than Chattel: Black Women and Slavery in the Americas*, edited by David Barry Gaspar and Darlene Clark Hine, 279–97. Bloomington: Indiana University Press, 1996.

Soltow, James H. *The Economic Role of Williamsburg*. Williamsburg: Colonial Williamsburg, 1965.

Sosin, J. M. "English Colonial and Overseas Commerce: The Nexus of Kinship and Trade." In *English America and the Restoration Monarchy of Charles II: Transatlantic Politics, Commerce, and Kinship*. Lincoln: University of Nebraska Press, 1980.

Speth, Linda E. "More than Her 'Thirds': Wives and Widows in Colonial Virginia." In *Women, Family, and Community in Colonial America: Two Perspectives* 5–42. New York: Institute for Research in History and the Haworth Press, 1983.

Spruill, Julia Cherry. *Women's Life and Work in the Southern Colonies*. 1938; reprint, New York: Norton, 1972.

Stanton, Lucia C. "'Those Who Labor for My Happiness': Thomas Jefferson and His Slaves," In *Jeffersonian Legacies*, edited by Peter S. Onuf., 147–80. Charlottesville: University Press of Virginia, 1993.

Staves, Susan. "Chattel Property Rules and the Construction of Englishness, 1660–1800." *Law and History Review* 12 (1994): 123–53.

———. *Married Women's Separate Property in England, 1660–1833*. Cambridge, MA: Harvard University Press, 1990.

Steele, Ian K. "Empire of Migrants and Consumers: Some Current Atlantic Approaches to the History of Colonial Virginia." *Virginia Magazine of History and Biography* 99 (1991): 489–512.

Stoler, Ann Laura. *Race and the Education of Desire*. Durham: Duke University Press, 1996.

Stone, Elizabeth. *Black Sheep and Kissing Cousins: How Our Family Stories Shape Us*. New York: Penguin, 1988.

Stone, Lawrence. *Road to Divorce: England 1530–1987*. Oxford: Oxford University Press, 1990.

Stone, Lawrence and Jean Fawtier Stone. *An Open Elite?: England, 1540–1880*. Oxford: Clarendon, 1984.

Stretton, Tim. *Women Waging Law in Elizabethan England*. Cambridge: Cambridge University Press, 1998.

Strobel, Margaret. *European Women and the Second British Empire*. Bloomington: Indiana University Press, 1991.

Sturtz, Linda L. "The Eighteenth-Century 'Bokorah Woman' in Jamaica." In *Differentiating Caribbean Womanhood*, edited by Jacquelin Stevens, 1–17. Mona, Jamaica: Centre for Gender and Development Studies Working Paper Series 3, 2000.

———. "Catherine Blaikley," *Dictionary of Virginia Biography* edited by John T. Kneebone, J. Jefferson Looney, Brent Tarter, and Sandra Gioia Treadway, 534–35. Vol. 1. Richmond: Library of Virginia, 1999.

———. "The 'Dim Duke' and Duchess Chandos." *Revista/Review Interamericana* 29 (1999), <*www.sg.inter.edu/revisa-ciscla/*>.

———. "'Dining Room Politics': Lady Berkeley of Virginia." Paper presented to the Courts Without Kings Conference, Society for Court Studies, Boston, MA, September 22, 2000.

———. "Innovation and Tradition in an Imperial-Colonial Contest." Paper presented to the International Seminar on the History of the Atlantic World, 1500–1800, Harvard University, Cambridge, MA, 1997.

———. "The Ladies and the Lottery: Elite Women's Gambling in Eighteenth-Century Virginia." *Virginia Magazine of History and Biography* 104 (1996): 1–20.

———. "'Madam and Co.': Women, Property and Power in Colonial Virginia." Ph.D. diss., Washington University, 1994.

Tate, Thad W. *The Negro in Eighteenth-Century Williamsburg*. Williamsburg: Colonial Williamsburg, 1965.

Tate, Thad W. and David Ammerman, eds. *The Chesapeake in the Seventeenth Century: Essays on Anglo-American Society and Politics*. New York: Norton, 1979.

Terry, Gail S. *Documenting Women's Lives: A User's Guide to Manuscripts at the Virginia Historical Society*. Richmond: Virginia Historical Society, 1996.

———. "Family Empires: A Frontier Elite in Virginia and Kentucky, 1740–1815." Ph.D. diss., College of William and Mary, 1992.

———. "An Old Family Confronts New Politics: The Preston-Trigg Congressional Contest of the 1790s." In *Diversity and Accommodation: Essays on the Cultural Composition of the Virginia Frontier*, edited by Michael J. Puglisi, 233–1. Knoxville: University of Tennessee Press, 1997.

———. "Sustaining the Bonds of Kinship in a Trans-Appalachian Migration, 1790–1811." *Virginia Magazine of History and Biography* 102 (1994): 455–76.

———. "Women, Property, and Authority in Colonial Baltimore County: Evidence from the Probate Records, 1660–1759." Paper presented at the Forty-fifth Conference on Early American History, Baltimore, 1984.

Thomas, Keith L. "Age and Authority in Early Modern England." *Proceedings of the British Academy* 62 (1976): 206–48.

Thompson, Roger. *Women in Stuart England and America: A Comparative Study.* Boston: Routledge and Kegan Paul, 1974.

Thorndale, William. "Flowerdew and Rossingham." *Virginia Genealogist* 34 (1990): 205–6.

Thorpe, Daniel B. "Doing Business in the Backcountry: Retail Trade in Colonial Rowan County, North Carolina." *William and Mary Quarterly*, 3d ser., 48 (1991): 387–408.

Todd, Barbara J. "Free Bench and Free Enterprise: Widows and Their Property in Two Berkshire Villages." In *English Rural Society 1500–1800*, edited by John Chartres and David Hey, 175–200. Cambridge: Cambridge University Press, 1990.

———. "The Remarrying Widow: A Stereotype Reconsidered." In *Women in Tudor-Stuart England*, edited by Mary Prior, 54–92. New York: Methuen, 1986.

Ulrich, Laurel Thatcher. *Good Wives: Image and Reality in the Lives of Women in Northern New England, 1650–1750.* Oxford: Oxford University Press, 1983.

———. "Of Pens and Needles." *Journal of American History* 77 (1990): 200–207.

———. "Martha Ballard and Her Girls: Women's Work in Eighteenth-Century Maine." In *Work and Labor in Early America*, edited by Stephen Innes, 70–105. Chapel Hill: University of North Carolina Press, 1988.

———. *A Midwife's Tale: The Life of Martha Ballard Based on Her Diary, 1785–1812.* New York: Knopf, 1990.

Underdown, D. E. "The Taming of the Scold: the Enforcement of Patriarchal Authority in Early Modern England." In *Order and Disorder in Early Modern England*, edited by Anthony Fletcher and John Stevenson, 116-–36. Cambridge: Cambridge University Press, 1985.

United Nations Department of International Economic and Social Affairs, Statistical Office and International Research and Training Institute for the Advancement of Women. *Methods of Measuring Women's Participation and Production in the Informal Sector.* Studies in Methods Series F, no. 46. New York: United Nations, 1990.

Varon, Elizabeth R. *We Mean to Be Counted: White Women and Politics in the Antebellum South.* Chapel Hill: University of North Carolina Press, 1998.

Vickery, Amanda. "Women and the World of Goods: A Lancashire Consumer and Her Possessions, 1751–81." In *Consumption and the World of Goods*, edited by John Brewer and Roy Porter, 274–301. New York: Routledge, 1993.

Walsh, Lorena S. *From Calabar to Carter's Grove: The History of a Virginia Slave Community.* Charlottesville: University Press of Virginia, 1997.

———. "'Till Death Us Do Part': Marriage and Family in Seventeenth-Century Maryland." In *Chesapeake in the Seventeenth Century: Essays on Anglo-American Society and Politics*, edited by Thad W. Tate and David Ammerman, 126–52. New York: Norton, 1979.

Ware, Vron. *Beyond the Pale: White Women, Racism and History.* London: Verso, 1992.

Wawrzyczek, Irmina. *Planting and Loving: Popular Sexual Mores in the Seventeenth-Century Chesapeake.* Lublin: Uniwersytetu Marii Curie-Sklodowskiej, 1998.

Weatherwax, Sarah Jane. "The Importance of Family in the Community of New Poquoson Parish, York County, Virginia, in the Late Seventeenth Century." M.A. thesis, College of William and Mary, 1984.

Wheeler, Marjorie Spruill. *New Women of the Old South: The Leaders of the Woman Suffrage Movement in the Southern States.* New York: Oxford University Press, 1993.

"Wiatt Family." *William and Mary Quarterly*, 1st. ser. 7 (1898–99): 35–45.

Wiesner, Merry E. *Women and Gender in Early Modern Europe.* Cambridge: Cambridge University Press, 1993.

Wilson, Lisa. *Life After Death: Widows in Pennsylvania, 1750–1850.* Philadelphia: Temple University Press, 1992.

Withington, Lothrop. "Virginia Gleanings in England. *Virginia Magazine of History and Biography* 20 (1912): 372–81.

Wulf, Karin A. *Not All Wives: Women of Colonial Philadelphia.* Ithaca: Cornell University Press, 2000.

Zahedieh, Naula. "Making Mercantalism Work: London Merchants and the Atlantic Trade in the Seventeenth Century. *Transactions of the Royal Historical Society,* 6th ser. 9 (1999): 143–58.

INDEX